Planning and Creating Better Direct Mail

Planning and Creating Better Direct Mail

JOHN D. YECK

Partner, Yeck and Yeck Advertising Agency
Graphic Service, Direct Mail Agency, Dayton, Ohio

JOHN T. MAGUIRE

Associate Professor of Business English
University of Illinois, Urbana, Illinois

McGRAW-HILL BOOK COMPANY, INC. 1961

New York   Toronto   London

PLANNING AND CREATING BETTER DIRECT MAIL

789-MAMM-7987

72264

Foreword

When the word reached me that my two relatively young friends, Jack Maguire and John Yeck, were in the process of writing a new book on direct mail . . . I wondered how in the world they could tell the story differently from any of the other many books on the subject.

When I was asked to write a foreword, I accepted . . . but with mental reservations. What could be said honestly if Jack and John should fall flat on their faces? After all, I have a reputation to uphold as a no-holds-barred caustic critic of anything wrong in or about our favorite medium of advertising.

The advance manuscript has now been read carefully and sent back to the publisher. I could make this foreword short by just saying, "The whole book is wonderful . . . I endorse it 100 per cent without qualifications." But a foreword writer must prove he has actually read the book. So . . .

Without detracting from the fame of other writers on the subject, most books on direct mail have been written in a factual, detailed style which sometimes gets boring, especially to those who know most of the details.

But these "young fellows" have succeeded in creating a "new frontier" in the teaching and explaining of direct mail. Jack Maguire is a professional teacher, accustomed to dealing with young people who must be kept alert in spite of themselves. John Yeck came up the hard way . . . selling direct mail to thick-skinned prospects, then selling, creating, and producing direct mail for an ever-growing number of satisfied clients. So this combination of professional teacher and hard-boiled practitioner shines out brightly in every chapter. And behind the studious explanations of details . . . there is a rare combination of psychology, logic, philosophy, and sometimes humor.

For instance, articles about lists and list maintenance are often dull . . . but the two chapters devoted to this subject make the problems exciting. The problems of maintenance are grouped into six major divisions, with a half-dozen or so subdivisions under each. The student or reader is told exactly *how* to tackle each subdivision of the problem. Then *what* will happen if the advice is followed. Excellent teaching technique . . . backed by sound advice gained from experience.

Every media salesman should be induced to read at least parts of this book . . . especially the chapter which logically explains the real differences between direct mail and other forms of advertising. There would not be so much petty competitive nonsense written or spoken against direct mail if media salesmen recognized the differences between types of impressions and the differences between cost per shot and cost per hit.

The motivation research experts who talk and write abstractly about motivations would profit by reading the down-to-earth, easily understood, friendly descriptions in the chapter devoted to simplified research.

The chapter on how to deal with women by mail is a courageous undertaking and an exciting analysis of this delicate art. The How to Build Believability chapter is wonderful. Don't miss it. It's worth the price of the book. If the advice is followed, much of the deserved criticism of some kinds of direct mail would vanish.

I like particularly some of the tongue-in-cheek spots of humor . . . where the authors seem to poke fun at themselves or at the seriousness of teachers and textbook writers. And all through the book you will find pleasing examples of exceptionally good writing. For instance, in the chapter on different kinds of copy styles, such as narrative, dialogue, benefit appeals, humor, etc., you will find this gem of psychology:

"High-level Josh plays an important part in the use of humor in copy style. In approaching the suave and the smooth, a 'near-flip' attitude can sometimes be effective. People of high levels of sophistication, those who settle for nothing less than triple *entendre*, who love the subtle flavors of language, who like to play with words, can be approached with a tongue-in-cheek style of 'josh.' These people form an elite audience, measured not always in money, but always in taste and in knowledgeable perception. This class of people is the hand-made lace on the satin petticoat which hides the sameness of the human animal. Decorative, artistic, they make the drabness, the dullness, the monotony of 'the everyday' seem more interesting, more satisfying to those who know not such circles. They don't need the money if their taste is right, if they can see that human antics, foibles, peccadilloes are merely scenes to be enjoyed from the wings on the stage of life, where the drama of the main act is made the more real by contrast with its own parts. With these people the fabric of conversation is an artistic needlework of kindly snide syllables, cut with the shears of caustic comment, and bundled into a genuine appreciation of and love for all things human."

I believe this book will become a standard textbook for the teaching of direct mail for years to come. It would be difficult to improve on its content. There will be better direct mail practitioners in the future when young people in college advertising courses use this book as a guide, and when their elders set them a good example by following its simple logic.

One critic of direct mail recently wrote, "There is a fairly safe rule one can adopt toward mail: Its uselessness increases in direct ratio to its errors." In spite of the critic's negative approach . . . the rule is true. This book will help to eliminate the errors and increase the effectiveness of all direct mail.

Henry Hoke

Preface

This is a coauthored book. So you ought to like half of it, anyway.

It wasn't easy to write because John T. Maguire and John D. Yeck are opposites. Jack Maguire is a professor. John Yeck is in business. Jack's a bachelor. John's happily married. Jack eulogizes with flowery and lyrical language occasionally. John likes writing that's short and sweet. Jack sits serenely after hours and contemplates the whole broad field of direct mail. John has twenty irons in the fire at once. Jack carefully annotates his references and leaves a lot of helpful footnotes in his wake. John chews up his reading, digests it, adds some "experience" and "opinion" flavor of his own . . . forgets where he read it first.

How they ever managed to write a book together, nobody knows.

Not even Jack and John.

Maybe it's because they are both intensely interested in and love to talk about direct mail and the skills of persuasion and conviction through the written word . . . and because Jack (the professor) likes to talk about business and John (the nonprofessor) likes to talk about education.

You can probably tell, before you're through with the book, who wrote what originally . . . but both have gone over every word, and this is a book they agree upon.

Budding writers will find it invaluable. Old-time direct mail men will find some new profitable ideas. Teachers and students will find it useful. You'll like it.

We hope.

John T. Maguire
John D. Yeck

Contents

Introduction

A sales manager of a fairly important company reported to his boss the other day, somewhat discouraged.

He'd just finished a sales meeting with his staff: two star salesmen, eighteen mediocre ones, and four he would fire tomorrow if he could replace them.

"We could easily be doing a better selling job," he said, "if we had more and better manpower. I'd like to go calling on all our prospects myself. But there just isn't enough of *me* to go around."

That predicament, shared by most businessmen, is the reason for this book. There's more selling and more communicating needed in Marketing today than there are good men to do it in person. But through business mail, businessmen can "go calling on all the prospects" and "spread themselves around." They can get a better job done.

For well-prepared business mail has many advantages.

Well-prepared mail is a personal call. A *good* personal call. On paper. To a carefully selected group of readers. Its ability to be *personal* and *selective* makes it substantially different from "mass" advertising . . . to a degree where it probably shouldn't be called "advertising" at all.

Well-prepared mail is economical. It costs perhaps one-hundredth as much as a personal call . . . and can call on thousands or millions in a day. This has resulted in greater and greater use of the mail as the cost of a man-hour steadily rises.

Well-prepared mail is efficient. Because a sales manager, for example, can tell his *one best sales story* in a mailing piece, . . . making sure each prospect is exposed to exactly the same story, the way he wants it told.

Well-prepared mail gets attention. It gets read. It gets action. It gets—

1

but just read this book. You'll soon have a better appreciation of what well-prepared mail can do for *you*.

Don't overlook the suggestions here simply because you write your "direct mail" one letter at a time to one person at a time, either. This book can help you even more. Because there's a good chance, on the average, you aren't giving your letters as much attention as the people who prepare mail for thousands to read.

Incidentally, this is *not* just another book about "mail order"—that is, the kind of mail that initiates and completes a sale all by itself. While it does include one chapter on selling by mail, the book is primarily concerned with the kind of mail prepared for an ordinary business, using the normal channels of distribution, run by businessmen who realize there isn't enough manpower to go around and simply want to use mail efficiently . . . to do a better job.

With intelligent use of the mail they can do it . . . for substantially everything an individual can do, personally, in the fields of communication, information, and persuasion *can* be done by mail. The trick is to do it well and profitably.

Perhaps this book can help.

1

Direct Mail Is
Effective Advertising

Advertising Is Salesmanship in Print

Advertising has been called "salesmanship in print." And, be it in print or on the airways, all advertising should be *part* of a sale. Most advertisers are not trying to close the sale in print or over the air. When they do, they are called "mail-order advertisers," because readers or listeners must ordinarily complete the sale by mail. Most advertisers are simply trying to create an *atmosphere* in which a sale can be made . . . to "cultivate the ground" so that a dealer, a salesman, or some kind of follow-up can make the actual sale . . . or to bring the prospect to a point of sale in a retail store.

People *advertise* to make a point, to create a favorable atmosphere, to let others know about, to prejudice in favor of. Express it as you will. But it comes out: *People advertise to make mental impressions.*

And what are impressions? To understand the value of direct mail as an economical advertising tool, you have to understand a "secret" of communications: "*A message is not a message until it is received.*" Or, better yet, "*An impression is not an impression until it has impressed.*" But that sounds like Gertrude Stein. So let's pin it down.

That Advertising Impressed Me. Webster says an impression is the *effect* produced by a stimulation of the senses. That's what we think of

3

when we talk about an advertising impression. That's what we *want* the word impression to mean. Let's, then, call this IMPRESSION 1.

That Advertising Is Impressive. Webster, however, goes on to say that "impression" has also come to mean the stimulation itself, whether anyone pays attention to it or not. Let's call this IMPRESSION 2.

Five Million Impressions per Issue. Some advertising men go one step further and define an impression as a *potential* stimulation. For example, X magazine boasts of 5 million "impressions" per issue. They talk of a cost of a fraction of a cent per "impression" . . . when they *really* mean "per copy sold" or "per reader." Let's call this IMPRESSION 3.

Of course, IMPRESSION 3 is off base. IMPRESSION 2 is often a vain hope. The only "impression" that really counts with an advertiser is the first one—an *effect*. And if this effect is not produced on a *prospect*—or at least a suspect—it's not worth much.

It's the Cost per Hit that Counts. A message that reaches you, if you're a prospect, through the mail has at least as good a chance to make an impression on you as one that actually reaches you through other advertising media. Some advertisers, however, reject direct mail as a pure advertising medium on the basis of *cost*. They say "cost per impression" is too high.

But they are often comparing "apples with oranges" . . . or IMPRESSION 1 with IMPRESSION 3. It is not the *cost per potential stimulation on the mass* that matters. It is the *cost per impression* actually produced on a prospect.

It doesn't really matter how many *printed* impressions your printing presses make. What's important is the *psychological* impressions on prospects that your *printed* impressions make.

Let's think of it another way. Remember the sergeant at Fort Dix who checked the targets of a new recruit and failed to find a single hole after 100 shots? "Son," he said, "where are all the bullets going?" "I dunno, Sarge," was the reply. "They're leaving here all right."

The moral is perfectly obvious to any soldier, hunter, or trapshooter: It isn't the cost *per shot* that counts. It's the cost *per hit* . . . *on target*.

A typographer we know belongs to a trade group. As a group, they advertise in national publications when they want to influence the thinking of each member's prospects. They advertise in magazines which people who are likely to buy typesetting are also likely to read.

When an actual buyer of typesetting reads such an ad and makes a mental note about it, the ad has made IMPRESSION 1.

When an actual buyer sees the ad but pays no attention to it and can't remember seeing it, it makes IMPRESSION 2 . . . not worth very much.

When a person getting the magazine doesn't open it to that page or doesn't buy typesetting, his "impression" is IMPRESSION 3 . . . worthless.

But the typographer we're familiar with knows we're prospects. So he doesn't take a chance on our seeing the ad. He knows that readership studies show, *on the average,* that even if it's an exceptional ad . . . less than 10 per cent of the circulation is likely to read most of it. So in addition to shooting copies to thousands of magazine subscribers, he shoots *one* copy to me, direct, through the mail. I *see* that one for sure.

The mail effort costs him more *per shot.* But it may cost him a lot less *per hit.*

When you use direct mail as "advertising," then, you will measure it on the same basis as you do other advertising. This will often be on the basis of *readership* rather than *traceable sales.* You will expect to get more "impressions per dollar." You'll choose your media that way.

If you think more *actual prospects* will read your ad in $1,000-worth of magazine space, you'll use that. If you think more actual prospects will read it in $1,000-worth of direct mail, you'll use direct mail.

And when you *advertise* with direct mail, you'll use more of the traditional advertising techniques. You'll think in terms of repetition, impact, color, less copy—more art, moods, etc. You'll be less concerned about reply cards and descriptive literature, for example. You'll think simply in terms of making an impression (number *one* if you can) or an announcement.

In fact, a lot of direct mail lore will be useless to you. "Facts" about direct mail successes are usually compiled by people who use direct mail to do the complete selling job, or, at least, to produce inquiries.

Direct Mail's Place

To place direct mail "advertising" in its proper perspective, it would be useful for direct mail people who plan and create direct mail to think of the medium in three *new* categories instead of the *ancient* three which have been used for so long. These ancient categories were called Direct Mail Advertising, Direct Advertising, and Mail-order Selling.

Direct Mail's Modern Divisions. The first category is *Direct Mail Advertising.* Attempts, through the mail, to influence people favorably toward a product or service. This kind of direct mail has the same goals as general advertising—to inform, influence, make friends, build a popular-brand image, bring prospects to dealers, etc.

The second category is *Direct Mail Sales Promotion.* This division includes that type of direct mail which seeks to get a response from prospects: to get information, to get qualified leads, to open the door for salesmen, to "involve" prospects.

The third category is *Selling by Mail* (or *Direct Mail Selling*). This is where the sale is completed through the mail without the use of salesmen or dealers. The use of the term "mail-order selling" is deliberately avoided because that term logically includes selling by "mail order," through newspapers, magazines, radio, and TV. Even car cards. Wherever the *order* comes through the mail. In any over-all *functional* view of advertising, "selling by mail" is a logical division of "mail order."

Another category, which is really a stepson of the direct mail fraternity, but which is necessary for a complete picture of this medium—be it ancient or modern—has to do with *Direct, Nonmail, Advertising, and Promotion.* This classification includes printed materials not sent through the mails but conveyed directly to the recipient: distributed from door to door, passed to pedestrians on the street, placed in parked automobiles, handed to customers in retail stores, included in packages and bundles, delivered by salesmen or messenger.

This last category has many of the same *functions* as the others: to inform, influence, build a popular brand, get qualified leads, "involve" prospects, make friends, even, on occasion, to sell. It requires entirely different handling, however, because it lacks two major elements of direct mail—selectivity and personalness.

These categories are rather clear-cut in actual practice. Writers and counselors tend to find themselves becoming proficient in one area or another, and they find it relatively difficult to work in the other fields. There is some overlapping, of course, and some organizations develop specialists across the board.

Direct Mail's Uses

To help define direct mail more fully, let's see what it can be used for. Remember that direct mail can be used advantageously in many cases where other media are also used. However, it has limitations and sometimes is not adaptable to some uses.

Here are five of the principal types of selling jobs direct mail can do for you:

1. You can get orders directly from consumers or users.
2. You can get responses indicating interest.
   a. To be followed up by more direct mail
   b. To be followed up by salesmen
   c. To be followed up by telephone
3. You can put the prospect into position for personal selling.
   a. In a retail outlet or showroom
   b. In front of an exhibit of products . . . particularly those which salesmen cannot take to the prospect for demonstration
4. You can create a receptive atmosphere for your salesmen.
   a. Through cordial-contact mailings which build an "image" of your company.

b. Through institutional types of direct mail (for example, mailings such as the paper and printing companies use to illustrate the product's or the company's abilities) which function like cordial-contact mailings.

c. Through the "impact" created by any type of mailing you send out. Any mailing will create some kind of impression. Well-executed mailings will identify you favorably to prospects. The impression given may set up good will, or leave a latent desire, which can be triggered into action by a later mailing.

5. You can influence selected groups to action.
   a. Building salesman incentive
   b. Seeking and obtaining employees
   c. Obtaining credits and collections
   d. Building mailing lists
   e. Developing political campaigns

6. You can make more effective the impact of advertising through other media.
   a. By gaining the cooperation and building the enthusiasm of all persons involved with your advertising efforts, through keeping them properly motivated and informed
   b. By helping to convert impressions created by other advertising into sales through:
      (1). Bringing the prospect and product together at point of sale
      (2). Following up inquiries developed by other media
      (3). Using your ad from a newspaper or magazine as a mailing piece or part of a mailing unit . . . to precede or follow up the issue of the magazine or newspaper in which the ad appears

Direct Mail as "Pure" Advertising

Since direct mail is used for so many other specific *selling* purposes, some people forget it can be used, profitably, as a pure "advertising" medium . . . *to create impressions.*

When a manufacturer reprints a trade-paper ad and mails it to his best prospects, he is using direct mail as "advertising." The same thing is true when a dealer sends out post cards to advertise a three-day sale. They are simply trying, as advertisers do, in newspapers, magazines, billboards, radio, and TV, to create favorable impressions about their brands or to make announcements.

An Example of Direct Mail as "Advertising." The following letter is an example of how to use direct mail as a pure advertising medium . . . to create impressions. This letter does not try to close the sale. It tries to create an atmosphere in which a sale can be made. It tries to set up an "impression" with the reader, which will create a favorable situation for selling, for the salesman. Note that the letter does not ask for any action. It merely "advertises."

PRICE BROTHERS COMPANY
1932 East Monument Ave.
Dayton 1, Ohio

WHEN A DROP OF WATER (a plastic, golden water drop was glued here) LOOKS LIKE A DROP OF GOLD . . .

Sometimes even today *water is worth its weight in gold.*

In case of fire, for instance.

Insurance underwriters know this. That's why fire insurance rates are higher wherever water mains are *too old, inadequate,* or *subject to breakage.*

As Fire Chief Elmer M. Cain of Cleveland told the *Cleveland Plain Dealer* not long ago:

> "Of the seven major factors in grading a city (for instance), the most important is water supply. We get a lot of deficiency points from the underwriters because much of our 1,500 miles of water mains are *old,* and *tuberculation* has reduced their capacity."

Old-fashioned water mains are costing Cleveland thousands of dollars a year, today . . . long after they thought they were "paid for" . . . because of *low* capacity and *high* insurance rates.

In judging water pipe, you—like insurance underwriters—should look for the "Big 3" requirements of economical water lines:

Long Life . . . Sustained Capacity . . . Great Strength

No other pipe meets these *3 big requirements* as well as Concrete Pressure Pipe.

For buried concrete is ageless as limestone. Its high flow coefficient stays high indefinitely . . . with *no corrosion or tuberculation* under ordinary conditions. It's *shatterproof* . . . so you avoid the constant threat of sudden, complete failure.

Next time you approach water line problems, remember those "Big 3" requirements: *life; capacity; strength.* . . .

Think of the gold that foresight can save and you'll . . .

Think first of PRICE,
/s/
Harry S. Price, Jr.
Vice-president

Direct Mail's Advantages

The main advantages of direct mail are personalness, flexibility, selectivity. So, when you want your advertising to have these qualities, consider first direct mail.

Here are ten advantages which direct mail offers you when your advertising needs personalness, selectivity, flexibility:

1. You can be more exact in selection of and delivery to individuals or markets you wish your advertising to reach. From the list of the "Wisest Men at $1 for 7 Names" offered by one list house, to the massive National Occupant lists which carry the addresses of most American homes (98.5 per cent accuracy guaranteed), to that list right in your lap—present customers, past customers, and the people they would recommend—you can hit exactly at the market you wish.

2. You can be personal and confidential with direct mail . . . you can wrap a personal message in the secrecy of an envelope when the message is the "between-you-and-me" type.

3. You have less competition for the reader's attention with direct mail. Because of its physical make-up, direct mail doesn't have to compete with other advertising or editorial matter, to the same degree, or in the same way that display advertising does. When the reader has a mailing in his hand, the "distraction" from other elements is less.

4. You have few limits in format to restrict the creative impression of your advertising ideas. The selection of color, shape, size, and format has few restrictions except those of feasibility, practicality, and the U.S. Post Office. For this reason, creative ingenuity in expressing an advertising idea is almost unlimited.

5. You have great flexibility in the selection and use of creative materials and reproduction processes. All forms of the graphic arts, all those elements which can give direct mail a third or fourth dimension—die cuts, folds, sound, smell—can be adapted to give you a custom-built advertising impact.

6. You can interpret your advertising story . . . with a "reader-only" individualism, with novelty, with realism. You can get attention with such things as odd shapes, pop-ups, cutouts, folds, etc. And at the same time, you can get the difference of novelty . . . the impact of realism in your advertising message.

7. You can produce direct mail as you need or want it. No publication date will make you wait for the impact of your advertising to be felt in your market. You can make a quick promotion when needed, make "emergency mailings" when circumstances call for them.

8. You can use the "control" inherent in direct mail for research, for testing—appeals, ideas, etc.—for reaching highly selective audiences. The individual, personal qualities of direct mail are ideal for research. And with well-selected portions of lists, you can test mailings before you throw your whole advertising effort in the hopper.

9. Your timing of mailings can be accurate, exact. To help you hit your market at the time you wish, mail departure and arrival schedules can be obtained from your post office. This means you can have mailed material hitting at its target, as planned.

10. You can offer a complete "reply" package so that the reader has ease of answering. With an enclosed, easily mailable, postpaid reply piece—business reply card, envelope, order blank, and the like—you can get easy, immediate action from readers.[1]

Just to Complete the Record, here is a list of forty-nine ways in which *Direct Mail Can Be Put to Work in Your Business.* This list was developed by the Direct Mail Advertising Association. It has had wide acceptance as a tool in using direct mail effectively. Maybe you can get some good, applicable ideas from it. First, here is your key to the symbols used:

M—Manufacturers   S—Service Organizations and Associations
W—Wholesalers   MO—Mail Order
R—Retailers   P—Philanthropic and Welfare Agencies

WAYS YOU CAN PUT DIRECT MAIL TO WORK [2]

In Your Own Organization

1. Building Morale of Employees. A bulletin or house magazine, published regularly, carrying announcements of company policy, stimulating ambition, encouraging thrift, promoting safety and efficiency, will make for greater loyalty among employees. M-W-R-S-MO-P.

2. Securing Data from Employees. Letters or questionnaires occasionally directed to employees help in cementing a common interest in the organization and bring back practical ideas and much useful data. M-W-R-S-MO-P.

3. Stimulating Salesmen to Greater Efforts. Interesting sales magazines, bulletins, or letters help in unifying a scattered selling organization in speeding up sales, and in making better salesmen, by carrying sound ideas which have made sales, by success stories, etc. M-W-S-P.

4. Paving the Way for Salesmen. Forceful and intelligent direct mail, persistent and continuous, will create a field of prospective buyers who are live and ready to be sold. M-W-S-P.

5. Securing Inquiries for Salesmen. Direct mail can bring back actual inquiries from interested prospective customers—inquiries your men can call upon and sell. M-W-S-P.

6. Teaching Salesmen "How to Sell." A sales manual sent to salesmen at one time or in the form of a series of messages will educate them on "bagging more and bigger" orders. M-W-R-S.

7. Selling Stockholders and Others Interested in Your Company. Enclosures with dividend checks, with pay envelopes, or direct messages

[1] DMAA *Presents the Story of Direct Advertising,* Direct Mail Advertising Association, New York, 1959, pp. 18–19.
[2] Published with the permission of DMAA.

will sell stockholders and employees on making a greater use of product or service and in suggesting its use to others. M-W-R-S-MO-P.

8. Keeping a Contact with Customers between Salesmen's Calls. To assure your firm of receiving ALL the customer's business you should send messages to these customers between salesmen's visits. M-W-S.

9. Further Selling Prospective Customers after a Demonstration or Salesman's Call. Direct mail, emphasizing the superiorities of your product or service, will help in "clinching" sales. It will make it difficult for competition to gain a foothold. M-W-R-S-P.

10. Acknowledging Orders or Payments. An interesting letter, folder, or mailing card is a simple gesture which will cement a closer relationship between you and your customers. M-W-R-S-MO-P.

11. Welcoming New Customers. A letter, welcoming new customers, can go a long way toward keeping them sold on your company. M-W-R-S-MO-P.

12. Collecting Accounts. A series of diplomatic collection letters will not only bring and keep accounts up to date, but will leave the recipients in a friendly frame of mind and hold them as customers. M-W-R-S-MO-P.

Building New Business

13. Securing New Dealers. Direct mail offers any concern unlimited possibilities in lining up new dealers. M-W-S.

14. Securing Direct Orders. Many organizations have built extremely profitable business through orders secured only with the help of direct mail. There are many concerns not now selling direct by mail that can, in like manner, do the same thing. M-W-R-S-MO-P.

15. Building Weak Territories. Direct mail will provide intensified local sales stimulation wherever you may wish to apply it. M-W-S.

16. Winning Back Inactive Customers. A series of direct mail messages to "lost" customers will revive a large number of them. M-W-R-S-MO-P.

17. Developing Sales in Territories Not Covered by Salesmen. Out-of-the-way communities and unassigned territories offer an alert organization vast possibilities to develop direct sales by direct mail. M-W-S.

18. Developing Sales among Specified Groups. With direct mail you can direct your selling messages to those you wish to sell and talk with them in the language they will understand and act upon. M-W-R-S-MO-P.

19. Following Inquiries Received from Direct Mail or Other Forms of Advertising. A series of messages sent to those who have expressed their interest in your product or service, outlining the reasons why your product or service should be bought, will increase the number of sales. M-W-R-S-MO-P.

20. Driving Home Sales Arguments. Several mailings, each planned to lay stress on one or more selling points, will, point by point, educate your prospective customer on the many reasons why he should buy your product or service . . . and from you. M-W-R-S-P.

21. Selling Other Items in Line. Mailing pieces, package inserts, or "hand-out" folders will educate your customers on products and services other than those they are buying. M-W-R-S-MO.

22. Getting Product Prescribed or Specified. Professional men, such as physicians and dentists, will prescribe a product for their patients if they are correctly educated on its merits and what it will accomplish. Likewise, consumers and dealers will ask for a certain product, by name, if they are thoroughly familiar with it. Direct mail can be profitably used for this purpose. M-S.

23. Selling New Type of Buyer. Perhaps there are new outlets through which your product or service might be sold. Direct mail is a powerful selling tool in the development of them. M-W-R-S.

24. Bringing Buyer to Showroom. Invitation through letter or printed announcements will create the desire for prospective customers to visit your showroom or factory. M-W-R-S.

Assisting Present Dealers

25. Helping Present Dealer Sell More. Assistance given your dealers through the mails and through the use of "point-of-purchase" helps will receive the dealer's hearty cooperation, for it will sell your product or service faster. M-W-S.

26. Merchandising Your Plans to Dealer. You want as many of your dealers as possible to use your material, for the more of it used the more sales you make. Use direct mail to sell the use of this material to your dealers. M-W-S.

27. Educating Dealers on Superiorities of Your Product or Service. All our memories are short when it comes to remembering the other fellow's product or service and its superiorities. It will pay you to keep telling your dealers the features of your product or service. M-W-S.

28. Educating Retail Clerks in the Selling of a Product. Clerks are the neck of the retail-selling bottle. If they believe in a company and a product, their influence is a powerful aid to sales. If they are indifferent, the manufacturer is losing an effective helper. Direct mail, addressed to the clerks, will bring you their cooperation and more sales. M-W.

29. Securing Information from Dealers or Dealers' Clerks. Letters, printed messages, a bulletin, or a house magazine will bring back helpful data from the individuals who actually sell your product or your service— information you can use to your profit by passing on to other dealers or sales clerks to help them sell more. M-W-S.

30. Referring Inquiries from Consumer Advertising to Local Dealers. Direct mail should be used to refer quickly any inquirer to your dealer in his territory, and to inform the dealer about the inquiring prospect. Not to do so is to pass up many sales. M-W-S.

The Consumer

31. Creating a Need or a Demand for a Product. Direct mail, consistently used, will stimulate the demand for your product or service and will remind the customer to ask for it by name. M-S.

32. Increasing Consumption of a Product among Present Users. Are your consumer customers putting your product to all the uses they might? If not, it is probably because they do not know how else they might. Package inserts, booklets, etc., should be used to educate them on all uses. M-R-S-MO.

33. Bringing Customers into a Store to Buy. This applies to retailers. Personal, friendly, and cordial direct mail messages, telling your customers and prospects about the merchandise you have for them and creating the desire to own that merchandise, will bring a large number to your store to buy. R.

34. Opening New Charge Accounts. This also applies to retailers. There are many people in every community who pay their bills promptly and will do the bulk of their buying where they have accounts. A careful compilation of such a list with a well-planned direct mail program directed to them, inviting them to open charge accounts, will bring considerable new business. R.

35. Capitalizing on Special Events. Retailers in particular can make capital, through direct mail, of such consumer events as marriages, births, graduations, promotions, etc., to help them sell more. Likewise, letters should be sent to select lists featuring private sales and other lists to feature general sales. R.

General

36. Building Good Will. The possibilities of building good will and friendship through direct mail are unlimited. It's the little handshake through the mail that cements business relationships and holds the business of your customers even though your salesmen leave you to go with a competitor . . . or your competitors are aggressive in trying to wean your good customers away from you. M-W-R-S-MO-P.

37. Capitalizing on Other Advertising. Direct mail will permit you to capitalize on your other advertising investments and bring back more in sales for each dollar spent. M-W-R-S-MO-P.

38. As a "Leader" in Other Forms of Advertising. To make the ultimate sales of a product or service, more words are oftentimes necessary than publication space or radio or TV time will permit. A booklet or attractive folder can be featured in this other advertising, which when asked for and sent to prospects, will help to make more sales. M-W-R-S-MO-P.

39. Breaking Down Resistance to a Product or a Service. Oftentimes sales are hindered because of resistances in the mind of prospective customers. Direct mail will help to overcome these resistances. M-W-R-S-MO-P.

40. Stimulating Interest in Forthcoming Events. Such an event might be a special "week" or "day" devoted to a greater use of a product, an anniversary, the taking on of a line by a new dealer, an "opening" . . . or scores of other happenings. Direct mail, built around such an event, can help greatly to increase sales. M-W-R-S-MO-P.

41. Distribution of Samples. There are thousands of logical prospects who could be converted into users of your product if you proved to them its merits. There is no better way to do this than by letting the prospects convince themselves by actual test . . . provided your product lends itself to sampling. M-S.

42. Announcing a New Product, New Policy, or New Addition. There is no quicker way to make such announcements, to create more sales, to stimulate greater interest in a concern and what it is doing than through the personal, action-producing medium of direct mail. M-W-R-S-MO-P.

43. Announcing a New Address or Change in Telephone Number. When such important changes are made, a letter or printed announcement sent through the mail has a personal appeal which will register your message better than any other form of advertising possibly could. M-W-R-S-MO-P.

44. Keeping a Concern or Product "in Mind." Blotters, calendars, monthly mailings will all assist in doing this—a most vital problem with any concern faced with the keen competition of others who are trying their hardest to take customers away from you. M-W-R-S-MO-P.

45. Research for New Ideas and Suggestions. Direct advertising research is a powerful force in building sales. Direct mail can be used to find market facts, to eliminate sales fumbling, and to chart direct, profitable trails to sales. It furnishes all the important tools for sales research, in order to discover what to sell, how to sell it, and to whom to sell. M-W-R-S-MO-P.

46. Correcting Present Mailing Lists. The average mailing list will be 25 per cent or more out of date by the end of a year if it is not corrected. Direct mail can be employed to keep your list accurate. (See Chapter 5.) M-W-R-S-MO-P.

47. Securing Names for Permanent Lists. Direct mail can be used to secure lists of prospects from dealers, to write municipal clerks or other influential people in a community for names of a certain type, to secure names of friends of customers who might be prospects for you, . . . and in many other ways. M-W-R-S-MO-P.

48. Protecting Patents or Special Processes. Shouting forth the ownership of such patents or processes by direct mail can leave no question in the minds of your customers—present or prospective—to whom they must come for such a product or process. At the same time it gives you greater protection from possible infringers. M-S.

49. Raising Funds. For directing appeals to a selective list of prospective contributors, direct advertising affords an effective economical method of raising funds for worthy causes. P.

2

Direct Mail's
King-size Readership

"Look-See's" Impressions

Readership is a measurement of a possibility or a probability that people have taken a "look-see" at your advertising and that you have created an impression.

And direct mail, aimed with intelligence on the bow and arrow of competence toward its target—the prospect—hits a bull's-eye in readership. In such instances of competence in direct mail:

> Readership-recall scores of less than 40 per cent are *almost unknown*.
> Recall scores of up to 90 per cent are not unknown.

If you don't get at least 40 per cent recall, you haven't properly planned and executed the mailing. Because less than 40 per cent recall means you have failed to interest your audience. Captive is the audience, with a captured interest, and highly successful is your mailing . . . if you get 90 per cent recall. And the ball doth bounce in such fashion at times.

Readership in Direct Mail Differs, however, in its meaning from that given to magazines and newspapers. In 100 per cent of the direct mail deliveries, at least one person gives the mail attention. That isn't true of magazine and newspaper ads. Each magazine or newspaper ad is not necessarily, not even probably, given attention. This situation of direct mail's contact with recipients, incidentally, helps to show that you don't have to hit your readers over the head to get attention. Attention is not direct mail's first problem.

Direct Mail's Readership Scores are, actually, measures of memorability, because direct mail pieces do not have to compete with other ads and editorial matter, as do magazines and newspaper ads. Admittedly, direct mail must compete with other mail, as well as the reader's choice of what he will do at a given point in time. But by the same token, so do other media. Competition is decreased by the physical make-up of direct mail. Usually, one reads a letter or a brochure all by itself. Direct mail, for that reason, does not have the competitive distraction which magazine and newspaper pages have.

Memorability, as a definitive perspective of readership in direct mail, seems largely a function of product interest. Thus you invariably get a higher readership from those persons who already have an interest in the product (see Chapter 3 for a study of carpet) or from direct mail which immediately arouses interest.

Why does direct mail attain such favorable degrees of readership? Well, let's look at the consumer's attitude toward it. Then we can take a look at direct mail and the business and professional man.

Consumer's Attitude toward Direct Mail

Contrary to popular opinion, consumer direct mail is neither unpopular nor is it buried in a large volume of mail. In fact, quite the reverse is true. For example, take these figures from R. L. Polk & Co., Detroit, one of the largest directory publishers and direct mail list houses: [1]

The average number of pieces of all kinds of mail—letters, post cards, bills, advertising, magazines, newspapers, etc.—received daily by upper-income families . . . (such as users of late-model cars) . . . averages about 3.2. . . . (and . . . less than one of these pieces is advertising). . . . Spread over all families in the United States, there is only about one piece of mail per day.

As evidence to prove that the consumer is receptive to direct mail, take these statistics from Polk's research: [2]

1. Like to receive 38%
2. Don't care much one way or the other 49
3. Dislike to receive 13

[1] Lawrence G. Chait, *Those Little Golden Lists,* R. L. Polk & Co., Detroit, Mich., 1955.

[2] "The Handling of Advertising by Its Recipients," *DMAA Research Bulletin,* vol. 1, no. 2, May 11, 1959, p. 5.

On the basis of these figures, then, which show the amount of mail delivered per family per day and the figures which indicate the consumer's attitude toward the medium, there is little truth in the notion that direct mail advertising is a waste-basket barrage—disliked by the public. Shucks! Many people wrap their garbage in newspapers. But who complains about that?

Direct Mail and the Businessman

To Business All Mail Is Important. From his mail, a businessman gets orders, inquiries, checks. He also gets new, money-making ideas and useful information.

A businessman is trained on letters. He gets his most important, most personal business information from them. Many a businessman, as a matter of habit, makes marginal memos as he reads, then tosses the letters to his secretary for handling. His office, as well as his mind, is set up to handle them. They fit his permanent files, his "bring-up" drawers, his "do-today" baskets. Letters, one might say, are a familiar, understood part of the "culture." And by and large, the closer your advertising letter resembles the businessman's day-to-day personal communications, the better chance it has to hit home.

If a businessman is to stay on top of the newest information in his fields of interest, he *must* read his mail advertising. Well-adapted mailing lists will bring him such information, sooner, usually, than he can get it otherwise.

Actually, in business, all mail is given consideration. Industrial and commercial advertising, furthermore, account for a good-sized part of all direct mail. And this advertising pays.

What Happens to Direct Mail in the Office?

Waldie and Briggs, Chicago, had a study made which, among other things, was set up to determine ". . . how many of the prospects receiving the mailing discarded it without reading; read and remembered it; filed it for reference; passed it along to an associate." [3]

And here are the results of how the mailings were disposed of: [4]

	Company A per cent	Company B per cent
How did you dispose of this mailing?		
Discarded without reading	4.5	9.1
Read and discarded	34.8	27.3
Filed for reference	7.6	15.2
Passed along to associate	33.3	24.2

[3] Robert F. DeLay, "It Can Be Done: Let's Put More Science into Direct Mail," *Industrial Marketing*, vol. 42, no. 10, p. 50, October, 1957.

[4] *Ibid.*, p. 51.

The outstanding result of these studies was the disposition of the mailing. In the case of Company A, where 33.3 per cent of the respondents passed the mailing along to associates, the "multiple readership projected over a total mailing list means in Company A's case that one-third additional prospects received the mailing. In the case of Company B, nearly one-quarter additional prospects were contacted." [5] The "true" readership, not precisely measurable because we don't know the eventual results of "filed for reference" and "passed along," must be high. And that percentage of "filed for reference" indicates two things:

1. That your mailings in industrial direct mail and for certain types of consumer products should be so conceived, depending of course on the circumstance of product and purpose, that they can be readily filed or kept.

2. That you have created an advertising "impression" which could possibly be triggered into action by later mailings. This shows a need for continuity in your direct mail efforts.

And Who Sees the Business Mail First? Based on a study made by H. Huntly Geddes, Director of Research, R. L. Polk & Co., Detroit, among truck owners as representing a cross section of American business, Polk learned that the following is:

. . . what happens to truck advertising among businessmen.

The Man of Decision—the man who makes the major decision—sees all the mail first in 60% of the cases. The occupational level of the first person to see the mail is:

Owner	39%
President, vice-president	10
Manager	16
Clerical	15
Driver, mechanic	17
Family member	1
Other	2
	100%

A *Broad Picture of What Happens* to business mail in the office was revealed by the Polk studies. These are more of the Polk study results:

Here Is What That "First Person" Does with Mail Advertising:

Looks it over and passes it on for others	34%
Looks it over and keeps it for reference	12
Looks it over and discards it	33
Passes it on without looking it over	13
Discards it without looking it over	8
	100%

[5] *Ibid.*, p. 50.

Thus:

79% is looked over by the first person to see it.
47% is passed on by the first person to see it.
41% is discarded by the first person to see it.
12% is filed for future reference.

Here Is the Occupational Level of the "Second Person":

Owner 49%
President, vice-president 10
Manager 25
Clerical 5
Driver, mechanic 4
Family member 4
Other 3
                                                   ─────
                                                   100%

On the Second Level, the Man of Decision Sees the Advertising in 48% of the Cases, and the Second Person to See the Advertising Handles It Thus:

Looks it over and passes it on 12%
Looks it over and keeps it for reference 16
Looks it over and discards it 45
Passes it on without looking it over 0
Discards it without looking it over 27
                                                   ─────
                                                   100%

(The figures given in this section are averages from a series of studies. They reflect the conditions which existed "at the time and under those circumstances." They are believed to be applicable in a general way to similar conditions elsewhere. *However, it is always dangerous to apply data obtained under one set of conditions to different conditions.* In other words, regard these figures as a general guide. This is what they are intended to be.) [6]

Another Look-in on Mail Advertising's Reception in the Business Office is found in the Dickie-Raymond continuing studies on direct mail readership. These facts are taken from several of their studies. They give even more proof that your advertising by mail gets to your target. And gets read: [7]

1. . . . 84% of those surveyed (in a study for Pitney-Bowes) claimed that they see all third-class mail addressed to them.

. . . 52% of those surveyed . . . also claimed that they open all mail and remove the envelopes addressed to them personally.

2. . . . 86% of those surveyed (in a study made for Air Express) claimed that all third-class mail reaches their desks. And of those who recalled the

[6] "The Handling of Advertising by Its Recipients," *DMAA Research Bulletin,* vol. 1, no. 2, May 11, 1959, p. 4.

[7] "The Effectiveness of Direct Mail as a Pure Advertising Medium," *The Reporter of Direct Mail Advertising,* vol. 19, no. 12, pp. 25–26, April, 1957.

mailing, 94% always see the third-class mail addressed to them. . . . Of those who did not recall the mailing, one-third . . . receive their mail after it has been screened by another person.

3. . . . 85% of the entire group (in a study made for Air Transport Association of America) claimed that they see all third-class mail. This is the fifth (Dickie-Raymond) survey . . . [which] . . . inquired about readership of third-class mail, and it is interesting to note that from 71% to 86% of the respondents claim to see all third-class mail.

4. . . . 79% of those surveyed . . . (in a study for Dickie-Raymond Mailing Service) . . . claimed that they see all third-class mail addressed to them personally. . . . Of the 21% who answered negatively, it is important to note that more than one-third stated that their mail is screened prior to reaching them.

No matter how you look at it, then, your mail advertising sent to the businessman gets an extremely high degree of readership. With the experience of Waldie and Briggs, Polk, and Dickie-Raymond, it's obvious that the use of direct mail advertising—when it is the proper vehicle for the purpose—can bring you a good response. And a great deal of pure advertising value.

Direct Mail and the Doctors

Doctors Have an Interest in their pharmaceutical direct mail—when, as evidenced by part of the information to be given you here, it's prepared with proper care. It is, after all, a source for the latest information which helps the doctor do his job. For example, take this paragraph from the July 15, 1959, president's report to members of the Direct Mail Advertising Association:

An eminent doctor told surveyors for Fisher-Stevens, the medical direct mail house, that mail ads are so important to him he'd be *willing to subsidize* the drug companies if necessary to keep his name on their lists! This and other enthusiastic comments came as replies to a questionnaire mailed by F-S to 1,000 M.D.s. Of the 600 replies, *520 doctors favored remaining on mailing lists even after sixty-five.*

To Give Doctors what They Want in pharmaceutical direct mail, Buckley-Dement Direct Mail Advertising of Chicago researched the medical markets to determine what the doctors preferred in direct mail.

Here are answers to some of the questions put to the doctors—answers that can help you in planning pharmaceutical direct mail which will get the readership you want. These figures indicate the proportions of "yes" and "no" answers as taken from the questionnaires. The other figures indicate proportions per answer as taken from the questionnaires.

1. Do you make a practice of going through your mail personally?

Yes . . . . 4½   No 1

2. Do you give reading preference to first-class mail over second- or third-class?

          Yes .... 6½   No 1

3. Do you usually file worthwhile information received in pharmaceutical manufacturers' mailings for future reference?

          Yes 2   No 1

4. When samples and informative literature are sent you by mail, do you prefer quantities for clinical testing or only a few?

          Clinical 2   Few 1

5. Of the following types of mailing, which would you be most likely to read with interest?

          Company magazines 2
          Newsletters 3
          Case reports 4
          Medical-journal reports 1

6. As to physical form of mailing, have you any preferences among the following types?

          Booklets 1
          Folders 3
          Enclosed letters 4
          Mailing cards 2

7. Do you like to have reply cards enclosed in mailings to assist you in requesting more information, samples, etc?

          Yes 3   No 1

8. Does the occasional use of a humorous approach in pharmaceutical mailings tend to add interest in them for you?

          Yes 2   No 1

9. Do references to medical literature lend greater authority to the mailing piece?

          Yes .... 2½   No 1

Here, Too, Are Some Widely Held Opinions about Medical Direct Mail, as elicited from the 22 per cent of those doctors who took time to write comments on the questionnaire. These opinions are offered merely as guides in planning pharmaceutical direct mail—as an indication of the types of "booby traps" you can fall into. They by no means cover the entire range of these physicians' comments. They are merely some of the criticisms most frequently discussed:

1. Large mailing cards are not liked, especially when they show illus-

trations of skin diseases, etc., which may distress patients or the public who happen to see them.

2. Tricks and gimmicks create resentment in many doctors. Straight, factual presentation of the product's uses is preferred.

3. Illustration of products and packages should be exact and accurate for easy recognition.

4. Information about products should be complete, including data on side effects and contraindication.

5. Dosage, cost to patient, and packaging form should be clearly specified, preferably on a standard-size card for convenient reference filing.

6. Unsolicited advice on how to conduct his practice is resented by the physician.

7. Small-size mailers, which tell story concisely but completely, are preferred to large mailers containing lots of "hard sell."

8. Specialists are annoyed when they receive materials which have no application to their specialty.

The answers to the questions can give you a general point of view as to classes of mail and type of format which will get readership. But only as a *general* point of view. The doctors' own comments give an indication as to how pharmaceutical direct mail best fits into a doctor's professional life, how he can best utilize it. The restraints indicated in such things as illustration and gimmicks seem to "fit in" with the generally dignified concept of a doctor's profession.

For a Broader Perspective about Doctors and Direct Mail, we offer you information from an address by D. B. Mahoney, Advertising Manager, Frank W. Horner Ltd., Montreal, given at the Ontario Medical Association Convention, May 13, 1958.[8] Here are some of the facts about readership which Mr. Mahoney presented:

1. In . . . "a survey of 1,000 physicians in the United States by personal interview . . . 94% claimed to see all samples sent to them." This percentage would indicate a high degree of contact—readership—with the mail advertising which brought the samples to the doctors' attention.

2. "A survey by the American Medical Association (of) 500 physicians by personal interviews ranging from 45 minutes to 1½ hours each" . . . revealed this information: The first question asked what the last drug was which was new to the physician and which he had prescribed for the first time. Then the physician was asked this question: "Where did you happen to get information about it which led you to prescribe it?" And here are the answers:

Detail men	44%
Direct mail from drug firms	22
Papers in journals	17

[8] D. B. Mahoney, "There Is Method in Our Advertising Madness," reprinted from *Ontario Medical Review,* February, 1959.

Advertising in journals 15
Discussion with other doctors 11
Staff meetings at hospitals 5
National medical conventions 2
Other medical meetings, etc. account for the balance.
Some physicians gave two sources.

This same question, broken down on a "general-practitioner-versus-specialist" basis and compared with the general division of the drug companies' promotional dollar, gives you this interesting comparison:

The promotional dollar of the drug industry is divided, generally, this way: *

Detail men 45–55%
Direct mail 15–20
Medical journals 10–15

The G.P. prescribed the last new product through information received from: †

Detail men 48%
Direct mail 30
Medical-journal ads 18
Medical-journal articles 14

A good degree of correlation exists, then, between the advertising effort and the result, in these cases. Figures, of course, vary among the different drug companies. "Obviously the representative is considered the most effective, mail next, and then journals. However, some companies rate journals over mail. But all of these media are complementary—not competitive. The nub of this question is how best to present a new product, to dislodge someone else's by pointing up the advantages of yours through a succession of communications to bring an awareness and then physician conviction. A mixture of forces that leaves as little as possible to memory, chance or time."

The Ages of Physicians seem to have a pertinent impact on their source of new drug information. For when this question was asked: "Where did you get information about the last new drug you prescribed . . . which led you to prescribe it?" . . . these were the answers:

Detail men

Doctors under 40 .... 48%
Doctors 40–59 42
Doctors over 60 41

Papers in journals

Doctors under 40 .... 22%
Doctors 40–59 17
Doctors over 60 7

Direct mail

Doctors under 40 .... 20%
Doctors 40–59 19
Doctors over 60 32

Journal advertising

Doctors under 40 .... 19%
Doctors 40–59 13
Doctors over 60 12

The conclusion, of course, is that . . . "Physicians over sixty depend heavily on direct mail for new product information."

* The other 10% of the drug industry's promotional dollar is made up of convention displays, hospital displays, medical films, sponsorship of seminars, closed-circuit television, and visual aids for salesmen.

† Many physicians gave more than one source. The total, therefore, is more than 100%.

Mr. Mahoney's Third Study was conducted by a large American pharmaceutical house. This company had a three-year-old competitive product which was not doing too well. In fact, it didn't seem to be doing much of anything. So the company took these steps:

1. Reduced all national advertising of this product.

2. Selected four geographically separated territories for a direct mail experiment. Three of these territories had sold less than the national average for the product and one considerably more.

3. Salesmen in these territories knew nothing . . . were told nothing of the experiment.

4. The company mailed eight modest mailings for one month.

5. Then the company mailed one mailing per week for the next three years.

And here were the results:

Sales before the test: $ 690 per territory average sales
Sales after 3 months: $1,900 per month. . . .179% increase
Sales after 6 months: $2,530 per month. . . .265% increase
Sales after 3 years: $5,727 per month. . . .725% increase over the original $690.

Readership, Responses, and Bonus Impact

Direct responses of any kind are, of course, important. But it's equally as important to have your sales messages *remembered* in the future when your prospects consider use of your type of product.

Several years ago Dickie-Raymond, Inc., Boston, conceived the idea of a readership survey to measure the real effectiveness of direct mail over and above the percentage of direct responses. Beyond your direct responses lies an effectiveness in readership and retention value—a bonus impact. You try for and get direct responses. But you also create favorable impressions of your product with a good percentage of the readers who did not respond.

This area of effectiveness of direct mail implies a need for the development of well-planned, skillfully executed mailings which give you continuity. A follow-up mailing can take advantage of the impact created by earlier mailings to which some readers did not respond. It can help to create a cumulative effectiveness derived from continuously pounding at your market.

Here are some of the results of the Dickie-Raymond studies:

A Major Airline, in an effort to influence business travel via its facilities, mailed a memo, descriptive booklet, photo illustration, and business reply card, to a list of 210,000 business executives.

This mailing pulled 6,300 replies or approximately 3%. A survey of *non-respondents* was made in three areas from one week to eleven days after mailing.

It was found that City A had 39% *proved readership;* City B had 48%; and City C had 52%. Or, averaging these figures out, we find that the mailing was read by 46% or 96,500 executives. This was in addition to the 6,300 who replied directly.

The 6,300 replies, or approximately 3 per cent, are a precise measurement of the effectiveness of the advertising (a stimulus which creates a mental impression). But there is a *bonus* in pure advertising, measured on the basis of readership, which gives, actually, a much larger and more powerful effect from this advertising. For it got 46 per cent readership among nonrespondents. Responses were 3 per cent. But that's only a fragment of the "advertising" story. Since 46 per cent of the nonrespondents read the mailing, the advertising's effect created some kind of mental impression in 49 per cent of the people on the list. This means that the aim of the mailing, when measured as pure advertising, was "on target" almost half the time.

A Manufacturer of Business Machines was interested in placing an interesting booklet in the hands of as many prospects as possible.

The company used a simple sales letter and an unusual reply label which offered the free booklet. It mailed to a list of 400,000 of its prime prospects.

Besides the thousands of booklets that were distributed, a survey of those who did not respond showed that 62% or 248,000, had read at least part or most of the sales letter.

In this example the "bonus" in readership was the 62 per cent who did not respond. Your readership score, however, is really higher. Because the percentage of those who responded should be included.

A Leading Manufacturer of Electrical Equipment wanted to arouse the interest of architects in a heat-pump unit for both heating and cooling homes and commercial buildings.

The mailing piece consisted of a sales letter, a four-page booklet and a file folder. There was no reply feature. The mailing was directed to a list of 5,600 architects.

Total indicated readership of the mailing was 68% or 3,800.

Over 50% of that group reported having saved the folder for reference purposes.

The readership is 68 per cent. But *add* the impact of the future "impressions" which will result from the folder's being saved for reference purposes. Here's where your need for continuity shows up. A mailing piece which can be filed and saved for future reference can use the support of follow-up mailings to trigger action.

These studies point to this conclusion: If you use direct mail to reach a selected market, a market which should have need for your particular product or service, and if adequate skill is brought to bear in planning and executing your mailing, you can score unusually high in readership and retention value. If your skills in planning, in carrying out, in interpreting products in terms of needs, in timing, rate high on the scale of competence, you can be assured that direct mail will do a bang-up job for you.

3

How to Increase
Direct Mail Readership

Jes' Say, "Yes, Ma'am"

The best way to increase the readership of your direct mail is to be like
Marshall Field: "Give the lady what she wants." Because of the infinite
dimensions with which you can work in direct mail, you can "marshal
your creative forces" to develop the kind of impact that will increase
readership—through interest and curiosity—by remembering to "give the
lady what she wants."

Bright Individuality: A Difference

To increase readership, create the unusual, the dramatic, the "newsy,"
the eye-catching, the brightly individual. Leave the run of the mill to
your competition and create a difference in *any possible way* in your
mailings. For example, be different . . .

- in your wrapping or envelope, for that's your original contact.
- in your creative materials in format, for that's the "bearer" of your
  message.
- in the opening (or envelope teaser) copy itself, for that's the "impact-
  key" to reader action.

The Outside of Your Mailing makes it contrast with other mailings,
stand out, and compete with other mail. (Granted: Some people receive

their mail without the cover from a secretary or a mail room. But since you don't know specifically how many do or don't, don't miss the chance of competing for attention at this point. Your format, beyond the cover, should be designed to snap up those who don't see the cover.) To get a first impact of difference, then, start with the wrapper, the envelope.

In fact, probably it's a good idea to have a change of pace in any series of mailings. You should never put a reader into the position where he can assume he knows what's in your mailing, unless that is precisely what you want him to do. You can accomplish this difference of change of pace on your envelopes in several ways:

1. Change the size of the mailing unit.
2. Change the color of the unit.
3. Change the envelope teaser copy.
4. Change the finish of the paper.
5. Change the type of postage.
6. Change the color of your postage indicia.
7. Change the envelope illustration or corner card.
8. Change the type of envelope—window versus closed face.
9. Mail from a place with a "strange" postmark (Economy, Indiana, for example).[1]

Note that the "key" to *difference*, to bright individuality, is CHANGE. Don't do the same thing all the time . . . create a *difference* in what you do—to gain the kind of attention in the right places to increase the readership of your mail. For further discussion of creating a difference in your mailings, see the chapters on creative materials. (*Caution:* Don't, whatever you do, let yourself get so tied up in the attempt for "difference" that you lose the proper perspective. Actually, your selling *strategy* is the most important part of your planning. If you don't have the right strategy —expressed in a suitable offer and in well-executed copy, the dress your mailing wears can't possibly overcome strategic flaws.)

The Format of Your Mailing can make a "difference." For example, to make your mail stand out—to demand readership: If your competitors are using one type of format, you use another. "If your direct mail has developed a kind of *sameness,* is quickly recognized by those who receive it as coming from you, thereby giving too many an opportunity to prejudge the contents, then you'd be smart to start giving its appearance" . . . a difference.[2]

This statement applies first to your mailing's cover, but it applies equally as well to the format. Change your formats. Vary them. If for

[1] Kurt Vahle, "Does the Outside Affect Inside Readership?" *Convoys,* vol. 12, no. 2, pp. 3–10, Cupples-Hesse Corporation, St. Louis.

[2] Edward N. Mayer, Jr. and Earle A. Buckley, "Let's Make Direct Mail More Profitable," *Bulletin of the Buckley Institute,* vol. 1, no. 17, Philadelphia (n.d.), p. 1.

some reason you wish to use a format continuously, say, for example, a French fold, then change the color of the paper, of the ink, of any dimension which can be altered—add die cuts, etc. Admittedly, there are certain types of mailings where the format must be kept constant, to reinforce continually your advertising impression. For example, newsletters. But these are not the competitive types of messages which try to persuade to action. In some types of campaigns which aim only to advertise—to create a favorable impression in the minds of readers—to be followed by personal selling, you want to create such a *difference*, to make yourself such a standout, that your advertising's impact becomes deeper with every mailing. (See the description of Union Bag-Camp Paper Corporation, Chapter 15.)

The Familiarity of an Old Friend Who Calls by Mail

Many mailers send out an item which has a *sameness* to it which increases readership by creating favorable original reactions and by reactivating former impressions in the minds of readers. The idea of repeating is to create a continuity of impression, to reinforce the previous "punch" of your advertising's impact. The reader feels, when he receives this type of "sameness" mailing, "It was pleasant once. . . . It will be pleasant again." As an example, the cordial-contact (reminder) letters in Chapter 23 always maintain a certain sameness. They use the same letterhead. They have the same "touch" in the copy. (Occasionally, a holiday type of letterhead is good in a cordial-contact campaign. But, the copy's style should remain constant . . . to sustain your continuity.) It's this sameness that makes them successful. Actually this type of sameness is bright individuality . . . a difference itself. Because it takes talent and skill to maintain the same friendly pitch which this type of letter must needs have.

Another example of sameness, of a reminder from "an old friend," is the Executive Pocket Appointment Calendar which Names Unlimited, New York, mails. Always it is the same. But always it keeps their reminder of their available services *fresh*. And always it fits the pocket . . . does the job of keeping track of things. Sameness, in some ways imperative, in others undesirable. You have to avoid it or adapt it according to the type of advertising job you're trying to do.

The Readability of Layout

Copy layout is another important way of increasing readership, by making the copy *appear* to be easy to read. You can get two kinds of attention—both of which lead to readership. One is Voluntary Attention, the other Involuntary Attention. If a person wants something from a want-ad section of a newspaper, he'll plow his way through the bewildering clutter to find it. He'll do this hunting because he already has an interest or a need that asks satisfaction. This is Voluntary Attention.

If you'll recall, however, the full-page spreads which stores like Marshall Field's place in newspapers, you'll notice that the ads have lots of white space . . . a focal point to draw the reader's eye. The white space, the result of wide-open layout, is to make the ad *seem* easy to read. This is an attempt to get Involuntary Attention. It looks so easy to read. The reader resists it less.

This same principle applies in direct mail. If you'll break up your paragraphs, simplify your punctuation, make the copy *look* easy to read, you'll increase your readership. You'll overcome that problem of the reader's innate inertia. Take these following examples. The same copy is used in both. But, notice how much easier it is to read the second one. Because the copy has lots of "air." It breathes. While the other example is too jam-packed . . . doesn't look inviting or easy to read. One is a solid block of uninviting print. The other, through broken, parallel, indented layout and more "liberal" punctuation, creates a more inviting, more readable setup. (At this point, apologies to The National Research Bureau, Inc., Chicago, for the way their copy has been mangled, in the first example, to make a point.)

Example 1:

Here is what the Newspaper Working Press of the Nation and the Magazine Working Press of the Nation can do for you: You will find at a glance the key individual or contact you are seeking for any of the nation's newspapers, allied services, or important magazines. You will receive more publicity by addressing to the right name, title, and affiliation. You will find hundreds of new channels for publicity and promotion. You will save time and money by increasing accuracy and efficiency, eliminating the costly process of compiling and keeping mailing lists. These volumes offer the most comprehensive compilations of key personnel on the nation's systems of communications ever published.

Example 2:

Here is what the Newspaper Working Press of the Nation and the Magazine Working Press of the Nation can do for you:

   . . . You will find, at a glance, the key individual or contact you are seeking . . . for any of the nation's newspapers, allied services, or important magazines.

   . . . You will receive more publicity by addressing to the right name, title, and affiliation.

. . . You will find hundreds of new channels for publicity and promotion.

. . . You will save time and money by increasing accuracy and efficiency, eliminating the costly process of compiling and keeping publicity mailing lists.

These volumes offer the most comprehensive compilations of key personnel on the nation's systems of communications ever published.

What "Snaps Up" Reader Interest?

The "snapper-upper" of reader interest is the subject of the advertising, with the necessary techniques of copy, layout, etc., properly applied.

And interest is as variable as the weather, among groups of people as well as among individuals. Anyone's interests vary with the circumstances of his life. Vary from day to day, week to week, season to season. Things which modify the mental emphasis persons or groups have in a product include their age, the weather, their financial and emotional circumstances, and the like. Never to forget their ever-prodding egos and the state of their amours.

An individual's interest also varies with his attitudes toward what he considers proper status symbols for himself. The man climbing to the next rung, for example, of the fragile ladder of success doesn't have the same type of interest in cars that an eight-kid pop with a median income does.

Groups vary in their interest, too. Lent makes quite an impact upon food choices. So it evolves into this: Too many situations have too much impact on individual and group interests, at too many different times, for people to have a straight line of constancy in their interest patterns. The wise direct mailer will cotton to these variations and adapt to them—where he can.

What Determines Interest is presented in a *DMAA Research Bulletin.* This bulletin reports on an attitude study made by a well-known magazine that ". . . wanted to know the attitude toward mail advertising of the upper-income class which constitutes their market. This group reported an average of about 15 pieces of mail advertising in a single week. The median works out at about 12. The highest-pieces-per-week group (60 pieces and over) constituted 1% of the total market; the lowest group (9 pieces or less) constituted 11%.

"The largest single category of mail . . . [received by this group] . . . was from magazines. Next in order were retail stores, then insurance, book clubs, furniture mail-order houses, and so on through twenty categories of advertisers.

"Now here are the 'payoff' figures in answer to the probing question on attitude. . . . But . . . first . . . these figures are from an attitude study within a certain group of people. They are not necessarily universally applicable." [3]

Whenever I receive advertising mail, I am . . .

Always interested 30%
    Read all of it 20%
    Read, then decide 8
    Take home, read later 1
    File after reading 1

Sometimes interested 47%
    Read if of interest to me 12%
    Read if right product 3
    Read quickly 13
    Sometimes read 1
    Throw away after reading 18

Never interested 23%
    Throw away 15%
    Am not interested 5
    Get annoyed 1
    Don't receive any 1
    No answer 1

And here we have degrees of interest as applied to the several types of products advertised by mail:

Subject	Degree of interest		
	Always interested, per cent	Sometimes interested, per cent	Never interested, per cent
Product DM	31	44	24
Book	49	26	24
Magazine	29	27	43

Next we find the results in this attitude survey of "the kind of advertising mail I like to receive" and "the kind I do not like to receive."

The kind of advertising mail I like to receive

Looks like . . .

1. Something friendly 30%
2. Something informative...... 30
3. Something factual 25
4. A concise letter 10
5. Something uncluttered...... 3
6. The prices are included.... 2

                100%

And it tells me . . .

1. What it can do for me...... 42%
2. About quality and price.... 25
3. Something concisely 20
4. Something gaily and color-
    fully 5
5. World news 7
6. No answer 1

                100%

[3] "The Handling of Advertising by Its Recipients," *DMAA Research Bulletin*, vol. 1, no. 2, May 11, 1959, pp. 2–3.

The kind of advertising mail I do not like to receive

Looks like . . .		*And it tells me . . .*	
1. A gimmick	36%	1. Something in a misrepresented way	28%
2. Misrepresenting	14	2. A lot of nothing	26
3. Bulky mail	8	3. About worthless bargains..	15
4. Noninformative	8	4. Something in a high-pressure way	5
5. Something for nothing....	8	5. Something flattering	3
6. It's patronizing	1	6. Something patronizing	3
7. High pressure	1	7. Soft soap	3
8. Flattering nonsense	1	8. What to do	3
9. No answer	6	9. Same old stuff	1
10. Doesn't like any advertising mail	17	10. No answer	4
		Not interested in any advertising	9
	100%		100%

Copy Openers "Pick Up" Interest. Your copy opener may be exciting, or, if you wish, startling, but it *must* be interesting enough so that the reader wants to read on. One way is so to relate your product's benefits to a fulfillment of a reader's needs or desires that he wishes to finish reading the letter. (Creating attention has been discussed in Chapter 8.)

An example of a direct mail opener which immediately hits at the reader's interest was mailed to teachers of English. The Mid-Century Book Society, Inc. hit at the English teacher's desires—on the envelope—in this broadside, appealing fashion:

> A few remarks
> addressed to those
> who really like books
> and need them . . .

The envelope carried a picture of Jacques Barzun, W. H. Auden, Lionel Trilling (all familiar to English teachers) sitting around a table. They were, the copy stated, "holding this meeting for you." A good appeal. Because those on the list felt themselves on familiar ground of mutual interest with these three men. They are "involved," in essence, in the same or similar type of interest. The enclosed letter repeated the envelope's teaser copy . . . then went on to say:

> This letter is directed to those who delight in literary discovery, relish good writing, enjoy the appearance of a well-made book. And take pride in gathering a library.
>
> We feel that you, as a person of independent mind, will recognize what this letter has to say can be important to you.

From a picture which creates an immediate acceptance of mutual interest or involvement between reader and mailer, from a teaser on the envelope which hits hard at one of the reader's primary interests—books, to the opening paragraphs, this letter has what it takes to get the reader started reading.

Personal Involvement and Product Interest

For further illustration of how a person's involvement with a product has a very positive effect on the readership of advertising of that product, we'll take up another DMAA case study.

This was a study made of a mailing used by a nationally advertised brand of carpet. The mailing included a booklet, a letter with a one-line fill-in, and a coupon for $5. It was sent to householders who recently had moved into newer homes. Several local dealers were identified in the letter.

The booklet was designed to display the product's patterns and colors in such a way that the housewife could get ideas for the decoration of her home. It had well-developed suggestions for interior-décor ideas— everything from colors, to carpet, to ideal wallpaper designs. The cover had a lilting mood, showing a lovely blonde (naturally!) and a picture of carpet fading into an abstract of the ever-ever land of beauty and happiness. The title, well calculated to keep most women in suspense, was: *The Masland "Happy Mood" Book of Color.* From the gaiety of the blonde, to the impact of the words *happy mood,* to the note, "Price, 25 cents" (and what woman doesn't like *that* kind of bargain?), the cover had an almost irresistible personality. So the mailing, *in toto,* said more than, "Yes, ma'am." It said, "Yes, ma'am, and How!" [4]

Meanwhile, back at the enclosed letter, the plot was thickening. . . .

C. H. MASLAND & SONS
Carlisle, Pennsylvania
MASLAND
Weavers of Fine Rugs and Broadloom Carpets

Date

Dear Mrs. _____ [The one-line, individualized fill-in]
Since you have recently moved to your new address, it is most likely that you, like nearly all "movers," have decorating problems.

If so, you may welcome some of the very practical suggestions in our *Masland "Happy Mood" Color Book,* a complimentary copy of which is enclosed. Many thousands of these have been sold and put to good use.

You may be particularly intrigued with the pages of wall colors and fabric patterns in the back of the book, which can be torn out and laid against the carpet colors to work out your own color schemes.

[4] "Direct Mail Case Studies," *DMAA Research Bulletin,* vol. 1, no. 3, July, 1959, p. 1.

Unfortunately, no printed picture can capture the really distinctive beauty of Masland "Happy Mood" Carpet Colors. You can see the actual colors, however, by calling at any of these fine stores:

[List of stores]

To make this doubly worth your while, I am also enclosing a special certificate good for $5 toward the purchase of any Masland room-size carpet from any of the stores listed above. This certificate is good for 60 days and may be used for a lay-away purchase if you do not need new carpet immediately.

Yours very sincerely,

Note in this letter how the copy gets on common ground at once by showing the writer knows the reader has recently moved. Note also the third paragraph, where the copy tries to involve the reader, the booklet, and the reader's home into a unified knot of interest. Note, too, the mention of the coupon. All these were calculated to establish a rapport between the ideas of the mailing and the desires of the reader—to get personal involvement through well-developed interest.

To Determine the Effectiveness of This Mailing, interviews were held with a representative sample of the mailing list. The interviews were started within ten days after the date of the ad's delivery. And they were completed within a week. Here are the results of the study: [5]

61% of the respondents recalled the booklet.
57% of the respondents recalled the letter.
43% had read all or some of the booklet.
37% still had the booklet in the house.
13% had used the materials to work out a color scheme.
3% had gone to a store.
7% intended to go.
3% intended to buy this carpet.

Personal Involvement's Cause of Degrees of Interest shows up in this study. This mailing, sent to new occupants, also included renters. Note, in the results of the interviews, how renting brings a lower degree (in this instance) of interest in the product—carpet—and therefore lower degrees of involvement with house furnishings of this type. Note these data: [6]

Only 24% of the renters recalled this mailing, while
. . . 86% of the homeowners recalled the mailing.

Here it's obvious that ownership of one's home projects a greater degree of interest in certain types of products—here, carpets—which have to do with the home. This is just a tenuous inference . . . but when a person is "involved" financially with a situation, his "care" for that

[5] *Ibid.*
[6] *Ibid.*

situation, his pride of ownership, create a greater degree of interest in maintenance, development, and improvement.

But on with our data: To show how renters lack an interest in this type of product, look at these facts: [7]

1. Only 20% of the renters had purchased any carpet within the previous six years.

2. 56% of the homeowners had purchased carpet within six years, and well over half had purchased within two years.

The study revealed further that . . . "One-third of the homeowners who received the mailing were the original occupants of the house in which they lived," while . . . "only 4%" of the renters were original occupants.[8]

These facts show how circumstances influence interest in products . . . how they can affect the degree of a reader's personal involvement.

The Answer to Creating Involvement, then, boils down to a well-defined list, the right product, properly meshed in the copy's appeal with the reader's interests and desires, at a proper place, mailed at the right time. It's a case of "giving the lady what she wants, how she wants it, when she wants it." Neat trick . . . if you can do it. And you can. Others have.

A Potpourri of Points

Here are several lists of points, with a potpourri of ideas, to consider when you plan a mailing. These ideas are the result of many years of experience by competent direct mail practitioners. They are well based in professional competence.[9]

TEN TIPS FOR BETTER READERSHIP FOR LETTERS

1. Have an opening that promises the reader a benefit (free booklet, time or money saving, etc.).

2. Ask a question that gets the reader mentally to nod his head.

3. Get "news" into the headline.

4. Keep opening paragraph short—mix up long and short paragraphs.

5. Address the reader as an individual. Don't write a headline, "To all our good customers," when the letter presumably will be seen by only one.

6. Come to the point quickly. Don't start off with an irrelevant story or anecdote, no matter how good it may be. It's a sure sign you don't know *how* to get started.

[7] *Ibid.*
[8] *Ibid.*
[9] "The Effectiveness of Direct Mail as a Pure Advertising Medium," *The Reporter of Direct Mail Advertising,* vol. 19, no. 12, p. 28, Garden City, N.Y., April, 1957.

7. Don't annoy the reader—and lose him—by telling him obvious things about his own business.

8. To carry reader along through the entire copy—and to smooth transition from paragraph to paragraph—use conjunctions liberally—especially at the opening of sentences and paragraphs.

9. Try to make your letter personal, low-pressure, friendly, sincere, informal.

10. After writing your first paragraph ask yourself, "Is that what I'd say right after the handshake if I were calling in person?"

NINE TIPS FOR GETTING READERSHIP FOR PRINTED PIECES

1. Use interesting and easy-to-read testimonials.

2. Have eye-catching illustration.

3. Use a fresh, "off-beat" approach—humor, old-fashioned type, layout, copy.

4. Try for a dramatic layout: use unusual camera angles and effects in photographic illustrations.

5. Use unusual folds or die cuts.

6. Try sending *pre*prints of space ads instead of *re*prints—with a letter.

7. When mailing helpful, technical, or semitechnical information to people like engineers and architects, lean the other way and avoid *all* tricks or frills—pack your mailing with helpful facts.

8. When preparing a booklet to be offered, don't fill the entire booklet with "nuts and bolts." Make the first half of the booklet objective, helpful, informative—without any "sell."

9. Enclose your booklet or printed piece in an envelope and have a letter of transmittal *selling* the piece—rationalize why you have sent it.

But It Takes "Know-how" for Results

The Dickie-Raymond studies (Chapter 2) pointed out that they . . . "so far have dealt with material properly and professionally planned . . . [and] . . . no one . . . [should] . . . get the idea that all direct mail gets as warm a welcome, or high a percentage of readership." [10] You can't just throw something together, toss it in the mail, get it back, and know you're successful. Sometimes it may work that way. But, as in anything that is really effective—be it writing, be it painting, be it sculpture, or even conversation—it takes *know-how* to create the most effective results.

This need for "proper, professional" planning for creating (or obtaining) readership does not apply only to direct mail. It applies to any kind of advertising. In one Daniel Starch study, it was determined that "top copy writers get top readership." This study showed that forty-two top-

[10] *Ibid.*

rated ads . . . got ". . . one-third more observers, three times as many thorough readers as average ads."

As Mr. Starch notes, "These favorite advertisements prepared by top copy writers were, to be sure, materially above average in attention-attraction power, but their outstanding strength was in *their power to get copy read.*" [11]

Skill, then, in properly planning, properly creating any kind of advertisement, is a prerequisite to most effective readership. Surely, many things affect readership: timing, color, shape and size, competition with other mail (or ads) and other events, even the amount of previous mail contact with the reader. "But," as Mr. Starch further notes, . . . "nothing equals a fertile imagination applied to an empty page. This is what makes the big difference. Whether the dreams of the imagination are practical and effective must be determined by experience and inquiry." [12] There is no substitute for imagination in creating advertising. There is also no substitute for research to test the product of creative imagination.

Toward an Improved Medium

To make direct mail an even more effective advertising medium than it is, to add stature to this "Cinderella" of all advertising media, various organizations are dedicated to research, education, and the sharing of knowledge and experience.

In their conventions, workshops, institutes, meetings, they exchange ideas for the benefit of all . . . and for the benefit of direct mail itself. Chief among those groups and institutions which are working to further the interests of direct mail through high standards of ethics and performance are:

The Direct Mail Advertising Association, 230 Park Avenue, New York, New York

The Business Mail Foundation, 230 Park Avenue, New York, New York

The Mail Advertising Service Association, 622 Fifth Street, N.W., Washington 1, D.C.

The American Business Writing Association, 1007 West Nevada Street, Urbana, Illinois

The National Council of Mailing List Brokers, 55 West 42nd Street, New York, New York

[11] Daniel Starch, "Do Top Copy Writers Get Top Readership?" *Printers' Ink,* vol. 254, no. 3, p. 32, Jan. 20, 1956.

[12] *Ibid.,* p. 34.

4

How to Handle Lists

The Importance of Lists

"I learned how to play golf in two minutes this morning," the dizzy blonde said. "There's nothing to it, really. All you do is hit a ball with a club until it goes in a hole. When you can get in the hole every time with one hit, you're perfect."

Alas! When you start to learn golf, there's no end to it. There are always more things to learn. Something new always goes wrong. The ball *never* goes in the hole, every time, with one hit.

And so it is with lists. There's "nothing to it," really. All you do is put *all* your prospects on a list and take *all* your nonprospects off. As soon as that's done, you're perfect. You can stop worrying about your list, for the moment.

Please don't take that lightly. Prospects on, nonprospects off. That's your goal, as a hole in one is your goal in golf. It's a goal you should constantly strive for. And one you'll probably never reach.

But your striving is as important as anything else you can do to improve your direct mail. Some direct mail men say the list is 50 or 60 per cent "important" in direct mail results. Actually, if you think about it, it's 100 per cent important. Because if your list is 100 per cent nonprospects, your mail will be a 100 per cent failure. But your list will never be that bad. Neither will it be perfect very often. So keep working on it.

The list is the weakest spot in many direct mail programs, because it is taken for granted. A large company may require ten O.K.s on the copy and art. An advertiser hovers over the printer's shoulder to see that the ink matches his sample exactly. Photos may be carefully retouched to bring out the product's name. But most people just *assume* that their list is in good shape. And that's dangerous. It's natural, though.

A perfect list, like a hole in one, is just about impossible. So working on a list is frustrating. And, besides, in all other forms of advertising, someone else develops the "list," or audience, for you. You buy it ready-made, "as is," and use it all. They analyze it for you. They keep the addresses up to date; you don't have anything to say about it. So, you don't worry about it.

But direct mail's greatest—its most important—reason for being is *selectivity*. That advantage is lost unless:

1. You build a good list to begin with.
2. You *keep* it good.

Building Your List

How do you build a good list? What sources do you use? How do you judge the names? When are you satisfied? The answer varies with each problem, of course, but here are some usual sources:

Your own organization. When you mail to the customers or former customers on your books, or to the prospects your salesmen call on regularly, a good list is easy to build. Because you have the records in your office. You can also go through your correspondence files and take the names and addresses of people with whom you have corresponded. Some of these can be added to your prospect list.

You can, however, often build a list of additional good prospects, yourself. Have your salesmen develop a list for their own territories. Or, if you are in retail business, use some method or form to get the names and addresses of cash customers. Delivery slips, repair tags, etc., when completely filled out, will help. A "contest" of any sort will also bring in names and addresses.

Compiled lists. Another approach to the list problem is to compile your own lists—getting the names and addresses from other lists. This is the best solution to many problems—especially local ones. Remember, there are two parts to list building. First, define your prospect. Second, get his address. But, if you have defined your prospect as "anyone who lives within ten blocks of my store" and if you have a city directory or criss-cross phone book that lists these names, it would be silly to cover the ground on foot, ringing doorbells to get names and addresses. If people who play golf tend to be good prospects for you . . . and you can get membership lists of local country clubs, that's easier than asking questions at the nineteenth hole (although that too may have its rewards).

Current directories offer you precisely the kind of selection you need for your good prospects. But a *warning:* Almost every directory is out of date by the time it is printed. A city directory may be 8 to 10 per cent wrong before the ink is dry. But it still may give you the best list you can get for a start.

Here are some suggested sources for directories or similar publications from which you can compile lists:

City directories
Telephone directories
Telephone "yellow pages"
Telephone, "crisscross" (owners of telephones listed by address)
Organization membership lists
Automobile or other property lists
Auto-license lists
Thomas's *Register*
MacRae's *Blue Book*
Industry "Buyers' Guides"
State or local manufacturers' lists
Credit-rating books
Who's Who
These, and many, many more

Most associations publish a list of their members.

B. Klein & Company, 27 East 22nd Street, New York 10, New York, publishes a *Mail-order Business Directory* and *A Guide to American Directories for Compiling Mailing Lists.*

There are, however, a couple of major disadvantages to directories. First, they're often out of date, since directories usually aren't corrected after they are printed. Second, there's a danger in using a directory, because it *is* relatively easy to get and inexpensive. You may find yourself mailing to a group of names which does not actually have better-than-average prospects for you. So be sure, when you compile, that you are compiling the names of *true* prospects.

In addition to directories there are many other sources of list data, particularly in the local-list field. Some of those are:

Voting lists
Tax lists
City or county records, showing property transfers, building permits, liquor licenses, etc.

Other sources, in addition to directories and prepared lists from which you can compile your own lists:

Coupons from your own newspaper or magazine ads
Listing of rural-route quantities from postmaster
Occupant lists
Birth lists from newspapers
Engagement and marriage notices

Publicity stories in newspapers or magazines
Trade-show attendance
Telephone or personal call
Open-house attendance
Enclosures in your mailings on which you ask prospects to suggest other prospects.

Your regional office of the U.S. Department of Commerce is one of your best list sources. The department personnel keep government-compiled lists available, both domestic and foreign, and they'll also furnish information about lists and directories available elsewhere. They're eager to help you.

Sometimes your only possible source is a personally compiled list. And sometimes compiling it takes real ingenuity. Some years ago a reducing studio, wanting a list of rich, fat ladies in Manhattan, hired "spotters" to roam the Park Avenue and Riverside Drive area with an eye out for avoirdupois. Whenever a prospect disappeared into an apartment building, the spotter would walk past and say to the doorman, "That was Mrs. Johnson, wasn't it?" "No, the doorman would respond, "That was Mrs. _____," and another name was on the list.

Another practical way to compile a list is to give away something that interests *only* people who need or use your product. In such a case, you can use mass-advertising media—magazines, newspapers, radio, television, publicity, trade shows, etc.—to get requests. But here again, be careful. Don't choose your give-away because it is generally *popular*. You'll get too many requests from nonprospects. Give away something which *only* better-than-average prospects are likely to want at all.

Rent or buy your list. Sometimes a list you want exists right now, in a "list house" or in someone else's files. For example, you can almost always buy a national or regional list if your best prospects are grouped by occupation, neighborhood, income (if it's high), auto ownership, or if you sell to a particular type of business.

There are hundreds of sources for purchased lists, national, local, general, and specialized. The largest general list houses are Donnelley,* Polk,* Ponton *; and the U.S. Department of Commerce * has compiled a list of list sources. Also the DMAA is happy to make specific suggestions. Your local direct mail shop may be able to help with local lists and, through contacts with national sources, with national lists.

Normally, you'll buy those lists outright and maintain them yourself. Some folks prefer to let the list house keep the list clean. So they buy the list "fresh" each time and have the list house type it directly on the envelopes they expect to use. Some list houses have special rates to encourage this. If you mail to the list frequently, however, the ideal way

* See SOURCE LIST for full names and addresses.

is to buy the list and let your direct mail house maintain it for you. And occasionally—every year or two—buy the list again to get the new names and the changes you've missed.

Then, too, you can often *rent* the use of a mailing list from another list user whose customers or prospects are likely to be better-than-average prospects of yours. You probably can't rent your direct competitor's list, but some mighty similar ones are often available.

The usual rental procedure has three steps:

1. You arrange for the use of the list you want and for a particular date.

2. You prepare the mailing completely, "except for the address," and ship it to the list owner along with a check for at least the postage involved.

3. He addresses the pieces. Then he either mails them from his post office or ships them direct to your postmaster.

In some cases, your direct mail shop may be able to arrange to have the list addressed onto empty envelopes for you, under a guarantee not to copy the list. Then you can mail from your own post office and control the mailing date without the cost of shipping back and forth.

The three major sources for rented lists are:

1. The list owners themselves.

2. Magazine publishers, who often rent their subscription lists (in some cases, only to their own advertisers).

3. List brokers, who keep detailed records of thousands of available lists. And who are always eager to search their files for the answer to your particular problem. They are paid by the list owners. So their service is free to you.

All three sources will usually make arrangements for you to rent part of a list for testing if you want to.

Rented lists, if you can find the right ones, are often your best and least troublesome source. The list owner has all the maintenance headaches, and the cost is often about the same as commercial-typing charges. Of course you can't refine the list or check for duplications. Your mailing schedule is slowed, and sometimes you lose control of your mailing date. But unless these are serious disadvantages for you, it will pay to investigate rented lists.

Don't ever try to rent empty envelopes and "steal" the list, though. (You wouldn't try that. But some renters have. And they're always caught. List owners are suspicious folk, and they sprinkle each list with an occasional "imaginary" customer at the address of a friend or change the middle initial of a cooperative customer. When an "extra" mailing shows up from a renter, they know exactly what's happened.)

Sellers and renters of lists usually "guarantee" 100 per cent (sometimes a little less) accuracy. This means they'll refund postage. And sometimes they limit that to one unit of first-class postage per piece on all mail returned to you as undeliverable or through your use of Section 3547 (see page 50). They do *not* guarantee that every address on their list is correct. That would be impossible. Even if it *were* 100 per cent correct when they sold it to you, some people would have moved or died while you were getting out the mailing.

On the average, about five people out of every thousand *move each week*. Even more change jobs. In business, about nine or ten executives out of every thousand change something (titles, location, etc.) in any given week. You can see what happens in a year to a list.

So don't get excited when the postman brings back a stack of returns after a large mailing. After all, that's what you've asked him to do. But if you do buy or rent a list with a "guarantee," be sure to claim your refund, even if it's only a few cents. Then the list will be in better shape for the next user. This continuous cleaning of the list is one of the reasons it pays the owner to rent. The list is in better shape when he wants to use it.

These returns, or "nixies" as the list people call them, are a positive, continuous reminder that your list-building job is never finished. And it certainly isn't, for other reasons than changing addresses, too.

Charles Kettering once said, "It's much harder to improve selling techniques than production techniques, . . . and the reason is, people change from morning to afternoon, but pieces of metal don't."

He was talking about attitudes, interests, motivations, etc. So when you realize that people not only move around physically but also change from prospects to nonprospects and back again, you'll understand why eternal vigilance is the price of a good list.

Once you have compiled or purchased your list, you may want to sit back and relax. Don't! Your first step is to find out how good your list is, whether it has weak spots, how it can be improved. Depending on your situation, you'll probably do this in one of two ways:

1. *If you know the characteristics of your prospects very well and feel you have a list that matches them:* Your job, then, is to find out whether the names on the list are the kind of people you want. So you'll take some small samples. If you buy a nationwide list, you'll probably turn immediately to the names for your own town. If you have salesmen, it will be best to have them spot-check their territories too. If you use a local list, you might want to drive by some of the addresses, or phone some of the names at random. However you do it, you'll soon find that checking on *specific* names or addresses helps to show up the list's strength or weakness. Your next step might be to use some form of list-cleaning device, as mentioned in Chapter 5.

2. *When you cannot define your prospects very well or cannot find a*

list that matches them exactly: About the only way, then, that you can judge sources is to test them. Take samples of each of a number of lists. Then mail the same material to the whole group. You assume that the samples which give you the best returns represent the best lists for you.

Folks who sell by mail do this all the time, of course. They evaluate their list opportunities by direct test. But those who simply "advertise" by mail have a harder time measuring results. Sometimes they'll offer a catalogue or booklet and figure that the number and quality of requests show the interest and relative value of the list. Or they'll send out questionnaires, ask the recipients to reply if they ever expect to be interested in the product, and compile a "prospect" list from the "suspects."

Bob Crawford, in Akron, used this technique to develop a list for a men's-clothing store. He simply mailed to every promising local list of men that he could get his hands on. His letter offered to include the reader on the list of men who received presale announcements. He enclosed a reply card ("Yes, I would like to receive notices about the private-sale dates") and, from the returns, compiled a fine list of interested prospects, who, incidentally, had now *asked* to receive the store's advertising.

Well, then, let's assume you have your list. Next you must decide how to keep it so it's most usable. You have many choices. And the best way for you will depend upon:

1. The turnover in your list
2. The frequency of use
3. Whether you want subdivisions
4. The quality of reproduction you want
5. The price you are willing to pay

No method we know about is "best" under all conditions.

Maintaining Your List

Here is the true story of an AaA1, multimillion-dollar manufacturing plant. They hired a direct mail agency to do all the important work in connection with their mailings, but pointed out that they "had" a list of customers and prospects. Was it up to date? Certainly!

So their office service addressed the envelopes and sent them to a letter shop . . . where they would meet the rest of the job. After a few months, the letter shop called the agency and said, "Look, it is none of our business, but there's something fishy about that list. We have mailed *exactly* the same number of pieces for three straight months." When word got to the advertising manager he pooh-poohed it. But he decided to check the list. He found it had not been checked for *seven years*. They had used none of the simple methods of list cleaning. They had used no methods at all. The only time a man got off that list was when he died and someone else wrote them. The only time a new man got on was when he asked to be put on. The ad manager found the names of local men who had been dead four years. And, to his consternation, he failed to find the firm's three *best* customers.

If you plan to use your list over a long period of time, it's important, then, to set up a method to keep it "clean." When you expect to use a list for only a few weeks or months, you probably would not bother. In such a case, it is usually cheaper to waste a few mailing pieces than to set up a correction system.

MAILING LIST CHANGES Additions, Deletions and Corrections. Send White and Yellow copies to Graphic Service (COMPANY NAME & ADDRESS) _____		Sheet No. _____ Date _____ 19__				
NAME AND ADDRESS (Firm Name, Street, City, State) (Name and Initials of Individual)	Class. Code	Action Required			OLD ADDRESS & REMARKS
		Add	Drop	Cor.	
1.					
2.					
3.					
8.					
9.					
10.					

Here are the major areas of list maintenance:

1. *New names.* The world has not stopped just because you have your list on plates. You should, then, have a plan and system for adding new names.

2. *Duplication of names.* Particularly when you maintain more than one list. But you would be surprised to know how easy it is to keep two identical addressograph plates in one file, indefinitely.

3. *Errors.* Names, addresses, spellings, etc., when incorrect, can cost you money through undeliverable mail. And, through creating antagonism by mishandling a person's proudest possession, his name.

4. *Changes.* This is the most difficult, of course. People move, die, get

promoted and fired, change jobs. Something is happening to the names and addresses on your list *all the time*.

Naturally, one of the first things you need is a system for changing your list physically. That is the easy part. You *can* give corrections verbally, jot them on a piece of paper, or circle the name at the bottom of a letter. That is, you can handle the problem casually. If you do, however, sooner or later you will be sorry. You must keep at it to keep a list *fresh*.

You should treat the names on your list like money (which they certainly represent if they are any good) and have systematic "bookkeeping" transactions. On page 47 is an example of the correction slip used by Graphic Service, a direct mail agency in Dayton.

Customers using this sheet prepare an original and a carbon, listing the corrections, additions, or deletions for their list. They keep the carbon as their record, to compare with proofs of the new or corrected plates, and send the original as instructions. Because it is handled in an organized way, the plating goes faster; there is less chance of loss or error. And any "interpretations" of signature, title, etc., (which are often necessary when reading names and addresses originally written en route by salesmen or mailmen) can be made in the customer's office.

You also need to know what corrections to make. And it is good to tackle many of the areas—individually.

1. New names: If you have compiled your list, keep on compiling it. If you've purchased it, plan to get an up-to-date revision in a year or so. But, whatever you do, set a date—six months, a year, eighteen months, two years ahead—for a complete revision. How long you wait between revisions depends on the turnover among your prospects, of course.

2. Duplication: Code the various categories of your list and keep them in one file . . . if that is practical. If not, it pays to run off a set of 3- by 5-inch cards for each list and consolidate them into one alphabetical or geographical order. Then, whenever an addition, correction, or deletion is made, you can check for duplications when filing the new card.

3. Errors: Typing errors seem to be part of life and one of the strong reasons for the increase in mechanical addressing. On the other hand, a mechanical error is perpetuated. So at least a couple of proofreadings are advisable when the plates or stencils are first cut. The occasional use of an "Is-your-name-and-address-correct?" list cleaner will help, too.

4. Changes: There are a number of standard, reasonably satisfactory ways to get those changes which are known to the post office. And most list changes are.

However, the post office cannot tell you whether your addressee has left a large company, changed his title, ceased being a prospect, etc. You will have to work that problem out yourself. There are many ways. The most important and effective ways are discussed in the next chapter.

5

How to Keep a List
Up to Date

List Stability Makes a Difference

Naturally, the amount of attention that must be given to a list depends on the stability of the list itself. If, for example, you have a mail-order business aimed at young people, who are constantly moving, getting married, and changing jobs, your list will be in constant turmoil. And the percentage of change per year will be astronomical. If you are addressing businessmen, the change will be smaller. If your mail is directed to a business firm itself, the change rate is lower yet.

Among service professions, the most stable classification is that of architects, who have only a 5 per cent change a year in normal times. At the other extreme are barbers, lists of whom will be found to change 37 per cent a year. The average change in the professions, according to the large mail-order houses, is about 15 per cent a year.

Among the retailers the higher mortality rates occur as follows:

Retail florists	27%
Drugstores	27
General stores	27
Men's-clothing stores	29
Floor-covering and drapes stores	29
Women's-wear stores	29
Delicatessen stores	32
Furriers	32
Retail auto accessories	33

Manufacturing companies are comparatively stable. But the constant activity in mergers, name changes, and new plants means there is much change even in this category.

The most stable addresses, obviously, are those of a business or organization (not an individual) in a category which tends to be long-lasting and which owns its own building—banks, YMCAs, etc.

Tips on Keeping Mailing Lists Up to Date

Here are the recommended methods for keeping a list's accuracy high by keeping it up to date:

A. Correct wrong addresses, removals, etc., which keep mail from being delivered.

    1. Use "Return Requested" on third- or fourth-class mail.

    How: Print the following legend in the lower left-hand corner of your third- or fourth-class mail: "RETURN REQUESTED." Your own name and address must appear in the upper left-hand corner.

    What happens: If the person is no longer receiving mail at this address, the carrier will write the reason for nondelivery and the forwarding address, if known, and return the mail to you. You'll be charged a minimum fee for this service or the regular rate of postage for the piece . . . whichever is higher.

    These Return Requested provisions apply only to mail sent out in the regular course of business for purposes other than to obtain the address of the person to whom the mail is being sent. You may not use Return Requested in connection with mail sent primarily for the purpose of collecting past-due accounts.

    Return Requested may be used on third- or fourth-class matter and on post cards but is not necessary on other forms of first-class mail. This is so because first-class mail (except post cards) is returned to the sender automatically when it is undeliverable, without any additional charge. Post cards, however, although receiving first-class treatment in every other respect, are not returned when undeliverable unless the Return Requested procedure is followed.

    There are similar provisions for the use of Return Requested on second-class mail (newspapers, magazines, and other periodicals).

    When you use a number of lists for the same piece of mail, you'll find that tracing down the original name in order to make the correction is an expensive, time-consuming job. It will be wise, therefore, to add a code to the address itself. A key letter or number following the state name or on a line below it will do the trick. Of course if you code the returns, either by code number on your reply card or envelope or by coding your return address in your corner card, you'll be able to identify the correct list that way.

It's important to remember that this type of list correction goes only as far as the postman. As long as your mail is accepted at an address, he will have no reason to return it. So this method of correction is limited. It will not correct misspellings, will not announce the removal or promotion of a person within a business concern unless the mail is refused by the concern, and will not even announce deaths in a home if the mail continues to be accepted.

2. Have post offices correct lists for you.

How: Submit your mailing list on cards to each post office, and they will correct the cards at a nominal charge for each one you send. There is also a minimum charge per post office. That is, you pay for a minimum number for each post office whether you send that many or not. You should prepare your list in card form, the size and approximate weight of a post card. Put one name and address on each card, in the same location you would normally put an address. Put *your* name and address in the upper left-hand corner.

What happens: Your cards will be separated and given to each carrier. He checks the names and addresses. But, as in the case of Return Requested, he cannot vouch for titles or correct spelling of individual names within a company. You will not get any changes in personnel. Names to which mail can no longer be delivered or forwarded will be crossed off. New addresses, when known, will be added. Corrections in street numbers, initials, etc., will be made, but *no new names* will be added.

Although the *Postal Manual* does not require it, postal authorities suggest that you put the words "Mailing List" on these cards. This reduces the possibility of a carrier erroneously delivering some of the cards.

One word of warning about using this method. If your list cards are imprinted from stencils or by other mechanical means, you can ship them to the post office at parcel-post rates. *But, if you type or write the cards in longhand, you must pay first-class postage.*

There is some feeling that lists submitted in this way get slightly better attention from the average postman than do Return Requested mailings. Neither is perfect. While the Postmaster General is anxious to provide completely accurate list-cleaning services and is constantly reminding postmasters of the importance of accuracy in this regard, his determination does not always filter down to the individual carrier. Nevertheless, you will get a very high percentage of corrections. And the corrections which you receive are nearly 100 per cent accurate.

Post Office Will Zone Your Mail.

It helps your mail to get faster delivery if it is properly zoned. There are now 106 large cities in the United States that have postal zones. The post offices will furnish the zone numbers for each name on your lists for their respective cities. No charge is made by the post office for this service.

3. Use first-class mail as a final check.

   a. How: After receiving a "Moved, left no address" or "Undeliverable" notice, or other vague wording on a Return Requested report, send your next mailing to the addressee by first-class mail. If this mail is *not* returned to you within a reasonable amount of time, you can assume that it *has* been delivered. You then write the postmaster concerned, stating the facts: Return Requested mail was undeliverable on such-and-such a date, but subsequent first-class mail has apparently been delivered. Why the discrepancy?"

   What happens: This letter will put the postmaster on his mettle, and you will receive a high percentage of new, corrected addresses.

   b. How: Another method of using first-class mail after third- or fourth-class has been returned is to write the recipient, first-class, with a reply card enclosed and ask the recipient to give you his correct address.

   What happens: Either you get the reply card back with the correct address and correct your list, *or* you get the first-class mail back, which indicates that the post office really couldn't deliver, *or* you get nothing back (which will frequently happen if the recipient is not particularly interested in your mail at the moment). In this case, you proceed on the assumption that the mail was delivered and write the postmaster as indicated above.

   The Grolier Society, Inc., developed the following plan some years ago. It is reported in current terminology.

   "To keep our list up to date, we use *Return Requested* on our mailings twice a year. And because we have found that not even the post office is infallible, we have developed a special follow-up procedure. If the post office returns mail marked, "Moved—left no address," we immediately remail the offer to the customer via first-class mail. If it is not returned, we assume that delivery was made, the post office now knows the new address, and another offer is mailed under Return Requested to obtain it. If it *is* returned, we remail the same offer under Return Requested. We keep remailing to nixies, alternating between third-class with Return Requested and first-class, for eight months before we finally give up. At that point, less than 1 per cent of our customers will have been lost."

4. Use a certified letter with return receipt requested. Because the generally high quality of postal service is not universal, you may have a few important names which cannot be cleared by Return Requested or first-class mail with a follow-up to the postmaster. In these cases, certified mail can be used.

How: Send a certified letter to the last-known address.* When you send it, you may:

a. Ask for a return receipt, which will show to whom, when, and where delivered.*

b. Ask that it be delivered personally to the addressee and request a return receipt, showing to whom, when, and where delivered.* (Note: Be sure to ask for the receipt, which includes *where* delivered. A return receipt showing only to whom and when the mail was delivered is also available.)

What happens: In either case, after the letter is delivered, the return receipt will be returned to you and will show to whom, when, and to what address the letter was delivered. If a certified letter is returned to you as undeliverable, you can be sure that the addressee is really lost. (Note: You may also use a registered letter in the same way. It would cost you more, however, and serve no particular purpose as a list cleaner.)

5. Make corrections as shown in *Postal Bulletin*. If you want the best possible accuracy in your list and if you mail a reasonable amount of mail to small towns, either in urban or rural areas, you might want to correct addresses wherever post-office names have been changed or eliminated.

How: Subscribe to *Postal Bulletin* and make changes as they are announced.

What happens: The *Postal Bulletin* is a weekly news bulletin issued by the U.S. Post Office to give instructions and information to its employees. Any interested citizen may subscribe, however. And, since all post-office changes are listed in the bulletin, you can make corrections in your lists as soon as such changes are made.

* For the current costs of these special services, check with your local post office.

6. Use the services of Western Union.

How: Use Western Union and "interview forms," which they will check out and return to you. Take them to your local Western Union office.

What happens: Western Union distributes your forms, with the latest names and addresses on them, to its offices all over the country. Western Union operators contact the individual company by phone or in person, and verify the name and address or correct it. At the same time, they can handle any other information which you might want or need. It may take them a month or two to correct completely the entire group, and an estimate of costs may be from 25 to 30 cents per completed interview plus postage, and any long-distance phone charges . . . but you will actually have a personal follow-up on each name and address.

B. Correct names, spelling, etc. and eliminate removals, deaths and incorrect addresses on mail which is being delivered by post office but is not reaching the correct person satisfactorily.

1. Put notice on the envelope, asking for corrections.

How: How you handle this method will depend upon your list. If your mailings are generally to individuals at their home addresses . . . any message on the envelope would presumably be addressed to the recipient. It would probably read . . . "We are anxious to address you correctly. If your name and address are not exactly correct, please make the corrections and return this envelope to us." The notice-on-the-envelope technique, however, is usually used when mailings are addressed to persons within a large business or organization. In most firms of over two or three people, the person who opens the mail is not the addressee. On the other hand, she does dispose of the mail addressed to people no longer with the firm, using judgment on whether to forward the mail or destroy it. A message addressed to her might read: "To the person who opens this mail: We want to be sure that the information we are sending reaches the right person and that we have correctly spelled the name and address. If the person to whom this mail is addressed is no longer with your company or if the name or address is inaccurate in any way, won't you please make corrections and return the face of this envelope to us?"

What happens: Naturally, you don't get cooperation from all secretaries. But you'll get corrections from a reasonable number. Some of them will even write notes indicating that you are addressing the wrong man in the company or that your addressee has a new job. While this is probably the least effective of the methods used to make these corrections, it is also the least expensive and does get you some corrections without much effort.

2. Insert with mailing a slip or reply card requesting corrections (effective for lists which recipients want to be on).

How: What sort of slip you include is limited only by your imagination. But probably the most common one is the simplest. It provides space for the previous name and address and present name and address. It may or may not be a reply card.

What happens: Obviously, unless you are mailing to people who are definitely interested in your mailings, you get relatively low returns. They improve with the use of a reply card. When enclosed with dividend checks or informative or interesting mailings, however, a reply card will correct a high percentage of errors.

3. Addressograph name on reply card.

How: Instead of including the usual "name, firm, and address" blank lines on the reply card, use your addressing plate for both the envelope and the reply card itself. Then, at the bottom of the reply card, include the line "Is your name and address correct?" Of course, this method will secure corrections only from those who reply to your mailing. But, if you use it consistently, it will improve your list. In addition, this method has an added value. You'll undoubtedly get a greater number of inquiries from a mailing when you prepare the reply card in this way.

4. Write the entire list asking for help.

How: Prepare a post card or letter and return card (business reply is usually more economical than a government post card) asking for assistance in correcting your list. If the mailing is on the humorous side, or otherwise "unusual," it will generally pull better returns. Stagger these mailings so that an even flow of work can be maintained, avoiding a sudden burden on your clerks.

What happens: Even if people aren't particularly anxious to receive your mailings, many of them will almost automatically make the correction and return the card if you take the trouble to write them a carefully worded letter about it and provide the postage for the return of the correction. They feel it's only good manners. This is an excellent method of correcting your list.

5. Phone, on local lists.

How: Simply call the company and ask for the personnel department. This department is usually willing to help you correct the names and titles of a reasonable number of people in the firm if you are mailing to them on business matters. If a firm is obviously too small to have a personnel department, or if the telephone operator indicates that they have none, just ask whoever answers the phone.

What happens: This method gives you about as close to a 100 per cent correct list as you can obtain. While it may seem comparatively expensive, it is not nearly as expensive as an incorrect list.

6. Take off names which have not purchased or responded in a reasonable length of time.

   How: To do this correctly, you must keep track of the date on which each name was placed on the list (otherwise you would be tossing off your newest prospects), and you must have an easily accessible record of purchases. With these two sets of facts, you merely check the one against the other and remove the inactive names. Possibly, as part of your final mailing, you may enclose a note expressing regret at the fact that they have not purchased and asking if this is due to any fault of yours. Indicate that you intend to drop them from the list after the current mailing unless you hear from them in the meantime. Such a note often produces response when normal methods have failed.

   What happens: It is obvious that you have eliminated a good deal of dead wood at the risk of very few potential future sales and have, therefore, increased the effectiveness of future mailings by a considerable degree. Now you can add more "live" names without increasing your promotion budget.

   Even those potential future purchasers may come through if you add a "last-mailing" warning. Some subscription-renewal efforts, for example, are continually rejected by subscribers until they are notified that they aren't going to get any more appeals (perhaps with their address plate enclosed). Then they hop to it and send in their subscriptions. In any event, it's a wise idea to make some kind of special mailing slanted particularly to the nonbuyers before you throw them away.

7. Print, "Is your name and address correct as we have it?" on invoices, delivery slips, and other communications containing names.

   What happens: Like printing a notice on the outside envelope, this method produces a low percentage of corrections. However, since it costs practically nothing and is constantly at work, it does have a good effect on the list.

8. Encourage customers to shop under one name.

   In mail-order selling to individuals, particularly, many members of the same family are likely to sign orders from time to time and find themselves added to your list as "new customers." This can even happen on some lists when a "Mr. Jones" living on a rural route signs his given name on one order and his initials on another. Since all the duplicate names on the list are "correct," you can easily mail indefinitely to a list that is full of duplications.

How: Put a message on your order blank suggesting that all members of the same family shop under the same name. It is also practical, in some cases, to include this suggestion in your catalogue or mailing piece itself. You can imply that it helps the customer's credit record to be listed as a larger buyer or that it can help reduce your selling cost and eventually your price by eliminating duplication. Include a note, "If you have moved or changed your name since your last order, please give old name and address below."

C. Review your entire list periodically.

    1. Use your salesmen, servicemen, technicians, distributors or dealers.

How: Send each person, salesman or other, a copy of the list for his territory. Enclose a business reply envelope and a little note. In the note brag a little bit about the list and its accuracy and about how careful you are to keep it up to date. Imply that you are sending him the list to help direct his activities toward the best possible prospects. Don't come right out and say so, but suggest vaguely that some changes might be required, because of upheavals in the last week or so. Indicate that some unique situation might make an addition practical if he feels he can defend his choice. *Don't* ask him to do a list-cleaning job.

What happens: He'll show you! He'll go over your list word for word, searching for errors, and will enjoy eliminating the non-prospects and adding new prospects to your list. If he is the spirited-salesman type, you will probably get back the most accurate list you have ever had in the files.

    2. Check against newer directories.

How: If your list has been built from directories, list the source, if possible, beside each name. Order the new directories as soon as they are available. Once in a while, it will be possible to get the publisher to send advance proofs.

What happens: To a certain degree, of course, directories are out of date before they are received, so it's important to use directories as soon as you can get them and to be careful that you are not "correcting a more recent correction." (You may have received a post-office correction that is newer than the directory material.) Nevertheless, if your list source originally was based on directories, you need the constant review, or your list will gradually die out in effectiveness.

Following this practice, you should be able to make a 10 to 15 per cent correction in your list before you make your next mailing. (This will be smaller or larger, depending upon your ability to keep the list up to date during the time between directories.) Theoretically this should increase returns on your mailing by 10 to 15 per cent.

3. Have an executive review 8 per cent of your list each month.

How: Arrange with the company maintaining your list to run off 8 per cent of the list, as currently corrected, each month.

What happens: This method is practical for companies who are mailing to reasonably high-quality lists, . . . where many of the names are known to executives of the company. A personal review of such a list is practical because no method of list correction is 100 per cent perfect, particularly when the list contains the names and titles of people in business.

Regardless of the list, the typical executive finds it "impossible" to review an entire list at one time. He keeps putting it off, even when he is convinced that the idea is a good one. On the other hand, when he is faced with only one-twelfth of the list each month (and knows that another one-twelfth will be coming around in four weeks), he is more likely to find the time to give the list a brief review.

4. Send names to local sources, other than postmasters, who can check on the individuals.

How: Group names for each post office and send them to people in that post-office area who have access to lists of names or who have general knowledge of inhabitants. In larger towns, you might send to letter shops, in smaller towns to lawyers, justices of the peace, express agents, or bank clerks.

What happens: Of course, you will use this method only when you have "lost" very good prospects, customers, or members. It's a last-ditch and relatively expensive method of obtaining a list correction. In addition to the cost of the mailing, you should either provide some sort of a "reward" for the person who is doing the job for you (money will do) or use some common interest for your contact. (If there are only three or four names in a town to check, for example, then you might ask your own lawyer to send letters to small-town lawyers . . . or exploit some similar relationship. People are usually willing to do reasonable favors for a stranger if they can identify themselves with the stranger in any way.) Since you are probably using this method only for difficult cases, you will probably not get a very large response.

5. Check the list itself for duplicates.

How: A skilled person, with a feel for mailing lists, reviews the list occasionally, in search of obvious or suspected duplications. What happens: She finds some obvious duplications and removes them. She also finds "suspected duplications." These generally occur through misspellings or errors which are not incorrect enough to interfere with mail delivery. "John S. Jones" and "J. L. Jones" at the same address may be father and son. But they may also be the result of poor handwriting of an "L" at some time in the past.

In alphabetical filing, a slight misspelling of a man's last name may cause duplications. If a good memory during the list review, or the geographical refiling of mailing pieces as they are about to be mailed produces a "John F. Jones" and a "Jone F. Jones" at the same address, the reviewer has a suspected duplication. In the same way, slight errors in spelling of street names will not affect delivery . . . since the postmaster will deliver a package to 846 S. Main St. even if it's spelled "Mane" St. But the two streets, in a geographical file (which often prevents duplication better than an alphabetical file), will not be in the same place. Communities across the country are constantly changing street numbers, too. And the discovery of "two" men with the same name living at different numbers on the same street is cause for a little investigating. Rural routes are often loaded with similar names living at difficult-to-distinguish different addresses.

At Aldens, for example, when they find suspected duplicates, they put all the similar names on a card. If there are ten names or less they send the card to one of the names on the list and ask whether the names are duplicates or members of the same household. If there are more than ten, they send the list to the postmaster asking for the same information.

D. Rent your lists. Let the owners keep them clean.
   1. *List houses* have lists available by business category, etc.
   2. *List brokers* are able to rent you lists owned by others, classified by interests.
   3. Magazines or similar list owners rent them direct.
   4. Names of phone owners, home owners, "occupants," parents, brides, high-income people, etc., are available, locally and nationally.

   How: Literally hundreds of organizations throughout the country are in the business of compiling or renting lists. Some of them may contact you by mail. However, your most practical approach is to make a careful study of the type of people you want (their occupations, characteristics, or whatever aspect tends to qualify them as your best prospects) and turn this description over to your local direct mail agency. From their extensive files of list sources, they can either recommend or get in touch with a number of sources to obtain the best list available. No one list source is "best" for every purpose. Almost every large list operator has some specialty which makes his list superior in some area.

What happens: Since you are renting the list, the list renter addresses your mailing piece for you as part of the rental price. You pay this rental each time you use the list. However, it is the list owner's obligation to keep the list clean. Some list owners are more effective than others in this regard. And part of the service of your direct mail agency is an intelligent selection of the best (highest-quality) list source. When you do get corrections to lists which you rent, it helps to return these corrections to the list owner. The more renters who do this, the cleaner his list remains. Lists which are constantly used, by many users who cooperate in keeping them clean, are obviously in excellent shape.

E. Keep your list growing. A list is not up to date as long as any good prospects are missing.
  1. Ask customers to add names of others who might be interested. How: If you are selling by mail, it is not unusual to add a few lines to your order blank, with room for the recipient to add the names of friends he thinks might be interested. If your unit of sale is a large one, you might be willing to offer him a premium for the name of a friend who then purchases within a certain period.

If your mailing is informative or especially interesting, you can get some additions by enclosing a business reply card with room for names on the back and a request for the names of friends interested. Sometimes a company's house organ or small printed leaflets or folders are used for this purpose.

What happens: Generally speaking, the names which are suggested to you are reasonably well "qualified." That is, your customers or prospects will not normally recommend people who are not likely to be customers too. This is another instance of improving your list inexpensively, since the requests go as part of another mailing, and the names they produce are usually good ones. While it's unusual to get great numbers of names this way, some companies have been quite successful. One company (mentioned by Metropolitan Life Insurance) sent a processed letter to 4,000 customers, together with a prospect blank, asking for names and addresses of prospects. Replies were received from 492 customers, who furnished 2,180 names of prospects. Sometimes a company will ask if there is any objection on the part of the customer to using his name in soliciting the prospects he has listed. In the above case 33.4 per cent of the customers replying gave this permission.

2. Mail to a broader list with some kind of offer to "qualify" prospects.

When a mailing list has too many nonprospects on it, your mailings are bound to be ineffective. So you'll aim to do most of your mailing to known prospects. Broader or more general lists, with a *low* percentage of prospects, can be valuable, however, if you use them as a *source* for more prospects to add to your regular lists. Your objective, when mailing to this broad group of "suspects," is to get the prospects to "raise their hands" and identify themselves, or to "qualify" themselves as prospects for your product or service.

How: Develop some kind of free or special offer which will have maximum appeal *only* to your good prospects. (A booklet entitled "Hints on Keeping Mailing Lists Clean" will be requested primarily by people who have mailing-list problems and are, therefore, qualified prospects for a mailing service.) Mail to the general list, making this offer and enclosing a reply card or envelope to make it easy for your prospects to answer.

What happens: People who are interested in your offer (and are, therefore, qualified prospects) send in for it. The more restricted your offer (the *less* interest it has for nonprospects), the fewer returns you will receive. But, since you *want* to restrict replies to qualified prospects worth adding to your mailing list, you don't want very many returns. In fact, a *high* percentage of returns to this type of mailing is an indication of failure, rather than success. Assuming that your judgment on the original list is correct (that it was a general list containing only a small percentage of prospects), too high a return indicates that your offer was of interest to nonprospects as well as prospects. Next time you will want to define the values of your offer more carefully, so that they will appeal only to your prospects.

You may or may not follow up the offer with a salesman's call to substantiate the customer's qualification. If your mailing program is extensive enough, this may pay, since you do not want nonprospects on your basic list. And, no matter how restricted your offer, a few replies will come from nonprospects.

3. Use mass-media advertising with coupons or editorial releases to make special offers "for prospects only."
How: This method of adding names to mailing lists follows the same technique as outlined in the suggestion above, except that the offer is made through a press release or through advertising.

In most instances, any mass medium reaches many readers who are not prospects for your particular product or service. Any offer of general interest will bring plenty of response, but not necessarily from prospects. So here again, as in the suggestion above, you offer material or information which is of interest *only* to your prospects.

A typical offer for this purpose is a booklet. And the selection of a title for the booklet is important since this is often your only offer ("Send for our free booklet _____"). Typical titles on booklets used for qualifying prospects are: "How to Solve _____" (insert the *problem* which creates the *need* for your product); or "How to Enjoy _____" (insert the *benefit* which your product brings). Obviously . . . a high percentage of the requests for those booklets will come from qualified prospects.

What happens: As in the illustration above, qualified prospects for you have a tendency to respond to your offer. After getting their inquiries, you either add their names to your mailing list directly or make some further effort (by salesman, follow-up letter, etc.) to make sure that they actually are qualified prospects.

4. Enclose guarantee cards with your products to get names of users or dealers.
How: It's a common practice of manufacturers to offer a warranty against defective materials or workmanship with each of their products, contingent upon the return of the warranty card properly filled out. A simple business reply card, enclosed with the product, will do the trick. (This card is often used for other purposes as well, a survey of buying influences or motivations, etc. But we are concerned here only with its use as a source of customer names.)
What happens: A good percentage of the purchasers will return a warranty card, particularly on items which they think may cause some trouble. In time this produces a fair list of users and an excellent list of dealers, particularly the larger dealers in that item.

5. Attach cards to cartons to get names of dealers. Sometimes distributors are reluctant to provide names of dealers. Since you

cannot write the dealer, you must devise a method of getting him to write you. You can use much the same system as is used with customers and warranty cards.

How: Offer a dealer co-op advertising, sales-promotion tips, information for his service department, or some other attractive offer. Put this offer on a business reply card or on a larger, attention-getting piece and attach it to your cartons. If the dealer customarily unpacks your product for delivery to the final customer, you can pack your dealer message inside the carton.

What happens: Unless your offer is unusually attractive, you will not get a very high response by using this method. But it is inexpensive and may be the only practical way you have of getting dealer names. If the practice is continued, possibly with a variation of offer from year to year, you will soon build a substantial dealer list.

6. Include space for list information on salesmen's reports.

How: There are all kinds of opportunities in this area. If your salesmen make written reports without using a form, you just keep reminding them to check the mailing list against their knowledge of the firm. In these cases, it's best to provide salesmen with 3- by 5-inch cards or similar records containing the current list. Whenever a salesman makes a call, he returns the card for that company with any corrections which he may have discovered. When this card is received at the mailing house, the corrections he recommends are made to the list and a new card is processed and returned to him. Ordinarily, no attempt is made to keep his list up to date on post-office changes, etc., received by the mailing house.

When salesmen have printed forms on which to report, leave room on the form for list corrections. It's even more effective to require an answer to the question: "Should any changes be made in our mailing list for this company?"

What happens: This depends upon the salesman. Some salesmen will report list corrections regularly, and others will not. However, if space for corrections is made available, and if a particular salesman never makes any, it's obvious that he is not keeping in close touch with the personnel changes in his prospects' companies.

7. Use newspaper or trade-paper clippings to correct and revise current lists.

How: Review each issue of the publication which best covers your list. Clip announcements or news stories which might affect your list immediately. File them, and before each mailing, make the corrections which have developed in the meantime.

What happens: This is a relatively expensive method of list control because it takes a good deal of time. But it is also one of the best methods for keeping lists really current.

8. Use "investigators" who search for prospects.

How: You simply hire people to go out and look for prospects. This goes one step beyond the newspaper or trade-paper clipping area because you send investigators into the field to gather your own "news."

What happens: Your results depend upon the quality of your investigators. And of course this frequently depends upon their rate of pay. If you are a local concern and hire an investigator to develop a list of cars with worn tires, houses that need paint, sidewalks that need repair, etc., it is usually best to spot-check the investigator before adding all the names he furnished to your list. However, if your investigator is dependable, this can be one of the most effective of list-building methods.

9. Be sure to add *new* customers as you get them.

For many businesses, customers are the most valuable prospects. Yet customers' lists are often "built" and then forgotten, as far as adding new customers is concerned.

How: One method is to check all new invoices against current mailings lists. If a company's business consists primarily of reorders, however, this can become an expensive operation. In such cases, someone who is familiar with the names of old customers can do an initial screening. Another method is to make periodical additions from ledger cards or similar records.

10. If using a purchased list, buy a new one occasionally.

A 1935 list of barber shops, even if cleaned constantly and efficiently through the years, would be far from up to date by now. If you purchased a list originally, the chances are that the same problems that kept you from building your own list then, still remain. Perhaps you don't really have the facilities to develop a *complete* list, or perhaps you find it less expensive to buy a list than to build one. The list house where you purchased the list, on the other hand, has gone right on compiling new lists from the original sources. Warning: Even list houses aren't perfect. And you may have live names on your current list which will not be included on their new one. So a check of the new list is in order.

How: Purchase the latest list from your list house. If you have made few corrections or additions to your list, just substitute the new list for the old one. However, if you have made regular corrections, you should check your old list against the new one. When you find completely new names, add them to the list. When names are on your list but not on the new list, or are on the new list at different addresses, take them off your list temporarily and use one of the methods suggested under *B* above.

Do not do this just "any time." Ask your list house to tell you the best time of the year for a revision. (Some lists are based, primarily, on annual directories or registrations. Obviously, if auto licenses are purchased each December, you won't want to buy a new list of car owners in November.)

11. In retail stores, get clerks to obtain names and addresses when making cash sales.

How: If you are using sales slips for every customer, simply ask the clerks to get names and addresses for cash sales as well as credit sales. If you do not offer credit or don't use sales slips for cash sales, you will have to provide special slips for clerks to use. What happens: All names and addresses obtained by the clerks are reviewed to see whether they fall in the store's trading area, etc. Qualified names are added to the mailing list.

Incidentally, the decision to obtain the names of cash buyers is usually followed by a flurry of activity, which then gradually tapers off. Clerks must be reminded of the policy frequently. And sometimes it is necessary to provide some kind of a small cash bonus for obtaining the names. In other instances, the number of qualified names you receive may be increased by making the request selective, asking only for names of people who purchase over a certain amount or who purchase certain items.

F. Reduce errors in handling and maintenance. No list is up to date if it's full of misspellings or other errors.

1. Use skilled typists for typewriter addressing.

How: If you type your addresses in your own office, recheck the addressing of each typist periodically to see that she is taking sufficient care with the addresses. Many typists consider envelope addressing a burdensome chore and are not especially concerned about accuracy when addressing. Sometimes their attitude will change, if you make spot checks of their work.

If you purchase typewritten addressing outside your own office, be sure that you are getting the quality of addressing you want. Commercial firms often give you the choice of various addressing methods: (*a*) full address, (*b*) use of normal abbreviations where possible, or (*c*) "skeleton" addressing. Unless you specify full addressing, you may be receiving "skeleton" addressing (with Mr., Miss, or Mrs., Street, Road, or Avenue all omitted, street names abbreviated, the word "City" used, etc.).

2. Use mechanical addressing when possible.

Mechanical addressing provides greater accuracy. Once an addressing plate has been prepared and proofread, it remains accurate. Mechanical addressing, in addition, is *much* faster than typing, so that mailings can be produced more quickly.

A common rule of thumb indicates that your mailing list can be switched to mechanical addressing at a lower cost if you intend to make six mailings or more of the list. In the interest of accuracy, some people put their lists on mechanical-addressing equipment for even fewer mailings. (The number six is not entirely accurate, on a cost basis, for every list. The exact number will depend upon the anticipated number of changes in the list and the frequency of mailing. If a list is to be used for ten years, but only once a year, it should probably never be plated. On the other hand, if it is to be used for four quick mailings, without time for list changes, it will probably be economical to use mechanical addressing, even if it is never used again. If the list is to be used over a long period of time and a number of address changes are anticipated, it may be necessary to count on eight or ten mailings before it is economically feasible to switch to mechanical addressing. This computation, of course, ignores the matter of accuracy, which is important in keeping lists up to date.)

Obviously, it is not necessary (nor usually desirable) to obtain your own mechanical-addressing equipment. Commercial addressing services are available, where skilled help provide good service at reasonable prices.

Even with the Best of List Maintenance, Lists Get Out of Date

George J. Cullinan, former vice-president of Aldens, Inc., now president of the George Cullinan Organization, Chicago, once said:

Very probably most mail-order people think they do a good list-maintenance job, and the efforts they make are imposing enough to give credence to that thought. But can our own list-maintenance program, however imposing, be called good when:

1. On each of 8 media mailed annually we have 2% nixies or 16% in all?
2. When one-third of a "clean," "purged," and "pure" list of customers, who have bought substantial amounts of merchandise in the past six months, fail to buy at all from a series of mailings aggregating 3,000 pages over a period of a year?
3. When a company makes over 1,500,000 "new" customers a year over a period of 20 years, and yet its total has never exceeded 3,000,000?

Yet this is what actually happens in all of the major mail-order companies and is very likely happening to other direct mail companies, . . . and this despite a list-maintenance program involving daily, monthly, semiannual checking of the list file.

Have List Specialists Maintain Your List. Direct mail advertising has such tremendous *power* that much of it is successful *in spite of* poor list maintenance. Yet how much better it could be if lists were given regular doses of "Tender, Loving Care."

Good lists mean *more sales and higher profits for the same promotion money.*

So it makes sense, and dollars, to have list specialists maintain your list.

Although it would seem to be routine, list maintenance is not an "easy" job. Even when you follow all of the above suggestions, the problem of keeping the physical list corrected is a ticklish one.

When you try to maintain lists in your own offices, you find: (1) The job gets put off, because it's tedious. This increases costs, since it is usually cheaper to make a correction than to mail even a single extra mailing. (2) Because maintenance *is* difficult, unskilled people tend to compound errors. And the high-priced people who can do it satisfactorily are more profitable on other work.

So turn the maintenance of your list over to a specialist. Skilled list workers develop a sixth sense for slightly different duplications; learn to decipher the scrawls of postmen; practice methods that reduce errors; and understand the need for extreme care in list handling.

Take Your Mailing List Seriously

If—as the result of reading this chapter—you think that building and maintaining a good list is a lot of hard work, you are absolutely correct. But so is any form of *successful* selling. And time spent with your list will often pay off at a higher hourly rate than time spent any other way. Your list is the *heart* of your direct mail.

Remember, the basic philosophy of mailing lists is as simple as golf: "Get all prospects *on* your list. Get all nonprospects *off*."

"On" and "off" are equally important. Do not slight either.

6

Direct Mail Costs:
A Perspective

Profits Measure Success

We must all agree that the *control* of costs is an important factor in business success. We should also agree that *profit* is the measure of success in business. It is not a nasty word. Money was invented to *measure* the relative value of anyone's contribution to another or to many others. And profit merely measures the *excess* of your contribution over the cost to you. Ideally, at least, "He profits most who serves best."

A great profit can be produced out of a given operation *either* by increasing the value or by reducing the cost.

This is just a way of saying that the discussion of the "cost" of various types of direct mail or of various types of advertising is a waste of time. Low "cost" or high means nothing by itself, except in relation to the profit that it generates. This is a lesson yet to be learned by many in direct mail.

Let's take an example to demonstrate how this works. Some years ago, the Dumpcrete division of the Maxon Construction Company was sending out monthly letters to get inquiries for Dumpcrete bodies. (These are specially designed truck bodies used for hauling air-entrained concrete.) After two or three years of monthly mailings, it was determined that each inquiry was eventually worth about $844 in sales. It had provided a good profit on the mailings.

However, it was suggested that monthly contacts could be made at a substantially lower cost by shifting to a mailing card in place of a mailing that consisted of a letter, a folder, and a reply card. As a result, a series of mailings was developed, four of them in the letter–insert–and–reply-card tradition, and the other three using mailing cards. At the end of the season, the results were as follows:

Number of
inquiries

Mailing no. 1 (letter)   65
Mailing no. 2 (mailing card) ..   3
Mailing no. 3 (letter)   31
Mailing no. 4 (mailing card) ..   7
Mailing no. 5 (letter)   36
Mailing no. 6 (mailing card) ..   1
Mailing no. 7 (letter)   32

The total mailing list was somewhat under 6,000 names. And even the most expensive letter mailing did not cost over $500. So you can see there was nothing "less expensive" about "saving" money by the use of mailing cards.

Therefore, we must understand that any intelligent approach to direct mail costs must take into consideration the profit factor:

Successful direct mail never "costs" anything. It returns a profit.

Unsuccessful direct mail costs more than it produces. It, therefore, generates a loss.

There is no correlation, at all, between "low cost" and success, or, for that matter, between "high cost" and success.

It is only the *profit* that counts. This thinking should not be restricted to mail order, where the profit can be determined with relative ease. The thinking is true in any use of direct mail, although some forms of direct mail advertising are so far from the ultimate sale that any actual and accurate estimate of the profit is extremely difficult.

The Ford Motor Company, for example, does not sell Fords by mail. But they do use a great deal of direct mail. The objective is simple: to make certain that people have a friendly feeling toward the Ford Motor Company, think of Fords when they decide to buy a new car, and know where to go to find a Ford dealer. By the time any actual dollar "profits" accrue to the Ford Motor Company, the effects of any particular direct mail piece are pretty much lost in the shuffle.

In Ford's case, their investment is so great that they employ research firms to sample the results of their direct mail and tell them which mailings received the greatest recognition and which helped the greatest number of people to identify their Ford dealer.

Of course, most people who use direct mail to help their salesmen or to encourage people to visit their store can't afford the research that Ford can. So, unfortunately, they may never know whether certain "economies" or "extravagances" have hurt or helped the effectiveness of their campaign.

Measure Direct Mail "Value"

If we keep this in mind, we'll measure all direct mail efforts on the basis of their "value," which might be expressed in an equation:

$$\text{Value} = \frac{\text{effectiveness}}{\text{cost}}$$

Don't get the idea that this is easy to measure, however.

All forms of advertising try to measure value. Magazine and newspaper publishers count the readers; . . . they sell circulation at a fraction of a cent a "reader." Broadcasters sell ratings, or the number of sets presumed to be turned on at a given time. Outdoor people sell exposure. They count the number of cars going past all your boards and let you divide the dollars you spend by the number of cars to get your "cost per exposure."

All of these ways of measuring have some relative value. It's better to know *something* about the effectiveness of your ads than to know *nothing*. Besides, "numbers" have a certain soothing quality. They give you something to hang on to and to "believe." They have the look of "facts."

So a "cost-per-impression" measure is often used, not only in choosing outlets within a medium but also between media . . . and even, in direct mail, between proposed pieces or methods of mailing.

On a pure basis of numbers, direct mail would appear to "cost" hundreds or thousands of times as much as other media. How, then, can it survive? It survives, of course, because the count of people exposed to advertising means practically nothing at all. What counts is not the number of people who might see an ad, or even the number who read it, but *the number of real prospects whose minds have been changed by it.* It is the effectiveness, then, not the cost, which is the most important member of the equation.

$$\frac{\text{Effectiveness}}{\text{Cost}} = \text{value}$$

(Parenthetically, direct mail *advertising* or any other kind of advertising has some problems here. In the average manufacturing business, top management is often more sensitive to effectiveness than to cost. But the person who develops the direct mail is given a budget, and—since quality is often very hard to measure—he plays safe and buys quantity.

In *mail order,* on the other hand, top management is generally in command of the decisions. And it's easier to measure the quality, too. So the choice of media and type of mailing is more likely to be based on *value.)*

However, even though it is the effectiveness rather than the cost that is the most important factor in the equation, any reduction in cost without corresponding reduction in effectiveness obviously adds to the value.

While working with direct mail you'll find many opportunities to reduce costs without reducing effectiveness. That's because there are so many details to direct mail, each one a factor in cost.

But each effort to reduce cost and each added expenditure must be measured against the possible reduction or increase in effectiveness. Let's take a few examples.

1. It's perfectly obvious to anyone experienced in direct mail that eliminating a reply card in a mailing going after inquiries is poor economy. You simply won't get as many replies.

2. Typing the recipient's name on his reply card will increase the "cost." But, it will also, undoubtedly, increase the number of inquiries, requests for information, or leads for salesmen. (There's no way to generalize on this as an expense or economy, however, for such a move might reduce the quality of the sales lead, discourage the salesmen from following up on any of them and therefore reduce profits.)

3. The extra expense of hand stamping rather than metering mail may be worthwhile when mailing to housewives, but may be wasted on presidents of large corporations, whose mail is opened for them.

4. Processed letters may save cost and prove just as effective as automatically typed letters . . . but probably not when a charity appeal is addressed to top executives or a new product is being discussed with potential wholesalers.

5. Mailing cards are cheaper than letters; one-page letters are cheaper than two-page; one-color printing is cheaper than four-color . . . but not necessarily as effective. The list is endless. Only one constant remains: *There is no correlation between cost and value in direct mail.* Cost alone means nothing . . . only its relationship to the effectiveness of the mailing.

Get Rid of Waste

The best way to reduce cost in direct mail is through the reduction of waste in direct mail programs.

The greatest waste comes through lack of thorough planning originally, when the purpose, objectives, and possible results of direct mail are not thought through completely, so that money is spent saying the wrong things to the wrong people.

Another great waste appears when lists are not carefully developed or selected.

A *third waste* develops when lists are allowed to continue in use without proper maintenance—constant attention and care.

A *fourth waste* is in the lack of plans for effective follow-up . . . by mail or by salesmen . . . so that an otherwise effective direct mail program is wasted. A great deal of advertising is designed to interest (or "half-sell") prospects, or even simply to *locate* them. Such campaigns can be 100 per cent wasted and frustrating to boot. For a half sale is no sale at all . . . and no profit, either.

A *fifth waste* is in the frequent use of high-priced (and limited) time in the *production* of direct mail by users. This waste is built into the medium by the fact that little investment is necessary to become a "publisher" of direct mail. The post office sells stamps to anyone.

As a result, manufacturers or retailers—whose total business experience is along other lines—will try to produce their own direct mail "economically." They wouldn't buy a newspaper plant to run a newspaper ad, or a radio station in order to run a radio commercial, because the capital investment is too great. But the elusive "economy" of rolling-their-own direct mail is too enticing to overlook. (Elusive, because the economy is always "about to be," but never quite here. . . . "Once this new girl gets broken in," all will be well. "When I get a chance to review that list," life will be rosy, etc.)

But purchases of equipment lead to the training or hiring of skilled operators, the need for more space, the extra load of payroll, and the constant need of "supervision" on the part of people whose skill and training and value is in the field of the original business—*not* in direct mail production. The following mailing, sent out by a member of a direct mail production association, says it well:

What is it, about human nature . . .

That makes *big chunks of money easier to spend than little chunks?*

You may think this isn't so, but we see it all the time. Business firms "do their own" duplicating and mailing. They buy expensive machinery; assign space (which sooner or later costs rent money); hire extra people, with all the extra, hidden costs of employment, taxes, overtime, vacations, and human conflicts that come with them. They take their own really valuable time, or that of some supervisor, to try to cut down on errors . . . and, to top it all off, *they reduce their quality standards to meet those of the people they hire,* because "people just don't do things as well as they used to."

They spend $2,000 to $10,000 for machines; thousands for wages; $1,000 up for rent; who-knows-what in lost time of their own or an expensive supervisor. . . . In order to avoid occasional, relatively small "outside" invoices.

If they'd ever stop to figure out their *real* costs, they'd soon see that they're actually spending *extra* money in order to "enjoy" the troubles and irritations that go with doing their own work . . . and often not getting what they want, anyway.

The idea that it "pays" to put out *big* chunks of money for equipment and manpower to do something yourself, rather than to spend *little* chunks of money to have it done for you, is, to say the least, open to doubt.

Next time you have a mailing to get out, duplicating or printing to do, or a direct mail advertising campaign to develop, give Graphic a ring. You'll find snappy service, top quality, and a right price.

It's BA 2-8317

/s/

Kay Laird

JS:gi

P.S. Some of our customers *have* investigated their own costs . . . apparent and hidden. They've concluded that they can make more money in *their* business than they can in ours, and they've turned over their duplicating and mailing troubles and mess to us. Think about it.

HOW TO SAVE MONEY ON YOUR MAILINGS

The Mail: Your Personal Messenger

Of all forms of written communication, mail is the most personal. This "personalness" has great advantages.

It allows you, in your communications, to be specific, selective, persuasive. It gives you more freedom in format, timing, and style. Your company can more accurately reflect its own personality . . . its own high standards.

In other forms of written communication, in mass-media advertising, your personality is tempered by the personality of the magazine, newspaper, or catalogue.

When you use the mail, however, your own reputation and personality are directly reflected in the mailing piece itself, and you help to establish your company's "image" quickly. Of course, the tone of your message, the style of your mailing piece, your offer are all important. But equally significant is the appearance of the piece, its accuracy, its timing, and all the other elements concerned with its *production.*

If the address is inaccurate, the reproduction inferior, the timing off . . . if the quality of the production is below your company's standard, your firm's image suffers.

Practically everyone with high business standards agrees that this is so:
> The *mail* which they receive direct from other companies affects their opinion of these companies more than any other written or printed material.

Executives who think about it are just as concerned about the tone and looks of their mail as they are about the appearance of their salesmen and their telephone operators (two other important reflectors of a company's character). They carefully review the message and style to be sure that the mailing says exactly what they want to say. And they want the production and mailing to be of top quality, too, especially on mass mailings, sent to hundreds or thousands at a time, where executive review of each piece is impossible. They want their mailings to go out *right* and *on time.*

There are two traditional ways to handle this:

1. Keep all duplicating and mailing operations inside the store or plant "where we can keep an eye on them."

2. Turn the responsibility of maintaining high quality in mailings over to a specialist . . . an outside mailing house.

The failure of the first is well known. The firm, large or small, which is able to produce, year in and year out, top-quality mailings from an internal mailing service is the outstanding exception. Probably not one in a hundred manages to do it. (This is not to suggest that the organizations *couldn't* do it, for some have, . . . but simply that setting up inside mailing departments means entry into a second "business," which generally gets only secondary attention from management.)

How well the "outside" method works depends, of course, on the firm selected to do the mailings. But this is no more difficult than choosing any other supplier, and a good professional mailing house will have established a reputation in the field—where good reputations are earned only through high quality and accuracy.

The Disadvantages of an "Inside" Mailing Room

While many executives wince slightly at errors and become somewhat frustrated at the constant emergencies among mailing-room personnel, they still continue to justify the addition of equipment and the continuation of internal mailing rooms on the theory that this *saves money.* They are encouraged in this theory by:

1. The office manager, machine operator, or whoever is responsible for the work produced.

2. Equipment salesmen, who keep their eyes firmly fixed on the part of the "iceberg" of costs which lies above the water (like an iceberg, six-sevenths of the cost of internal mailing rooms is not apparent at first glance) and on the quality and speed of work which can be reached only by the finest operators.

3. "Experience" of their own and others, running back to the days when mailing-room labor was both inexpensive *and* willing to do a good job.

4. The idea that they can get work done "quickly."

But, nine or more times out of ten, in addition to lowering the quality of mailings and, therefore, downgrading the firm's image in this most personal of written communications, the internal mailing room does not save money, but actually *increases costs*.

Here are some of the things which often *reduce quality*:

1. *Semiskilled help.* At least until departments become large enough to have one skilled operator for each machine, they get the equivalent of "semiskilled help." That is, they are not highly skilled in the work they are called upon to do, even though they may be of *very* high caliber in their own field. Like a college professor required to dig a ditch, they are not the best or quickest on the job.

2. *Employee problems.* Sickness, vacations, other responsibilities, resignations, etc., call for substitutes or replacement even less skilled in the art of producing top-quality mailings. In a large mailing house, with many skilled workers, these emergencies average out.

3. *Attitude.* Possibly most important is the difference in the quality of production a firm requires from a *supplier* and from a *coworker*. The pressure is always on the firm to reduce its quality requirements to the capacity of its equipment and the quality standards of its employees.

Here are some of the costs that you *don't* see in an internal mailing room:

1. *Material waste.* The idea that the "cost" of paper, for example, is $10 if the paper merchant's price book lists it at $10 fails to take waste, spoilage, investment, storage, etc., into consideration.

2. *Time waste.* No one is 100 per cent productive. Many mailing-room people don't come close, and seldom are they working at their highest skills.

3. *Delay.* The theory that production is "quicker" is often the poorest of all. If a mail room is actually staffed for quick service at all times, it's probably overstaffed, and the cost really skyrockets. On the other hand, if it is generally loaded with work, internal stresses between offices begin to pile up. Most mailing departments soon fall into one of two categories: the harassed, always-behind type, with constant shifting from one partially finished job to another, or the "take-charge" type, where the operator or supervisor begins to make executive decisions on timing of work.

4. *Attitude.* To an outside mailing service, your firm is a *customer*. To the internal department, your secretaries (and even some executives) soon become "coworkers," and the attitude is different (the customer is always right, the coworker always wrong). Petty differences create problems and add to cost.

5. *Supervision.* This is often the greatest cost of all . . . not only in the cost of executive time that is used to hire, direct, correct, console, and organize the employees of the department, but also in the doubly hidden cost of the supervisor's distraction from the producing side of the busi-

ness. Most executives find themselves most valuable to their own business, not to a second one, inside.

6. *"Fringe" labor costs.* It's easiest to figure costs on the basis of hourly rates, but the actual rate for *productive* time on the job is much, much higher. Vacations, holidays, coffee breaks, and a host of other costs (some of them, like unemployment compensation rates, pension plans, etc., building up problems for the future), increase the true hourly rate substantially even before the nonproductive time is taken into consideration.

7. *Space and storage.* Even though some departments begin in an "unused corner," the natural growth of most firms soon develops the need for more space; so the cost of space occupied is important, whether the department requires, eventually, an addition to the building or whether it simply cramps other departments which could use the space more profitably. Since supplies and materials always provide "savings" through quantity purchases, storage space is an expense that soon joins the parade.

8. *Machinery.* Machinery costs are generally quoted on a "depreciation" basis, along with the statement that "the government pays 52 per cent of *that.*" The government, of course, does nothing of the kind, unless you want to assume (and this is a perfectly reasonable assumption) that the government "pays" 52 per cent of *all* expense checks. In any event, depreciation expense is no better than others . . . actually not as good, since you must spend the money now and get credit for it later.

In addition, depreciation has a way of teaming up with "obsolescence" nowadays, to make the value of your investment drop very rapidly, almost immediately. Most machinery which is not in constant use gets out of date long before it wears out.

Repairs (or "service agreements"), maintenance, and the lack of return you would otherwise get on your investment add to the true cost, too.

9. *Inaccuracy.* There's plenty of opportunity for inaccuracy in mailings, in lists for example. And while there is *no* way to keep large lists 100 per cent accurate (people move and are fired and die while your mail is on its way, for that matter), lists that are not watched *very* carefully can create huge wastes that add to cost and reduce effectiveness.

10. *Loss through slow or inaccurate list correction.* Good, speedy list maintenance doesn't *cost*, it *saves*. The big cost connected with list maintenance does not come from the charges you pay to keep a list up to date. It comes from the *waste* of unnecessary mailings which do not reach the correct people.

11. *Useless production.* An internal department encourages production that would never be dreamed of if it were not "free." Some of this is business production caused by Parkinson's Law: "Work expands to fill the time and materials available." The production would not occur if it re-

quired purchase. Some is "monkey business," which helps fill up otherwise empty hours.

12. *Profit loss through omission.* Advertising and sales-promotion programs, which should be timed to fit the needs of the sales department, are frequently "retimed" to meet the schedule of the office service department. Mailings are late—or don't get out at all. This affects sales and, therefore, profits.

Advantages of an "Outside" Mailing Specialist

With all those costs, and more, to be carried by an inside department, it's no wonder that many large firms, with accounting departments and comptrollers who run down hidden as well as obvious costs, are turning more and more to outside specialists for their mailings.

The assembly-line efficiency, machinery effectiveness, and skilled help at a top-quality mailing house obviously provide plenty of room for a good profit at prices well under the *true* cost of internal work.

In addition to lower cost and better quality, there are many "bonus" advantages that normally come when dealing with a professional in any line. There's the extra knowledge at your disposal . . . new ways to cut costs, or to make mailings more effective. Knowledge of postal regulations. An extra, practiced eye to spot errors in planning.

And the virtues of confidential handling . . . not only because of the confidential nature of all clients' business, but because of the complete lack of personal interest in mailings when they are not connected with the employee's own business.

Other advantages to buying a speedy, accurate, worry-free service:

1. Your work goes out on time.
2. It's neat, professional-appearing. It lends dignity to your message.
3. You have no supervision cost.
4. You are not at the mercy of an operator's health.
5. You spend your energy improving your own business, not a duplicating and mailing business.
6. You don't have a heavy investment in space, machinery, storage space, paper stock, etc. (Machinery starts as a duplicator or addressing machine; . . . soon includes a plate maker, camera, cutter, folder, storage racks or cabinets, graphotype, postage meter, etc.)
7. There's no *mess.*
8. Your mailings meet postal regulations. You mail under the most economical conditions.
9. You avoid waste; pay only for what you get.
10. "Monkey-business" duplicating and mailing are eliminated.
11. The mailing house has a greater selection of addressing methods.

12. The mailing house knows hundreds of sources for building, buying, and renting lists.

13. Lists are more accurate. A tested system of list maintenance is handled by skilled people who know how to interpret post-office returns.

14. Every dollar invested in prompt, accurate list maintenance brings in dividends of $5, $10, or more through money *saved* by *not* wasting future mailings. Professional list maintenance is insurance against future losses.

15. Most important of all: The standards for your work are high . . . your firm is a *customer*, not an "unreasonable coworker."

7

Creative Copy Writing

PRELIMINARY TEST: PICK A WINNER

Just because, dear Reader, it may make reading these copy chapters more interesting for you, . . . we'd like to suggest that you pit your own opinions against those of some of the experts. And see if you can "Pick a Winner."

Here's the idea: The four letters which follow this introduction were used most successfully by the company which mailed them. As a challenge to their ability to tell how well a letter will work, the members of the Dayton Ad Club and selected members of the Mail Advertising Service Association International were asked to see if they could evaluate how these letters pulled.

We have given you their answers on page 150. (Don't look!) See if you can outperform these people in selecting the order in which these letters pulled.

You can have this much information as a starter: The returns per 1,000 were 44, 52, 40, 56. Can you match these returns with the letters?

Read the letters now. Write down your guess. Then read the copy chapters. And guess again. See if you'll change your mind. Then look up the results on page 150.

C'mon . . . you'll enjoy it.

No. 1

G. W. SMITH & SONS

Manufacturers of Protect-O-Metal Products
116 South Spring Avenue
Dayton 3, Ohio

Date

Dear Superintendent:

In just a few days I'm going to send you a free small can of our Protect-O-Metal No. 2, the new miracle spatter-proofing compound.

Protect-O-Metal can be brushed or sprayed on the metal, as long as a week before welding. It's a simple process, but look what it does!

· It cuts after-welding cleanup time *ninety per cent*. It stabilizes the arc. It improves the weld. It carries additional flux. It fights rust. It's an improved paint base. It prevents annealing scale. It *wipes* off. And it does all this with NO SMOKE, NO SMELL, NO FUMES. So welders swear by it, and plant superintendents "fight for it."

You might suspect that such a compound would be very expensive. Maybe cost half to three-fourths as much money as it saves. That would be reasonable, and mighty worthwhile. Well, you're in for a surprise. The cost is amazingly low . . . only one-tenth of a cent per foot . . . nowhere near the labor cost of grinding, hacking, and filing spatter.

Now I don't expect you, or your welders, to believe such statements on my say so. You'd be fools if you swallowed everything you heard. I just want you to prove it to yourself, and I'm going to back up what I say.

I'm going to send you that free sample without any catch at all . . . except this. I want you to promise to *try* it. That's all. I'll pay for the compound. I'll pay the shipping costs. I'll even pay the postage on the return card enclosed. And I'll mail you the sample with absolutely no obligation, except the obligation to try it—free. Because I know that once you try spatter-proof welding, with NO SMOKE, NO SMELL, NO FUMES, you'll never send your welders back to slow, tiresome, time-consuming hacking, grinding, and filing.

But catch me while I'm generous. Don't let me change my mind. Send the card today—save cleanup time tomorrow.

V. W. Smith

P.S.   This compound is patented. It is the only compound we know of that improves the weld, *wipes* off with the spatter, and has NO SMOKE, NO SMELL, NO FUMES.

No. 2

DO YOU HAVE P.W.A. WORKERS
ON YOUR PAYROLL? ? ? ? ?

Remember the "relief" workers of 1933 . . . leaf raking, snow shoveling, ditch digging, and such?

Nonproductive work.

Well, if you have men spending valuable time grinding or hacking off weld spatter, you're supporting a miniature P.W.A. today.

BECAUSE PROTECT-O-METAL CAN CUT YOUR CLEANUP TIME 90%.

Put all of your man-hours on productive work. Use the welding compound that paints on and wipes off, absolutely eliminating spatter problems.

It cuts cleanup time, stabilizes the arc, improves the weld, carries flux, fights rust, grips paint, prevents scale . . . all with NO SMOKE, NO SMELL, NO FUMES. The folder tells the whole story.

Get that P.W.A. atmosphere out of your shop. Mail the yellow card today.

Enjoy a little "relief" yourself,
V. W. Smith

P.S. What does the card bring you? Just this. A FREE trial can of PROTECT-O-METAL No. 2. Then you can prove to yourself that this welding compound does everything I say it does. We'll let the product be our salesman. You're under no obligation, of course.

No. 3

1666% INCREASED EFFICIENCY ON WELD CLEANUP.

How? . . . Look!

A large steel-fabricating company hired a laborer to clean weld spatter. He was good. He cleaned up for three welders.

Then they tried PROTECT-O-METAL No. 2.

Now he cleans up for 50 welders. (A 1666% increase)

❀ ❀ ❀

2,000-pound bombs in a California welding company got a hot, cleaning bath—but first they passed twelve men removing weld spatter.

Then they tried PROTECT-O-METAL No. 2.

They closed the "cleanup" department—the hot bath cleans it alone.

❀ ❀ ❀

A boiler manufacturer in Minnesota and his time-study man checked off 19½ hours cleanup time for every 6 hours of welding on a unit.

Then they tried PROTECT-O-METAL No. 2.

Now an hour-and-a-half cleanup time is top for the same job.

❀ ❀ ❀

Those stories may sound as fantastic as hair-tonic commercials, but they're true. There are a hundred other stories like them. Every one of our customers is saving time and money daily. The enclosed folder tells why. Read it carefully.

Then YOU try PROTECT-O-METAL No. 2 . . . "on the house."

We'll send you a trial-size can FREE. You'll be under absolutely no obligation. Just fill in the enclosed card and slap it in the mail today. It will bring you real money in time savings . . . and better welding jobs.

V. W. Smith

P.S. The compound is a favorite of welders, too. It not only reduces cleanup time, it quiets the arc, strengthens the weld, inhibits rust, makes a better base for paint, prevents annealing scale . . . all with NO SMOKE, NO SMELL, NO FUMES.

No. 4

"Blow it off," we said . . . calmly.

That welding superintendent almost brained us with his chisel. "Blow off weld spatter?" he screamed. "Are you nuts? You can't get that stuff off with an axe."

"Blow it off," we said . . . calmly.

"Listen, brother," he listen-brothered, getting redder in the face, "In case you don't know it, we have ten men who do nothing but hack off weld spatter. Blow it off yourself."

So we blew it off . . . calmly.

It was so quiet you could hear a chisel drop. His did.

"How long has this been going on?" he whispered.

"We've been selling the compound about two years and it—"

Then he *did* get mad. "Why you °#$°°#%¢," he sputtered. (Postal laws forbid literal translation.) "Do you mean to tell me you've had something that licks cleanup time, rust, scale . . . makes a better weld and doesn't make a welder sick, and you've been hiding it under a bushel for two years?"

Then it was my turn. "Look," I said, as calmly as possible from under the bench, "We've advertised until we're blue in the face. Hundreds of other plant superintendents have become our customers. We just can't come out and 'blow it off' for everybody. The trouble with you is you won't believe anything until you see it."

He's one of our best customers today.

V. W. Smith

P.S. Come to think of it, maybe people shouldn't believe things until they see them. Maybe you feel that way. Well, send the yellow card today. We'll mail you a *free* sample of PROTECT-O-METAL No. 2. There's absolutely no obligation—just try it.

And here is the copy from the card used with G. W. Smith & Sons' letters:

O.K. SMITH
BUT YOU'VE GOT TO SHOW ME!

I'll believe those NO-SMOKE-NO-SMELL-NO-FUMES-SAVES-90%-CLEANUP-TIME claims when I make them myself.

Send me that FREE sample and I'll try it out. I understand I'm under no further obligation.

NAME_____

FIRM_____

STREET_____CITY_____

A Point of View

When artists or experts in any field explain their methods, they are likely to talk about techniques, "how" a particular thing is done. But if they (or anyone else) try to teach others by discussing techniques alone, they produce sterile, dull imitators instead of a new generation of artists.

Great direct mail writing comes only from people who know "why" and "when" as well as "how" to do their job . . . who understand the abstract requirements of their work.

So the emphasis in this chapter is not on sales-letter formulas, check lists, and the like. Here the emphasis is rather on perspective, on point of view, on a way of looking at working words (for a discussion of formulas, see Chapter 28). An attempt has been made to penetrate some of the depths of language—of which direct mail copy is but an offspring. In later chapters you will find patterns which you can adapt to your copy problems. Without the *perspectives,* the *specifics* supplied you—in the patterns—have no real depth in applicable meaning.

Patterns for selling letters are presented subordinately. Because none of the elements of the persuasion process are separable. They are not individualized parts of a whole . . . but, instead, are integrated, blended, unified parts of a process—picking up a reader's interest and leading him through to a suggested action.

Included also are several check lists. These check lists are better used as guides, not as strait jackets. They are particularly effective in checking copy after you have written it, to see if everything has been included. Better it is . . . *not* to sit down with a check list in front of you and try to force yourself to write a letter to fit it. If you do, you strangle the creative impulses as they become warm and filter through your hand, onto a page, from your pen.

The copy chapters have been set up as they are for these reasons:

1. To give you a general perspective of the creative processes available in language. You will find that in this chapter.

2. To give you the four steps of the selling or persuasion process . . . in perspective. These steps are found in the chapters on "Attention," "Interest," "Belief," and "Action."

Before we define what working words are, what copy is, let's see what copy's job is. The copy job is twofold:

First, *Copy must inform.*[1] You have to tell your reader something . . . something worthwhile. Otherwise, why should he read your copy? You owe your mailing list the courtesy of saying something worthwhile.

[1] Edgar W. Bolles, "Good Business Writing Makes Good Sense," *The ABWA Bulletin,* American Business Writing Association, Urbana, Ill., vol. 22, no. 4, January, 1958, p. 5.

Second, *Copy must influence.* The reader's reaction will depend upon the type of message presented. If you are selling by mail order, chances are you will want an immediate reaction. If your message seeks to build an "image" to represent you, if you build influence over a period of time, then the reaction may be cumulative or delayed.

But copy should give the reader something more, something over and above the information and the persuasion. "Pete" Hoke suggests that copy should give inspiration as well as information. When possible, then, give a little humor, stir the depths of nostalgia. Take this example from Charles W. Groves Company, Michigan City, Indiana. This is just part of a letter. But it taps the wellspring of human sentiment and appreciation. This copy explains why the cordial-contact handshake from Groves is a welcome guest on any desk. The "something more" of this copy is childhood wrapped in a halo of nostalgia. Remember, it's only part of a letter. Here's the copy:

AN EIGHT-YEAR-OLD

has a little bit of daring, a big dash of shyness and is more curious and noisy than anyone else in the world. He can buzz like a jet, roar like a rocket and tell stories that seem to have no end. He's curiosity with a smudge on its face . . . friendship with a freckle or two. And when he writes with crayoned letters, "TEACHER . . . I LOVE YOU" . . . he makes her queen in her classroom kingdom . . . a queen with a smile in her heart.

What, then, is copy? Copy is words, words applied to a selling problem, in such a way they interpret products and services in terms of a reader's needs and wants. But, what are words?

WORDS ARE COLD THINGS, DROPPED FLAT ON PAPER.[2]

Words, cold as they may be, are, however, the most powerful invention of man. Words are the key to everything in man's civilization. A man lives by words. A man loves by words. A man prays with words. And a man dies for, by, and with words. Every human animal is wrapped in a fabric of words. Should that fabric tatter, should that fabric tear, a man can also go mad—by words. They are the key to understanding and appreciation, to emotion and reason. Because they are the symbols of IDEAS, but . . .

What Are Ideas? According to Ernest Dimnet, author of *The Art of Thinking,* ". . . the flux in our brain carries along images . . . feelings, resolves, and intellectual, or partly intellectual conclusions, in vague or psychological confusion. . . . All we can say is: that most of our mental operations are inseparable from images, or are produced by images . . .

---

[2] An excellent example of the something extra which copy can offer in the way of wisdom. This sentence is from copy written by Dorothy Malbon Parker for Fin 'n Feather Farm at Dundee, Illinois.

that these images closely correspond to wishes or repulsions, to things we want or do not want, so that this wanting or not wanting seems to be the ultimate power in our psychology, probably in connection with elementary conditions in our being." [3]

To create an effect within a reader's mind, then, we must first interrupt his "vague or psychological confusion." This is a problem of developing attention—the presentation of an image which will immediately interest the reader. There is no intention here, however, of implying you have to hit a man over the head to get attention. Direct mail will get read. But the point of departure in copy can help sweep up a reader and get him into the copy. An *image* can be of several types: offering a benefit through copy, creating interest through copy style, developing attention through format. Actually, it is a combination of all these that develops our effective images.

How to Develop Usable Ideas

Before you can create effective copy, before you can develop usable copy ideas, you must do two things to build a base from which you can be creative:

1. Find out what you have to work with.
2. Determine what the *purpose* of your direct mail is.

To achieve both of these objectives, you must fill your mind full of familiarity, full of ideas. You cannot write without familiarity with your subject matter and purpose. To accomplish this state of mind you have a three-step process. This process is part of a method developed in the *Manual* of the Brooklyn Press, 335 Adams Street, Brooklyn 1, New York.[4]

1. *Compile all the background material available to you.* Before you tackle any copy job, you should compile all the information you can about the company, your product or service, your market, your method of distribution and selling, your media, and your sales objective.

2. *Group in importance.* After you have compiled your material, you come to the second step in developing a creative base. *Group your material into categories of importance*—importance to your reader . . . importance as it affects his life, his needs, his wants or interests.

3. *Select a CSP.* Our third step in determining purpose through knowledge and familiarity is the selection of a CSP—*Central Selling Point.* This is the feature, appeal, image which is most promising for your marketing success. And remember that it's based on what's most important to your reader.

[3] Ernest Dimnet, *The Art of Thinking,* a Premier book, Fawcett Publications, Inc., New York, 1955, pp. 18–19.

[4] "How to Develop Ideas," *The ABWA Bulletin,* American Business Writing Association, Urbana, Ill., February, 1948.

Activate the Imagination

According to Alex F. Osborn, the functions of creative imagination are twofold: "One to *hunt*, the other to *change* what is found." [5]

In the process we have been developing here, we have been doing the *hunting*. We have thought in terms of *what we have to work with*. Now we are at the point where we want our imagination to change what we have found, to help us develop usable ideas. At this point, we go through another process in which we think of our product or service, its appeals, its uses in terms of how we can deal with it—imaginatively—in copy. This process includes these three steps:

1. **Create New Combinations.** The first step in creating imaginative copy ideas is to *create new combinations of things already in existence*. As an example, tying instant coffee to the fact that workers produce more when their morning or afternoon stretch includes a short relaxing period . . . and coming up with the idea of a "coffee break."

2. **Shift Attributes.** The second means of creating ideas is to *shift attributes or characteristics from one thing to another*. The most effective method of doing this in copy is to give human qualities to inanimate things—an object, an ideal, an animal, a product, or a quality of a product. Abstract ideas or product qualities can be well described by giving "life" to them. With the aid of vividness from words that whiff life into the nonliving, the punch in copy can drive home its message more deeply.

The interest created by giving life to the inanimate is derived from the seeming paradox of inert matter or intangible concept entering into the realm of human reality, through actions and expressions limited ordinarily to the human animal. These examples from the Fin 'n Feather Farm catalogue are excellent in their treatment of this technique:

Such Happy Flavor!

Giving happiness to flavor carries the connotation of a satisfying, smiling-fresh taste to the food described. By reducing the intangible of flavor to the specific feeling of *happy*, the copy writer activates the imagination of the reader. And since the concept of happiness is an individual thing, the impact of the copy is personalized.

Nothing to Cope with, except Runaway Appetites

Here the copy writer has achieved the almost impossible. By using the words *runaway appetites,* she (Dorothy Malbon Parker of New York City) has described *drooling* in colorful fashion without using the word *drool*

[5] Alex F. Osborn, *Applied Imagination: Principles and Procedures of Creative Thinking*, rev. ed., Charles Scribner's Sons, New York, 1957, p. 105.

—not exactly a pleasantly descriptive word. The human ability to run away, when given to *appetite,* lifts this copy from run-of-the-mill into the unusual.

This Hickory-smoked Bacon of Ours Never Saw a Butcher Shop and Would Wince at a Slicing Machine.

No store-bought bacon this! It's kitchen-fresh from a home-made atmosphere. Not only that—it's tender, extremely sensitive, and you can slice it to any convenient thickness. The human ability implied in "saw a butcher shop" and "wince" bring life to the greasy slab.

In this next example of giving life to the inanimate, the copy writer's pleasant touch of humor has potted plants whispering among themselves. It also attributes the human ability of feeling pain to the flowers. This copy is from *Sand and Spray,* a house magazine published for Chalfonte-Haddon Hall, Atlantic City, New Jersey.

Chuck, a man of gentle touch with the scissors, also supplies the cut flowers for our dining room. He's so gentle, it's whispered among the pots, that not one of the hundreds of dozens of flowers he must amputate for us ever feels a twinge of pain.

3. **New Qualities.** A third way of creating interesting ideas is to *give new qualities to a thing*—qualities which are not ordinarily ascribed to it. And one of the best ways of doing this is to develop new ways of measuring it. Here are examples where the usual method of measuring things is changed to get good copy.

There's a Dab of Nostalgia in a Slab of Our Bacon.

Dab is a good measurement for the immeasurable parts of nostalgia.

Next, we have an example from a letter which describes teacher dedication:

Things like . . . values—lofty ones which are a teacher's own and which shine through her *little bits of people.*

Little bits of people is an effective, and unusual, description of children. Actually, this measurement of children has all the depth qualities of poetry.

But with these cold things—*words*—however, you have problems. Words are not what they seem. Connotations of words are individual. So it is necessary to choose very carefully each key word we use. Language has limitations; it is imperfect. And within these limits we must work with words.

1. *Doesn't fit.* The first limit of language is: It doesn't always fit a given situation. Take that small but important little word "No." Does "No"

always mean a negative answer? Not necessarily. It may mean, "Well maybe" . . . or "Perhaps later." It may mean, "I'm too busy now." You never know.

2. *Can't stop it.* Language is dynamic. No matter how the grammarians protest, language will continue to change—as it has changed through the centuries. And you *can't stop it* from changing. Language belongs to the people who use it—not to the scholar and the pedagogue. For example, take the *Winston* ad:

> Winston Tastes Good Like a Cigarette Should.

According to the rule, *like* is not a conjunction. If it were, Shakespeare would have called his play, "Like You Like It." But the latest reports from Webster's indicate that *like* as a conjunction is now acceptable on the colloquial level of speech.

3. *Can't pin it down.* Among areas, regions, cities, usage in language varies. You *can't* take every word and *pin it down* as the only way to express an idea, everywhere. Take one example—that spot of grass between your sidewalk and the curb in front of your home. Ordinarily, the most widely used word for this grassy plot is *Parking.* However, you'll find different words used in various parts of the country to describe that spot of grass. Some of the words are: Boulevard, Banket (New Orleans), Parkside, Parkway, Tree Lawn, Terrace, Berm. None of these words is wrong. In fact, they are all right . . . if you judge them by the area in which you find them. They will, however, cause confusion in some cases when used out of the context where they exist.

4. *Can't count on it.* You can't count on a word to mean the same thing to another person that it means to you. As an excellent example of this kind of confusion, take the example of former Vice President Richard Nixon. While traveling in Asia, he gave one talk where he received an ovation every time he said "Dwight Eisenhower." Actually, he probably thought he was in a Republican precinct. It wasn't until later that he learned that the sequence of sounds in President Eisenhower's name—in the native tongue of Nixon's audience—meant Free Beer.

You get results only from copy that packs a wallop. Now, how do you put a wallop into your copy? Well, knowing that we should use interesting ideas, ideas which we CONTROL to get our desired effect, we set up a three-part Pattern for Creating Reaction in the minds of our readers. The three parts are: EMPATHY . . . MOTION . . . IMPACT.

Empathy

Empathy is *Sympathy*, the rapport created by copy. It is the spirit of copy that bridges the chasm between people—the chasm which exists because each individual sees the world a little differently. It's the ability to wear another man's shoes, to see the world through his glasses, to listen to his boss's growl, his wife's chatter.

Empathy is *Heart*. And, heart is sympathy, sincerity. It's the hand shake in copy, the display of interest in those things, persons, ideas, nearest and dearest to the reader. It's the attitude which you display to indicate that you wish the reader well.

Empathy is *Balance*. Balance means that copy has the proper amounts of appeal to reason and to emotion. Since reason and emotion are inseparable, no decision is made purely on the basis of one or the other. You must have both.

Empathy is *Insight*. Insight is a writer's perception, the ability to see the world through his reader's eyes, to see and understand the reader's problems, his perspectives, as he does. And, importantly, it means the copy is presented from the reader's point of view.

Empathy is *Harmony*. This means copy is written within the language level of the reader. It means language is adapted to the reader's intellectual capacities. It's good, old-fashioned, colloquial English set down in proper language disciplines.[6]

Motion

Motion is the second part of the Pattern for Creating Reaction. Motion in copy is moving the reader from the state of mind you find him in to the state of mind you want him in. And, besides the persuasion content your copy must carry, copy must be put together so that it flows rapidly.

Language without discipline and proper order can result in a chaotic presentation of ideas which arrives at no agreement or assent from your reader. Disciplines and orderly presentation apply most forcefully to written language. Speech for coherence needs some order and discipline. But, in conversation, how often do we fracture the rules? How many fragmentary sentences, for instance, do we leave hanging on the clotheslines of conversation? This happens in speech because continuity is carried by two or more people.

In writing, on the other hand, the continuity and coherence are up to the writer, for he does not have all the atmosphere of conversation to assist him. For this reason, proper language disciplines and good, coherent organization are important. Admittedly, there are times when the grammatical rules against sentence fragments, etc., may be discarded. But the copy writer must have a certain degree of sophistication with language before he can break the rules effectively. Good organization, also, is not possible without a thorough knowledge of the subject written about.

[6] Harper's *American College Dictionary*, 1948, defines colloquial English as ". . . the words, expressions, and the structure of the informal but polite conversations of cultivated people. . . ."

Create Orderly Movement of Ideas. Before you can make copy move, you must know exactly where you are going. This means you must have compiled all the possible facts about your copy problem before you have started to write. It means you know what the purpose of the copy is. It means, too, you understand completely the point of view of the person you are writing to.

Without all the facts, without knowing your objective, without understanding your reader, you cannot properly organize your copy into the proper pattern of persuasion which will move the reader from where he is to where you want him to be. Because you will not be sufficiently familiar with the ideas to emphasize for persuasion.

Good organization makes ideas move, flow. And good organization will help your copy move from its opener through a logical development to the desired conclusion. The enemies of fluid copy movement are improper analysis of the problem, poor logic, unbelievable statements, awkward sentence structure, and inadequate or improper transition.

You would not cross the United States without a road map (unless you had taken the same route before). You wouldn't fly without a flight plan. Neither should you try to write copy before you have first of all determined your objective and then decided which is the most logical, effective, and desirable way to achieve that objective.

After you've outlined and started to write, don't swing back and forth over the same idea trying to clean it up. Say it and be gone. Get to the next idea, and the next, always on a bee-line toward your goal—creating a well-constructed message which gets the reaction, the assent, the agreement you want from your reader.

Use Active Voice. After good organization in copy writing, active voice is necessary to make your copy move. To effect this, use active verbs and active sentence structure. Active verbs give good mental imagery and therefore make a deeper impact on the reader. They put "punch" into copy. They put the necessary rhythm of the heartbeat in your copy. Active voice usually makes a sentence more forceful, more emphatic.

Create Copy Rhythm. One discipline which a copy writer can use to keep his copy moving is rhythm. Let us first define rhythm; then see how we can create it. Rhythm is measured movement, the uniform recurrence of a beat. The key words here are *uniform, recurrence,* and *beat.* Implicit in these words are the ideas of repetition and emphasis. How rhythmic the use of repetition and the application of emphasis turn out to be depends upon how skillfully these two writing tools are applied. Let us have a look at the means of creating rhythm.

Eye Rhythm is our first means of creating measured movement. This type of rhythm is created in your layout and punctuation. It is also part of the problem of design and format. To get eye rhythm into your copy, break up the paragraphs. Vary their size. Indent some of them—but see that you create good margins for balance and so that the indention repeats. Change the color of the type in alternating paragraphs.

See the National Tag Company letter, page 175, for a good layout. This example shows how the size of paragraphs has been varied to give a seeming ease of reading through rhythmic placement on the page.

Structural Rhythm is the second method for creating movement in copy. To get structural rhythm, select carefully the types of sentences you use. Vary the sentence types. Use a combination of long and short sentences. Then, to create a staccato effect, use a series of very short sentences—all of the same type. Do not use the same sentence length or type over and over again, however. You will get monotony instead of rhythm. Usually for the most effective writing, you should put the subject first, the verb next, the object last. This simple declarative sentence is effective because the reader will then visualize the ACTOR going through the ACT of the verb in the direction of the object.

Here is an example from the booklet which Hart Schaffner & Marx used to introduce Viracle. Note the varied sentence length. Note the "recurrence" of the short-sentence type to create a series of quickly understood images and a staccato effect.

A HAPPY UNION

Once upon a time there was a genuine synthetic prince. His name was Dacron. He was strong. He was handsome. He was versatile. He'd even been on television. But still he was unhappy. He felt he was missing something. But he didn't know what.

So he went to see the old family psychiatrist. The doctor stroked his goatee and told him: "You're living too artificial a life. Get out of that laboratory and find yourself a mate. It'll make a world of difference in the way you look and feel."

So Prince Dacron donned his neon crown and made a scientific search. But it was no use. Downhearted he shed a test-tube tear. He was just about to give up when he saw HER and fell head over electrons in love. He heaved a synthetic sigh and clanked, "It had to be ewe."

He proposed, "Lambikins, be mine, and you'll never have to worry about wrinkles. I'll make you stronger, lighter, and cooler, too. You'll live to a magnificent old age. And you'll never have to fear wet weather again."

She made sheep's eyes at him, promised to love him forever, and to give him her wool-soft hand. She plighted to share her famous affinity for fine tailoring. She vowed that her rich and luxurious beauty would henceforth be his.

In time they were blessed with an heir, who combined the best qualities of both. Richness and resilience. Style and strength. Luxury and long life. At first sight, Prince Dacron exclaimed, "It's a miracle!" "No, dear," said his wife, "It's a Viracle.*" And they were both right!

* Reg. U.S. Pat.Off. HS&M Chicago.

The picture of the part wool, part Dacron Viracle tropical on the opposite page shows you why. Or better still, come down to the store and try on a Viracle. Hart Schaffner & Marx sent us one in your size that's up for adoption right now.

Parallelism of Sentence Structure is the third method for creating copy movement. Using the same example from Hart Schaffner & Marx, let us look at how parallel structure in sentence type gives a quick-paced, staccato effect. These short, terse sentences develop the story quickly. And the copy movement is rapid. The double bar is used to show how the copy writer developed his parallelism for the repetition of the beat.

His name	was Dacron.
He	was strong.
He	was handsome.
He	was versatile.
He	'd even been on television.
But still	
He	was unhappy.
He	felt
He	was missing something.
But he	didn't know what.

In this case the copy writer has used the same sentence type. But notice that, although they are all the same type, they are not all the same length. This is one way of avoiding monotony.

Structural rhythm can also be created by a series of sentence fragments. In this technique you create a series of images with vivid verbs. Then you separate them with leader dots (...) to give the reader sufficient pause to absorb the imagery. Note in the following example how the series of images is created by a series of sentence fragments. Note also that part of the rhythm is created by the pause which you get from the leader dots. The effect is this: an image is created through a verb. Then the pause is created by the leader dots. You get an image, then a pause, an image, then a pause.

Wild Berber tribesmen *riding* through Morocco streets . . . the Queen of Greece *frolicking* with her children . . . pilgrims and beggars *crowding* about spiral domed Moscow churches . . . a French premier *fighting* to stay in office . . . torrential rains *pouring* misery on millions of people in Pakistan. (*Look Magazine*)

Alliteration is another method of creating copy rhythm. From the earliest poets to the twentieth-century copy writers, alliteration has been used as a means of putting impact into writing. And alliteration is more than the repetition of the first letter of a word. It can be achieved by repetition of the same sound—regardless of where that sound appears in

a word. Here are some examples of alliteration from a Christmas catalogue
of Fin 'n Feather Farm:

Lazy Little Plumes of Smoke

In this instance, "L" creates the alliteration. The "S" sound, however, gives
the *overtones* of the hushed movement.

The next example gets its alliteration from the "F," "S," and "W" sounds.
Note that these sounds appear at different positions in the various words.

Pacifists Fight for a Drumstick. Stoics Swoon for a Wing.

Shifting moods is the next method for creating rhythm in copy. Mood
rhythm is developed by the skillful selection of words which swing the
emotional pendulum of the reader from a negative reaction to a positive
reaction (or vice versa). The noted semanticist Hayakawa has labeled
these mood words as *Snarl* (negative) and *Purr* (positive) words.

A snarl word creates a negative reaction in the mind of the reader. He
is "agin" the situation being described. He is against the meaning of that
word because it symbolizes something of which he disapproves. A purr
word creates a positive reaction in the mind of the reader. He is "for" the
situation being described. He is "for" the meaning of that word because
it symbolizes something of which he approves. To create this mood
rhythm, you should develop ideas (with snarl words) which will create
disapproval in the mind of the reader. Then shift to other ideas (with
purr words) which you know will bring approval in the mind of the
reader. In this shift from mood to mood you get a rhythmic emotional
swing in reader reaction.

By skillful selection of snarl words and purr words in developing his
ideas, a copy writer can create a subtly rhythmic appeal to his reader.
This copy from Boys Town is an excellent example of mood rhythm and
swings from emotion to emotion. Note how the copy writer leads the
reader into ideas he knows the reader dislikes. Then note how he shifts
that mood to gain reader approval.

Just a few years ago they were homeless, destitute, and forgotten. Many of
them were abandoned because of the tragedies of death, divorce, or crime.
Some, friendless and without hope, became wanderers on the face of the earth.

They have now joined the thousands of other former citizens of Boys Town
as proud, productive American citizens, who today live and work in the largest
cities and the smallest towns across the nation, where yesterday they were
destitute, without homes, and without friends. We gave them a home and an
opportunity, and in turn, they are giving America their toil, their skill, and
their devotion.

Knowing the universal appeal of boys, this copy writer has two strikes
against his reader before the reader opens the letter. When most readers

hear of boys who are *homeless, destitute,* and *forgotten,* when a reader thinks of boys who are *friendless, without hope,* his reaction can almost be assumed. He is "agin" it. But when the copy shifts to a new environment for boys, when the boys become *proud, productive American* (any reader is for that!) *citizens,* the reader heartily approves. The solution to a *homeless boy,* the way to make him a *productive American* citizen, is to contribute to Boys Town.

In this example from an AMVET's letter, you get a combination of rhythm based on repetition in the use of prepositional phrases to set the scene and the rhythm of shifting from one mood to another.

In foxholes, on battleships, in planes—millions of American boys faced death and dreamed of peace and all that it would bring.

Here you get a shift in mood words when you swing from "American boys faced death" (and that is a swing within itself) to "dreamed of peace." This creates a snarl image, then moves into a purr image. The change from snarl to purr gives the swing, the rhythm, the change of pace to revive and renew reader interest.

Impact

The third way to create copy with the Pattern for Creating Reaction is *impact.* Impact is the bounce of the ball, the force with which the message hits a reader, the degree to which a message penetrates. Impact is measured by how well it diverts a reader from what he's doing to what you want him to do—read your mailing and act upon it.

Impact is depth penetration, the carry through into and throughout copy, to reach the reader's mental and emotional levels of persuasion. Depth penetration works on all the possible combinations of reason and emotion which help move the reader from where he is to where you want him—to a state of belief in what your message says and a readiness to act upon what you request.

Hit the Reader's Senses Hard. A light scratch on a polished surface soon wears away. Cut deep and the mark lasts.[7] If you want copy which cuts deep into the mind of the reader to leave a lasting mark, use those words which convey vivid sense imagery. Select words which force the reader to see, to feel, to smell, to taste your product or service—to feel it physically, psychically, and, if possible, spiritually. Such words give you more impact, a deeper cut, a keener impression, with the result that your copy is more effective in helping the reader visualize how your product or service benefits him.

This technique is not applicable to all copy because some products are

[7] Milton Wright, *Managing Yourself,* 2d ed., McGraw-Hill Book Company, Inc., New York, 1949, p. 77.

not adaptable to such a presentation. There are, however, two ways of using this type of description with almost any product or service:

1. Write about the product or service per se—when it is adaptable to descriptive copy which appeals to the senses.

2. Write about the product or service *in use*. Pictorialize benefits in imagery by projecting the reader into a mental state where he can see himself using and benefiting from the product or service.

A word of caution: Beware of that undefinable *line* where your reader admires the copy but does not want the product. This *line* is determined by the mailing list and the product. The sophisticated audience of Fin 'n Feather Farm would appreciate the casual word play of Fin 'n Feather direct mail. A less sophisticated audience would get caught up in a mis-understanding of the copy writer's intent—a smooth and suave approach with an implied overtone of a select, in-group belongingness.

Smell: This copy excerpt presents appeals to several of the senses per se. It also has sound, alliteration, rhythm.

I wish I had you here on the Farm. To hear the Whir-r-r of Pheasants rising from the fields. To sniff the smoke from the smokehouse fires—fragrant on the frosty air. You'd go for it all right.

The act of "sniff the smoke" sets the reader's reaction for the satisfaction of the sense of smell. From *smoke, smokehouse, fragrant,* and *frosty,* the reader's sense of smell has been appealed to.

Taste: Taste, of course, has a close correlation with smell. In this example from Fin 'n Feather copy the sense of taste is appealed to. The idea of delicacy is conveyed by the copy writer's restraint in these phrases: *dainty sliver, tinged, just gamey enough, accented with wood smoke.* Taste is appealed to by *tender, sweet, wood smoke, rich, gamey,* and *accented.*

Every dainty sliver is tender, sweet, and subtly tinged with wood smoke. Each thin dark slice, each coveted wing or leg is tender . . . rich . . . just gamey enough . . . and accented with wood smoke.

Sight: In appealing to the sense of sight, you have shape, color, line, and movement to work with. And if you can get action into your descrip-tion, so much the better. Action is easily visualized.

In this example of copy which appeals to sight, the vividness and imagery are developed by the use of the participial form of the verbs *prodding, tweaking, wrestling.*

When we're not prodding a pig or tweaking a turkey, we're wrestling with shredded cellophane and balls of ribbon.

The next example creates vivid imagery to appeal to sight through description of the product *in use*. Since the product is nose drops, color, shape, and smell do not offer the possibilities of good description as well as the product *in use* does. This is Horner Pharmaceutical copy directed toward doctors. Part of its appeal lies in the amusement value it gives with its humorous tone. Imagery is created through the use of action verbs: *lie down, bend over, stand on his head.*

For until just recently, the administration of nose drops started with contortions and ended in a degree of futility. Whether the patient would lie down, bend over, or stand on his head to put in the drops,—he'd still feel them trickle out soon after he became perpendicular.

Change of Pace. In developing impact, you have a writing technique which helps to freshen your writing, helps to keep reader interest alive. This is the use of a change of pace. The technique is based on the psychological concept that comedy relief improves the quality of drama, on the idea that you should provide entertainment for your reader, and on the idea that sustained attention needs relief for holding or renewing interest.

The best way to get a change of pace in writing is to use a quick shift in levels of language. Here are two examples of change of pace based on language-level shifts. Note that the first starts on a high level of josh, moves into French, then abruptly swings into American slang—to give the reader an abrupt change of pace. The second example, directed toward the same audience, starts out on an almost stilted (though joshing) plane. Then swings abruptly from stilted formalism into slang.

1. Feel luxurious and festive! Roll your eyes like an epicure and throw in a little French, even if it's only an ooh la la. That's the effect pheasant has on people. It's rare . . . it's distingué . . . oh *nuts*, it's darn *good.*
2. Dear Discerning One:
   We know you *are,* since you're on our lists as having been given some delectable Fin 'n Feather Food. And Friends don't send such food unless they deem you worthy. Yep, it points straight to the savvy on your part.

Let It Incubate

So that we can get our ideas loose and on paper, we now let the whole thing—our study of the product, market, etc., and our attempts to deal imaginatively with our sales problem—*incubate.*

If copy doesn't come easily after you've worked your way through this process, just turn the problem over to your subconscious for a while. Go golfing. Go to a concert, a play. Read. Do anything that stimulates you. In so doing you are letting ideas develop.

To quote Milton Wright on this topic: "Your brain is active all the time, whether you are conscious or not, and it does accurate work—constructive work—when you give it an opportunity."

Fill your mind, then, with facts, perspectives, ideas, notions, attitudes. Let your subconscious work it over.

How to Create Copy

Now we reach the blood, sweat, and tears of creating good copy. You have sufficient information, a good backlog of material. Your ideas are beginning to pop loose. Now you're ready to go to work. This is the place where you have to compress ideas into a piece of good copy.

Write. Sit down, take your pen or typewriter, and start. Now write, and write, and write. Then rewrite—rewrite—rewrite. If you'll remember that everything good has been rewritten, you'll realize how much the preparation process means to good copy.

Seek Criticism. After you've written what you think is a good piece of copy, *seek the criticism of someone else,* preferably someone who has no familiarity with the subject you're writing about. In this way the reader can tell you where the copy has faults. When you write from familiarity, you sometimes omit ideas which are necessary to proper transition and development of thought. Then, when you read what you've written, your head supplies omitted ideas—and you don't spot their absence.

Change the Setting. The next step is to change the setting of the copy. When you read your copy in a new atmosphere, you can see things which escaped you previously.

One good copy writer we know mails his copy to himself at home. Then he can read it in another atmosphere. You may not always have the time to mail it home before it's printed. Do it anyway. You'll learn something which will be valuable in future copy writing.

Let It Age. The last part of this compression of copy is let it age. When you have the time, let your copy get stale for a few days. Then go back to it. In a few days, your own moods, attitudes, perspectives have undergone a change—no matter how small or subtle—which will give you a new look at your copy. Age it. Then, change it if you will.

One important thing: You can "fuss" too much with copy. You can kill it, emasculate its impact by *over*working it. The time to quit working on a piece of copy—to accept what you have done as adequate—is something which only experience can tell you. With practice, you'll develop this skill.

8

How to Create Copy Attention

Copy Openers

The success of any copy opener is determined by one thing: Does it get the rest of the copy read? This includes all types of openers: envelope teaser lines, letter attention lines, the opening sentence of a letter, the first paragraph of any piece of copy, the title of a booklet or brochure.

Supported by the creative materials you have for developing visual impact—paper, color, types, die cuts, folds, etc.—to give its background a contrasting difference over other mail and other events, an effective opener can give the immediate impression of being in the reader's interest. Or it can amuse him, arouse his curiosity. Many ways are available to you as a means of getting started in your copy.

But an incentive to read further should be kindled in the reader's mind. And how do you create this incentive? You relate your headline to a reader's needs, his wants, his interests, his habits, the roles he plays, the way he sees himself in contrast to the way he wants to be, his pattern of reference, and those things, people, and ideas in which he is interested.[1]

To illustrate the diversity of the human personality facets and interests to which your opener can appeal, let's look at the comment Douglas B. Mahoney, advertising director of Frank W. Horner, Ltd., makes on his own copy. Mr. Mahoney uses cordial-contact direct mail to keep the Horner "image" constant and fresh with doctors. Here's what he has to

[1] Wilbur Schramm (ed.), *The Process and Effects of Mass Communications*, University of Illinois Press, Urbana, Ill., 1954, p. 31.

say about the diversity of the approaches of copy as it attempts to get the reader's attention:[2]

Rapport can be best achieved by a piece that hits first at the human. One that erupts out of the pile with warmth, humour, whimsey, or pure crash. A rendering that plucks a nostalgic string. One that enlists the senses through associations with well-known persons, places, sayings, objects—visually and/or verbally. Having stirred an emotion, we meet the reader on a ground common to both of us. Then lead him seductively into the commercial.

Your copy opener is the "greeting," the "handshake" between you and the reader. To be effective, and to assure you that the "greeting" leads the reader clear through the conversation (your copy), the opener has the mission of achieving three things:

1. It should establish rapport between the writer and the reader. Or, call it "getting on common ground" with the reader.

2. It should contain an incentive, a reason why the reader should read your message.

3. It should *lead* the reader logically, coherently, and easily into the copy.

The means of establishing rapport and creating incentive to read are many. In these examples, note how well integrated the opener is with the rest of the copy. Notice that the movement from the opener into the commercial messages is smoothly logical and leads the reader easily into the selling message. The openers given you here are from various types of letters—mail-order, cordial-contact, prospect-selection, etc. They have been combined into one chapter to show you various ways of getting your copy writing efforts "off the ground." Since this book is intended for college students as well as businessmen, the emphasis on "how-to" copy has been made extensive.

Amuse Your Reader. One of the effective types of copy openers is that which amuses your reader. And amusement is much more than provoking a "thigh-slapping guffaw." It moves full circle from the guffaw, through the chuckle, into the grin—and fades into the very personal areas of memory and nostalgia.

McCann-Erickson uses the amusement approach in its highly creative and very effective direct mail campaign for Standard Oil of New Jersey. To quote the late Mr. Ferd Ziegler of McCann:[3]

We strongly believe in paying for what we get—*we never ask for something for nothing* from our audience. And we pay off in entertainment. This is

[2] D. B. Mahoney, "The Eldest Is Always Called 'Percy,' Dear," *The Reporter of Direct Mail Advertising,* vol. 17, no. 11, p. 17, March, 1955.

[3] Ferd Ziegler, "What's the Big Idea in Direct Mail?" Speech on Chicago Direct Mail Day, May 25, 1956.

precisely the same principle used in TV and radio—and magazines and news-papers.

When we try to reach a person via direct mail . . . in the Esso Dealer Program, we find that the best incentives we can provide are amusement and useful gifts.

The specific approaches which amuse the reader in some way would form a long list. Here are a few:

Start with Satire. Depending upon the sophistication level of your audience, satire can be an effective way of creating rapport between you and your reader. Satire, too, can create the kind of interest which gives an incentive to read the rest of your copy.

This example from Frank W. Horner, Ltd. (pharmaceuticals), uses satire to attract its rather sophisticated readers—the members of the medical profession. This is a good example of satire because it treats very lightly the drastic act of suicide.

Dear Doctor:

Anyone bent on doing away with himself has a wide selection of weapons. There's poison, rope, carbon monoxide, a high building, a motor car, or the river.

But another weapon, still unrecognized as such, is gaining much favor. It is a combination made up of a knife, a fork, and a spoon. It's not as fast, of course, but much more pleasant . . . and the results take a few years to show. Soon obesity ensues to increase the incidence and speed the course of diabetes, heart disease, arteriosclerosis, and renal involvement.

In this copy, rapport is established and incentive to read is developed by the tongue-in-cheek humor which enumerates the various means of deal-ing death unto one's self. The transition from attention into the com-mercial message is developed by continuing the list of weapons of suicide, by continuing the *tone* of the opener, and by tying the attention into the commercial.

Create a Paradox. People enjoy seeing the context of life out of kilter. They enjoy seeing the usual patterns of life set up into casual and con-tradictory conflict. Here, again, the audience to whom you write will de-termine whether you can use such an opener. But, so long as your paradox is well handled, it should be effective in creating reader interest. Here is another example of a Mahoney/Horner opener; again, it is copy directed toward doctors.

Dear Doctor:

Sometimes the straight and narrow is deadly dangerous.

At least that's what highway engineers tell us. For apparently a road with no turnings exerts some sort of mesmeric effect on the average motorist. And when the ensuing stupor disappears, he awakes to find his car bent around an elm at the side of the road. So curves and corners are built into highways to keep the driver awake and alert.

And this procedure has a medical parallel. For in treating mixed or doubtful infections, the straightforward approach again carries well-defined risks. An antibiotic injection may not have enough scope to affect offending pathogens . . . a sulfonamide in sufficient strength to arrest the infection courts crystalluria.

Horner establishes rapport through the natural human interest in the seemingly contradictory situation. In this day of so many automobiles and so many drivers, the information about highways should have an almost universal appeal. The smooth transition from the opening line and the first paragraph is based upon building a parallel figure for the commercial—using the keynote of the attention opener: the straightforward approach.

Pluck a Nostalgic String. Nostalgia is that human feeling for the old-fashioned, for childhood, for the past—when the world seemed smaller, more pleasant, more secure—before the piper of time had to be paid in grey, and lines, and sometimes disappointment. Dip into this area of "human interest." Select a string from the harp of nostalgia—the people, the events, the shows, the styles, etc.—and play upon this emotion. Pluck a nostalgic string—to make your reader remember the "good old days." Lead him from that point into your copy.

This example, from Charles W. Groves (teacher lists) of Michigan City, Indiana, recalls, subtly, the romance of childhood. Copy like this— which is handled with a kind and gentle touch—lets the reader savor that early experience of a child's love for the unknown, helps the reader recall what is meant by bright-eyed innocence, implicit faith. This copy, though low-keyed to act as cordial contact only, has a depth of persuasion in plucking at nostalgia to create reader interest.

TO BE A CHILD . . .

is to believe in love . . . to believe in belief and to be so little that the elves can stand on tip-toe and whisper magic secrets in your ear. His griefs, his treasures, his field of vision and his world are small . . . because so is he. But his impressionability is keener than ours.

Behind his words, "My teacher says . . ." is an utterly inflexible conviction. His teacher, you see, holds the key to belief that unlocks the door to his world, where she enters and talks his talk. That is why you as an advertiser need to be very conscious of the nationwide impact of teacher opinion.

Notice how very smoothly the copy writer leads the reader from a child's impressionability into the specifics of the child's conviction of the truth of what his teacher says and then into the general impact of teacher opinion.

Horner has used the nostalgic appeal in another way. Assuming that many of the doctors on their list remembered the great Lon Chaney, they wrote the following copy to appeal to the feeling that (despite movie publicity to the contrary) movies were better, more thrilling—in the good old days. Here they used, as the opener for the letter, the symbol most closely associated with the name of Lon Chaney—"the man of a thousand faces." From there the reader is led into a nostalgic reminder of the chills, thrills, of Lon Chaney movies:

Dear Doctor:

Who was the Man of a Thousand Faces?

If once in a darkened theatre about 25 years back, you sat petrified through the "Phantom of the Opera," you'll never forget Lon Chaney. He is the man who spent a lifetime twisting and torturing his nice normal self into ghouls that scared a generation of us. And decades later, this artist of make-up and disguise is still remembered as the master of transformation.

But some transformations go deeper than Chaney's grease paint and straps. One familiar to you is that tense, agitated, anorexic patient, who strives to regain peace of mind and capacity for work and enjoyment. And your task is to bring about this change.

In this example, notice how the lead from attention into the commercial is based on a parallelism in imagery and the repetition of a key word. *Transformation* is the key word which swings the transition. The parallel imagery is found in these two sentences: one about a normal man, one about a patient—both about people with difficulties.

1. He is the man who spent a lifetime twisting and torturing his nice normal self into ghouls that scared a generation of us.

2. One familiar to you is that tense, agitated, anorexic patient, who strives to regain peace of mind and capacity for work and enjoyment.

Tell a Story. People like stories. They like to read about people, about people in action. People like to be caught up in the clutches of drama, the intensity of conflict, the excitement of romance. They like to wrap themselves in the wistfulness of the love story—to make routine less drab, more endurable. The number of magazines which offer fiction both to men and women, the variety of fiction available in paperbacks (plus the constant outpouring of new and revised titles) attest to this popularity. People are friendly toward narrative. They like story telling. And enjoy it. You have a good chance of holding their interest once you have attracted them —if you use narrative writing.[4]

One important problem though: The story you tell should be relevant to the message you are trying to convey. It should not be so long that the

[4] Melvin S. Hattwick, *How to Use Psychology for Better Advertising*, Prentice-Hall, Inc., Englewood Cliffs, N.J., 1950, p. 263.

reader wonders why he should plow through your introductory copy instead of enjoying your story and getting your message.[5] If you use a story to create an opener in your copy, you have the special problem of building the transition into the rest of your copy. Unless the entire piece of copy is a sales message integrated with narrative, the movement from attention into the sales message can become awkward. To create good transition, you can tell a story with a "moral" and then project the reader into a similar situation in your sales message. This is a problem of creating a parallelism in imagery. This example from a mailing of DeVry Technical Institute, Chicago, illustrates this point. The letter merely requests an inquiry. After the inquiry is received, other direct mail is used to sell the Institute.

> Did you ever hear the story about the two frogs who fell into a jar of cream? They struggled and struggled to stay afloat.
>
> Finally, one frog said, "What's the use?" He stopped his struggle and sank to the bottom. But the other frog continued to thrash and churn about—and lo, an island of butter began to appear under him. During the night, a rainstorm raised the butter to the top of the jar. The frog escaped.
>
> Today, many men flounder around, give up, and remain in low-paid work—when all that's needed is just a little added effort and help to start earning real money. And THAT'S OUR BUSINESS—*to provide this very help you need.*

This letter uses a story opener to illustrate the main point of the whole message—*keep trying* and you'll make the grade. Especially, with the help of DeVry. The correlation of basic sales offer and story is very good in this letter.

The next example of telling a story is from a *Reader's Digest* letter. In this example, part of the narrative was printed on the envelope. Then the copy was broken at a crucial point in the story. The rest of the story then appeared at the top of the enclosed letter. The narrative is from a *Reader's Digest* feature, "Life in These United States."

[Envelope copy]
LIFE IN THESE UNITED STATES

> "Mother, I wish I didn't look so flat-chested," said my 15-year-old daughter as she stood before the mirror in her first formal dress.
>
> I remedied the matter by inserting puffs of cotton in strategic places. Then I hung around Mary's neck a string of seed pearls—just as my grandmother had done for my mother and my mother for me.
>
> At midnight her escort brought her home. The moment the door closed behind him, Mary burst into tears. "I'm never going out with him again," she sobbed. "Mother, do you know what he said to me? . . ."

[5] Howard Dana Shaw, "How to Start to Write a Letter," *The Reporter of Direct Mail Advertising,* vol. 11, no. 10, pp. 11–16, February, 1949.

At this point the story breaks and the reader is led inside the envelope.

[Letter copy, continued from envelope]
. . . He leaned across the table and said, "Gee, you look sharp tonight, Mary. Are those real?"

"I hope you told him they were," I said indignantly. "They've been in the family for three generations!"

My daughter stopped sobbing. "Oh, the pearls! Good heavens, I'd forgotten all about them."

—from "Life in These United States."

YOU Can Have *The Reader's Digest* at Half Price . . .

Use a Startling Statement. To startle a reader is to take him by surprise. To startle him is to present him with the unexpected, something out of its usual context—a word, a person, a situation, a thing, or idea. And the degree of a "startle" can run the gamut from a raised eyebrow to a loud and screaming "EEK!" Startling statements seem to present a contradiction —an impossibility as a truth. They sometimes give life to the inanimate, put the inanimate through human action.

Closely related to a paradox (which *can* startle), a startling statement's effectiveness is based on the degree with which it "snaps a reader to" . . . because he can't believe what he has read. Well stated, this type of opener can give the kind of contrast with other mail and events that the writer seeks.

This example is especially startling because it arrives in an envelope from the *Journal of Commerce*. One doesn't ordinarily associate the dignified stature of the *Journal* with the contents of this opening line. However, people do business everywhere. But you read it:

THEY WALK TO PRIVIES IN THE RAIN,
AND NEVER WET THEIR FEET.

Everything was up to date in Kansas City at the turn of the century, when indoor plumbing was a novelty, according to the popular song from *Oklahoma!*

The people there had "gone about as fur as they could go." But they hadn't heard a whisper yet about the electronic brain, or nuclear fission, or the guaranteed annual wage, . . . and "automation" was a cloud upon the sky no bigger than a man's hand.

A great many other things have happened in recent months that have a direct bearing on the operation of your business . . . its present position and its future prospects . . . things that you must know in order to stay comfortable near the top in the competitive picture today.

Start with Humor. One way of attracting the reader is to approach him from the "funny side of the street." When you start with humor, you are "paying off in entertainment." For, everyone likes to laugh. And a smile is the key to ease and acceptance, opens the door to rapport. Make the reader smile. Make him laugh. And his incentive to read has been created. A warning, however. Watch the use of humor. Nothing can kill attention like a flat joke or a story which strains for its point. Unless it's well handled, humor can *block* your copy rather than get it read.

This tongue-in-cheek humor from a Belford Company "Corncard" (Creative Binders, 317 West 47th Street, New York 36, New York) should score a hit with the reader. Belford uses only two short paragraphs on their Corncard mailings. The humor has been so well handled on these cards over the years that the result of sending them has been most gratifying.[6] The cards, which have been used for about six years, have kept the name of Belford before prospects. And the humor which arrives by mail becomes the "point of departure" for conversation when the salesman calls, a *key* for establishing rapport between the company's representative and a prospect.

One of our salesmen, who reads the financial section of his newspaper, has noticed a trend that he feels should not go unrecorded. He found that immediately after Belford delivers a bookbinding job to an account, the stock market reacts by boosting the account's stock by several points. We cannot explain this strange activity other than to observe that somehow word gets around.

Offer Psychic Rewards

This type of opener is based on the human desire for self-improvement, for release from tensions, for developing personal adequacy and success in social and business relationships. This type of opener is also one of the most important because it covers such a broad scope of human interest. And with the development of more adequate and effective research techniques, these psychic needs of your readers have been revealed more closely.

Help the Reader "Play His Role" Better. Researchers in motivation have clarified the need for solutions to the problems of the individual in the roles he plays socially and in the business world and professions. To quote from *Business Week*, April 30, 1955:

The motivating drive to buy can be plotted as a physical force exerting pressure on the individual's own present view of himself. The strength of that force depends on how far his present concept of himself falls below his goal (desired self-concept).

If you can offer a reader that type of product or service which will assist him in developing from his present "self-concept" toward his "de-

[6] Dudley Lufkin, "Just Two Short Paragraphs on a Post Card," *The Reporter of Direct Mail Advertising*, vol. 19, no. 8, pp. 16–17, December, 1956.

sired self-concept" (or to maintain what he considers his self-concept in his social and business associations), you will be giving him ample incentive to read your copy. If you can offer the reader an opportunity to feel more adequate in some way *important to him,* you will succeed in getting that copy read.

The National Research Bureau, Inc., Chicago, uses this type of opener —an offer which "helps the reader play his role better," helps him maintain his self-image as he sees it. This sample copy opener appeals to the desire to be liked, to keep one's "popularity image" at the desired level. The example also ties in the idea of personal success (self-concept) of the individual in his business endeavors with the image that his customers hold of him—their preference for him as a personality over his competitors. Based on the idea that "it's the little things that count" in human relationships, this opener has an effective appeal. It should create the incentive to read the entire letter.

Dear Customer:

It doesn't show on your balance sheet . . . but a good percentage of your profits are traceable to one basic fact—*your customers like you.*

Yes—you could open your books today and show me account after account who favor you over competition . . . *just because they like to do business with you.*

And when you stop to explain this favoritism toward you . . . isn't it the little things that create good will for you? That extra measure of service, fair dealing, *appreciation.* These are the measures of success. There is no substitute for friendship in business.

(The National Research Bureau, Inc., Chicago.)

This next example from a Dictaphone company letter offers the reader the opportunity to "play his *job* role" better by increasing his capacity to get things done. Implicit in any man's job performance is the desire to step up onto the next rung of the ladder toward success. Increased capacity to get things done will assist the reader in moving toward his *desired* self-image, toward his next "rung"—that promotion, that new job, that raise. This copy opener offers the reader part of the means toward accomplishing such a goal.

[Picture of a Dictaphone]

PUT THIS ON YOUR DESK . . .

And something wonderful will happen:

Your capacity to get things done will quickly increase—probably double. And yet—you'll work no harder or longer! In fact, the convenience of always being able to "DO IT NOW" makes extra accomplishment seem like *less* work. The routine jobs that often clutter our desks and minds never pile up when you use a Dictaphone Time-Master dictating machine.

Tap the Imagination

As an opener designed to get attention, you can offer the reader many different types of "voyages" which may not otherwise be available to him. You can offer voyages that he cannot otherwise afford. You can make available those things which are seemingly impossible for the reader to obtain because of the restrictions of time, distance, seasons, or his own limited situation.

To tap the reader's imagination, take him on an imaginary voyage. Project him into a hypothetical situation you know he will enjoy. Create an appealing image, which moves him from the commonplace into the realm of pleasure, appreciation, self-improvement, possibly escapism. Then offer him the means of fulfilling a desire for this image, for the "essence" of this voyage.

This type of opener is good for magazines, travel services, music, books —any type of product or service which can build an appeal to pleasure, appreciation, self-improvement or similar wants.

The following opener from a letter of the "Around the World Program," sponsored by the American Geographical Society, taps the reader's imagination through an offer of a "Magic Carpet Tour of FRANCE." Note that the opener offers to . . . "unlock for you and your family all the fun and educational adventures of a trip around the world." This offer makes possible the adventure, the fascination of travel, which is otherwise unobtainable to the reader. It offers him the pleasure of travel without leaving home, the appreciation of knowledge of faraway places, the educational self-improvement of at-home travel.

Read Below How You Can Take
A "Magic Carpet Tour" of FRANCE
. . . Absolutely FREE!

Dear Reader:
The stamp at the right is worth far more than its face value. It is actually a key that will unlock for you and your family all the fun and educational adventures of a trip around the world!

To enjoy its full value, paste it on the enclosed card and mail it today. By return mail you'll receive FREE—and without obligation—the American Geographical Society's brand-new "Magic Carpet Tour" of FRANCE, containing a big guide-book ALBUM filled with absorbing, fascinating facts about this fabulous country.

But that isn't all . . .

With your Album will come a large sheet of 25 full-color photographic reproductions, gummed and perforated, that bring many magnificent scenes of French cities, villages, and farms vividly to life. By reading the exciting, educational story in the Album—and at the same time studying each picture as you place it in position—you and your children will acquire an astonishing fund of travel experience, without ever leaving the comfort of your favorite easy chair!

Ask a Question

If you use a question as an attention lead, the question should be so phrased that it maintains control of the copy. A question should be so stated that the remainder of the copy has a chance to do its job—persuade the reader. If a reader can make his decision about your offer after reading the question, your copy's persuasion has not had a chance to work. Have caution, too, that you do not ask too many questions. The reader may lose interest.

To create copy attention with a question, try to get some of these qualities into that question:

1. Tap some vital interest in the reader's personal or professional life.

2. Do not ask a question that can be answered "No" unless that is the logical lead into the copy.

3. Ask, whenever possible, a question which elicits an equivocal answer from the reader and leaves his curiosity aroused.

4. When you ask a question, the most logical transition into the copy from that point is the answer to the question or an indication that the answer is coming. Otherwise, the reader may lose interest; or he may "flip" to the end of the copy looking for the answer and not read the whole message.

The Wall Street Journal uses a question in this next copy opener. As soon as the letter asks the question, it gives the answer. Then the writers lead logically into another question, which is a good way to build transition.

What Is the Most Powerful Force You Can Use to Make Money in Business? . . . the one ingredient for getting ahead fast, without which no amount of thinking, determination or stick-to-itiveness will work?

The answer is IDEAS.

Yes, good ideas are the stuff that success in business is made from. They make the difference between getting along and getting ahead . . . between making out and making money.

WHERE DO YOU GET IDEAS?

(The answer: *Wall Street Journal*)

Note that the question taps a vital reader interest—the desire to "make money in business." After the question has been answered, a new appeal is made to the reader's desire to be competent. In this case, the copy touches upon possible reader problems and offers solutions. The means of "getting ideas to get ahead" is, of course, through reading the *Journal*.

Offer the Reader a Benefit

One of the best types of copy openers is the offer of a benefit. A benefit, according to Harper's *American College Dictionary*, is "anything that is good for a person. . . ." If something is good for people, they usually want it. This word *good*, however, must be taken within all of its possible meanings. Anything which contributes to a person's material or psychic betterment can be considered "good for him." And a person's desire for betterment can be viewed from a double-edged perspective—his desire for gain and fear of loss.[7]

So, you have, then, two ways of offering services and products on the basis of the benefits they give your reader:[8]

1. You can offer betterment through material or psychic gain. Desire for gain can be interpreted as a desire for:

Recognition	Advancement: social—business
Popularity	Improved appearance
Self-confidence	Comfort
Prestige	Security
Pleasure	More efficient performance on the job

2. You can offer betterment through *avoidance* of material, or psychic loss. Desire to avoid loss can be interpreted as a desire to avoid:

Discomfort	Risks
Worry	Embarrassment
Work	Insecurity

These examples will illustrate how benefits, as they apply to the satisfaction of a desire for gain, have been applied in copy:

1. How the product or service offers psychic rewards
   a. Aesthetic gain. This offer combined aesthetic gain with the saving of money.

THE FIRESIDE THEATRE BOOK CLUB
Garden City, New York

These theatre stamps are worth up to $10.45 to you!
See details below for "cashing in" on their value!

Dear Friend:

The Theatre Stamps enclosed are a MONEY-SAVING SPECIAL prepared especially for you—as part of a spectacular introductory offer from the

[7] Frank Bettger, *How I Raised Myself from Failure to Success in Selling*, Prentice-Hall, Inc., Englewood Cliffs, N.J., 1957, p. 66.

[8] Victor O. Schwab, "Writing Mail-order Copy that Sells," in Louis Kleid, *Mail-order Strategy*, The Reporter of Direct Mail Advertising, Garden City, N.Y., 1956, p. 50.

country's only theatrical book club. Today, the impact of good theatre is felt everywhere—and you can keep up with the very best of Broadway theatre—easily and inexpensively through the Fireside Theatre!

b. Gain of confidence. This opener offers the psychic gain of ease in public speaking.

NOW—YOU TOO CAN TALK
TO AN AUDIENCE
. . . with confidence
and enthusiasm

Dear Friend of NRB,

Many promising executives stumble on their climb to success . . . *because they can't face a live audience with confidence!*

Yet every executive *on the way up* . . . is expected to talk before the public. For with success . . . your public speaking days begin.

And to help you become just as confident on the speaker's stand as you are behind your desk . . . we'd like to send you with our compliments a copy of—

How to Make Blue-ribbon Speeches
– 28 Check Points for Talking in Public –

With a copy of this 28-page Speaking Guide . . . you're prepared for every conceivable speaking engagement. You're ready to face your public with confidence and assurance.

(The National Research Bureau, Inc., Chicago.)

2. How the product or service offers material benefit
   a. Save money. This example is a combination—pleasure *at a saving.*

   If you'll take advantage of your A-1 credit rating with Look and mail the enclosed Special Money-saving Subscription order card today . . . you'll have your first copy of Look in less than 21 days—AND you'll enjoy Look every-other-Tuesday for the next 18 months AT JUST HALF THE NEWSSTAND COST!

   b. Save money. This opener offers a product—Changing Times—as a means toward making money go farther.

   Dear Reader:

   You and I—and all the other folks who are alive and kicking today—have one big thing in common.

   We are all trying to find ways to make today's puny, shriveled-up dollars do as much and buy as much as the old-fashioned "buck."

   Of course, you and I know that in lots of cases it simply can't be done—but by buying wisely at the *right* time, and using other dollar-stretching techniques, you CAN make your dollars cover more ground.

   Anyway, this is the tack that the Changing Times editors take, and you'll find at least one or two suggestions in every issue for ways to make your money go farther.

c. Save time. (Letter had a small hourglass sketched beside the copy opener.)

TIME
is money.

If there's any lesson contractors have learned lately, it's that TIME is MONEY . . . sometimes is even more important than money.

That's why close-figuring contractors are turning more and more to Dumpcretes . . . which save them both time and money.

The Dumpcrete body—cheaper in the first place than truck mixers— mounts on a light truck—takes an average 2800 pounds off the wheels and consequently saves time on every load.

Means many more loads per man per day.

With your same crew, you can pour more concrete faster than with truck mixers. Those minutes saved every load mean hours gained every day and days cut from every job.

d. Make more money.

McGRAW-HILL
330 West 42nd Street, New York 36, N.Y.

No matter *what* you sell
you can make MORE MONEY
 . . . *with these tested methods used by top salesmen*
 earning $25,000 and more a year

Now you can cash in on the experience of specialty salesmen who average $25,000 to $100,000 a year in commissions. Famous sales consultant Bill Rados lets you in on the exact methods, techniques, and procedures these top-income earners use to make *more* and *bigger* sales.

Whether you sell insurance, housewares, advertising space, industrial products, or any other item, the author shows you—step by step—how to apply these specialty selling ideas for *quick payoff results!*

A full discussion of ways for creating opener copy would, if adequately covered, fill a good-sized book. Many additional ways are available to you. With your own perspective on language and psychology, you can probably add many more. Here are, however, a few additional ways for you to think about:

1. *Start with current news.*
    a. Sometimes green is rather wearing. But certainly not so in this week of March the 17th. (Horner, Montreal)
    b. What makes 20,000 fairly normal people scream and stamp when an ordinary-looking human races goalward with a hockey puck? (Horner, Montreal)

2. *Challenge the reader.*
    a. Are you daring enough to wear the mysterious fragrance of Tobruk? (Michele Pasquier, Perfumes)

  b. Test the *"collection power"*
  of these *stickers for 30 days* . . .
  and if they don't bring you more money, faster . . .
  return the unused portion and owe us nothing.
      (The National Research Bureau, Inc., Chicago.)
  c. Dear Friend:
      Let me send you 100 EXECUTIVES—full 4⅞-inch perfectos—on open
  account. Smoke a few with my compliments.
      This may seem a funny way to sell cigars—but most men like it.
  I don't ask for cash in advance—I don't offer to ship c.o.d.—I just send all
  delivery charges postpaid and without any obligation—100 EXECUTIVES
  for you to try. If you don't like them after you have smoked a few—send
  them back. I'll pay the return postage. That's all there is to it.
      (Thompson & Company, Inc., 200–220 N. Edison Street, Tampa,
  Florida.)

3. *Start with a testimonial or success story.*

   Dear Professor:

   "Time packs in the background information."

   "Time's readable style and classified news permit one to follow develop-
   ments systematically—"

   "Time gives students an analysis of the news by experts—acquaints them
   with innovations in many fields."

   —wrote three Professors of Journalism in recent letters to us, telling why
   they use and like TIME in their classes.

   (All of these testimonials to *Time* were processed in simulated
   handwriting—*Time*, Inc., New York.)

4. *Offer a premium or a bargain.*

   a. Dear Friend of NRB:
   This stamp is worth $5.05 to you!

   Return it today on the enclosed registered certificate and we will send
   you *all expenses prepaid* . . .
               WEBSTER'S UNIFIED DICTIONARY AND ENCYCLOPEDIA
                          – New 1955 Edition –

   Here, without a doubt, is the most valuable reference work a business
   man could own. Beautiful and practical beyond description—Webster's
   UNIFIED gives you, as only Webster's can, the facts and knowledge you
   need about *important persons, places, things and events.*
       (The National Research Bureau, Inc., Chicago.)

   b. If I sent you a 'round-the-world ticket for only $3 . . . would you accept
   it? Of course you would.

And that, in effect, is exactly what I am doing when I send you the enclosed $3 certificate. *For you can use that certificate to get 40 issues of* LOOK—issues that will bring the entire world right into your living room. Regularly, every-other-Tuesday (for a full 18 months) LOOK will take you across the nation and over the seas—to wherever there are happenings of interest to Americans.

(*Look* Magazine.)

5. *Give him an exclusive.*

You have the exclusive rights . . .
to the beautiful 19— Christmas Greeting Letter you select from the folder enclosed. And, if you will endorse and *return the registered agreement now* . . .
. . . no one else in your line of business in your area can use this Christmas Letter. Only *your customers* will receive this warm, friendly greeting during Christmas season 19—.

And that is so important. For the good will you enjoy with your customers is *personal*. And only in a letter can you express your sincere feelings in such a personal way. (M. P. Brown)

6. *Offer him a first.*

This year, for the first time . . .
. . . you can have *your own* complete FOOTBALL HANDBOOK. You will win the thanks of your employees, your friends, your customers . . . *from September right through New Year's Day.*

And this booklet *will bear your firm name and address,* as well as your advertisement, if you wish. Your booklet will bear *the stamp of authority.* For it is edited by the sports department of International News Service—key source of information to America's leading newspapers.

(The National Research Bureau, Inc., Chicago.)

9

How to Create Copy Interest

That's What Interest Is

Interest, according to the *American College Dictionary,* is ". . . the feeling of one whose attention or curiosity is particularly engaged by something."

The key words here are feeling and engaged. Because copy interest grows out of the relation of a person's needs and wants with the benefits your product or service offers. It engages the benefits you offer with the things he wants in such a way that he feels you offer him a solution to a problem or the satisfaction of a need.

It's sort of like a handshake where your hand is the benefit and his hand the need. And the over-all attitude which you project to him makes him feel glad to have met you. Interest is achieved when the reader feels what you offer is important or beneficial to him, or to those persons, things, ideas in which he is interested.

Human Interests: A Listing

Before we go into a perspective on men and women in this chapter, let's take a look at Victor O. Schwab's list of desires which "Make People Tick." This list of desires bridges and mixes the sexes. This chapter's perspective will attempt to separate desires by sex. Keep this list in mind as you read through the sections on men and women. Ideas for the application of these human interests will, then, pop into mind more effectively on the basis of what motivates people into these desires.

114

The Schwab List: "What Makes People Tick." [1] These are the interests or desires which Mr. Schwab uses to move people to read, to believe, and to buy. This is an excellent list of human desires. Use them as the "hooks" upon which to hang your copy appeals.

People want to gain	*They want to save*	*They want to do*	*They want to be*
Health	Time	Express their personalities	Good parents
Popularity	Discomfort	Satisfy their curiosity	Creative
Praise from others	Risks	Appreciate beauty	Efficient
Pride of accomplishment	Money	Win others' affection	Recognized authorities
Self-confidence	Worry	Resist domination by others	Up to date
Time	Embarrassment	Emulate the admirable	Gregarious
Improved appearance	Work	Acquire or collect things	"First" in things
Comfort	Doubt	Improve themselves generally	Sociable, hospitable
Advancement; social—business			Proud of their possessions
Security in old age			Influential over others
Leisure			
Increased enjoyment			
Personal prestige			

Let's now take a look at what a man and a woman want—generally. Then we can see how some copy examples have attempted to engage product benefits with man's and woman's wants—specifically.

WHAT DOES A MAN WANT? A PERSPECTIVE

In his actions, of course, the modern domesticated American male operates on nature's plan of survival first, other things later. Although survival can come to mean many subtle and complicated things within the complex twentieth century now that much of the "risk" in gaining the primary needs of food, clothing, and shelter has been reduced.

"A loaf of bread, a jug of wine, and thou" may have been sufficient for Omar Khayyam. Not so for the American male. The only thing American men have in common with friend Omar is the need for "thou." Today's

[1] Victor O. Schwab, "Writing Mail-order Copy that Sells," in Louis Kleid, *Mail-order Strategy,* The Reporter of Direct Mail Advertising, Garden City, N.Y., 1956, p. 50.

loaf of bread and jug of wine are much more complex, complicated, and varied.

But, no matter how you define it, his need for sex or a need for "thou," for his wife and child he'll put to work the greatest force given to nature —the ingenuity of man. And with his ingenuity, man has a great deal of "try" in his heart, a powerhouse of performance, to which his woman has the key. Because the more he has to believe in, the more powerful is his desire to achieve.

A man performs better when he does things for someone else—his wife, his child. He does something better for others than for himself because his identification (his main problem in life after survival) is to him a reflection of his own impact upon the world.

A man's identity also becomes apparent to him in his position in the social structure as it relates to the positions of other men. In his relationships with and expressions of worth from his colleagues and associates. Importantly, in the products of the twentieth century, a man can assert his preferred self-image.

For example, on the achievement or social-status plane, the Cadillac has come to be the ". . . symbol for the man of achievement, the realization of . . . [the] . . . American dream of business success." [2] And . . . "the man who owns a car, or even the youngster who is driving a borrowed car, feels more important, more substantial, more achieving, more masculine than the man without a car." [3]

One of the key words is masculine. Masculine has to do with manliness. One who feels he has at his control all the power of the modern automobile feels he has an extension of his own power. Man, being limited in his impact on the world without an extension of his arm, his voice, his character, finds satisfaction and greater meaning for himself in objects which help him increase his own impact. The reflection of a man's impact on the world, measurable in material things and psychic rewards, is the basis of his meaning or identity.

Examine man's life: You have baseball, football, the airplane, the auto, the rifle. All are part of the interests of a man. And each one of these items helps extend man's masculinity beyond the length of his arm or beyond the sound of his voice. All of these represent the male need for self-assertiveness—for achievement within his world.

Man has a need to control not only himself but the forces which surround him. Control is an instrument for creating order. And a man's need for order stems from his need for identity. Because, as he controls his own world, he puts purpose and meaning into his life.

[2] Pierre Martineau, *Motivation in Advertising*, McGraw-Hill Book Company, Inc., New York, 1957, p. 74.

[3] *Ibid.*, p. 71.

Man, lonely seeker of identity, adventurous, explosive by nature's pattern, is basically an animal of vision. Because his deep-seated need for identity causes him to seek meaning more deeply than a woman does. She can be gratified with, "This child is part of me." But a man needs more. And as an animal of vision, he also has a dreamer's turn of mind.

Vive la Différence

The differences between a man and a woman can more or less be symbolized by their shoes—woman's toeless shoes reveal the delicacy of foot, flatter the ankle, and put poetry in the calf—all part of the beauty which fascinates a man.

The delicate and stable, yet unstable, balance of m'lady's self atop the platform on which she walks also reflects her own make-up of sometimes unreasoned reason. Part of which a man sometimes doesn't see or appreciate properly—to his regret. But a man's brogans are so built that he can easily keep his feet on the ground, literally and figuratively.

His meaning, his survival, then, becomes a development of personal worth through translation of his "try," his abilities, into tangibles which reflect his creativity and imply his status.

Life's Play Bill

Since a man does play roles and since we can appeal to this manly pastime, let's break the male roles into man's four basic approaches to life. But, before we do, a note of thanks is due here to psychologist Donald Laird, for this chapter leans heavily upon his excellent work, *What Makes People Buy.*

We come, then, to *Life's Play Bill* for a man. Here are his leading parts in the earthly drama. Importantly, although we separate these roles, they are actually all part of a well-knit psychic fabric. Only for the convenience and emphasis of several perspectives do we distinguish among them.

> Role No. 1—Mr. Adam
> Role No. 2—Mr. Atlas
> Role No. 3—Mr. Babbitt
> Role No. 4—Mr. Methuselah

Mr. Adam. Here is the male role which has to do with man's relationship with his woman. And that relationship has a lot to do with how *he thinks* he appears in her eyes. This role is the need for romantic attachment within the framework of home and marriage. It is in his relation with the other sex that a man gains a sense of completeness. And where he generates his sense of personal worth.

Mr. Adam is the role a man plays, for which he buys items which will add to his attractiveness to the opposite sex as a single man, any item that helps a married man maintain the romance and the man–woman satisfaction in his marriage.

To show you how you can appeal to a man by assisting his Mr. Adam role, we'll take an example from those eminent psychologists—Hart Schaffner & Marx. This mailing piece is a 6- by 9-inch mailing card. The illustration is an attractive, broad-shouldered man (naturally looking dashing in a Hart Schaffner & Marx outfit). He dominates the domestic scene in which we find him.

His suit has a touch of masculinity to satisfy a man's basic need for attractiveness to the opposite sex. It's "in style" to satisfy his desire for high-class appearance. The woman and child quietly admiring the man of the house in the background are an indication of the man's ability factor as it relates to his Mr. Adam's need for a pretty wife and his Mr. Atlas's need for a child-bearing mate. A subtle touch of impact is also found in the overtones of masculine virility in the cut of the suit and the broad-shouldered build of the model. The copy reads:

It's a man's day-by-day record that adds up to praises, raises, or even a Vice-Presidency.

That sentence is an *Interest* appeal to a man in his attempts to adjust successfully within a social group. It's an appeal to the need for status and recognition within the social group. It's an appeal, very indirectly, to the need for self-preservation within the economic setup.

This next bit of copy is the tie-in of the opening appeal with a desire for status, with the specific product which will help satisfy this need.

The way you dress can have a lot to do with it . . . which is why we recommend our Scotleigh tweed suit by Hart Schaffner & Marx.

Mr. Atlas. This role is the need for a display of masculinity and virility, the need which calls for a display of manly prowess. This is the role a man plays for which he buys items which add to his athletic ability, his ability to perform physical feats, his desire to appear virile. Whenever you have a product or service which fills a man's desire for a display of masculinity, for virility, then you appeal to him by applauding his Mr. Atlas role. Part of a man's identity is his profession or career. Part is also the kind of clothing he wears, as we saw in the previous Hart Schaffner & Marx mailing piece.

These next copy examples have more to offer than a Mr. Atlas appeal. But, then, we can't separate all of a man's roles . . . or he'll end up a schizo!

Again, we're going to turn to Hart Schaffner & Marx for the perfect example of direct mail which offers various aids at playing the roles a man selects. This copy has a tongue-in-cheek overtone of humor. Because when you appeal so directly to an unconscious or near-conscious human need, you have to be more subtle than a sailor on a six-hour pass.

This mailing piece, a double-folded leaflet, had the masks of tragedy and comedy—below the question, "Which secret role do you play?" This question, because of the word "secret," appeals to the Walter Mitty complex in all of us. And, whether you'll admit it or not, it's there.

The next questions offer the reader a selection of roles. They're a trifle more serious. Because we're leading our reader by his hot little hand into "the something more we're going to give him" before we raise the sound on our commercial. Here are the lead-in questions:

> Man of learning?
> Prince of industry?
> Chargé d'affaires?
> Carefree *bon vivant?*
> Pick your part . . . here's how to play it . . .

Now we get to the "something-more-than-information" part of this mailing piece, for we open the first fold on the leaflet. Here it is. And it appeals nostalgically to the little boy in a man, the age he liked the best . . .

> How long since you left a Western movie patting an imaginary six-gun at your hip . . . ready for the first varmint who'd dare to make trouble for the fastest gun in the West? Some years, perhaps—but a bit of actor remains in each of us. And why not! The "Secret Roles" we all occasionally play are a welcome diversion. With our new Hart Schaffner & Marx clothes for Fall, we'll be your wardrobe master. Fold this flap back for some handsome examples.

The fold, incidentally, helped maintain the dramatic suspense of what was to come. We flip back the second fold, and we have more copy which appeals to our need for role playing, and which offers us a mixture of the various roles.

First Role: "Professor":
> Professor:
> Are you well-read and inquiring . . . always pleased to learn something new . . . and even more pleased to tell others about it?
> Hart Schaffner & Marx tweeds are for you—they're soft-spoken, masculine . . . with a rich surface texture and deep colors. Trim-Trend styling, too.

This copy appeals directly to a professor's own estimate of himself— through "well-read and inquiring," through "soft-spoken." The Atlas role of a man is appealed to through "masculine" and "Trim-Trend styling"— Trim-Trend having to do with an athletic figure.

Second Role: "Executive":
> Executive:
> Are decisions your stock in trade? Is your mind analytical, your bearing confident, and your sense of business judgment keen?
> Hart Schaffner & Marx worsteds are your answer—the patterns are dignified and correct—but never stuffy. Trim-Trend styling adds distinction.

This copy appeals directly to a businessman's own estimate of himself—through "decisions . . . analytical . . . confident . . . business judgment." The Adam and Atlas roles are appealed to through "dignified . . . correct . . . Trim-Trend styling." The leaflet's illustrations of healthy, handsome, provocative males were obviously set up to appeal to the Adam in Man . . . a desire to be attractive.

Mr. Babbitt. This role is the need for measurable status, through the ownership of material things. It is the most obvious of the roles through which a man seeks identity in the world. Because a man measures part of his identity, position, or status in society on the basis of the material rewards which society gives him.

In this role, man wants symbols which indicate his ability to perform. He wants evidence that he is a person of stature. This is the role for which a man buys Cadillacs, expensive ties, a home in the best subdivision, to prove to the world at large and to the little woman in the suburbs that he's really quite a capable guy.

Many products are adaptable to this need. We'll take an example of a letter from Prentice-Hall. This letter offers a book entitled *How to Be a Success before 40* as a give-away if the reader will buy the *Business Executive's Encyclopedia*. But, from the *Success before 40* book, the reader can obtain all of these *Babbitt Benefits*. Here's some copy:

> . . . Double your productive power with half the effort.
> . . . Sell your services for more than *you* think they're worth.
> . . . Spark big-money ideas and ride them to the payoff.
> . . . Handle a business problem with the skill of a man 20 years your senior.
> . . . Always be on the spot *where* and *when* the "breaks" occur.

That copy offers the reader the means toward satisfying a need for material things and the need for stature.

Mr. Methuselah. This role shows the desire to save time through doing things efficiently. And it also shows the human desire to stay young, to live longer. In this role we have also a projection of man's need for a son —to conquer (a manly endeavor) time.

Products and services which help a man become more efficient in his work so that he can save time or perform rapidly, products and services which help a man stay relaxed and in good health, satisfy this craving for more time. You can appeal to a man's need for more time, his desire to stay young, or his desire to live longer by marketing Mr. Methuselah.

If your product or service in some way helps him cut the corners on time, if they shave the minutes necessary to do a job, if they give a man a "seeming" youthfulness, then you can appeal to him by marketing Mr. Methuselah.

AND NOW TO WOMEN

We've discussed the male roles. So what about the female? Well, then, first of all,

What is Woman . . .

Roman philosopher Lucretius, back in 54 B.C., thought she was just a "little, tiny, pretty, witty, charming darling."

And "only one of Nature's agreeable blunders" was playwright Hannah Cowley's opinion in 1779!

But . . . regardless what ideas have held sway until now, there's no question that today's modern woman is regarded as much more than a frill or a mistake! In fact, nowadays she is expected to be—

A skilled, imaginative chef and then, a few minutes later, the poised and well-informed hostess . . .

An economy-wise homemaker who can make her clothes look like Paris models, her home a comfortable showroom, and still have the budget balance.

And at various times through the day, a doctor—tailor—hair stylist—psychiatrist—nutrition expert—often a combination of executive and window cleaner.

Yet always attractive and energetic, fascinating fun to the men in her life!

So wrote *McCall's Magazine* in a sales letter. Thus *McCall's* presents most pithily the roles a woman plays in modern American life.

With all the things she must do, all the responsibilities she must face, woman must be a composite of all the talents available at Hollywood's Central Casting. Show her ways to weave the various faces she must wear into an orderly, integrated tapestry of living. She'll be interested. Shall we, then, cast her into the roles she plays so well? Shall we break them down into categories like . . .

Role No. 1—Ms Eve [4]

Role No. 2—Ms Constance

Role No. 3—Ms Home Maker

Ms Eve. This is her need for romantic love, desire for fulfillment as a helpmate and mother, desire for the biological and psychological satisfactions offered her in marriage.

This is the compulsion, the infinite talent, which fulfills man's need for

[4] Ms is acceptable as Miss or Mrs. When in doubt as to the marital status of a woman, use Ms.

the composite of companion, sweetheart, wife, mistress, mother, and fall guy. This is the ability which assuages the ache of man's bruises, bloats and builds his wounded ego, tends his passion's needs, puts him and keeps him together when the forces of life shatter what he is.

Here is the ability to reassure the quizzical eyes of a child, to twist pain into pleasure with the "awarding" of a Band-Aid or a Curad, to create the foundations of faith, consideration, and kindness which project themselves—through her progeny—throughout the time-fabric of mankind. Women want marriage for the affection involved and the children they can have.[5] To help women fulfill this desire, many industries are dedicated to their beautification, to the intent of keeping "youth" alive, to making women more attractive to men.

Products and services which paint, pound, shake, bundle, and tie . . . products and services which shape, hold, raise, cover, and lie . . . are consumed yearly by American women—to the tune of billions of dollars. And, for the results achieved, it's worth even more.

Many of these products and services are calculated to give women that "Daffodil Delicacy," that fragrant femininity, to attract man, the Polygamous Bee. But caution: When you talk of romantic love to women in advertising, you should *stay with* the idea of romantic love. You must use appeals which offer either beauty to attract the male or youthful appearance or zest to hold him. For, there is a fine line of taste and propriety which never should be crossed in selling to women. Because you may bring about resistance by invading areas she doesn't want invaded.

Woman's resistance to the invasion of areas of her existence is, of course, based on words and their meanings which she finds objectionable. Customs and the conditioning process—that hang-over from the past, through which the present suffers for the foibles of its forebears—make the use of some types of words unwise for the advertiser.

Men have no objection to the use of many words women find repugnant. A man's development, his male make-up, lead him to an interest in a vocabulary which a woman often considers uncouth.

While a woman may marry for the security of a man's affection and the creativity of childbearing, it's also important to *keep a man*. Her effort continues through life—paralleling his Mr. Adam compulsion. And she knows that every guy (especially that very important one called *the guy*) gets a slight "puffing of the chest" when he's with a woman who's lovely.

One of the services which offers woman the kind of attractiveness that in turn gains for her romance, affection, a more stable emotional plateau is the "bouncing Betty" of the Smithers System. Tables of all conceivable types shake, shimmer, and circulate woman into a new and more attrac-

[5] Janet Wolff, *What Makes Women Buy?* McGraw-Hill Book Company, Inc., New York, 1958, p. 137.

tive figure. Admittedly, the patron must cooperate on the food intake. 'Cause Smithers' sincerest efforts can't compete with a knife-and-fork fixation.

This example of Smithers copy offers a vitality in beauty—obtainable through better circulation from the table's passive "exercise." It offers a new morale based on knowing that most figure problems can be solved through the mutual cooperation of Smithers Salon and the client. Make her figure attractive. Her confidence soars.

SMITHERS

Champaign, Illinois

Because so many of our patrons are happy with new figures—from provocative bustlines . . . to slender hips and thighs—we decided to make this *special introductory offer of a new loveliness* to you.

With the enclosed coupon . . . you may have the complete series of 25 visits for *only* $50. This is a savings of $12.50 over the usual rate of $62.50. And . . . it's made to introduce you to these beauty benefits:

A Fresh Vitality in Your Beauty: From stimulated circulation and new figure control . . . just by relaxing on a motorized Smithers Salon table. Let the motor do the huffin' and puffin'!

Relax (even sleep) your way to new-complexion, new-figure beauty. Get refreshed and vibrant skin . . . a head-turning figure. The motor whir-r-rs its way through the panting (and the sometimes ranting, too) with you at ease —if you please!

A New Morale in Your Heart: Based on a new confidence in knowing you have a fabulous new figure (in some cases, even the old YOU). In the informal atmosphere of the Smithers Salon . . . and with your own cooperation in the push *away* from high-calorie foods . . . you'll be slim, trim, smooth, and saucy—with a feeling of new confidence.

In this copy, the appeal to romantic love is found in the inferences a woman can make from these words and phrases:

". . . from provocative bustlines . . . to slender hips and thighs . . ."
". . . stimulated circulation and new figure control"
". . . new-complexion, new-figure beauty"
". . . refreshed and vibrant skin . . . a head-turning figure"

This copy also offers—implicitly—to give her security—especially in the social sense through being "slim, trim, smooth, and saucy . . . with a feeling of new confidence."

The sense of "doing it easily and saving time" (as per the Mr. Methuselah attitude which also appeals to women) is found in the phrases:

". . . let the motor do the huffin' and puffin' "
". . . relax (even sleep)"
". . . the motor whirrs its way through the panting (and the sometimes ranting, too) with you at ease—if you please!"

A woman's prime motivation as Ms Eve is to be a better mother and a better wife. This is not only an expression of her egoistic desire to be the "mother hen" in the family nest. It's also an expression of her feminine selflessness, which dedicates itself to others—implicitly on the survival basis. An offer, then, which helps her integrate the role of Ms Eve with the other roles she must play should be effective.

An example of copy which illustrates the appeal to a woman's concern for both husband and children is found in these *McCall's Magazine* sales-letter paragraphs:

You're a better mother for reading the authoritative and understanding *McCall's* articles on child rearing, written by the nation's foremost child specialists (as well as by successful parents).

You're a better wife for the knowledge that *McCall's* discerning and helpful articles on marriage and family relations bring you in every issue.

Ms Constance. This role of the woman is her need for safety in the world, for security in the social sense. One of woman's basic emotions is fear, a sensitive sense of insecurity, which manifests itself in the protective urge in her relationships with her family and the less fortunate—as well as the (consistent, not contradictory) need for the protective shield of the male.

She needs a sense of order, a feeling that things are "in their place," that the boat won't rock, that life's vicissitudes will not shatter her security, that all is *safe* in an economic and social sense.

This need for security in the social-economic sense has several, inter-related, overlapping aspects:

1. *The need for economic stability.* If she is not a career woman satisfying this need for herself, it is provided by Mr. Adam's crescendo pattern of proving his masculinity. And she can help in maintaining a constant economic stability through her own efforts—by work or by inspiration for the male breadwinner.

The unmarried career woman takes care of herself—in most cases. The married woman who works outside the home makes varying contributions to the family's economic welfare. But the wife who doesn't hold a job outside her home can't always help out financially unless she does sewing or babysitting, or holds some other not-always-too-lucrative job. She wants, however, to help in any way she can to preserve the family's economic stability. And Knipco Company of Dayton, Ohio, realized this when they set up their "Cheery Word at Breakfast" campaign. The idea behind the campaign was a deference to "the power of a woman."

Realizing that a woman can help motivate a man through the application of some of those facets which make her his fascination, Knipco Company asked for cooperation in setting his mood, his disposition, into a pleasant and favorably aggressive mold . . . so that he could sell more Knipco Heaters. And they were willing to reward her for her assistance. The reward was $5 for every Knipco dealer he signed up.

An excellent idea for Knipco to use. Women want that economic stability. They also have a devotion to their families. Combine the two motivations into a campaign of this sort, and you'll get results. If she wanted the Knipco fivers for luxuries she couldn't otherwise afford, budget money could be used or saved as she wished. The results of her efforts to help the man of the house would be better performance by him, more economic stability for her.

What were the results of the Knipco campaign? Eighty-six salesmen's wives "inspired" them to sell 600 new dealers.

2. *The need for psychic security.* Her psychic security has to do with how she gets along with her world . . . with herself. It is derived from the satisfaction of being liked socially, appreciated as an individual, and approved of by family and friends.

Show a woman, then, that she is secure, needed, wanted. And she will plunge into the worthy projects of her home and community—and with her constant tenacity—will whip things into shape.

The female reaction to psychic security is an inclination to perform at a high level of effectiveness. It is similar to Mr. Babbitt's reaction to material rewards. Because approval of performance through additional rewards motivates for even better performance.

This paragraph from a *McCall's Magazine* sales letter appeals to this inner feeling a woman has—a desire for peace of mind or spirit based on the confidence in knowing that she's appreciated:

What a bargain in happier family living, in added peace of mind and entertainment, in confidence and competence you get from reading *McCall's* authoritative, up-to-date articles on all the many things you're expected to know and do.

Women, as the source, have always been the ones to look out for the children and for the unfortunate. Once upon a time it was the "gracious lady from the hill"—who could afford it—who helped the less fortunate. Today's women, in their need for more personal expression and for group (and group approved) activities, have organized charities to a "fare-thee-well" of efficiency.

Since the average American home no longer has an extra woman— maiden sister, aunt, grandmother, etc., . . . because custom has changed with the unfettering of women and because gadgets help her short-circuit the time needed to do her home job—the twentieth-century female must have more out-of-the-home interests.

Women not only love and care for their own children. They also can't stand seeing the unfortunate abused—particularly if they are children. Because, when things are "secure" elsewhere (outside her own home), a woman feels happier. When Peggy Greenlaw, copy writer at Charles W. Groves Company, was asked for an opinion as to what makes a woman tick, her long and enlightening letter contained a perceptive little gem on this maternal affinity women have. Here it is:

If it weren't for having so many of my own kids, plus mortgages, college tuition, and just little minor expenses like replacing lost gloves, bats, sweaters . . . and buying things for knees that get floor-burned during basketball games —I'd most surely be a foster parent to some little waif in Korea. It really hurts me to withhold the fifteen dollars a month that would keep some little kid from starving or buy him the warm winter clothes he needs.

Note the maternal quotient in "knees that get floor-burned" and "some little waif." Let alone the declarative "hurts." Note also the feminine protective of "my own" first, then those who need it badly (the human family). Typically American femininity (and aren't we proud of them!).

Ms Home Maker. The role of Ms Home Maker gives a woman satisfaction as an outlet for her creative impulses. And the more creative the job is the greater her enthusiasm for it. As an example, a woman's role as family chef gives her a great deal of satisfaction. Because in foods she finds a way of obtaining approval from her family and friends for being creative in a way which establishes her personal prestige.

Not only in food preparation can she gain the security she wants through the approval of the family unit for a job well done. In home décor she has an opportunity to be creative, expressive, individual—with resulting compliments which reveal appreciation.

Between Suburbia and the midcentury housewife, a great change has been brought about in America. With the growth of the use of autos, woman's world expanded. The auto helped her unshackle herself from the home. And smaller, more easily kept homes and more readily prepared foods left her time for social contacts, civic efforts. War scattered people to the now-no-longer-strange corners of the world, created contacts with distant cultures, mores, habits, foods. An interest in things "foreign," "from abroad," has developed. Foreign travel has grown by leaps and bounds. With vision based on keen observation of what was going on in the world—mail-order entrepreneurs made available gifts, food, and the cultural arts in the form of Hi-Fi records, etc., from all parts of the world. Supermarkets also got into the act . . . so that fried bumble bees, canned rattlesnake meat, and Philadelphia garlic cheese are amenable partners on American cocktail tables.

The result: Creative woman has been able to blend the products of many lands into an interesting and hospitable way of life on the prairies, on the hills, and in the city towers of America.

Suburbia took her out of town. The auto brought her back, expanded the possibilities of her choice of activities. Her natural affinity for things new, for change and variety, coupled with her power-of-the-purse at the point of sale, led to a rash of new products, new methods of marketing, a new kind of life for her and her brood.

As the focal point of the home, she applies all that is best in her make-up to create an informal, casual way of life that dips into the reservoirs of the world's culture, products, pleasures for its satisfactions. 'Tis nothing in Suburbia to drink whisky made in Scotland, from a glass made in Mexico, while eating hors d'oeuvres made in Japan or France, set on table linen made in India. And what does Ms Home Maker get out of it? The knowledge that her family thinks she's a pretty great gal . . . while her friends feel she's a talented, gracious hostess. It all adds up to the ability to "feel better about life." Because one is appreciated.

And the ingenuity of man, in developing gadgets to make her life easier, has led to more personal satisfactions for the home maker. She cottoned to the gadgets not unlike the proverbial duck to the pond. Ease of doing the job with modern kitchen and home equipment was only part of her motive, however. With the time-saving wife-savers which help her combat dust, disarray, and debilitation, she found a means of doing her job in such a way that she gets the approval which leads to greater self-esteem.

Gadgets and foods are not the only things that help her pry feelings of adequacy from life, though. The means she uses to make her children more articulate animals . . . her husband a more capable cuss . . . also reflect her wisdom as the hub around which the home's influences flow. When she can do things for Dad and "the demons" which make life better for them—in the form of pleasure, education, inspiration—she'll do so. And from doing so, she gains her confidence and security.

A child's balanced need for learning, romantic adventure, religious experience comes from woman's need to be "felt" in the child's blossoming life. Because she "feels" better about things when a child has hooks upon which to hang his emotional-intellectual security. An example of copy which offers to open up exciting vistas of adventure and education to the whole family is found in a letter of the American Geographical Society's "Around the World Program." Here's the copy:

The American Geographical Society's "Around the World Program" is a new educational effort to arouse interest in a broad, comprehensive, yet detailed knowledge of our wonderful world and its peoples . . . and to bring this knowledge into your home with story and pictures that both youngsters and adults can understand and enjoy.

A brand-new "Magic Carpet Tour" will be issued every month. This program will take you and your family across the Atlantic to visit the fabulous countries of Europe and the Near East. You'll know what it is like to bask in the sun of romantic Capri, ski in the snows of Tyrol—discover intrigue and adventure in romantic places like Tangier, Tunis, and Istanbul. You'll explore jungles and deserts, cruise among the lazy islands of the Indian Ocean. You'll wander through Baghdad, Calcutta, Saigon—and see the mystic wonders of the Far East!

Your world tour will cover in detail every continent, every important nation and exotic global area. You'll meet the people who live there, learn about their history, civilization, arts, economy, culture, tradition. The whole world will be your "stamping ground"—from the sultry shores of colorful Latin America to the frozen outskirts of the Polar waste lands—from the swank salons of Paris and Vienna to the tropic atolls of the South Seas!

From this copy comes a promise of adventure, education, pleasure. Most of all, though, comes a promise of a better understanding of the world the parents live in—the world which offers the child his many paths to fulfillment.

The "core" of a woman's motivation seems to be gaining the security she needs by giving satisfaction to others. The roles a woman plays against the backdrop of life give her a needed security through expression of herself in a unifying effort to keep a smoothly operating house, to maintain a "retreat" from job tension for a husband, to create a sanctum of security and happiness for her nestlings (with all the "care" she can afford for the less fortunate). And all of these things she does bring their own rewards as reflections of her tastes, abilities, character—in the eyes of her family, friends, the community.

10

How to Create Belief

Prove Claims to Create Belief

To convince a reader, you persuade him through making claims that your product or service will *fit his needs* and then *by proving* your claims. And you must persuade him, make him *believe,* that your offer is better than your competitor's.

Usually, people will *believe* what they *want* to believe. Ordinarily, people, being the obstreperous animals they are, do not know why they believe what they do. They just believe. Steuart Henderson Britt describes this cussedness in the human belief situation this way: [1]

Many people cling to beliefs because of their psychological value—they are happier to believe than to doubt. Perhaps they have climbed what William James called "the faith ladder" with its seven steps: [2]

1. There is nothing absurd in a certain view of the world being true, nothing self-contradictory.
2. It *might* have been true under certain conditions.
3. It *may* be true even now.
4. It is *fit* to be true.
5. It *ought* to be true.
6. It *must* be true.
7. It *shall* be true, at any rate true for *me.*

[1] Steuart Henderson Britt, *Social Psychology of Modern Life,* rev. ed., Holt, Rinehart and Winston, Inc., New York, 1949, p. 195.
[2] William James, *Some Problems of Philosophy,* Longmans, Green & Co., Inc., New York, 1940, p. 224.

William James's steps show how human self-defense—shield against vicissitude—is constructed from the tentative acceptance of an idea. They show how belief in the idea gradually grows through concepts based on words which (in each step) give greater strength to the belief—*might, may, fit, ought, must.* Then James illustrates how a declaration of belief develops—through *self-assertion* in the word *shall.*

But as Mr. Britt also points out, . . . "Many paradoxical things happen in connection with belief and doubt . . . [one] . . . paradox is the tendency to believe almost anything they . . . [people] . . . really want to believe." [3]

As a direct mail example we can look at Juan, the "poor peon" who languishes hopelessly in a Juarez jail, just waiting for some American to bail him out. Though he has had all kinds of debunking during the years, he *still* writes letters to Americans (probably others), offering to share a fortune with them if they'll send him bail money. The way it works is this: Poor Juan has a "Millyun Yankee dollaires buried in a Nogales corral." But he can't get out of jail long enough to get the money to bail himself out. He offers part of his fortune to anyone who will send him the bail money. Funny part is, many Americans who want "something for nothing" have fallen for this racket. Sent money. No Juan. No money back.

But the incredible thing about the situation is that people *still* fall for the old, old racket. Why does this nonsense continue? Because *people believe what they want to believe.*

Since people believe what they want to believe on the basis of their understanding of words, let's see how words work in eliciting belief.

To all human animals . . .

WORDS ARE FRAGMENTS OF EXPERIENCE

They are mere elusive wisps of memory, symbols for the many experiences which have had impact on a human nervous system. As a person matures, a word gathers more and more meaning for him. And the word is merely the skeleton of the experience. A person may not remember the "flesh" of the actual experiences. But the skeleton which brings forth a reaction—the meaning of the word—*is* there.

The meanings of words are like the drip of water which adds length to an icicle. A little bit more meaning is added to a word as a person builds contact with life. And, as the icicle of experience increases imperceptibly, so does belief grow.

Words and their meaning are like an iceberg. The part above the water

[3] Darrell Blaine Lucas and Steuart Henderson Britt, *Advertising Psychology and Research,* McGraw-Hill Book Company, Inc., New York, 1950, p. 71.

is the word, merely the symbol for the huge mass beneath the water. And, like an iceberg, a word may plumb depths deeper than one realizes.

Because the human animal has been conditioned to the use of certain words having greater depth of meaning than other words, copy writers must be extremely cautious in their selection of words—particularly when they seek to create belief.

Let's take several examples of the selection of words for getting impact, for hitting deep into that part of the iceberg below the water, for getting reaction which builds belief.

Let's take the Mark Twain statement that the difference between the right word and the almost right word is the difference between lightning and the lightning bug. And remember . . . these sample words were selected for their impact . . . because of the conditioned-reflex reaction which the writers sought.

Let's take Winston Churchill's famous line made in his first speech as Prime Minister to the House of Commons, May 13, 1940:

> I have nothing to offer but blood, tears, toil, and sweat.

Can you imagine Mr. Churchill using the word *perspiration?* No. It wouldn't be the *right* word. It wouldn't be the word which strikes deeply and convincingly at the need for sacrifice and effort, to save England.

There are more *guts*. There's more sacrifice and effort, more determination, implicit in the word *Sweat*. Why? Because *perspiration* has been reduced, in our twentieth-century culture, to a slight nuisance which can be "poofed" out of existence. Or, with a trifle more effort, "rolled off." People couldn't *believe* in the desperateness of Britain's plight . . . with *perspiration.*

Take this next example for deep . . . deep . . . deep meaning in a word. Remembering that words gather meaning as mankind marches through time, take this sentence:

> Jesus wept.

The *meaning* to Christians of the word Jesus goes *clear back,* all the way through recorded Jewish history, *clear back* to those hazy, misty times when the promise of the Messiah was made. When you consider the iceberg of meaning beneath the word *Jesus,* when you consider the importance to the Western world of the word *Jesus,* can you imagine using any other word than *wept?*

Because of the human experience with the word *Jesus,* back through the long shadows of time to the crucifixion and beyond into the ages of darkness when the Messiah was promised to man, *Jesus* calls for the *dignified sorrow* implicit in *wept.*

If the sentence had been written Jesus *cried,* the word *cried* would have been in conflict with the lower part of the iceberg of meaning in the word *Jesus. Cried* would make Christ sound like a neurotic, immature child. Because people have been *conditioned* to such a depth of meaning, in the word *Jesus,* they wouldn't *believe it.*

If you used these words, *Jesus Spilled Tears,* what would you get? The result, unfortunately, is comic. And comedy doesn't fit in with the deep . . . deep . . . meaning of the word *Jesus.*

And people wouldn't *believe* it.

With proper word selection, so that you do not set up conflicts in the minds of readers (your own experience will bolster your judgment of this situation most of the time), you have three primary bases for building belief in copy. The human animal, a complexity of conflict and consistency, runs through a long gamut toward satisfaction. To persuade him, you must "gear your appeal to his gamut." Usually, a combination of the three bases of belief is the result of a copy writer's effort. We can set up divisions or approaches for trying to persuade people to react. But we'll probably come out with a combination of the divisions. Here, then, are the three bases upon which most men build their beliefs:

1. **Seeing Can Be Believing.** This type of belief is based on man's power of observation, modified and articulated by his reason. It can be developed through the use of samples of a product. (New Process Company of Warren, Pennsylvania, uses the "swatch" samples most successfully in selling clothing.) It can be developed through pictures and brochures which illustrate a product in use, through displays of working models which a prospect can visit, through the samples and swatches, or by the trial offer. And the greatest benefit of the free-trial offer is the seller's display of confidence in the integrity of his prospect and the worth of his product. It's difficult for the prospect not to reciprocate.

Example of Free-trial Offer:

> Examine and use this guide for 10 days FREE!
> Mail the postpaid card . . . and I'll put in your hands "ON APPROVAL" the book experts use to get Direct Mail *results that sizzle—*
>   THE 19___ GUIDE TO AMERICAN DIRECTORIES
> With this guaranteed "no-risk" offer, you're trying—*not buying* . . .
> (B. Klein & Co., New York)

There's a most important CAUTION here on the use of "Seeing Can Be Believing" as proof claims, however. You can make and illustrate claims which are completely valid—but which your reader will not believe, *even if he sees pictorial proof.* For example, one advertiser showed . . . "a trunk [luggage] supporting the weight of a mature elephant." Another showed ". . . a fountain pen which withstood the weight of loaded buses rolling over it." [4, 5]

But many people who saw these advertisements didn't believe them.

What was the problem of creating belief? The people who didn't believe . . . couldn't believe. Such illustrated claims just didn't fit in with their own experience. Although the claims were valid, they were incredible because they had an overdramatic impact. And they failed to gain reader involvement.

Reader involvement is that "rapport" which you create—through copy which meshes reader need with copy benefits and through illustrations with which he can identify or into which he can project himself—to *involve* your reader personally. And this involvement is one of those intangibles which makes copy effective. In discussing the personal involvement of the reader through copy, Mr. Frank McGinnis, advertising manager of the Ford Truck Division, Detroit, has this to say: [6]

Involvement . . . is a rather intangible and hard-to-define thing. It's more the feeling you get when you read the message than anything else. It's a feeling that this message is not only directed to you, but that it *involves you* . . . because it says things that apply to you personally. This exclusive or elusive quality is one of the priceless ingredients in direct mail.

A copy writer can fail to get reader involvement because the *style* and *tone* of his copy may create disbelief instead of belief . . . because the tone is flip, or not fitting for the reader. Because false *tone* builds resistance and destroys "reader involvement" with the copy's offer. A copy writer can be too "cute." And, in so writing, cause the reader to be more interested in how the words are put together than in what they say. If he does that, the copy's emphasis—and its reader involvement—are lost.

How do you achieve this personal involvement of the reader in your direct mail copy? You get it . . .

First . . . through a knowledge of the kind of people who are on the list you are using.

This situation implies an understanding of people *generally*. And it implies an understanding of the motives which operate within the specific group of prospects toward whom your copy is directed.

Second . . . through a knowledge of the product that you are selling, and how this product can fill the personal needs of the reader. Familiarity gives depth involvement of the writer, makes possible his projection of ideas in such a way as to involve the reader.

[4] A. T. Poffenberger, *Psychology of Advertising*, McGraw-Hill Book Company, Inc., New York, 1932, pp. 544–550.
[5] Lucas and Britt, *op. cit.*, pp. 68–72.
[6] Frank McGinnis, "What the Client Expects from His Agency in Direct Mail," *The Reporter of Direct Mail Advertising*, vol. 21, no. 9, p. 21, January, 1959.

Third . . . From a facility for expressing his ideas, a copy writer can project honesty, sincerity, warmth which will mesh with the same qualities in the reader—to get *involvement* of the reader. An excellent example is the "to-be-a-child" letter on page 101.

Fourth . . . If illustration is used, it should defer to the reader's "ken" on the same basis copy should. And it should be able to involve him personally—based on an identity with the pictured situation, or an emotional or rational involvement with the illustration. For example, one competent New York advertising agency tested an ad which wasn't getting the desired results. The ad showed a man at the controls of a huge scoop shovel. The picture's perspective was from the side of the shovel. Man, by size, was subordinate to the mechanical strength of the shovel. A new illustration was used after researching the reaction of men who would have influence in the purchase of the shovel. The new illustration showed the man in control of the strength of the machine. The picture was taken over the shoulder of the man. The view was extended through the front of the shovel up the length of the boom.

The problem was: In the first illustration, man was not in *control*. It had a sort of emasculating impact which built a resistance to acceptance of, or belief in, the product. The interested reader was not properly "involved." He resisted identification with the man in the shovel. Because the shovel reduced him to a mere "cog." However, showing a man as the dominant force in control reduced reader resistance and led to greater acceptance of the pictured role—and a greater degree of belief and involvement.

2. **Others Do It.** This kind of belief is based on the pressure of the opinions or the examples of other men. Such belief is *manifested in* a "Keep-up-with-the-Joneses" desire (whether the Joneses are trying to keep up with you never seems to be considered) and a desire to "get ahead." Belief of this type has to do with group mores which call for certain types of behavior, attire, habits, and the like. It has another twist in the emulation need (people are actually *imitators* or we'd never have left the animal stage) that many people have. To be known as a member of a certain group calls for a home in a selected suburb, magazines of a given class, brands of liquor and clothing which symbolize group membership.

This type of belief is separable into two parts. One part has an appeal which takes care of a human's needs in his present situation; the other part has an appeal which takes care of a human's needs in his hoped-for future. The two parts are:

a. "Me-too-ism": The desire to be identified with a group, to seek group approval by adhering to the standards, customs, behavior of a specified group. This is the stuff of which security is made. But latent in its latitudes is the curse of static conformity.

b. "Get-ahead-ism": The desire to get somewhere by following the paths blazed by men considered successful. An effort of emulation, to "cross the creek" on the steppingstones set up by those who went ahead. This is the stuff of which star dust is made. These are the "boot-strap boys" who push themselves ahead with progress for humanity and profit and prestige for themselves as reward.

This next example of copy is keyed to that human desire to seek group identification and group approval, to seek and achieve this by adhering to the standards, customs, behavior of a specific group.

The copy sets up the average user of this product as a person whom you'd wish to be like. Then it tells you that you can be like the average user if you'll only use this product. The offer presents the security blanket of conformity with a desirable group through adherence to the typical habits of that group.

Well-informed people you know (and acquaintances you'd like to know better) talk news, news, news. . . . It's their chief topic of conversation, and today twice as many newsminded people read TIME as any other news magazine. . . .

There are many good reasons, in short, why TIME is so invariably voted first-choice magazine by business leaders . . . statesmen . . . educators . . . top-ranking professional men . . . by almost 2,550,000 discerning American families. I hope that you will want to join them as a regular member now.

The appeal in the first paragraph is to the "Me-too-ism" of the reader, the desire to keep up with the Joneses—particularly the Joneses who read *Time.* But the second paragraph (from another *Time* letter) uses "Get-ahead-ism" as an appeal for belief. We all approve of statesmen (particularly if their biases are cut from the same cloth as our own), professional men, business leaders. These may be the people toward whom we are "reaching," whose social and economic position we also want. In that case, *Time* becomes a steppingstone in the right direction.

The "Others-do-it" method of creating belief can also be broken down into types of testimonials. The types are:

a. Prestige Names: Experts in a given field can be used to verify the validity of claims either with a personally written testimonial or with statements made by them about how they progressed in their career. The next copy example shows how words of a business giant have been adapted to a letter addressed to businessmen. This is a powerful technique known as "favorable comparison" which plays up to the ego of the reader. (From a National Research Bureau, Inc., letter.)

"Though fire or storm destroy my fine buildings, fixtures, and merchandise, I have lost little as long as I keep the loyalty and good will of my customers."

John Wanamaker

Like John Wanamaker . . .

. . . your most priceless asset is the good will you can enjoy among your customers.

And the enclosed exclusive Christmas greeting can be your good-will message for Christmas 19___. No one else selling the same customers in your area can have this letter . . . *if you tell us to put it aside for you.*

This copy, using a quotation which epitomizes Wanamaker's opinion of the stuff success is made of, is the "get-ahead" type of belief . . . it's the "thong" which holds the "boots" together while one raises himself. Among the words which help build belief—other than the prestige implicit in the name *John Wanamaker*—are the *most priceless assets . . . good will . . . exclusive.* These words cover most of the "south forty" of the farm of persuasion. Every businessman deals in assets, and knows of the impact and the "forward thrust of his career" that *good will* and an *exclusive* can give.

b. In-group Names and Status: Identification Users. Specific people within our own state of social and economic existence, who use and endorse a product or service. And whom we can believe because of our similarity of experience and our belief in their status.

See page 177 for a letter created in testimonial style. In this example, the names of the universities represented by the testimonials have a prestige impact on the readers toward whom it is directed. The status within the profession, the academic rank held by those giving testimony, also lends credibility to their statements. From the experience of the readers, these colleges and the performance within the academic world, as indicated by the rank of the persons quoted, create belief. Because within the academic world is a great deal of mutual respect for the integrity indicated by college and academic rank.

This type of approach in developing belief can be used with any of the professions and with the business world. To create belief, a copy writer should use the symbols which indicate the status of the person giving testimony within his profession or in the business world. Effective, also, is the name of the clinic, corporation, institution with which the person is associated.

3. **I Feel Like It.** This type of belief is based on a person's feelings, emotions, moods, on that part of his make-up which develops anxieties. It is embedded in the point of view he accumulates as he matures. As man matures, part of the little boy tags along to become a factor in the reactions of the man. Early experiences leave a conditioned response, where boy later tugs man in a preset pattern. It's normal, natural, not

immature. Two of the several facets which develop in humans are the inclinations to be "for it" or "agin it" . . . and not always on a reasoned basis. For convenience, let's label these facets:

a. The Pleasant Picture: The positive approach; the "for-it" inclination. This is the human inclination to accept ideas which are associated with those things, people, and ideas which experience has proved acceptable, desirable, or profitable. (Part of this acceptance—which leads to belief— came along with the boy. Part is the experienced judgment of the man. All is a blend of experience seasoned with reason and cussedness.)

To create belief through copy of this type, the writer associates his sales message with ideas which he knows the reader approves. Acceptable ideas are symbolized by words which meet a ready-made preference among readers. In their process of maturation, readers have become in-clined toward the meaning of these words. Such words arouse feelings of kindliness, approval, pride, vanity, sex, love, brotherhood, and the like. They arouse mental imagery of the pleasant, the sometimes nostalgic, the things secure. Much of the credence given these symbols is based on man's ability to believe, to have faith, in the ideas which give meaning to his existence and validity to his civilized heritage. Examples are home, mother, courage, brotherhood, happiness, dedication, friendship, char-acter, honesty, integrity, loyalty, patriotism, democracy, justice, and freedom.[7]

These copy excerpts from the mailings of the Charles W. Groves Com-pany (teacher and high school senior mailing lists), Michigan City, Indiana, illustrate how the "Pleasant Picture" method of building copy belief can be used. The Groves mailings are a series of cordial-contact letters which arrive on prospects' desks once a month.

Pleasant Picture symbols	*Excerpts from Groves's copy*
Brotherhood	". . . the sweet music of brotherhood in each Pilgrim heart."
Happiness	". . . your own little corner of happiness."
Courage	". . . labor and courage of our ancestors."
Friendship . . . faith	"Friendship; fellowship; the right to call upon the Wisdom of the Great Planner. They are ours for the asking."
Teacher dedication	[The schoolteacher] "YOU DON'T OFTEN SEE HER NAME IN THE PAPER, and you'll rarely see her around . . . but you can get a good look at her picture . . . mirrored in the eyes of a child."
	"And sometimes you ask, 'Why not use your brains to get ahead?' To which, in quiet satisfaction, she replies, 'When the day's work means freedom for 26,000,000 children, what's ahead of that?' And sticks to her teaching."

[7] From *The Process of Persuasion,* by Clyde R. Miller. Copyright 1946 by Crown Publishers, Inc., New York, pp. 149–168.

Why does the Groves Company use the "Pleasant Picture" to create belief in its copy? The idea is to project the honesty and sincerity of the company into the copy, offer what the prospect wants to buy—integrity. Then approach the reader on a plane which he is *inclined to accept.*

But—let Peggy Greenlaw tell you about it. Here is an excerpt from a letter in which she explains Groves's copy approach:

After all we're only human . . . so our style is human. It is as natural as we are natural. Its personality is our personality. We're not cold as fish or stiff as pokers or antiquated old fuddy duddies. Neither are the people we select as logical prospective customers. They are warm and friendly . . . because they are people. We like what we know about their business life and want their friendship. So, our copy reaches across space to talk as one human being to another.

A dusty list of names isn't interesting or even important to write about because confidence, reputation, and integrity are the priceless ingredients a buyer seeks in a product. That is what we sell him. When he buys, that is what he gets . . . along with the money-saving circulation and efficient service which keeps him as a buyer.

Since the schoolteacher's dedication has community-wide approval, and since most humans have a love for the "little bits of people," the natural copy approach for the Groves Company is to associate itself with the symbolism inherent in the reader's love of children and his approval of a teacher's dedication.

There is, however, a necessity for restraint in this type of copy. It should not be too *hard sell,* too intense, or it becomes maudlin and lacks sincerity. The reader, also, may reject the copy if it is overdrawn. He may resent the exploitation of well-cherished ideas. The reader may feel that the copy writer intrudes too deeply into things personal.

The Groves copy has sensitive restraint. It is keyed as low as possible in its *sell.* The *sell* is so low-keyed that the copy carries only a brief reminder of the service available to the reader. But the copy packs a wallop which leaves an unforgettable impression with the reader.

b. Oh, No, Not That: The negative approach; the "agin-it" inclination. This is the human inclination to reject ideas which are associated with those people and attitudes in which we do not believe, those things which we reject because experience has proved them unacceptable or undesirable. (Here we find the basis for the "Thou shalt nots" which help hold society together. Unfortunately, we get the "apron-string complex" here, too—"Don't do it, Mamma spank"—so that the venturesome spirit sometimes dies aborning.)

In this persuasion process we apply "poison" words—or bad names, or symbols to arouse feelings of fear to make . . . people . . . reject, shun, disapprove of, condemn an idea.[8] We conjure in their minds unpleasant or undesirable pictures. We develop reaction against something to persuade people to fight against it . . . and buy the product which helps them "win."

In this copy sample from Boyce Morgan and Associates, Washington, D.C., the "Oh, No, Not That" aspect, the poison words, are presented in the ideas which no businessman wants his business to be guilty of, *if he can help it.*

Too many employees take the *telephone for granted.* They have received *little or no training* in its use. Without realizing it, they can easily *make mistakes that irritate customers, create ill will, give their company a bad name— actually lose customers and drive business away.*

From these phrases, Mr. Morgan develops a picture of what can happen in a business if employees do not have proper telephone training. He then explains how his telephone-training aids can eliminate these negative situations: *Mistakes that irritate customers, create ill will, give their company a bad name, lose customers, drive business away.*

Belief is a strange and a wonderful thing. It comes from the depth of human self-defense and self-confidence. Sometimes it's hard to shake, to destroy. Other times an unexpected off-key or off-color symbol, tied in with human moods, can destroy beliefs. At times it is coherent and logical, at others—thoroughly unreasonable.

Based on the conditioning process of man, his experience with the world, and his achievements and failures (within his own set of values), his belief is created by what he can see for himself . . . and by what he can read or see that others in whom he has confidence believe in. Strangely, however, the greatest strength of belief lies in his own desire to believe—*because he feels like it.*

To give you more, in this chapter, we are including a college-teaching aid on how to build belief. This was developed by Hugh W. Sargent, associate professor of Advertising in the University of Illinois. It is added here to give you a little more perspective, a little material with which to do your own writing more easily, effectively.

Some Ways to Help Build Belief in Your Ad Copy
    I. Guarantee
        Unconditional
        Conditional (time or some other limitation)
        (In the future, to abide by F.T.C. requirements, a guarantee will have to have these qualities:
        1. Must state exactly what guarantee offers.

---

[8] From *The Process of Persuasion,* by Clyde R. Miller. Copyright 1946 by Crown Publishers, Inc., New York, pp. 149–168.

  2. Must state how guarantee will be fulfilled.

  3. Must state exactly *who* is the guarantor: manufacturer, wholesaler, retailer, etc.)

II. See for yourself

 Sample (including swatches of cloth)

 Free trial

 Demonstration

 Pictures and brochures

 Working models

III. Evidence of authorities

 Qualified experts

  Examples:

   Liberace, Horowitz, Rubinstein, for pianos

   Director of a university ag experimental station; farm adviser, for fertilizer

   Athletic director or coach for football uniforms

 Genuine users

  Persons (if possible) in same occupational, income, and/or regional groups as prospects whom you are trying to convince

  Examples:

   Housewife for household product

   Business executive for automatic mailing machine

   Secretary-stenographer for typewriter

 Official recognition

  Professional, scientific, and standard-setting organizations

  Awards and prizes

 Manufacturer with established reputation

 Dealer or retailer with established reputation

 Reputation of media carrying advertisement

IV. Proof by performance

 Laboratory tests

 Sales records; facts and figures

 Dramatic performance of the product in use (not planned by manufacturer)

11

How to Create Action

Why is the action element more important in direct mail than in other forms of advertising? Why does it warrant special attention? In direct mail—and only in direct mail—is it possible to give your prospects the complete and actual means of taking action.

No need to exhort an audience to dash out to the nearest retailer or dealer. No need to send people hunting for envelopes, stamps, cards, or stationery on which to express their interest in your offer. No need to give them a minikin-sized coupon on the kind of paper that defies any pen or pencil.

In your direct mail, you can include everything, not only the urge to take action, but the means to take action.[1]

The action element of direct mail is one of its chief advantages. And by putting action into your direct mail, you not only get more action out of your market, but you also get an indication of the effectiveness of your mailing piece.

Action is as important as any other part of your selling message. Probably more so because it's the climax of a selling story. And its adequacy can make or break the effectiveness of your sales effort It must, therefore, be conceived and executed carefully. It takes thought, consideration, and skill to ensure that the reader takes action and that he takes the action you want.

[1] *How to Put Action into Your Direct Mail,* a booklet published by the Creative Division of James Gray, Inc., New York, (n.d.).

Ask for . . . and Hasten the Action

Too much direct mail trips gaily through the daisy patch of persuasion only to reach the rock wall of resistance on the other side of the valley and stand there stumped. Beyond this rock wall is the reader's readiness to act . . . to do as you ask him. To get over the wall, *ask . . . ask . . . ask*. Don't be bashful. *Tell* your reader what you want him to do.

If you're out panning the business-market streams for gold-flake leads for your salesmen, *tell* your prospect he can get the information, or possibly the price list, or whatever it may be—by having your salesman call on him. If you don't *ask* for permission for your salesman to call, or for the reader to request a salesman's call, you're panning fool's gold. And there's no nugget of profit in that kind of operation.

Maybe you're trying to sell a product through dealers. O.K. Then *ask* the prospect to go to the dealer's place of business—for a demonstration or whatever it may be in your case.

If you're mail-order bent, *ask* for that order. "Faint heart never won fair lady." And there'll be no dollars tossed across your personal Potomac unless you *ask* for the order.

The effectiveness of your direct mail is measured by the response it brings in, by the way it gets people to *act* as you wish. And they'll not respond, not act, to as sufficiently profitable a degree—unless you ask them to.

At this point in selling—ACTION—you run into the two barriers which Henry Hoke lists as (1) human inertia and (2) competition for your reader's money.[2] These barriers form that wall at the other side of the daisy patch of persuasion. And the wall is *resistance*. Resistance is based on a conflict between desire for a thing, consideration as to how the benefits it offers are going to work for the reader, and other latent desires which "push" a reader away from action—toward something else. Resistance is also based on the inertia inherent in making up his mind.

To get action, then, you must *ask* for it. But how do you *ask* for action? If your reader has responded favorably to the benefits you have described and believes the evidence you have presented to prove your claims, then you must leave no question unanswered in the action part of your sales copy. Tell him *completely* how to get what you offer and *ask* him to do so.

Action is a four-part process of helping fulfill the desire your message has created. The four parts necessary to help the reader do what you ask are:

[2] Henry Hoke, *How to Think about Direct Mail*, The Reporter of Direct Mail Advertising, Garden City, N.Y., 1951, p. 6.

1. **Tell Him What to Do.** The action you ask of a reader depends upon the purpose of your mailing piece. But regardless of what the purpose is, *tell him to do just that.* Here are some examples:

 a. Take advantage of this opportunity right now. (*Nation's Business.*)
 b. But do "clip" this saving coupon today while this special offer is open. (*Newsweek.*)
 c. But this special saving is available for a limited time only—so take us up on it today. (*Time.*)
 d. Why not share in this year-round buying guidance that helps 800,000 families get high-quality products and save shopping dollars at the same time? (*Consumer Reports.*)
 e. Why not give yourself and every member of your family a treat by sending for the introductory album today?

(Paragraphs *d* and *e* could be strengthened by omitting the first two words—*why not.* Because within these words is an implication that there may be a reason "why not.")

In these examples the reader is told "what to do" by:

 a. "Take advantage"
 b. "Clip this saving coupon"
 c. "Take us up on it"
 d. "Why not share?"
 e. "Give yourself and every member of your family a treat by sending for. . . ."

2. **Tell Him How to Do It.** The second part of helping a reader do as you ask is to tell him how to carry out the action. This means you lead him by his humid little forepaw to the action-piece you have enclosed—card, card and envelope, coupon, whatever. Here are some examples of copy which tell the reader *how* to act:

 a. Just fill in and mail the enclosed card today. (*Consumer Reports.*)
 b. But check the enclosed postage-free order card and mail it to us today. (*Good Housekeeping.*)
 c. Just fill in and mail the enclosed reduced-rate order form in the postpaid envelope provided. (*Hi Fi Review.*)
 d. Just slip 10¢ into the handy coin envelope, sign the enclosed card, and mail both back in the business-reply envelope provided. Do it RIGHT NOW. (American Geographical Society.)

In these examples the reader is told "how to do it" by:

 a. "Fill in and mail"
 b. "Check and mail"
 c. "Fill in and mail"
 d. ". . . slip 10¢ into the . . . envelope, sign the . . . card. . . ."

3. **Give an Impulse to Action.** The third part of helping a reader do as you ask is to supply an impulse to action. Again, the impulse used depends upon the type of mailing you are using and upon your purpose. And though these methods of creating an impulse to action are listed here separately as examples, please note that the copy samples actually combine several methods—to get deeper impact on the reader. So don't necessarily limit yourself to one "action impulse" if your offer is adaptable to more than one. Here are a few methods of developing impulse to action:

a. Describe the benefits: Remind the reader what he or she can obtain in return for action. This is a very brief restatement of your Central Selling Point—the main reason why the reader should do as you ask.

In this next copy, another sample of Smithers Salon direct mail, a last "dart" is thrown toward reader desire in the complimentary close. Here is an effort to synthesize the essence of a whole letter:

> Between us . . . in an informal salon . . . we can cooperate in creating a new figure for you—to give you the impact which "stars" you in any role . . . on any stage. And *Smithers* guarantees satisfaction . . . with your help. For calorie control is a "cue" in the script for building a better figure.
>
> Bring the coupon in . . . by February 28, 1959 . . . or call for an appointment.
>
> 'Cause . . . Loveliness Awaits, M'Lady . . .

In this example, the space ordinarily given to the complimentary close is used for a last effort to tap a woman's desire for loveliness. Depending upon the purpose of your mailing, the type of person on your list, and the product or service you are offering, the complimentary close can be used effectively to add an impulse-reason why the reader should act.

b. Inspire confidence: [3] Offer a money-back guarantee by offering to send your item on approval or by telling the reader . . . "No need to send your check now; we'll be glad to bill you later." (*Newsweek.*)

This next example inspires confidence through offering to send an item on "approval," through a stated guarantee of satisfaction or money back, and through the idea that the reader doesn't have to pay until he has judged the product for himself. This action copy also contains a brief restatement of the benefits available: ". . . teach you and inspire you to achieve those goals dearest to your heart. . . ."

> Don't let this moment go by without action that may well lead to the big turning point in your career. Send for your free-approval copy of How To Turn Your Ability Into Cash.
>
> Please keep this in mind—if Earl Prevette's book is not everything I say it is in this letter—if it does not teach you and inspire you to achieve those goals

---

[3] Kenilworth H. Mathus, "Use Action Urges in Your Coupon Copy," *Printers' Ink*, vol. 237, no. 12, pp. 58–59, Dec. 21, 1951.

dearest to your heart—return the book instantly. You simply can't lose a dime. You, and you alone, are to be the judge of whether the book is worth the low price of $4.95.

But if you, like thousands of other worthwhile people, decide that you want to keep the book to read again and again over the years—send only $4.95, and the book is yours! SEND NO MONEY NOW. JUST MAIL THE ORDER CARD.

Parker Publishing Co.

c. Offer sample, free trial, or demonstration: Offer a sample for prospect's evaluation, a free trial where he can judge for himself (this is best when free-trial period is limited), a free demonstration either at his home or office, or at some other place. An advantage here: When you offer to let the reader examine your product before he buys, you create a feeling of confidence between you and him. For he realizes that you don't question his integrity. It should then occur to him that, by reciprocity, he should trust you. A good situation for selling.

This sample of Prentice-Hall copy offers a ten-day free trial to let the reader make his own evaluation of a set of books. It also helps make action easily palatable, by making payments for the books easy.

Send Your Free-trial Card Today for This Triple-powered
Speaking Tool—NO RISK . . . NO OBLIGATION

Here's what you do. Simply drop the handy reply card in the mail, and I'll send you the EXECUTIVE SPEAKING COURSE 3-volume set for 10 days *free* examination. You send no money. You pay nothing to the postman on delivery. No salesman will call on you after you get the books. All you do is send the free-trial card enclosed for your Special Preview.

When the books arrive, look them over for 10 days—then decide. If for any reason you do not wish to keep the books, just return them, and you owe nothing. But if you feel they are the best set of speaking and conversation books you've seen at any price, send your first payment of only $4.95, plus a few cents for postage and shipping. Then send just two more payments of $5 a month until the complete, low price of $14.95 is paid.

Imagine!—10 days free trial . . . and then easy payment terms. Send for your Special Preview set *today*, while you have the card handy.

d. Use an economy appeal: Remind reader how much he can save or how prices may be going up and buying now will save money. If prices for your product or service are to go up in the future, remind your reader of this fact. Emphasize it. He'll be more amenable to favorable decision and action if he knows he'll save money on your offer.

In this example of *Look's* copy, the fact of a price rise for subscriptions is made emphatic by being put at the opening of the paragraph and by the italics. To put more impact into this offer for the reader to save on his subscription, a time limitation is also added.

But Look's *subscription rates go up in February*—so right now, while you are thinking about it, initial your Discount Certificate and return it with your 63 Savings Stamps in the enclosed postage-free envelope.

Please don't delay. This offer is subject to withdrawal after 21 days and this is *the last time* we can make you such an offer before the rate increases. So— mail your order today . . .

. . . while this thrifty $3.85 trial rate is still in effect!

e. Offer a premium: If the reader buys now, you'll send something additional. This should be something which is logically related to the product or service you are selling. Or, it could be something which would aid the reader in his career. In highly specialized lists, the premium can be more readily adapted to the reader's interest, profession, or his typical forms of relaxation. This sample P.S. follows copy which the "Around the World Program" used to sell "Magic Carpet Tours" of the world—to be bound into an album supplied the purchaser. The gift of a wall map is a natural as a premium. Because it ties in with an interest in the "tours."

P.S. If you act on this offer within the next 10 days, we will include as an EXTRA FREE GIFT a colorful *Giant Wall Map of the World!*

f. Put a time limit on your offer: One of the best ways to overcome reader inertia is to put a limit on the time your offer is valid. Limiting the time for decision helps the reader make up his mind. He doesn't have as much inclination to delay, to "think about it later."

This sample from *Life* Magazine clearly states the time limit in which the reader must act. It "pulls out the stops" of reader reaction, and a hoped-for *action,* by giving a definite time for expiration of the offer.

But here's an important note: I am only authorized to make this offer to current subscribers, not to the general public—which means you can accept it only while your present subscription is in effect!

But you can also use some or part of the various persuasion devices as presented to you under copy styles. Such as humor, for example. In this letter from Tom Marker of Chrysler, as usual in hot pursuit of the effectiveness of his TV film clips, is the ineffable charm of the man, projected into a personalized, human, humorous "touch"—which got results.

And I swear that whatever you put on the enclosure will get a lot of attention. It will decide whether we go on making these things; how we'll change them for improvement; whether or not we'll continue trying to palm them off on you in particular; and possibly whether we stay here at Chrysler Corporation and shoot for the retirement age or stop now and go straight.

Cordially

Enclosures (1) incredibly easy answering gadget
                  (2) stamped envelope addressed to me
                  (3) good wishes

HOW TO CREATE ACTION

Here's persuasive action based on a light touch of "josh"—the use of the "enclosures" part of a letter for a dash of easygoing humor—to liven up the mixture of request and personality.

4. **Supply the Means of Action.** The fourth part of helping a reader do as you ask is to supply the means by which he can act. When you have asked a reader to act, pointed out how he'll benefit from action, given him an impulse to act, then you should have the means of achieving that action right before him.

Usually, the action piece is a card, or a card plus an envelope. If you want to give the reader a credit or c.o.d. shipment, a card is all that's necessary. If, however, you want a check with the order, a card and envelope, or just a properly designed envelope, are necessary.

And on the card use a succinct restatement of the offer. If you have started your copy by writing the card first, you're all ready—except for possible revision. If not, be sure the offer is clearly stated on the action card. For example, here is the offer in a letter from Reynal and Company, Publishers, New York:

We believe this book . . . [*The Reporter's Trade,* by Joseph and Stewart Alsop] . . . can be of great value to you in your courses. If you would like to examine it, we shall be glad to send it to you on approval if you will fill out and return the enclosed card. If you find after examining it that you would like to use it with your classes, we will be very happy to cancel the charges on receipt of the class order. (Distributed by Viking Press.)

In the first place, the copy writer has deferred to his academic audience by toning his letter down below the "hard sell," the insistence, the "push," which may be effective on other clusters of humanity. But which isn't too readily accepted in the academic world. The easy, quiet approach is probably more effective in dealing with college teachers. And, too, the dignity of this book calls for a dignified copy approach.

Here, then, is the copy of the action card which was enclosed with the letter from Reynal and Company:

To the Viking Press:
Please send me on approval a copy of *The Reporter's Trade* by Joseph and Stewart Alsop at $5 less my 20% educational discount, plus postage. I understand that this charge will be canceled if I return the book or if I adopt it for use in my class.

In this example the offer is rephrased into an "agreement" to accept by the reader.

Tests prove that a separate reply form—usually printed on a different type or color of paper—will bring in more inquiries than one which is part of the folder, broadside, or letter. And on this reply form ask for *only* that information which is *absolutely necessary*. The information should not stray in any way from the offer you are making, or from the objective of your mailing.

For better returns, include postage. Business reply envelopes and cards cost postage only if they are returned.

One of the many competent research studies reported by the Direct Mail Advertising Association has to do with the use of a reply card versus no reply card in a mailing.

The problem, as set up by the Provident Mutual Life Insurance Company of Philadelphia in making the mailing, was ". . . to determine the effectiveness of enclosing a postage-paid reply card as opposed to a suggestion in the mailing that information is available if it is written for."

The procedure for carrying out the test was that ". . . mailings were made to lists split in the following manner: 25 successive names were taken at a time and the mailing with the prepaid reply card went to the first 12 and the mailing without the card went to the succeeding 13." Here are the observations of the test:

Number Mailed	Response
580 (with reply card)	124 cards
586 (without card)	29 letters

The conclusions were that ". . . the difference in response was overwhelming enough to warrant the extra expense involved in using reply cards. As a consequence, all of the company's direct mail letters now have a postpaid reply card enclosed with them." [4]

As all research studies published by this association for its members state, however, "The conclusions reached by any single test do not necessarily apply in any future mailing either by the same or different mailer. Repeated testing is the only reliable procedure for reference . . . Reports should serve as guideposts in helping you conduct specific tests applicable to your own business."

Ready-mades

Ready-made, copyrighted, action-type mailing pieces are available to you. The most prominent producers of these mailing pieces are Reply-O,* Cabot Letter,* and Sen-Bak.* All of these organizations do more than offer mailing pieces with built-in action pieces. But we're interested only in action here. The advantages of this ready-made form of mailing piece are:

1. The action piece stays with the letter. Reply-O is slipped into a pocket on the back of a letter. Cabot Letter and Sen-Bak are "tipped"

[4] Published with the permission of the Direct Mail Advertising Association, New York.

* See SOURCE LIST for full names and addresses.

on the back of a letter with adhesive. And in this way the reader has the "response" mechanism as long as he has your mailing piece.

2. One addressing of the action piece gives you:
   a. The outside address on the mailing unit when window envelopes are used
   b. The inside address on a letter (through a cut the same size as the envelope's window)
   c. The reader's name and address on the reply card, ready for his signature

In all of these patented forms of direct mail format, the reply feature can be of any type you wish—card, envelope, or otherwise. One of the advantages of the ready-made is that, though the cost of addressing will vary with the method of addressing used, the one addressing operation helps hold costs down. Instead of three addressing operations, outside address, inside address, and reader's address on the action piece, you have only one addressing operation. And that is on the action piece. In this instance, then, you save the labor costs necessary in handling and addressing the three usual pieces—envelopes, letters, and action cards.

Here's the way the Protect-O-Metal letters pulled. Compare your guess with those of the Dayton Ad Clubbers and the M.A.S.A. experts. How'd you do? Interesting letter-success story, isn't it?

Here's the Way the Letters Pulled Returns:

> Returns per 1,000
>
> Letter no. 1: "In just a few days" 56
> Letter no. 4: "Blow it off" 52
> Letter no. 2: "P.W.A. workers" 44
> Letter no. 3: "1666% increased" 40
>
> 192 or 48 per 1,000
> Best previous letter 20

Here's how the Ad Club and M.A.S.A. Guessers Figured the Letters' Pull:

First-place Choices	Ad club	M.A.S.A. experts
Letter no. 1	7	13
Letter no. 4	13	8
Letter no. 2	0	2
Letter no. 3	7	2
"Fairly correct order"	5(14%)	14(48%)

And Here's More Information about the Test:

The best letter got 40 per cent better results than the worst.

To translate that into dollars and cents, let's assume (and we *are* assuming) that Protect-O-Metal Products' *average* customer is worth $50 profit per year . . . and that they lose 10 per cent of their customers every year. Let's also assume that 50 per cent of the inquiries received produce customers. (All these "assumptions" seem on the conservative side. . . . Customers, for instance, have been running higher than 50 per cent.)

On that basis, the best letter is worth $14,000 in profits when mailed to 1,000 people, and the worst letter is worth $10,000 in profits (over a ten-year period). The best previous letter that Protect-O-Metals sent out would have been worth $5,000 in profits.

No wonder Marshall Field once said, "The right letter can be worth a million dollars."

12

Marketing Research

Problems with Prospects

When a three-year-old doesn't like his girl friend, he hits her. When he hates spinach, he spits it out. When he's tickled, he laughs. When he's hurt, he cries.

With kids, you know where you stand.

Then kids grow up. They become adults. They aren't so direct. They hide their feelings. Past experience tangles their reactions. Their motivations become obscure. Even when adults *know* why they do things, they won't always *tell* why. They may deliberately give other reasons. This *reluctance* makes marketing and product research difficult.

Another serious difficulty for researchers is caused by *individual differences*. Since most markets are too large to "research" 100 per cent, samples are used. But small samples are always dangerous. The peculiarities of even a few people may throw results off badly.

Yet, to sell effectively, a manufacturer must know his prospects, what kind of people they are, where they buy, what they like and dislike about his advertising, why they buy or don't buy his products.

Personal Inquiry

So almost every manufacturer does some research, even if he only asks his friends, personally, what they think about his advertising or product.

Most know, however, that such opinions can't be trusted. Folks tell you what they think you want to hear. So, if you're headed in the wrong direction, you just keep getting wronger . . . and wronger.

Of course, if you ask enough people—particularly if you ask strangers—they'll tell you the major things. And some businessmen have learned a lot in lobby and waiting-room conversations during their travels over the country. But even on a large scale, *personal inquiry* has faults. Your own bias gets in the way. You lead people on. You get imperfect samples. And you tend to give extra weight to the opinions of the last few people you've talked to. So most manufacturers give up after a few tries.

Toward Scientific Research

Years ago, manufacturers began to replace personal inquiry with "scientific research." And, since then, researchers have tried just about everything. First, they sent college girls door to door to ask the question straight: "Why do you buy XYZ soap?" But they soon discovered that the housewife, anxious to make a good impression on the slick chick with the questionnaire, gave impressive, if not quite accurate, answers.

On the West Coast, for example, early radio-program surveys were door-to-door interviews with housewives. And, strangely enough, a symphony program always came out first. When more accurate measurements were developed, it turned out that soap operas were at the top and symphonies somewhat farther down the scale.

So college girls weren't good enough (to get unbiased results), and researchers "improved" on them (the research methods . . . not the coeds). They switched to "depth interviews" . . . where a skilled interviewer talked at length with a housewife . . . let her ramble, in the hope that she'd give herself away; then wrote a report on what the interviewer thought she thought. Naturally, those reports reflected the *interviewer's* bias.

So depth interviews weren't good enough, and the researchers "improved" on them. They took wire or tape recorders and made "secret" interviews, with no notes. And "unbiased" supervisors interpreted them in the laboratory later.

Recorders didn't quite ring the bell. So some researchers even tried hypnotism. They hypnotized selected users or prospects. And, while they were in the twilight sleep of hypnotism, the hypnotist asked them directly *why* they bought certain products. Naturally, this eliminated inhibitions and took care of fudging on the part of people who would not have told college girls their favorite radio programs were soap operas. But, obviously, hypnotism had other drawbacks, among them a difficulty in obtaining an accurate sample and even greater expense; so, this method never became popular.

Of course, there's still mind reading and the séance to be tried. But they're temporarily out of fashion.

The Cost of Research

You'll notice one consistent thing about the course of research. As surveys have been "improved," the price per interview has gone up. Lately it's gone up like a skyrocket.

Of course, because cost of research has to be kept under value of research, the extra cost of skilled interviewers usually results in the use of a smaller sample and sometimes (as in some television surveys) in the repeated use of the *same* sample which, aware of its importance, becomes nontypical.

The added *cost* is there, so the price had to go up. And successful research in this area has been valuable. The question is: Could successful research be done, in many instances, for less cost? It not only can be done. It is being done, every day.

One manufacturer, using a *simple, inexpensive* method of research, recently spotted a new fastening in his product that gave his users trouble, kept more from buying. He changed it, and sales improved. Another manufacturer discovered which trade magazines were *read and respected* by its top prospects. He concentrated his advertising money there, where his *prospects* wanted it.

A third learned the weak spots of a nationwide sales staff as seen by customers. A fourth changed product and advertising emphasis after learning *why* people were buying his product. A great retail store keeps tab on the opinions of its employees.

Through hypnotism? No.

They've done it in a way that is less expensive, per interview, than *any* of the methods of research . . . a method General Motors has used constantly, and successfully, for years.

The Anonymous Response

GM uses self-administered, anonymous response from *large* samples. Of course, these are on printed response forms. Most surveys of this type are done by mail. We might call this type of survey a Letterview.

The self-administered, anonymous survey all but eliminates those two major problems of personal interviewing—reluctance to tell the truth, even when known, and the danger of error in small or overused "samples." Because . . .

a. Answers are anonymous. The same people who will fudge a little to a college girl, a depth interviewer, a wire recorder, or a hypnotist *will* be honest when they feel their answers can't be traced. There's no prestige value in little white lies . . . if nobody knows who fibbed.

One thing all those other methods have in common: Between the respondent and the truth stands a second person. What is needed is a self-administered "interview" (or a self-stated view) which eliminates the other person.

There's nothing new or unusual about this. The *vote* took these steps. The vote is but an opinion of the voter on which person shall fill a governing position. But until the vote was *secret,* or anonymous, it never came close to the true reflection of the opinion of the people.

Same thing's true of any opinion. As long as some other person *knows* what your stated opinion is, the truth will have a tendency to be warped.

b. The size of the sample can be dozens of times larger than in personal interviews . . . at lower cost.

There are other advantages of self-administered surveys and polls . . . in addition to economy and anonymity. Written questionnaires ask everyone exactly the same question in exactly the same way. The "personality" of the "interviewer" is the same for all. Hundreds or thousands of people can be "interviewed" through a printed page, while a personal interviewer talks to a few dozen. And any gambler or mathematician will tell you the chances of error flatten out as you see more people, . . . as long as the people represent a fairly accurate sample.

Actually, there are two major schools of the "personal-interview" type. One is the "Question-Answer," which asks for typical "Yes," "No," or "Don't-know" answers to reasonably straightforward questions, then tabulates them and finishes with an interpretation of *statistics.* The other school is the "Depth" school, which usually deals with a smaller sample, asks the "Well-*why*-do-you-like-it?" or "Let's-talk-a-little-about . . ." type of question and then has social scientists interpret the response.

Though both schools deal in "motivations" as well as statistics, the term "Motivation Research" has been popularized by one group of Depth interviewers. Both kinds, of course, erect huge psychological barriers by putting a second person between the respondent and the truth . . . barriers that the anonymous, self-administered interview tends to eliminate. The anonymous, self-administered interview could be used for either type of study—the statistical or the psychological. But, in practice, the "Yes—No—Don't Know" type of answer is probably safer.

Of course, such surveys aren't *perfect.* Nor are they best for every problem. Many people, even when willing, cannot tell you, offhand, *why* they buy certain products, like cigarettes and pipe tobacco . . . and psychologists who do motivation research and hypnotism *do* frequently find hidden reasons for decision. So, in purely psychological cases, the personal interviews may very well be more helpful and worth the extra cost.

The chances are that no method of motivation and opinion research will ever be perfect. The "material" involved—the human, mind—is too tricky.

But let's face it. "Perfect" motivation or opinion research would find out *every* reason behind *all* decisions. No type of research does that. Most manufacturers wouldn't be able to use that much information if they had it. So, while not perfect, experience seems to show that the results from self-administered, anonymous surveys are *every bit as reliable and accurate as any other kind*. Certainly one of the reasons for General Motors' growth at the expense of others was that management said:

Find out what they want; give them more of it.
Find out what they don't want; give them less of it.

And they proceeded to find out through self-administered, anonymous surveys, at a fraction of the cost of personal interviews.

Besides, and here's the important point, the troubles of most manufacturers do *not* lie in their failure to find out *everything* about buyers' opinions, needs, and motivations. Many of them don't find out *anything*. They try to imagine what's wrong. They ask everybody (salesmen, wholesalers, retailers, their own wives) except the ultimate consumer.

Even a little information can help such companies. And *many products or services are liked or disliked for specific, known, factual reasons which people* Do *know and* Will *tell . . . anonymously.*

If 250 out of 500 purchasing agents say they don't buy your paper towels because they won't fit their dispensers, you don't need any more information to know what to do. If 10 per cent of your former dealers tell you they stopped buying because a small part on your machine was continually breaking, you don't need a psychologist to help make a decision. That information is *enough*. If 5 per cent of your customer pipe smokers say they like the odor of your tobacco and 43 per cent of noncustomer pipe smokers say they don't buy it because it smells like old rubber burning, you'll begin to think without further help.

Let's look at some actual cases, where the *objective*, self-administered survey, or Letterview served business:

1. *To measure effectiveness of direct mail:* A regional service firm had made a dozen or so monthly mailings to the presidents of banks and savings-and-loan secretaries in some of its territory. The purpose was to make its trade name favorably recognized. Simple, double–post-card Letterviews were sent to bank presidents and savings-and-loan secretaries in the entire territory. The questionnaire gave the president a list of twenty-four trade names, with the sender's and its major competitor's well hidden in the list. He was asked to check those he recognized favorably. The identity of the sender was hidden, and the respondent was not

asked for a signature. Over half were filled out and returned. Analysis showed the name was favorably recognized over twice as often by presidents and secretaries who had been receiving the mailings. The advertising pattern was considered successful. (A sidelight: At least one bank president was vacationing in Florida at the time of the survey. The Letterview followed him, and he answered it while on vacation.)

2. *To check on standing with wholesalers:* A manufacturer wanted the straight story on his reputation among wholesalers . . . wanted, particularly, to know his weaknesses. He dreaded, however, the psychology of having his salesmen ask their customers, "What's wrong with us?" He also wanted a balanced, impartial analysis of the customers' opinions.

Detailed Letterviews were mailed, by a direct mail research concern, to his major wholesalers. Each wholesaler was asked to report on *all* of his major suppliers in this line. The questionnaire asked the wholesaler to rate the suppliers as Excellent, Good, Fair, or Poor in the areas of product, company policy, sales representatives, delivery, advertising, and promotion. It asked specific questions in each area. The survey was completely "blind" . . . with no reason for the wholesaler to weigh his answers for or against the manufacturer.

Although the questionnaire called for sixty-one individual decisions of judgment, the majority were returned . . . enough to show the manufacturer two or three spots of unsuspected weakness and at least one point of unsuspected strength.

3. *To measure acceptance of name and main sales point:* The sales manager of an office-equipment company wanted to find out how well his product was known by business firms in various markets. His Letterviews, in the form of a double post card (Figure 1), asked three questions:

 a. Listed the names of seventeen office-machine manufacturers, asking the recipient to check the names of those which made adding machines

 b. Listed five advertising phrases, asking the recipient to fill in the name of the company using

 c. Asked for the name of their impulse-favorite

Questionnaires went to the presidents of manufacturing concerns of all sizes. They were coded by size of plant. A good per cent of the presidents replied, with little variation in the percentage of replies caused by the size of the company.

4. *To discover when people actually purchased appliances:* When one large manufacturer of home appliances, burdened with seasonal production problems, used this kind of survey, he discovered that while distributors *purchased* the appliances seasonally, the ultimate consumer bought at almost an even pace all year long. With these facts, plus an educational program for distributors, the manufacturer was able to level out production and reduce distributor investment.

MANUFACTURER'S MAIL RESEARCH
Chicago, Illinois

Will you
help us
help you?

So advertisers can serve you better in the future, we are studying the effectiveness of some current advertising methods.

This particular survey is on *portable, desk-type adding machines.*

Would you (or the person in your organization who makes final decisions on adding-machine purchases) be kind enough to answer the three questions attached?

Thank you very much.

/s/

for Manufacturer's Mail Research

P.S. We need only your offhand opinion, so it will take only a moment, but your answers will be most helpful.

SUBJECT: PORTABLE, DESK-TYPE ADDING MACHINES

A. Please put a check in front of all companies which you *know* make *adding machines.*

☐ R. C. Allen	☐ Monroe
☐ Avco	☐ National Cash Register
☐ Barrett	☐ Pitney-Bowes
☐ Burroughs	☐ Remington Rand
☐ Clary	☐ Smith-Corona
☐ Friden	☐ Swift
☐ Hobart	☐ Underwood
☐ IBM	☐ Victor
☐ McBee-Royal	

B. After each phrase below, please write the name of the company using it. Don't bother unless you *know. Please don't guess.*

"Sensimatic" by _____

"Thumb add bar" by _____

"Live keyboard" by _____

"Ten key ease" by _____

"Super-Quiet" by _____

C. If you were in the market for an adding machine, what make would you look at first? _____

No signature necessary

FIG. 1

5. *To discover customer preference for new credit plans:* A West Coast department store used anonymous Letterviews. It had its choice among a number of different types, but wanted to choose the one that most of its customers would prefer, not necessarily the type that appealed to its top executives, who were not typical shoppers. A simple Letterview

(Figure 2), in the form of a letter explaining the situation clearly and asking for help, brought the answer they needed.

CUSTOMER RESEARCH BUREAU
P.O. Box 1406—Del Valle Station
Los Angeles 15, Calif.

Date

Will you do me a favor?

I make my living by compiling information about customer likes and dislikes. You can help me very much by taking just a second to check the few questions on the bottom of this letter.

My client, like many other business firms, is anxious to improve service and the best way is to learn quite frankly what your ideas are. *You need not sign your name.* Your opinions are most valuable when pooled with those of others we're also questioning.

Thank you so much for helping. There's a postage-paid envelope enclosed for your reply. Will you please mail your answers today?

Sincerely,

- -

1. Is the 6-months' term Credit Account plan for purchasing personal and household merchandise attractive to you?

      ☐ Yes   ☐ No

2. What type of 6-month account appeals to you most?

   a. ☐ Contract type of account
   b. ☐ Coupon book type of account
   c. ☐ Merchandise scrip type of account
   d. ☐ Revolving charge account

3. From what store or stores have you purchased on the 6-month or more payment basis within the last year?_____

4. Why did you prefer this store?_____

No signature is necessary

FIG. 2

General Motors has used the interview by mail for years, and this is what they think of the technique: [1]

While we use many different methods to gather information (and find out what people want), we depend on mailed questionnaires for the majority of our surveys. We are able to ask everyone who receives one exactly the same questions in exactly the same way.

The average motorist cannot project his thoughts far enough into the future

[1] Quotes from a GM paper on "Customer Research."

to actually design the change he would like to see incorporated into a product. However, there is no question that he is an expert in the product's actual use. It is in this area that we seek his opinion.

One way of accomplishing it is to leave lots of room for people to write down any comments they may care to make. When these are tabulated, it is almost equivalent to thousands of "Depth Interviews," which would take infinitely longer to do.

A common characteristic (of questionnaires) is that people apparently take considerable time and care in filling them out, because it is very seldom that anyone goes right down the line checking everything "good" or even "fair" or "poor." The response is a deliberate, thoughtful one.

By making an intelligent appraisal of the statistical results, it is possible to initiate changes which will lead to greater owner satisfaction . . . our basic goal.

Scientists trained in contemporary psychology tend to believe that the personal interview is always superior in obtaining information. They consider the self-administered, anonymous questionnaire as a *substitute* for the personal interview. As you can see, the history of surveys has not substantiated this point of view. Quite the contrary. The personal interviewer has constantly tried to improve his techniques because his *results* were off (they don't always admit this . . . they say, for example, that the reason they've missed so badly on presidential elections is that so many people change their minds during the time between the interview and Election Day. Well . . .). General Motors, on the other hand, rode to undisputed first place in car sales by the other route; apparently the buying public told GM the truth on their printed, anonymous questionnaires.

The Mail Poll and You

Can you take mail polls and make such surveys yourself? Of course. Many companies do. But there's a real danger of serious waste without skilled, professional help on your questionnaire and message. And there's an even greater danger of unskilled or prejudiced interpretation of the returns when you do it yourself or have someone in your own organization do it.

On the other hand, if yours is a rather simple and uncrucial problem, there's no reason why you shouldn't have your fun. If you do decide to make mail polls or surveys yourself, here are some of the things to watch out for:

Don't ask unnecessary questions. Before you ask a question, you ought to have a clear idea of what difference the answer makes. If you don't know what you're going to do with the answers after you get them, or if you've already decided what you are going to do, regardless of the answers, don't bother to ask.

Be sure you do ask the necessary questions. It's easy for management to veto a question, "because we don't want to put *that* idea in their heads," only to find that the veto took the heart out of the survey.

Have enough alternatives. You might call this the "maybe" area. Questions which must be answered "yes" or "no" not only cut down on the percentage of returns; they frequently warp the results by squeezing the "maybes" into one group or the other.

"Split them down the middle." If you ask for evaluation, force the responders out of the middle ground. Example: "I believe the idea is _____Excellent _____O.K. _____Poor" will often find a huge percentage of the answers in the "middle" (O. K.) because they don't want to use the *extreme* words (Excellent or Poor). "I believe the idea is _____Excellent _____ Good _____Fair _____Poor" will force responders to go on one side of the middle or the other.

Interpret results objectively. The results will seldom speak for themselves. The figures will need interpretation. Never allow this interpretation to be done by someone with personal interest in the result.

The percentage of return necessary for success depends on a number of factors: on the homogeneity of the group being surveyed; on the size of the sample, its distribution, and the "tolerance" allowable in the answers. There's no "usual" percentage of return. Returns depend upon many factors. Some of the most important are:

1. The number of questions asked.

2. The difficulty of the questions asked. (One question which calls for looking up records will cut returns considerably.)

3. The difficulty of answering the questions. (This is different from No. 2.) The question, "How many dozen whingdiggets did you buy between April 10 and August 14 last year?" is a difficult *question.* The question, "Do you vote Democratic? _____Yes _____No" poses a difficult *answer* because there is no "sometimes." An *easier* answer would be "_____Always _____Almost Always _____Usually _____Half the Time _____Sometimes _____Seldom _____Never." While this answer *looks* more complicated than "Yes–No," it is actually much easier to answer.

4. The clarity of the questions.

5. The format of the questionnaire. It should appear to fit the problem. (There's no "best" format. Each situation has its own psychological factors.)

6. The phrasing of the request (quite important), . . . its apparent reasonableness, and the apparent need of its return.

7. The identity of the sender.

8. The method of return (obviously payment or nonpayment of postage has a great effect).

9. The occupation of the recipient.

10. Whether or not the interviewee is interested. (Try to make the

questions interesting to the reader. Some research people, when preparing a difficult or rather boring questionnaire, insert a question or questions which have no value at all to the client but which are of great interest to the respondent and improve their returns as a result.)

11. The readability of the questionnaire and accompanying letter (from all angles, including layout).

12. The relationship between the sender and recipient, if any.

13. The degree of anonymity (of course, in some cases it *increases* the returns to provide for identification . . . as when a highly respected member of a profession asks for the opinions of lesser professionals . . . or the boss asks opinions of branch managers).

It's seldom possible to have all factors favorable, but when some unfavorable factors are unavoidable (the answers to the questions you want answered *may* be difficult), you'll want to make a special effort to have as many favorable factors as possible.

One favorable factor may completely outweigh an unfavorable one. . . . For example, the questionnaire (part of which is shown in Figure 3) was prepared and mailed for a manufacturer of Power Mowers. While the format shows "only" nine questions, actually over thirty decisions are required of the person who fills out the questionnaire.

However, a number of favorable factors are present in this case. The questions are clear, the format is attractive, the request for information is reasonable and very friendly . . . and signed by the president of the company manufacturing the product. And the *satisfaction* of users of this product happens to be *very* high. These factors make the recipients quite anxious to cooperate, to the extent that the first mailing of the questionnaire pulled almost *60 per cent* return. And half of those returning the questionnaire wrote additional comments.

This unexpectedly high return brought back many more answers than were needed for a statistically stable sample and meant a considerable reduction in cost for the similar Letterviews taken in later years. The number mailed (still a careful sample of the whole) has been reduced a great deal without affecting the accuracy of the survey.

WILL YOU HELP US?

We want to make products that satisfy as many users as possible. The only people who can really help us do that are people who use them . . . including you.

Now that you've used your HUFFY MOWER for a while, will you take 30 seconds to tell us what you think about it?

There's no writing required. Just check off the answers to nine questions.

You'll help a lot.

H. M. Huffman, Jr.

HUFFMAN MANUFACTURING COMPANY
Huffy Mower Division, Dayton 1, Ohio

ANSWER EACH QUESTION AS WELL AS YOU CAN

1. Which Huffy model do you own?

   ☐ 16″ electric
   ☐ 18″ electric
   ☐ 16″ gas
   ☐ 18″ gas, 2-cycle
   ☐ 18″ gas, 4-cycle

2. How large is your lot (approximately)?

   _____ft by _____ft

3. Who uses your Huffy mower?

   (Check all who use it.)

   ☐ Man 16 to 30   ☐ Woman 16 to 30
   ☐ Man 30 to 40   ☐ Woman 30 to 40
   ☐ Man 40 to 50   ☐ Woman 40 to 50
   ☐ Man 50 to 60   ☐ Woman 50 to 60
   ☐ Man over 60   ☐ Woman over 60

4. If neighbors or friends have tried your Huffy, how many bought Huffys of their own?

   ☐ One   ☐ Two   ☐ Three   ☐ _____

5. Where do you live?

   ☐ Farm
   ☐ Village less than 5,000
   ☐ City 5,000 to 25,000
   ☐ City 25,000 to 100,000
   ☐ City over 100,000
   ☐ Residential suburban area near city
   ☐ Other _____

6. What about the Huffy do you especially like?

   (Check as many as you wish.)

   ☐ Cord control
   ☐ Cuts grass better
   ☐ Easy to sharpen blades
   ☐ Quiet
   ☐ The way it cuts terraces
   ☐ The way it cuts weeds
   ☐ Push-button starting
   ☐ Easy to use
   ☐ The way the blades swing back
   ☐ The low investment
   ☐ How cheap it is to run
   ☐ Light weight
   ☐ The flip-over handle
   ☐ You don't have to be a mechanic to operate it

   ☐ Easy to adjust cutting height
   ☐ Close trimming
   ☐ Mows backward or forward
   ☐ No turn-around trouble
   ☐ Easier to use than other mowers
   ☐ Does not make a racket
   ☐ The way the handle holds the the cord out
   ☐ No mess
   ☐ No fumes
   ☐ UL approval
   ☐ It's electric
   ☐ (Other) _____

7. Have you ever had trouble with your Huffy mower?

□ Yes   □ No

If so, was it

□ Motor or engine
□ Switch
□ Other
Describe briefly _____

_____

8. Does the extension cord give you any trouble (electric only)?

□ Yes   □ No

9. All in all, are you glad you bought your Huffy mower?

□ Yes   □ No

If not, why not? How could the Huffy be improved? _____

_____

(If more space is needed, use back cover.)

Of course, it's not necessary to sign your name. You may if you wish.

NAME _____
ADDRESS _____
CITY_____ ZONE_____ STATE_____

If you signed your name, may we tell others what you have said? □ Yes   □ No
If you have any additional comments, please make them here

_____
_____
_____
_____
_____
_____

THANKS for helping us. Now please enclose in the stamped envelope and mail.

FIG. 3

Naturally, the better the Letterview, the higher the return; and the higher the return, the smaller the necessary sample.

However, a tremendous percentage of return is seldom necessary. In mailings of reasonable size and simplicity, answers become fairly stable after the first few hundred returns have been tabulated. If the original sample is carefully selected and large enough to be representative, a 20 to 25 per cent return will be adequate. And a well-prepared Letterview will seldom fall below that. Unless obvious difficulties lead you to anticipate it ahead of time.

On small surveys, where a higher percentage is needed to get an adequate sample, or on very complicated surveys, where a poor return is only natural, one procedure is to key-code each piece and plan more than one mailing to those who do not respond to the first mailing. Usually the second Letterview (identical questions, of course) brings a greater percentage of return than the first.

Experience is a great teacher, not only in increasing the percentage of return but in anticipating the percentage of return. And sometimes it is more economical to predetermine the number of answers required and base the size of the mailing on this. That procedure is followed by the Annual Consumer Analysis of the Milwaukee *Journal* and other newspapers. First, on the basis of percentage of population, they determine how many questionnaires must be returned from each section of town. Then they mail .questionnaires into that area until they receive the predetermined number of returns. With this method, all sections of town are accurately represented, regardless of any variation in percentage of return.

In any event, you want the highest practical percentage of return. Here then, are some suggestions, based on the factors that influence returns, which should help you in preparing the self-administered, anonymous survey.

Techniques to Improve Returns

1. Use few questions for best returns—five or six at the outside. If you must have a lot of questions, either don't number them at all or number them by groups.

2. Require a minimum of writing. All check marks is par for the course.

3. On the other hand, leave plenty of room for comments. You'll get them from some of the respondents.

4. Include a "don't-know" or similar place to check for every question where this answer is possible.

5. Make the whole thing look easy, easy to fill out, easy to mail back. An easy-looking questionnaire is better than an elaborate one. Some people feel they get better returns from note-size questionnaires (even if more than one page) than from letter-size ones.

6. Leave *room* for a signature even though none is expected or desired. Some people just plain *like* to sign.

7. Be sure to include a response method that will not cost the respondent money or trouble. At least use a business reply envelope or card. Stamped, addressed envelopes will produce a higher return, and air-mail postage will increase returns even more.

8. Make your letter short. Make it personal. Personalize it if practical.

9. In your letter, make it clear that the survey is important and that the respondent is important to the survey. If you can also point out that the survey is important to the respondent, fine, but this is secondary to the

first two conditions. If there is likely to be any benefit to the respondent as the result of the survey, be sure to mention it. But don't try to invent a benefit. Your insincerity will show through and reduce returns.

10. Send a premium if you wish. Mailable premiums or even payments of 10 cents (Figure 4), 25 cents, or $1 have been used by a number of survey firms with some improvement noted. If this saves enough in mailing costs by cutting down on the number of mailings necessary, it's worthwhile.

BABY HEALTH RESEARCH INSTITUTE
216 West Jackson Blvd.—Suite 400
Chicago 6, Ill.

Date

Dear Mother:
May I ask a favor?
You have been selected as a representative mother in your community, who can supply us with important information that will help one of our clients in his efforts to give the best possible service to users of his product.
If you would spare me a minute of your time to answer the few brief questions on the enclosed questionnaire, I would be most grateful to you.
To thank you for your help I've enclosed a little gift for your baby—a dime for a can or jar of your baby's favorite food.

Cordially yours,
/s/ Susan Palmer
(Mrs. Susan Palmer)

P.S.   We are, of course, anxious for your answers to reach us as quickly as possible, so I hope you will be able to drop the enclosed stamped return envelope in the mail today.

FIG. 4

---

11. If the company taking the surveys is well liked or respected by the respondents, then its connection with the survey may improve returns substantially. But if there is any chance that the respondent might be reluctant to send a reply that might be traced, doubly protect his feeling of anonymity by interposing a neutral party (a survey organization, a professor, a chamber of commerce, etc.) to whom the questionnaires are to be returned. Point out that the actual reply will never be seen by the interested company. (If you are comparing your company against another, for example, you'll want to keep your name completely out of the picture, whether it would increase returns or not.)

12. You may mail out the questionnaires or pass them out to a group. But in your letter or announcement, emphasize that you are not interested in respondent's "personal" opinion as such, but only as he is a member of a group; that there is no way to trace his answer and no interest in tracing it; that all you want is the truth.

13. Offer to send results (if they'd be of interest) to the respondents, but (if the questionnaire is anonymous) provide a separate method of collecting the names, a separate slip to be enclosed with the questionnaire, a perforated section (if the reply is to go to a third party), or even a separate post card.

14. Pave the way or follow up with cards, letters, or other communication. For mailing to a whole community, some companies have announced the survey and asked for cooperation through newspaper ads or over the air. Figure 5 is a post card which preceded a questionnaire, to pave the way for it. And to alert the reader and create interest.

Dear Subscriber:

You are one of a representative sample of FORTUNE subscribers whom we are asking to take part in a special FORTUNE study.

Within the next day or two, you will receive a simple keyed questionnaire, which will require only a few minutes of your time to answer.

We will be especially grateful for your cooperation.

Sincerely,

/s/

Dr. Edgar Gunther

Director of Market Research

FIG. 5

Figure 6 is a post-card follow-up, which was used to trigger loose a greater percentage of returns.

A post-card reminder with an appealing picture of an infant and this copy:

I wonder if Mom returned that questionnaire (the yellow one)?

FIG. 6

Pitfalls to Avoid

Of course, there is more to successful research of any kind than putting questionnaires in the mail and getting a lot of them filled out and returned. One of the greatest dangers of do-it-yourself research is that the "survey" will be the beginning and the end of the research.

Since this outline on marketing research is from the direct mail point of view, most of the emphasis *has* been on the techniques in the "survey" or questionnaire area.

Direct mail people who have worked with organizations doing their own marketing research have noticed a certain pattern of difficulties, which often are discovered only *after* the survey has been completed. Some of the major ones are:

1. *Too many unimportant questions.* Because "it would be nice" to have the answers, additional questions were added, cutting the returns below the critical point for accuracy.

2. *One or more questions were too difficult.* Perhaps the respondents were asked to be too specific, to report matters about which they keep no records, report matters which they consider *too* confidential. (When you ask the average businessman what his profits were for the preceding year, his typical reaction—in a personal interview—is to lie. In a mail survey, he is more likely to tell the truth but even *more* likely to throw the whole thing away.)

3. *The most important questions weren't asked.* Somehow, after the returns are all complete and tabulated and the results announced, there is frequently a brief pause while someone asks, "Why didn't you find out about _____?" . . . This, everyone agrees, is a much more important question than one or two questions which were asked.

4. *The tabulating takes too long.* When tabulation is done manually and there are many variations, it can become quite time-consuming. This is not only costly, but it delays an analysis of the results. Consider the time necessary for tabulation when the survey is planned, and include machine tabulation in your plans if you want the results promptly. To make the most of machine tabulation, your original questions should be printed with the key-punch operator in mind.

5. *The analysis lacks imagination.* As in any other survey, the analysis or interpretation of the figures collected is as important as the figures themselves.

6. *The answers don't provide any help.* This can happen, of course, when the respondents are badly split, leaving you without a clear directive. But it also happens when a firm is committed to a certain course and will not change, *regardless* of the answers to the questions. In this case, there is no use asking them.

7. *The results are carefully noted, but nothing is done.*

All of these difficulties, except the last, can be eliminated by careful preplanning. Sometimes a dry run, either a small "test" survey (mail or personal interview) or a series of "What-will-we-do-if _____" questions, can precede the survey itself. During this dry run, you can find out whether the answers can be worthwhile and what is likely to be done about them.

No kind of research is worth much unless it has the capacity to produce action, . . . and the action must take place in the near future because the conditions revealed by the research will change.

It's been said that collecting information in this field is much like garbage collection: There's not much sense in collecting it unless you know what you're going to do with it . . . right now!

13

Direct Mail's Creative Materials

INTRODUCTION

Only in direct mail do you have the variety of applicable creative dimensions available for projecting the impact of your own personal commercial—right into your reader's hand.

But in direct mail, as in anything creative or expressive, "difference requires thought . . . sameness grows like weeds." To get "difference" in your direct mail, then, *think*. But first consider the sameness which plagues direct mail. Then, move your creativity to another place on the checkerboard of advertising persuasion.

Direct mail is as guilty as any other advertising medium when it comes to substituting "sameness," by imitating the successful efforts of others for the bright "difference" of individualized impact through creative imagination. Let the TV boys copy each other's Western heroes—let the beer and cigarette advertisers try to work out variations on the same theme—with the results which give only the impact of beer or cigarettes, not the individualized impact of "brand." And, at the same time, let other direct mail people have their own ideas.

Don't copy them. For you have so much to work with in direct mail, so many creative materials . . . that "thought" will produce for you a much better personality in your mail.

Admittedly, sometimes a variation of an idea *is* effective. But the more you copy, even in variations of others' ideas, the less creative work you'll do for yourself. And you'll not crash through that pile of mail as a "standout."

168

Nothing new under the sun? Don't you believe it. If not, how come all the fascinating campaigns, full of bright individuality, that appear on advertising's stage every year?

But let's take a quote from Leo P. Bott, Jr., Leo P. Bott, Jr. Advertising, Chicago, on the plea for standout creativity in your advertising in preference to the mediocrity of mimicry: [1]

David Ogilvy, of Ogilvy, Benson & Mather, has adopted a "Creative Credo." It includes: *In advertising, the beginning of greatness is to be conspicuous and different. The beginning of failure is to be invisible and orthodox.* And yet, many a fine advertising theme has died aborning because the copy chief or advertiser thought it too clever or wanted something conservative like competitor's advertising. So advertising gets or stays in the rut of mediocrity and indifferent success, and the client squawks and changes agencies once more.

Listen to Mr. Bott. Listen well and heed his wisdom. And if you need further evidence, abide by the words of the Great Seer—Burma Shave: "Substitutes and Imitations . . . give them to your wife's relations." 'Nuf sed.

What, then, are the ingredients you can use to create a selected impression in your direct mail? The number and the type you can bring to bear on an idea you wish to express are, actually, unlimited. For as soon as a list of creative materials is developed, someone will come along with a new material, a new ingredient, or a new combination of several older ingredients.

So, if you would be creative, start with the idea that you have unlimited possibilities—reducible to practicability by the necessary restrictions of costs, feasibility, mailability . . . and all other limiting factors.

Some of your creative materials with which you can work in direct mail include:

1. Copy Style: The way in which you weave a message into being—with words.

2. Theme: The thread of continuity . . . which ties your mailing or mailings into a unified or continuous impact.

3. Format: The clothes . . . the "dress" your message wears.

4. Reproduction Processes: The way in which your message is reproduced upon its format.

5. Envelopes. The "wrappings" of your direct mail package . . . the "hello" part of your conversation with a reader.

6. Postage and Postmarks. A grace note of impact . . . the glamour of faraway places.

The following chapters will discuss the various creative materials to use and how to use them in developing effective direct mail pieces.

[1] Leo P. Bott, "Ad Industry's Need: Few Mimics, More Gimmicks," *Printers' Ink*, vol. 266, no. 9, p. 92, Feb. 27, 1959.

14

Direct Mail's Copy Styles

Weaving of Words

Copy style is the way in which words are woven together into the fabric of language to produce the impact desired. Style is the means of combining ideas into a point of view which appeals to a reader. Or, if you prefer a literary allusion, take Lord Chesterfield's definition of style: "Style is the dress of thoughts."

Here we shall offer you different copy styles. They are adaptable to the various purposes and formats of Direct Advertising pieces. When you write copy, consider these styles on the basis of their adaptability to your product, your mailing list, and the purpose of your mailing. The copy styles are:

1. *Narrative:* The selling story is made part of another story—usually fictional. This style can take any literary form: short story, poetry, etc.

2. *Dialogue:* The selling story is made part of a conversation between two or more people. Dialogue, actually, is a form of narrative or an excerpt from a longer story. But it can be used as a style in Direct Mail Advertising. So it will be discussed as such here.

3. *The Worthy Word:* The selling story is based on the word of personalities whose testimony is acceptable to your mailing list as proof of a product's performance.

4. *The Benefit Approach:* The selling story is based on stating directly to the reader why he should use a product. This style is the usual, straight-selling, reason-why type.

5. *The Humor Approach:* The selling story is presented to the reader wrapped in the cellophane of laughter. Humor is given as a separate style here, even though it usually falls into the category of narrative, because of the pitfalls involved in its use. Special consideration should always be given to the use of humor. Wary should be the man who uses it in advertising.

A separate division under the Humor Approach is devoted to "High-level josh." This type of humor is deadly earnest in its selling job. However, it carries a light touch which is adaptable to the sophisticate. And a sophisticate here is considered to be the educated type of person who understands humanity pretty well, but loves people in spite of themselves.

Narrative. Narrative writing is the telling of a story. Written either in prose or verse, narrative is designed to interest or amuse a reader. And narrative writing has its own special and provocative appeal to the reader. The involvement of the reader with characters, plots, and situations in fiction gives him perhaps a feeling of escape, assuredly a sense of identification with people who do the things he would like to do. But, more importantly, this type of writing appeals to a reader's feelings and emotions.

This emotional appeal is narrative's best advantage. Because narrative appeals to feelings and emotions,[1] it leaves a deeper impression on the memory of the reader. Because the impression is deeper, it lasts longer.[2]

A copy writer who can "spin a tale" in which he interweaves his selling message can create a more lasting impression with his readers. The "story" can be a fictionalized account of the product in use or of the service being enjoyed. It can be a historical account of the product or service. It can be a news account of service or product. It can be an account of an incident within a company. Or a story can be used as the device which leads into a selling message. This special use of narrative is discussed under Attention in Chapter 8.

The second advantage of narrative copy is that it is easy to understand. Because narrative presents ideas in the orderly, normal sequence of events, the continuity in the writing follows naturally and easily. Since short narrative—if skillfully written—produces only one dominant emotional effect,[3] the writing has a unity of impression. The reader gets only one type of emotional impact.

The next advantage of narrative is that it attracts more people than other types of writing. It is the most familiar type of writing in the every-

---

[1] Thomas H. Uzzell, *Narrative Technique*, Harcourt, Brace & World, Inc., New York, 1923, p. 46.

[2] Milton Wright, *Managing Yourself*, McGraw-Hill Book Company, Inc., New York, 1949, p. 77.

[3] Uzzell, *op. cit.*, p. 44.

day lives of readers. Women admit that magazine fiction is of greatest interest to them (among forms of writing). Many men agree. Since narrative is the most familiar and seemingly the most popular type of writing among readers, you have a better chance of getting the attention of more people when you use it as advertising copy. You also have a better chance of holding their interest once you have attracted them.[4]

Narrative has advantages as a copy approach. However, it also has some very distinct disadvantages. These are not the fault of the style itself, but arise from the talent (or lack of talent) of the copy writer.

1. It takes a particular skill to create the unity of the one dominant emotional effect which puts the "punch" in narrative.

2. Narrative can be overdone, or be so self-consciously clever that the reader remembers only the narrative and not the sales message. This is the same thing that happens to too clever radio or TV commercials. People remember the commercial but not the product.

3. Narrative must have a very disciplined length. It should not be so long that the reader wonders *why* he should read it or *when* he is going to get to the point.[5] In direct mail, narrative length can easily be disciplined in all the various formats through judicious use of layout and illustration.

In the example of verse narrative from *McCall's Magazine*, the reader becomes easily "involved" in the story because it "tells the tale" of man's historic relation to woman. With the amount of newsprint dedicated to this "situation" in all the women's pages (and men's pages and magazines), there must exist an interest in the subject. The letters to "Woman's Page" editors indicate that the emotions are involved. But they would be, in this eternal battle of the sexes.

This copy goes through a logical sequence of events. It is short, easily read. And the writer, by using verse, employs the quality of rhythm in copy. Rhythm itself makes for easy reading, better memory of the reading.

The dominant emotional effect in this letter is humor, light and pleasant. Sketches were included in the letter to illustrate the development of the man-woman situation. They have been omitted because they are not necessary to our purpose.

McCALL'S LETTER

In days of old, when knights were bold,
And wives were hothouse beauties,
No man had any int'rest in,
A woman's household duties.

---

[4] Melvin S. Hattwick, *How to Use Psychology for Better Advertising*, Prentice-Hall, Inc., Englewood Cliffs, N.J., 1950, p. 263.

[5] *Ibid.*, p. 128.

She had her world and he had his,
And ne'er the twain would mingle.
'Twas hard to tell the married folks,
In those days, from the single.

She sewed and sang and poured the tea.
He hunted boar and pheasant.
She tatted while he roamed the fields.
It's not like that at present!

Today a woman's world is large,
And men have broader vistas.
Together now they live their lives,
The Missus-es and Misters.

The kids, the home, the meals, the school,
The "sitter" situation,
Are "Dad's" concern as much as "Mom's,"
And here's the connotation:

TOGETHER now they view the world,
Of fam'ly life and actions.
TOGETHER, as a fam'ly group,
And not as separate factions!

Together, too, they read McCALL's,
Together share its pleasure . . .
McCALL's—the fam'ly magazine—
The monthly reading treasure.

°Six million homes now get McCALL'S,
And read each worthwhile feature,
On fashions, hobbies, food and health,
For ev'ry human creature.

Now here's a special offer to
The folks who'd like to try it.
A DOLLAR, FOR THE NEXT EIGHT MONTHS,
IS ALL YOU NEED, TO BUY IT!

Just HALF the price subscribers pay.
$1.80 less than newsstand rate.
Return the card right now, today!
(Pay later, if you'd rather wait.)

Mary Mason

°Six million *and a half* it is.
 Six million, though, sounds neater.
 We lopped a half a million off,
 Just to preserve the meter!

The next example of narrative writing illustrates the use of a story to get to a key word—in this case "fit"—which is the "key" to the "sell" in the letter. It is a Dayton Rubber Company letter which does an excellent job of advertising Dayton Rubber cog-belts:

THE DAYTON RUBBER COMPANY

Dayton 1, Ohio

EVER BUILD A BOAT

IN A BASEMENT

. . . and forget to measure the door?

When the Great Northern built their first west-bound triple-decker construction cars, they had just one purpose in mind . . . to reach California before the Santa Fé.

Out of Minot, N.D., went the swaying, top-heavy cars—full of emigrant Irish and German crews, ripping across the plains, everything right on schedule. . . . 'til they hit that first mountain tunnel.

You guessed it. Somebody had forgotten to check for "fit."

Out piled the crews, cussin' in three languages, to trim the cars to size . . . and men who were there claimed you couldn't hear the saws for the sawers.

"Fit" is still important on the railway today.

Like the way Dayton Rubber Cog-Belts fit snug in the drive sheaves—stay taut in any weather to prevent slippage—yet "give" under pressure to protect expensive equipment.

Dayton Cog-Belts pack power into generators and safety into railroading . . . charging batteries for modern caboose lighting and two-way radio communication. The only V-belt with a preformed Cog built as an integral part of the belt —Daytons have more flexibility and grip!

No wonder when they talk about good fit on the railway today, you can be sure they're saying—

"Dayton Rubber"

/s/

Sales Manager

Railway Division

Dialogue. Dialogue is conversation. And conversation reads easily. It is interesting. It can be informal. It has a personal touch which adds to the reader's interest. And, importantly, conversation lends itself to the ideal, broken-paragraph layout.

When you use dialogue in advertising copy, you create short scenes or anecdotes in which people discuss the qualities, performance, uses, etc. of your product or service. You have, usually, a short narrative which frames the dialogue, which tells a story so that the conversation can be brought into time and space, and can be given a situation for its existence.

Dialogue, however, is not easily written. Difficult it is to portray conversation. Most writers put their own words into the mouths of the characters they create.[6]

To create effective conversation, let's take a look at the requirements for effective conversation as set up by Porter G. Perrin in *Writer's Guide and Index to English:*

1. . . . show the words and constructions of colloquial English, of the English spoken by the kind of person represented, not the more formal terms of typical written English.

2. . . . show the contraction, clipped expressions, and casual grammar of everyday speech.

The next copy sample shows how conversation can be used to get an easily read message across to the reader:

THE NATIONAL TAG COMPANY
344 South Patterson Blvd.
Dayton 1, Ohio

"NOW LISTEN HERE, HIME," . . . said the irate voice at the other end of the line, "Stop flooding me with letters about those Hot-Carcass labels."

"Something wrong?" I asked, worried.

"Plenty," the voice barked. "Ever since we asked for a full day's supply of your labels . . . free."

"You didn't get them?" I ventured.

"Sure, we got 'em," declared the voice. "Used 'em all day. That's when all the trouble began."

"They didn't stick?" I suggested, heartsick.

"Like magic!" boomed the voice.

"They didn't come off clean?" I tried again.

"Clean as a whistle, [he whistled] just like you said."

"Your men didn't like them?" I was getting desperate.

"They loved 'em." You could hear him smile. "That's the trouble. Your labels slap on and pull off so easy . . . and save so much time and mess . . . that they wouldn't wait for me to write up a P.O. Said I had to phone an order, even if I paid for the call myself.

"So look, pal," he pleaded, "stop writing me letters, won't you . . . and go out in the plant and rush a 10,000 order thru for me—today!"

I did.
/s/
Robert L. Hime
Sales Manager

[6] From *Writer's Guide and Index to English,* by Porter G. Perrin. Copyright 1950 by Scott, Foresman and Company, Chicago, p. 508.

P.S.   Turned out, the company treasurer liked them too. Here's why.

1,000 to 5,000	$9.94 per M	50,000......	$4.74 per M
10,000	7.64 per M	100,000......	3.98 per M
25,000	5.38 per M	250,000......	3.70 per M

P.P.S.   Like to see what the commotion's all about? Just send the card . . . and when you want to order, write, wire, or call (collect), we ship fast!

The Worthy Word. The Worthy-word approach in copy writing uses the testimonial or endorsement of the Worthy Man as evidence that what the copy says is true. Outstanding or newsworthy personalities—people with prestige or experience, men and women who are respected for success and achievement—are used as the voice of authority. Because readers will accept evidence from persons whom they know to be qualified to speak, testimonials and endorsements can effectively tap the wellspring of motivation whence flow human drives, desires, wants, and needs. In addition to being in a position to know, the Worthy Man should fulfill one of these requirements:

1. He should be nationally prominent, so as to have the necessary news value genuine testimonials need.

2. If he is not nationally known, he should be well known in the circles toward which the copy is directed.

3. He should be typical (if not well known) of the type of reader toward whom the copy is directed.

The Worthy-word copy approach is adaptable to direct mail in these two ways:

1. The major portion of the copy is nothing but testimonials. In this case, selling copy is cut short, and most of the persuasion effort is based on testimony.

2. The entire piece of copy is written by one man as an endorsement of a service or product. The mailing piece carries the letterhead of the endorser rather than that of the company which supplies the product or service.

The following copy example from McGraw-Hill Book Company illustrates the use of the Worthy-man type of approach, where the major portion of the copy is testimonials. The individuals giving testimony are identified as members of the profession toward which the copy has been adapted—college professors. This Worthy-word approach uses testimony from a given group or class. In addition, the evidence of the value of the product is attested by the use of the names of the universities and colleges which have adopted the product that this mailing piece sells. Note that the emphasis in this letter is primarily on the quotes of the Worthy Words of Worthy Men rather than on persuasive, selling copy. Page 2 of the letter presented quotes from the author's preface, the table of contents, and an offer (with reply card) of an on-approval copy.

NEWS BULLETIN   McGraw-Hill Book Company, Inc.
330 West 42nd St., New York 36, N.Y.

HAVE YOU
HEARD   — what professors are saying about
Haire

PSYCHOLOGY IN MANAGEMENT
Mason Haire
Associate Professor, Department of   *McGraw-Hill*
Psychology, University of California   *Series in*
Berkeley 4, California   *Psychology*

PROFESSOR Donald W. Taylor, Yale University
"You are to be congratulated on a book which deals effectively
with what, I think, are the central psychological problems for anyone
involved in administration."

PROFESSOR Irving C. Whittemore, Boston University
"I find it stimulating and thorough."

ASSOCIATE PROFESSOR Leonard Sayles, Columbia University
"This is a fine statement and analysis of a most appealing approach
to many problems in the field.
"Not only is the conceptual material excellent, but the writing is a
real delight. I am sure no educator in the industrial relations field
or administrator will be willing to be without a copy for very long."

The Benefit Approach. The Benefit Approach, or copy style, is discussed
in Chapter 22. Because the discussion there is thorough, we shall not repeat it here. But, we do wish to suggest you think of Benefit Letters in
terms of style adaptable to many situations as well as in terms of the uses
for this type of letter given you in Chapter 22.

The Humor Approach. "Humor," according to Richard Armour, "is a
sixth sense, and very nearly as important to us in making our way through
life as any of the other five senses." [7] Humor in advertising copy can be
story telling . . . actually a form of narrative. Or it can be any language
or "situation" *device* which points up the incongruities of life. Professor
Armour lists these devices: word play (puns), sentence play, exaggera-
tion, anachronism, burlesque, understatement, parody, *double-entendre,*
surprise (unexpected twists of thought or language), *non sequitur,* and
straight satire.[8]

Everyone (almost . . . we must except the devotees of the dour
dialectics) is pleased with a grin, enjoys a chuckle, likes to laugh, and
revels in hilarious uproar. And a copy writer can use this "sixth sense,"
this appreciation of things funny, to make his copy appeal to his readers.
Humorous copy can be effective in getting a reader's attention and in

[7] Richard Armour, "Of Humor and Humor Writing," *The Writer,* vol. 69, no. 10,
pp. 301–303, October, 1956.

[8] *Ibid.,* p. 301.

persuading him to read your copy. It can be effective in getting a reader to do you a favor: answer an inquiry, answer a questionnaire, etc. If you offer a reader the *reward* of humor, he will be more amenable to doing you a favor.

But there are problems involved in the use of humorous copy. Precisely what will provoke a grin, a chuckle, laughter, or revelry is an individual thing. When it comes to what is funny, the human race is not always in agreement. Professor Armour explains this problem: "Some people see the absurdities of life fleetingly, without much interest, certainly, without delight. Some people see them only in others, never in themselves." [9]

Everyone has had the experience of telling a story in one group and getting a hilarious reaction. He's also had the experience of having that same funny story draw an ear-splitting silence from another group. The reason is that people don't agree upon what is humorous. What's funny to a college student may be dull to an advertising man. What's playfully snide to one person may be scathingly mean to the person toward whom the humor is directed. Because of the differences in experience, bias, prejudice, perspectives, and inhibitions of individuals of different ages, groups, and professions, a unanimity of agreement as to what humor is seems to be impossible.

The direction of a humorous story or situation, however, *helps* to determine whether people will think it is funny. Stories are usually funny when the humor is directed toward another person or situation. They are not always funny when the humor is directed toward one's self. Men like jokes about women. Women like jokes about men. Neither sex, however, seems to like jokes about itself.

The *attitude* of the copy writer who is using humor also helps determine whether the reader will think the copy is funny. A copy writer's attitude should be one of playfulness, and he should convey this attitude to his readers. As Max Eastman said in his *Enjoyment of Laughter*, "The first law of humor is that things can be funny only when we are in fun . . . humor is play. Humor is being in fun. It has no value except the values possessed by play." [10] Richard Armour explains this attitude further: [11]

Involved in this whole matter of the *attitude* of a humor writer is a kind of playfulness and not taking himself or the day-to-day mishaps of life too seriously. His field is the minor faults and foibles of people. He leaves the major vices to the philosophers, the preachers, and the police. He laughs at the incongruities of life and cuts them down to size.

[9] *Ibid.*
[10] Max Eastman, *Enjoyment of Laughter,* Simon and Schuster, Inc., New York, 1936, pp. 3, 15.
[11] Armour, *op. cit.,* p. 302.

A humorist's restricting himself to the "minor faults and foibles of people" means that a copy writer cannot poke fun at things which are *serious* to his readers. Humor is not readily adaptable to advertising copy which has to do with sickness, accidents, health, savings—anything that is deadly serious to a reader. Humor has been used successfully with "serious" products, but the copy has not poked fun at that product or at the serious needs of the reader. Properly handled, however, humor *can* be used in product description, effectively.

This boils down to the basic rule for the use of humor in copy: *Don't poke fun at your reader. Laugh with him . . . not at him or his needs.*

This letter from *True* uses an interesting approach—with humor—to appeal to men. The copy might not appeal to women . . . but, then, *True* isn't writing to them:

TRUE
1 Fawcett Place, Greenwich, Conn.
The Man's Magazine

As ONE BUSY, discerning company president put it . . . "Cut out the pap—I'm already a subscriber to TRUE—have been for years. . . ." If you're in the same boat, please score two points by tossing this mailing piece into the handiest wastebasket. *But if you're not a subscriber to* TRUE, please, for Pete's* sake read on! (Reading time—45 seconds.)

TRUE is one of the few remaining sanctuaries for men only in the whole wide world. It is the be-all, end-all for the man who, shall we say, loves his wife, but, for Pete's † sake, wants an hour or two away from it all, in a world all his own. In the fields, maybe, or a trout stream, on the high seas, or in a bull-fighting arena, or any one or more of a thousand places where the male is King.

TRUE is high adventure by Hemingway, high humor by VIP, and highhandedness by Philip Wylie. TRUE is an inside straight, an outside bourbon and water, an upstairs maid, a downstairs billiard table. It's man-size reading, and Monroe-size looking. And, if nothing else, TRUE is *the largest selling man's magazine in the world.*

Put it this way: *Any man worth his salt wants* TRUE *to add just enough spice to his life to make it complete.*

The regular price of TRUE is 35 cents a copy or $4 for a yearly subscription, but right here and now I'm authorized to offer you a real bargain. It is almost too good to be TRUE.

10 ISSUES FOR $2.00   (Saving you $1.50)‡
or
22 ISSUES FOR $4.00   (Saving you $3.70)‡

I can keep this offer open for a month, but how about sending your order *right now* so we can shoot that first copy to you without delay?

Sincerely yours,
/s/
Ted Sloat

* Pete Barrett, TRUE's outdoor editor, very concerned about men who miss a lot when they miss TRUE.

† Pete Barrett again, still very concerned.

‡ If you enclose payment with your order you'll get an additional issue free. (This saves us a lot of bookkeeping.)

High-level Josh plays an important part in the use of humor in copy style. In approaching the suave and the smooth, a "near-flip" attitude can sometimes be effective.

People of high levels of sophistication, those who settle for nothing less than triple *entendre,* who love the subtle flavors of language, who like to play with words, can be approached with a tongue-in-cheek style of "josh." These people form an elite audience, measured not always in money, but always in taste and in knowledgeable perception. This class of people is the hand-made lace on the satin petticoat which hides the sameness of the human animal. Decorative, artistic, they make the drabness, the dullness, the monotony of "the everyday" seem more interesting, more satisfying to those who know not such circles. They don't need the money if their taste is right, if they can see that human antics, foibles, peccadilloes are merely scenes to be enjoyed from the wings on the stage of life—where the drama of the main act is made the more real by contrast with its own parts.

With these people the fabric of conversation is an artistic needlework of kindly snide syllables, cut with the shears of caustic comment, and bundled into a genuine appreciation of and love for all things human.

The next copy sample, which introduces a booklet, is a highly skilled presentation of a sales message within the flavorful confines of language at its best. It is handled with an affectionate appreciation of things human, an almost confidential tone, a dash of humor to spice things a trifle. This is Dorothy Malbon Parker—the copy writer—performing at her own high level of capability.

FIN 'N FEATHER FARM
R.F.D. 2, Dundee, Illinois

Revered Customer:

As if you didn't have enough on your mind—without Christmas! But it's headed for us, jet-propelled. The signs are everywhere, out here. There's the whir of wings overhead as birds with reservations down South take off. (Lucky bums! I can't even take Sunday off!) Underfoot, leaves crackle as squirrels scurry to their winter quarters—cheeks bulging like the mumps. (Nuts to them.) My youngest keeps pestering me to carve a pumpkin face, and it'll be Christmas-stocking talk, next.

Are you ready? Of course not! But I hope you're calm about it, knowing we'll be along to take care of you. Which we aim to do in bang-up style this year. Note *three* enclosures.

Game Birds, of course—just as you've come to count on 'em, in festive combination or solo performance. And we've added some irresistible new things in the food line. Like some very special and venerable Cheese.

We're doing more with Deerskin all the time, because people love the soft, practical stuff. And this year we decided to give everybody a chance at some of the hottest numbers in our Gift Shop. So take a look at that booklet. Might give you ideas for business gifts.

It's fine with us if you order 100 of everything you see. After 14 years at it we're set up to do things on a Big Scale. Wrapping fancy. Enclosing cards. Toting to the village post office. But we'll *live* longer if orders come before December 10th. And—this is our *un*selfish side—*you'll* have a lot Merrier Christmas if you get the whole works off your mind *now*.

Yours in a sweet burst of logic,

/s/

Carl J. Much

15

How to Develop
Theme in Your Mailings

Theme . . . Melodic Series

What is theme? Well, let's go to Webster and pick out a definition. Theme is ". . . a short, melodic series of notes constituting the subject of a musical composition or a phrase upon which variations are developed." What we want in direct mail theme creating, then, is a . . .

"*Subject . . . upon which variations can be developed.*"

And we'll get the same effect as a musical composition's rhythm—through its recurrence of a beat—in our repetition of an idea through different mailings or through different applications of our theme's subject.

Theme in direct mail can be quite a few things. Let's reduce it to three:

1. A *symbol* which is put to use in everything a business has—its mail, its packaging, its trucks, its personnel, its place of business.

2. The use of a subject upon which variations are developed to *unify* an impression which a *single* mailing piece seeks to create.

3. The use of a subject throughout a *series of mailings* in which variations on the subject appear in each mailing—to build a consistency of impression and a continuity of impact for the entire series.

Symbols as Themes

One of the most interesting symbols developed as a "corporate" theme during the last few years is the handshaking A's of Advertisers Associates, Inc., Pittsburgh, Pennsylvania. The late Les W. Gaupp, President, decided he needed a ". . . comprehensive redesign of every form of business stationery used by Advertisers Associates." [1]

The redesign job included ". . . letterheads and envelopes; invoices; quotation forms, business cards; blotters; checks; wrapping paper; shipping labels; identification labels; pickup envelopes; shipping cartons; truck lettering; decals; signs and logos as well as uniform insignia for messengers." [1]

All of the A-A stationery was analyzed in an attempt to develop a symbol which would fulfill these two objectives:

1. "To give basic identification to . . . [the] . . . business in many ways.

2. "To make a real salesman out of . . . [the company's] . . . identification." [1]

Several months and fifty "roughs" later, at a cost of $1,700, a basic design was worked out. Advertisers Associates came up with their—now copyrighted—trademark of two A's shaking hands. Why this design? We'll just lift part of a letter from Mr. Gaupp to explain. He tells us that:

> Since the very beginning of our business we have been known as a house of service; we managed to demonstrate our types of service many times by closely identifying ourselves with the sense of urgency, importance, and speed felt by the customer himself. What better way to display this feeling than by having the "Associates" shaking hands with the "Advertisers?"

If you'll notice, the *subject* of this theme—*the expression of an understanding of a customer's problems*—hits at the customer from every conceivable *variation* Advertisers Associates could work out in their contacts with a customer, by mail or through personal contact (truck lettering and uniform insignia). The theme is rhythmic in its consistency and in its recurrence of a beat—the repetition of the symbol.

Theme . . . Unity for a Single Impression

One good example of theme tying a mailing piece together is a self-mailer from Graphic Service, Dayton, Ohio. In this case the theme is "fasteners." The copy develops through telling of the progress made in the development of fasteners. It climaxes in the use of a most modern

[1] Les W. Gaupp, "Sales Pitch Shapes Redesign of Stationery," *The Post,* vol. 35, no. 4, p. 26, Mail Advertising Service Association (International), Washington, D.C., August, 1956.

plastic zipper to "separate" the self-mailer's action card. The copy opens with:

WHAT EVER HAPPENED TO

the hook-and-eye; the button; the lace; the elastic band? Well, most of them have zipped out of sight.

Then the contrast between the theme—fasteners—and the message—an offer to create professional direct mail for the reader—begins to develop:

And so it is with the catch-as-catch-can; homemade; often delayed; troublesome direct mail advertising that many companies used to do "internally."
Gone with the buttonhook.

Next development of theme is the transition from the "old-fashioned" fastener to the modern zipper. And this development is carried concurrently with the advantages of using professional skill in direct mail.

When your direct mail is turned over to specialists, it's done slicker, quicker, easier . . . like a zipper.
Pulls better, too.
In the end, that's what counts; whether the minds of your best prospects are "pulled" your way; "fastened" to your product or service.

In this preceding paragraph, theme is developed through the words "pulled" and "fastened"—to tie the advertising message tightly to the theme.

Direct Mail can do that . . . and direct mail prepared and produced by specialists usually does it best.
When you say "direct mail specialists," we come a runnin' . . .
So if you'd like to z-i-p your troubles away, direct mail—wise, just fill out the card below and . . . Z-Z-Z-Z-Z-Z-Z-I-P.

Note, in the illustration, how the "theme" climaxes in the drama of a real zipper, newest of its kind, which holds the reply card to the self-mailer.
And on the reply card . . . the theme carries through:

O.K., Graphic . . . Z-I-P over and see me.

This is an example of theme being developed in copy which is "tight" as it can be made. And which correlates the most modern of fasteners—the zipper—with the most modern of direct mail services—skilled professional talent. Many ideas—such as fasteners—can be used to unify a piece of writing. And at the same time to create drama and novelty, as this zipper mailing does.

Theme . . . Unity for a Series of Impressions

Notable among examples of using theme for consistency of impact is the spectacular, sixteen-piece Currency series which Union Bag–Camp Paper Corporation mailed in 1957.

The theme of Union's Currency series was the different mediums of exchange used throughout history. The idea was to present Union's "5-Star Plan" for selling Multiwall bags, by using various types of currency to illustrate that:

Money has value and usefulness only in terms of what it will buy. The test of an expert buyer is not alone the price he pays. The real standard is value received.[2]

Here is a descriptive list of the Union Bag–Camp Paper mailings as printed in *The Reporter of Direct Mail Advertising,* October, 1957, pages 28 to 33. Note how the use of currency unifies all the mailings into a continuous theme, how "Money should be measured according to value received" is hammered home again and again:

Mailing	*Description*
1	*Theme:* Mailed from Rome, N.Y., a small box with a real Roman Tetradachin over 1,600 years old. *Sales message:* "Roman Emperor Diocletian had budget problems, too."
2	*Theme:* Letter tells of exciting days in Roman economy . . . how Emperor Diocletian discovered "Money has value and usefulness only in terms of what it will buy." *Sales message:* "Shrewd buyers look beyond price alone."
3	*Theme:* A booklet tells of "financial manipulations of Jergen Von Schlick . . . how his currency capers resulted in the name 'thalers,' 'dolars,' then 'dollars.'" *Sales message:* "You should be concerned with what dollars buy."
4	*Theme:* A miniature bolt of Massachusetts-milled cotton as used by white and native traders in colonial days. Letter printed on bolt told how African corruption of word "American" named this cloth currency "Merikani." *Sales message:* "The test of an expert buyer is not price alone. The real standard is price received."
5	*Theme:* A folder with pictures of a 1516 taler and the Three Wise Men. . . . Christmas: "May the new year bring you the gifts of well-being, achievement, and peace of mind."
6	*Theme:* Folder tells of "The Man who Grew Money"—a colonist in the state of Franklin, now Tennessee. Goods were made legal tender . . . because of shortage of coins. *Sales message:* Short case history of sugar refiner who saved $510,000 through Union's "5-Star Plan" . . . pointing out the real value of money.

[2] "Union Bag–Camp Paper Corp. Campaign is Top Direct Mail Leader of 1957," *The Reporter of Direct Mail Advertising,* vol. 20, no. 6, p. 28, October, 1957.

7   *Theme:* Folder entitled "Wife Bait" tells of natives using feathers of rare birds . . . for wife trading.
Sales message: " 'Feather Money' . . . like other mediums of exchange . . . is important to the extent of what it will buy."

8   *Theme:* Booklet with *Treasure Island* motif . . . presents money-clip copy of "piece of eight." Copy tells derivation of "two bits," "six bits," from dividing piece of eight during shortage of small coins.
Sales message: "The dollars you invest in Multiwall (bags) also can be divided into parts . . . to save thousands of dollars."

9   *Theme:* Folder shows how rarely used sizes of bags just gather dust on shelf. Cover illustration of feather duster leads reader to inside spread of coins and Multiwall containers.
Sales message: "Whether you are operating the national mint or a business that uses large quantities of Multiwall (money in another form), the opportunity exists to save by eliminating unnecessary sizes."

10   *Theme:* Folder entitled "Money to Burn" tells how Chinese burn spirit money to ward off devils.
Sales message: "When you buy Multiwall bags, you expect the packaging service that accompanies your order to be more than a gesture."

11   *Theme:* A boxed salt disc with folder telling how Roman soldiers were paid in *salarium*—Latin for salt rations. Hence the English word—salary.
Sales message: "Whatever form it takes, the true measure of money is how much it brings in return."

12   *Theme:* Folder describes how nineteenth-century Borneo used human skulls as the standard monetary unit.
Sales message: Copy switched to new Multiwall package design.

13   *Theme:* Giant folder describes stone money—pancaked boulders ranging from 12 inches to 12 feet in diameter—used on the Pacific Island of Yap.
Sales message: "Massive or miniature, money is what you make it. What you make of it—value received—is the true gauge of the currency's worth."

14   *Theme:* A gate-fold piece with a die cut showing an original 10-heller (cents) piece . . . issued by the Vienna suburb of Hadersfeld during a shortage in 1920. Copy told of other countries—China, Germany, Canada, Greece, Sweden—using wooden wampum during crises and shortages.
Sales message: "All money, for that matter, has little real value—except what it buys."

15   *Theme:* Folder, which contained a magic paper cutting-mending trick, tells how reduced bag breakage means reduced labor cost.

Sales message: "The real power of pennies (or dollars), no matter how you slice them, is how much they buy."

16   *Theme:* A money-making machine which produced (1) a dollar bill, (2) a simulated check for $129,000 (representing money saved by a major Multiwall user), and (3) a bill-sized recap of Union's "5-Star Plan."

Sales message: Recap tells how "5-Star Plan" can make money for reader.

16

How to Select
Direct Mail Formats

The formats of direct advertising are limited only by the imagination of the creator. Direct advertising can be created to fulfill the needs of any user's problem. Size, shape, pictures, type, and colors give an unlimited scope to a direct mail man's ability to express ideas. Direct mail is unlike other media. It knows no predetermined specifications which limit creativity.

The following information and explanations are designed to give you a general picture of the elements that affect selection of physical form.[1]

In selecting the format for your direct mail, you should first consider:
1. The purpose for which the mailing piece is to be designed
2. The physical essentials of the format chosen

Any well-planned use of direct mail, naturally, defines the purpose for which the piece or pieces is or are intended—before the formats are selected. Then physical essentials in terms of purpose, necessary illustration, type of mailing list, budget, etc. must be considered.

Direct Mail's Four Purposes

Almost all direct advertising could be classified into four groups. Informative, Persuasive, Reminder, and Utility. Of course, some pieces

[1] *How to Build Sales by Mail*, Cavanagh Printing Company, St. Louis (n.d.).

have a dual or multiple function and would fall into more than one of these groups. However, for our purposes, here is a logical breakdown.

1. *First Purpose . . . Informative Direct Mail:* This includes any mailing pieces which merely give information. No immediate action by your reader is asked. Some pieces could, however, trigger a reader reaction. Changes in price lists, for example, could conceivably cause an action by the reader. But the intent of the price-list change is merely to inform. Types of formats which can be used to give information include:

Letters	Catalogues
Invitations	Price lists
Sales manuals	Survey, research, and informative
Instruction books	bulletins, and forms
House organs	Counter, store, and window displays
Package enclosures	

2. *Second Purpose . . . Persuasive Direct Mail:* This is the type of mailing which tries to get the reader to do something at once: send in an order; make an inquiry; telephone. This is where you find mail order selling. The types of formats which can be used for persuasion include:

Letters	Giant letters
Illustrated letters	Miniature newspapers
Folders	Post cards or mailing cards
Booklets	Die-cut action pieces
Broadsides	premiums, coupons
Brochures	Business reply action forms

3. *Third Purpose . . . Reminder Direct Mail:* This type of direct mail merely reminds the person who receives it of the sender, his product, and/or his services. This is an extremely effective area of direct mail. It ranges from "Cordial-contact" letters or cards, to blotters, to the fine "art" reproduction such as those put out by Lakeside Press. Formats which can be used as reminders include:

Letters	Cards
Calendars	Blotters
Printed novelties	Reprints
Preprints	Memoranda
Notebooks	Diaries
Pads	

4. *Fourth Purpose . . . Utility Direct Mail:* This is where you find the direct mail which may have a primary purpose of carrying out one job. But which, at the same time, functions in another way. The example of Advertisers Associates under "Theme" in this book shows you how utility pieces create a continuity of impact through repetition of a *theme.* And

this theme, in the case of Advertisers Associates, is carried out through the use of handshaking A's. The primary purposes of the pieces may be something else. But the actual formats have a utility purpose also. The A-A invoices request payment. The A-A tape seals. The A-A business cards announce. The A-A newsletter carries information. And so forth . . . all utilitarian jobs.

But, while being useful in helping a business function, they also hammer home that symbol, that theme—"A-A."

Formats which can be used as utility pieces in direct mail include:

Letterheads	Envelopes
Business cards	Business reply cards and envelopes
Labels	Order blanks
Printed packages and cartons	Tape
Wrapper paper	Newsletters

The Physical Essentials of Formats

After you have determined your *purpose,* ask yourself these questions to help determine which format best suits your purpose:

1. How long is my story, and how much will be copy, how much pictures? (If it is short, will a post card possibly do? If it is long, must I use a broadside to tell all, or can I use a folder, or a combination of letter and folder?)

2. How much space will be required for adequate display? (Can I show one small cut of my product and make my prospects understand what it is? Or must I show photos of it in use; cutaways to show how it operates; tables, graphs, and charts to show its performance record, etc.?)

3. Whom am I trying to sell? (Should the piece be designed to fit a filing folder in a purchasing office, a business office, or a teacher's files? Should it be designed to make a big but quick impression among many competing pieces of mail in a busy office or to be read more leisurely at home? Should it be simple or elaborate, dignified or corny?)

4. What is my limitation on the amount I can spend? (How many pieces will this amount buy? After dividing the number of pieces into the amount I have, can I buy post cards, letters, and folders or just letters or folders, envelopes, business reply envelopes and order forms . . . or must I leave out some of these . . . or should I cut my list?)

5. How will the piece be distributed? (Could it be a self-mailer and still do the job? Is it to fit into some other mailing device, into a package or into rack space, or both? Does it have to meet point-of-sale or other distribution requirements as to size, shape, and content? Must it take a beating in the mail alone, or will it be protected with an envelope? Is it small enough to go through handling without becoming too dog-eared?)

6. Does it fully meet postal requirements? Is the size mailable and mailable in the class I wish to use? If it is an envelope, have I used no more space on the front for advertising than regulations allow? If it is a gadget letter, have I chosen a gadget that is not mailable or one that will not survive cancellation and other rough handling? [2]

Direct Mail Formats

The major direct mail formats are highly varied. For almost any purpose, you can develop a format which will do a successful job for you. The advantages of the various formats . . . and when to use them . . . are presented to you here. Letters, as a format, have been presented briefly in this chapter. For a thorough discussion of the possibilities of uses for letters, see Chapters 22 and 23.

The Most Widely Used Format . . . in direct mail is composed of the outside envelope, the letter, a circular, an order card or reply form, a business reply envelope. This format is used particularly in mail-order efforts. It must be remembered, however, that . . . though this format may work well in many instances . . . it doesn't work as well as other formats under many circumstances.

The Letter . . . Direct Mail's "Work Horse." Letters can perform every possible direct-mail function. The letter is, actually, the work horse of direct mail . . . the format which is used—successfully—for more purposes than any other advertising form.

Letters, the most adaptable, most personal, most flexible direct-mail format, can do a good job—by themselves . . . or in conjunction with almost every other form of direct mail.

Letters can give economy to the mailer with a small list. In many cases, the cost of printed matter which involves typesetting and printing press work is prohibitive. Letters help overcome such a problem. For they are economical in large or small quantities . . . and can be produced by a variety of processes—multigraph, mimeograph, printing, automatic typing.

But, let's go to St. John Associates, a top-flight New York letter shop, for a further definition of a letter: [3]

A LETTER IS MANY THINGS . . .
ambassador and advocate, missionary and emissary, chronicler and counselor, salesman and statesman. It is as direct as a challenge, as disarming as a diplomat, as personal as a request. It can laugh, strut, amuse, assure, cheer, confront,

---

[2] *How to Use the Mails for Sales,* Bureau of Business Management, University of Illinois Bulletin, vol. 51, no. 65, University of Illinois Press, Urbana, Ill., May, 1954, pp. 10–11.

[3] *The Wolf Magazine of Letters,* The Wolf Envelope Company, Cleveland, pp. 11–12, April, 1958.

congratulate, offer, urge, request. It can propose with the imperiousness of an emperor. It can ask with the diffidence of a courtier. It can leap boldly to a proposal, lie in wait for a foregone conclusion, whisper a suggestion, plead for a cause.

To the Postmaster General, a letter is most of the billion pieces of mail his department handles in the course of a year.

To the Salesman, looking for a way to open a prospect's door, a letter is a chance to knock ahead of time.

To the Retailer, it is a way to let his best customers know he has something special for them.

To the Advertising Man, it is a way to merchandise an idea, to announce a campaign, to register a favorable impression.

To the Businessman, it is the way to say what he means and have it in writing—to reach the people he needs and wants to reach at the right time, at the right place, in the right way.

For a letter is, and always has been, *the next best thing to being there in person.* And in today's business world—when being there is as difficult as it is essential—as swift and inexpensive a device as a letter can put you almost anywhere you want to be by this time tomorrow.

The Penscript Letter . . . an imitation of handwriting, has been particularly effective with offers to women. Usually on a professional size, 7¼ by 10½ inches, they can be made up in any size or color you want. You can have a personalized fill-in which will match the letter copy, by having the person whose handwriting was reproduced to create the letter do the personalizing. Although penscript has been successfully used with women, it can also be used with other types of lists. (It is also effective when used as memos . . . and as a P.S.)

Giant Letters . . . are effective when you want to do something "special"—actually a type of broadside. Giant letters can be used to emphasize *bigness* as a product feature, to create "smash" in the opener of a campaign, to announce something new. Usually 17 by 22 inches, the giant letter can be personalized with a jumbo-size typewriter. Which, incidentally, can also be used to set up the copy.

Miniature Letters . . . can be used when you want to reinforce your selling message with the endorsement of satisfied customers. This is done by reducing customer letters to ¼ size and using them as testimonial enclosures. Edward N. Mayer, Jr., says that the miniature letter is ". . . particularly valuable in the sale of small products (and) . . . highly successful in selling feminine products to feminine lists." [4]

The Four-page Letter . . . called by some direct mailers the "combination letter and circular," can be created in a variety of ways. Using the 11- by 17-inch sheet folded across the 11-inch width, page 1, or pages

[4] Edward N. Mayer, Jr., *How to Make More Money with Your Direct Mail,* 3d ed., Printers' Ink Books, New London, Conn., 1957, p. 159.

1 and 4 can be used as the letter. The center spread then forms a circular. Some mailers have found it advisable in their use of this format to use pages 1 and 2 for the circular and page 3 for the letter.

The four-page letter can be used to answer inquiries . . . where you use the letter to answer, to introduce and draw attention to the information presented.

The Illustrated Letters . . . can be used for diverse purposes. Basically, they are used to create interest, to help your selling message by illustrating the product or service, to give a change of pace to a campaign, to create a difference in contrast with what you have been doing. You have three types of illustrated letters, each of which is effective:

1. *The Capers-in-context Illustrated Letter* is something like a cross between a comic strip character (taken out of his frame and put to work for you) and a regular letter. This type of illustrated letter replaces (or supplements) words, in the letter's context, with drawings or sketches of what the word means. Because of the difficulty of illustrating complex words in a drawing which will take the place of a word, or add meaning to it, the drawings are usually derived from simple words. Not always, naturally. The ingenuity of a copy writer and an artist can sometimes simplify complexities.

At those times, then, when you wish to give a letter a lilt, a touch of humor, an overtone of difference, use illustrations in the context of the copy. Maybe you want to add life to a page, make the words caper from the printed word into a sketch. This adds vitality to a page. In that case you have a caper-in-context type of illustrated letter.

What happens in this type of letter is that you have taken the idea of an attention getter and spread it throughout the copy . . . to renew attention, to build more interest, to help the reader get "involved" with your message.

2. *The Something-has-been-added* type of illustrated letter has some form of letterhead which illustrates the product, the sales curve, or anything else which can be used to tie in immediately with the opener and the main selling point of your letter. Your illustration can be at the top of the page . . . to one side of the opening paragraph . . . or down one side of the letter.

This type of illustration, which can be anything which has a relevant point in relation to the opener and your main selling argument, doesn't interrupt the copy in any way. You wouldn't illustrate down the center of a page. Because you would interrupt the reader's eye movement and make it difficult to read.

3. *The Other-sources* . . . *Other-talents* type of illustrated letter offers you the abilities of many people . . . on the basis of your own taste and

selection—for almost any purpose you can devise. For you can get from various sources illustrated letterheads—with or without appropriate copy.

This type of illustrated letter is excellent for use during the many national holidays . . . or for the many special occasions to which you can adapt it. The designs of these letterheads are greatly varied and offer you many provocative ideas. They are good for creating a difference, for a change of pace, for standout effectiveness.

Two of the many companies which offer these letterheads are the Arthur Thompson Company,* or Goes Lithographing Company.* See Chapter 11 for a discussion of the use of ready-made formats.

Folders . . . Inexpensive and Flexible. Comparatively inexpensive, extremely flexible, folders are the most commonly used of all forms of printed advertising. And like other creative materials available to you in direct mail, folders are virtually unlimited as to size, to shape, to style.

Folders are found halfway between letters and the booklet. They can be used to inform, to instruct, to persuade, to remind, or to bring back orders. You can use them:

1. To precede and follow more elaborate forms, books, presentations
2. To present brief messages which hammer home sales points concisely . . . and in a quickly grasped fashion
3. As a series of mailings
4. As "single-shot" efforts
5. As enclosures with letters

Booklets . . . the Longer Story. When you have a lengthy story to tell —and feel that you want to create prestige without elaborateness with your mailing—use a booklet.

Designed to give completeness to a story which calls for study or thorough reading . . . and with an overtone of "permanence" to imply it should be "kept" around a while, the booklet creates dignified impact. The booklet, to do its job (which can be as flexible as that of a folder), must be well written, well laid out for ease of reading. You can use booklets as instruction books, price lists, directories, catalogues, sales books, house organs.

Broadsides . . . the "Smash" of Bigness. The "size" of your message and the impact you desire determine the use of broadsides.

And when you want a "smash" impact and standout *emphasis* on specific ideas you are presenting . . . a surface which permits boldness of expression, and the psychology of size, use the broadside.

Actually large folders, broadsides can be used to put "smash" into your "kickoff" mailing in a campaign . . . or for special announcements which call for drama and size.

Skilled layout and design are imperative in developing broadsides.

* See SOURCE LIST for full names and addresses.

They should be easily handled by the reader. And should lead him in an orderly fashion from the beginning, through the various folds, clear to the end. Poor design will confuse. And, more importantly, won't sell.

In mailing broadsides, put them on their journey alone as self-mailers or in an envelope.

Brochures . . . Glamour, Richness, and Dignity. When you want to impress the richness and dignity of a product or service . . . and the stature of a company upon a reader, use a brochure.

The "glamour" girl of this Cinderella advertising medium, the brochure offers you elaborateness in a combination of creative materials: illustration, color, paper. The brochure implies power, worth, value, prestige.

Circulars . . . to Complete the Mail-order Story. Using a circular to accompany a mail-order letter is like copying the door-to-door salesman's pitch, once he discovers some interest in his product.

The letter and circular have to tell the prospect everything. In direct mail selling you have no one to answer any questions, except the direct mail piece. People who are definitely not interested will not even read a short circular or a one-page letter. Those who are mildly interested can be built up by giving all the information to push over the sale.

A circular must stand on its own, do its selling job. The elements which must be included in a circular are:

1. A graphic illustration (art) of what is being offered.

2. An illustration of the product or service *in use* . . . if possible.

3. Detailed information about the product or service. (A brief circular will bring fewer returns.)

4. A coupon which, when filled out and returned, will bring the product or service being offered (true even if you have enclosed a separate order form).

5. Inks and typography, appropriate to the product or service and to the message, and which make for easy reading.

6. A layout which is skillfully planned to lead the reader through the circular in proper sequence.

Mailing Cards . . . Inexpensive Brevity. Mailing cards, usually the least expensive of all forms of printed advertising, have great utility value. You can use mailing cards for brief announcements . . . not confidential; when budgets restrict you from more expensive forms; when you want to use "teasers" to introduce a campaign; when single messages or thoughts are desirable to influence prospects or obtain leads; when quick reminders are effective.

You can also use mailing cards when the time element is most important . . . when notices, announcements, invitations, and other short, direct messages lend themselves to this inexpensive, open, quick-reading format.

Unusual Forms . . . for Drama, Realism. Cutouts, pop-ups, novelties, and sample pieces can be used when realism is desired or when you want to add a touch of the dramatic to a mailing piece. Use them when you want to make a fast, simple impression on the prospect's mind—to gain his immediate interest.

When you want to show things, to emphasize a point that cannot be done in other forms of advertising, use the unusual form. Original, individual, effective presentations of products and services, or their features, can be effected through forms that are different and unusual. And your impact can be forcefully emphatic and appropriate.

Advertising Reprints and Preprints . . . to Double Your Impact. Reprints or preprints of your general magazine advertising always increase the effectiveness of that advertising. These reprints and preprints can be obtained from most publishers . . . on a rather inexpensive folder-type format, which includes the cover in full color . . . or as separate copies without the magazine's cover.

You can mail plain reprints or preprints as an enclosure with letters or memos. Or, you can use the folder-type format, which carries the magazine's cover, your ad, and more copy. Using the magazine cover gives the impact of "as advertised in," lets the magazine's prestige add to your story.

Simulated Telegram . . . for Urgency. A "take-off" on Mr. Western Union's favorite format, the simulated telegram is good for creating attention or for developing a sense of urgency. The message, too, should have the same impact of urgency as the telegram format has. Otherwise, the reader's conditioned attitude toward a telegram has not been properly appealed to.

Because of the touch of urgency based on the reader's attitude toward telegrams, this format can be used as a campaign "kickoff"—to get attention. And as an *imperative* campaign closer.

To carry through the integrity of the real format, combine your company name or campaign theme (or any other adaptable idea) with "-o-GRAM"—"PEP-O-GRAM," for a vitamin company, for example. Be careful. Don't bill it as a "telegram" or imitate one too closely. Mr. Western Union doesn't like it.

Self-mailers . . . Cost Reducers. Any type of direct mail format which can be mailed without an envelope is a self-mailer—folder, booklet, mailing card, circular, brochure, broadside, and others. But caution: Brochures imply top quality . . . so mailing them without an envelope reduces your quality impact.

The ability to withstand the trip through the postal system requires a piece of sufficient body and at times some kind of seal to keep the piece closed to comply with postal regulations.

Self-mailers help keep your mailing costs down. The advantage of lower costs, however, results in the piece being immediately recognized as advertising. To compensate, some mailers advocate the use of "teaser" or "benefit" copy on the outside—to lead the reader inside to your commercial.

Invitations . . . for "Newness" . . . a Change of Pace. Because the invitation format implies a "special" or "in-group" atmosphere, it is effective for special offers, for announcing something new. And it is effective as a change of pace in a series of mailings.

A "copy" of the personal invitation, this format creates an overtone of exclusiveness to help put *force* into the message it carries. And, like so many of your creative materials in direct mail, its shape and size are limited only by ingenuity, cost, mailability.

Blotters . . . Hard-sell "Reminders." The blotter is an inexpensive type of direct mail used to carry short, strong, sales messages, with or without illustration. It may carry product or service information, directions for use, etc. And it can be used as a miniature house organ. Blotters and calendars are leading forms of "reminder" direct mail, though blotters are becoming less popular year after year.

The Order Form . . . Reply Cards . . . Direct Mail's "Dotted Line." A wise direct mail man once said, "When you begin to prepare a mailing, write the reply card first, then you know where you're going." This is good advice. Even if your mailing will not, when completed, include a reply card, it's really profitable to prepare the copy for one.

What's the function of a reply card?

The reply card is the prospect's *reply* to you. And you assume that, as the result of the persuasive, convincing, believable story you've told in your copy, the reader will be brought around to your way of thinking and will send in the card. Fact of the matter is: if he *hasn't* been, he *won't* send it in, so that assumption is sound. Therefore, the typical reply card says, in the prospect's language and from his point of view, what you want him to feel concerning your proposition.

So you can see that this suggestion to "start with the reply card" is simply another approach to our admonition to begin by putting yourself in the reader's shoes.

A certain bit of human psychology gives us an additional opportunity on the reply card. Apparently a substantial percentage of readers, when opening a letter which contains a reply card, read the reply card first. *Then* they decide whether to read the letter.

For these readers your reply card must be interesting. It assumes the same importance as the opening sentence or headline in the letter, and it should probably answer or touch on the answer to the question, "What's in it for me?"

So a safe approach to the copy on a reply card is to restate, in the prospect's words, those *benefits* of the proposition which are most important *to him*. Then have him indicate that he wants to do what you want him to do.

Of course, curiosity can be used just as well. A reply card containing the one word message, "YES," with the recipient's name typed in, will carry the reader to the letter without difficulty.

There also seems to be a feeling, among expert direct mail users, that an attractive reply card has advantages, and that even the design of the front of a business reply card can have its effect on the reader.

Some illustration on the message side of the card seems to improve its readability and help point up its message, too. In many cases, particularly when the product being advertised is not completely familiar to the reader, an illustration of the product or of the part of the product which produces the greatest benefit will increase returns.

Many mailers improve the selling power of a reply card by adding a "flap" or perforated end, to put a message on both sides of the card. The reader tears off the message end before mailing the card. In this way a larger card can be used without paying extra postage.

As far as size is concerned, most mailings can use cards within the acceptable limits for mailing as a post card (3$\frac{1}{16}$ by 5$\frac{9}{16}$ inches, maximum, 2$\frac{3}{4}$ by 4 inches, minimum). Larger cards require a higher rate of postage.

Making the reply card an "air mail" one doesn't necessarily seem to increase its effectiveness. Though the returns, naturally, arrive a bit sooner. And that's important sometimes.

The use of stamps, on the other hand, frequently increases returns. And some fund raisers have found it well worthwhile to stamp their return envelopes. They collect some criticism from folks who feel they are wasting money. But they seem to collect a lot more in pledges.

Naturally all these elements are minor details in determining the response. The major element is the step you ask the reader to take. If your message now reads, "Please have a salesman call on _____, _____ at ____ o'clock," you'll get a high-quality response, but you probably won't be overwhelmed with returns.

If you run counter to all the technical suggestions listed here (use a dull-looking, all-type card, with no offer to pay the postage, for example) but change the message to: "Sign and mail this card for your chance on a free trip to Europe. . . . Only 100 of these cards have been mailed," you'll probably get about 95 back. The other five? Well, if your mailing list is typical, 95 per cent delivery is pretty good.

The House Organ . . . Promoter of Mutual Interests. According to Benjamin Fine, there are about 6,000 house organs (call them house

magazines if you will), which have a circulation of 150,000,000.[5] Printers'
Ink Books publishes a *Directory of House Organs,* which gives you a list
of house-organ titles and a list of those whom the magazines represent.
The 1954 directory listed 6,329 house organs of various types.

From the number of house organs circulated and the extent of that
circulation, you can infer the extent to which the house organ is used
to promote mutual interests, to develop and maintain good will, to help
promote sales, and the multitude of other purposes to which they are
devoted.

The S. D. Warren Company, Boston, defines a house organ this way: [6]

A house organ is a publication issued periodically by a person, partnership,
corporation, or association to help advance the mutual interests of those who
issue the house organ and those to whom it is distributed.

The types of house organs are then broken down, in the Warren definition, on the basis of who is to receive them. Here is that breakdown:

1. *House Organs for Employees*
   Purpose: To explain company aims and policies, to promote acquaintances
   between employees, and to stimulate the interest of each employee in his
   work and in the organization of which he is a part.
   To be circulated to: Office and plant employees, officers of the company.[7]
2. *House Organs for Dealers*
   Purpose: To furnish dealers information and ideas that will help them
   to sell . . . (a company's) . . . products. To give dealers full and complete information about *all* (that company's) . . . products.
   To be circulated to: Dealers and their salesmen; and to the office and
   sales force of the company . . . (which sponsors it).[8]
3. *House Organs for Users and Prospective Users*
   Purpose: To make customers more fully conscious of . . . (a company's) . . . products—what they are, what they will do, and where
   they can be bought. To inform customers how to use the products profitably.
   To be circulated to: All known customers and prospects; the office people and sales force of the . . . (sponsoring) . . . company; all dealers
   who may request it.[9]

The form of a house organ can vary anywhere from a post card, to a
one-sheet newsletter, to a newspaper, to the various magazine sizes. The

[5] Edward L. Bernays (ed.), *The Engineering of Consent,* University of Oklahoma
Press, Norman, Okla., 1955, p. 192.
[6] *More Business through House Organs,* rev. ed., S. D. Warren Company, Boston,
May, 1951, p. 1.
[7] *Ibid.,* p. 26.
[8] *Ibid.,* p. 40.
[9] *Ibid.,* p. 53.

physical form will depend upon what you are trying to achieve. If you are attempting to imply prestige as part of your house organ, then you get into the more elaborate forms and into the subtleties of paper quality, reproduction methods, color, and the like. If you're interested only in an occasional "reminder," then your form can be simpler. These factors, as set up by Harrie Bell, will help you determine what form to use: [10]

1. The amount of material and illustration you wish to use in each issue.

2. The way in which you plan to distribute the house organ. The size of the necessary envelope . . . or whether it's to be a self-mailer will both have a bearing. Is it easily and readily addressed and mailed—if you wish to mail it? Is it easily carried . . . if you wish its reader to "pick it up?"

3. The conditions under which those you expect to read it will read it. If it's distributed at the plant, is it of such a size that readers will take it home— easily? Or, is it conveniently read and handled, if read at an office?

4. The nature of the contents you will use. Maybe you'll use material which readers will wish to file for future reference. In that case . . . size will make a difference. You can, if your house organ has a continuing supply of information valuable for filing, have a form which carries punched holes for standard-size binders.

These are not all the means of determining the form of a house organ, but they will help you find your way to the best form for your purposes.

[10] Harrie Bell, *Getting the Right Start in Direct Advertising*, The Reporter of Direct Mail Advertising, Garden City, N.Y. (n.d.).

17

Methods of Reproducing
Direct Mail

Of course, after you have chosen your mailing piece, you still must decide what method of reproduction to use. You have many choices. And there's no one answer, for all processes have their advantages and disadvantages. So you'll make your choice, depending on the purpose of your piece, how much money you have to spend, what quality of printing or duplicating you want, the size of your mailing list, whether you want illustrations, whether you want your mailing "personalized," how quickly you must have it in the mail, and possibly some other factors . . . including your personal prejudices about a process.

For printed materials, the choice is not particularly difficult. Even so, it is well to know the various methods and their particular area of usefulness.

Letterpress Printing

The traditional printing method is letterpress printing. Almost everybody is acquainted with the steps involved. Pieces of metal type, an engraved piece of metal, or a piece of plastic with raised areas is locked in a printing press, covered with ink, and then pressed onto a sheet of paper. Wherever the type or engraving has been raised above the level surface, it has received ink. And this ink is transferred to the paper. Letterpress printing presses, used commercially, vary from the small multi-graph machine, job press, or flat bed to massive newspaper and magazine presses.

Lithography

A second form of printing is Lithography, also known as "offset lithography," "offset," "planographing," and "photo-lithography." The early lithographers used a huge flat stone, on which an image was drawn, in reverse, with a grease pencil or other greasy substance. Water was then spread over the stone, which accepted the water in all places except where the grease had been applied. Subsequently covered with ink, the stone refused to accept the ink wherever the water had penetrated (since ink and water don't mix), leaving only the greasy area to "ink up." When paper was pressed against the stone, of course, it accepted the ink from the greasy areas. And the impression was right side up.

Today's lithography, however, is done by the "offset" process on rotary presses. For offset lithography, a thin, flexible plate is processed by the same basic procedure as was used on the stone. That is, some spots on the plate are treated so as to receive ink and other spots to reject it. Of course, the process has become highly refined and is usually done photographically. With photography, the area which has an affinity for ink can be reduced to a spot the size of the point of a pin. So it is possible to reproduce gradations of tone just as accurately as with the letterpress method.

The plate, in offset lithography, is prepared right side up and put in a printing press. After the water and ink have been applied to it, via rollers, the plate passes a rubber "blanket," and the image is transferred from the plate to the blanket. The blanket then transfers it to a sheet of paper, where it is reproduced, of course, right side up and frontwards. One distinct advantage of this offset method is that there is no wear on the original plate. The blanket touches only the ink, which it removes. And the eventual wear on the rubber blanket, caused by contact with the paper, is not significant, because a worn blanket can easily be replaced.

The offset method of printing is not restricted to lithography. And "offset letterpresses" are also in use. But the term is so generally used with the lithographic process that the word "offset," when used by printers, is synonymous with lithography.

In both letterpress and offset, plates can be made photographically, so drawings and photographs may be reproduced. The lithographic plate, however, is less expensive to make. For this reason, you will find the lithographic process more economical for direct mail pieces which contain many photographs. In general, long runs seem to be more economical when lithographed.

If, on the other hand, a job is primarily the reproduction of some metal type, and the run is less than, perhaps 10,000, letterpress would be more economical, for the type can merely be set and run without the intermediate step of plate making.

It is not our place to say which of these two major methods produces the finest quality. However, it is fair to say that, to the layman's eye, beautiful reproductions can be obtained by either process.

Most common types of paper stock can be printed by either process, too. Paper with rather deep indentations, such as might be found in an imitation leather cover, cannot be printed satisfactorily by letterpress, but might be run offset.

Hairline register of any number of colors is available in both processes.

Intaglio

The intaglio process of printing is the one used for such items as "engraved" letterheads and calling cards. Since the word "engraving" is used quite generally to describe the metal plate (or "cut") prepared for letterpress printing, it is sometimes confusing to speak of engraving in connection with intaglio printing.

When the intaglio process is used, the image which is to be printed is cut *into*, that is *below*, the surface of a metal plate. Then ink is rubbed over the entire surface of the plate and subsequently wiped off. It remains, of course, in the grooves of the image.

When paper is pressed against this plate, the ink in the grooves adheres to the paper and pulls off. Because there is a "thickness" to the ink, it can be clearly felt by rubbing a finger over the surface.

An imitation of intaglio printing, which is done by letterpress, followed by the application of heat to raise the letters, is generally available, too.

Rotogravure

Rotogravure, a type of intaglio printing on high-speed rotary presses, is so seldom used in direct mail that it is hardly worth mentioning, except to say that if your material has many pages and you expect to run in the hundreds of thousands, you should investigate the possibilities of "gravure."

Silk Screen

If you want to put your copy on an unusual surface, like cloth, cardboard, wood, or glass, which cannot conveniently be run through a printing press, or if you have a relatively small run of many colors, you may decide to use the silk-screen process. Basically, in this process, a piece of silk is covered with a thin piece of nonporous, film-like substance, which is then carefully cut away (either by knife or through a photographic process) wherever you want ink to go through. The silk is tacked to a frame, making a sort of open-topped box with the silk as the bottom. A rather thick ink is spread across the silk with a squeegie, so that the ink goes through the silk wherever the film has been cut away. The process *resembles* mimeographing (described later) in that both processes press ink through a stencil. But the results are quite different because of the differences in the ink. Silk-screen ink is tacky and dries by exposure to air. So it does not have to penetrate. Silk screen can produce brilliant colors, printed (after drying) one on top of the other if desired.

Letters and Other Typewritten Material

When your direct mail consists of letters or other typewritten material, you have many more processes from which to choose.

While any of the previously mentioned methods of reproduction may be used for letters, there are a number of other processes in general use.

Automatic Typing. Letters can be prepared on an automatic typewriter which, of course, actually types them individually at considerably less expense than when they are personally typed. In this case a "master" is made, by using a roll of punched paper similar to a player-piano roll, or a paper tape to actuate the typewriter electronically, or by some other method.

Following the direction of this master, the automatic typewriter types letters approximately twice as fast as a speedy typist, generally with fewer errors.

The machine can be set to stop at selected points so that the name and address of the recipient and additional material in the body of the letter may be inserted by the operator, typing on the keyboard of the same machine. And, depending upon the length and complexity of a letter, one operator can keep four or five automatic typewriters going at one time.

Multigraphing or Flat-bed–press Processing. These methods of duplicating letters imitate typewriting as closely as possible. They use the letterpress process of printing, but with an *inked ribbon* replacing the printer's ink. You may use either a flat-bed letterpress with ribbon "tacked" over the type, or a rotary letterpress (the multigraph), which was originally designed to imitate typing closely and which contains a wide, moving ribbon. In either case, the type face is a duplicate of the type face on a typewriter. But it is set in the same manner as printer's type, either in individual pieces of type or in linotype slugs.

In both cases the action of the typewriter is exactly duplicated, in that pressure is applied on pieces of type through an inked ribbon onto a piece of paper, which, in the case of the multigraph, is even backed by a rubber roller. When well done, the result is very difficult to distinguish from typewriting done on a carefully adjusted electric machine.

With great care, the recipient's name and address may be "filled in" on the letter. But to get the best fill-in results, the wide ribbon used to print the letter and the typewriter ribbon used to fill in must be carefully matched so the density and color of the ink are the same after drying. A mismatched fill-in is generally considered *worse* than no fill-in at all.

Mimeographing. Mimeographing is a stencil process which is frequently used for form letters and even more frequently for such items as bulletins, instruction sheets, price lists, etc.

Mimeographing was originally a trade name for the A. B. Dick stencil duplicating machine and materials, but it has now come to mean any stencil duplicating.

Mimeographing is relatively inexpensive and quite easy to do. Unfortunately, it has a rather poor reputation for quality . . . quite undeserved. As in all of these processes, the quality depends on the operator. And mimeographing *can* be dark, neat, and clear when good operators and good paper stock are used.

It is true that the process works best on a rather porous paper stock (since most mimeograph ink must penetrate into the sheet to dry completely), and that many people tend to associate this soft-surface paper with cheapness. However, if carefully slipsheeted, smooth-finished sulphite bonds may be mimeographed quite satisfactorily.

In the process, a "stencil" is "cut" by typewriter, without the use of a ribbon. The stencil is a waxed paper of widely spaced fibers. And the typewriter actually cuts through the wax so that ink can penetrate in that area. A "stylus," or smooth, round "pen" can also be used to draw lines or add drawings or signatures. After cutting, the "stencil" is wrapped around a cylinder full of ink, covered by an ink-saturated pad. When the cylinder revolves, a sheet of paper is squeezed between it and a rubber roller, causing some of the ink to be squeezed through the lines in the stencil and reproducing the typed message on the paper.

Spirit Duplicating (Hectographing). The best known spirit-duplicating machine is manufactured by Ditto. This process is even less costly than mimeographing, but its quality is not high. And even readability suffers on runs of more than a few dozen.

For spirit duplicating, a "master" is prepared by putting a master sheet and a special carbon in a typewriter so that the typed message appears, backwards, on the reverse side of the typed sheet. The "carbon" actually serves as the "ink." And, when put on the machine and slightly moistened by a roller covered with the "spirit" or moistening agent, enough of it is released to "print" the message on paper fed through the machine.

Of course, the number of reproductions which can be processed by one master is limited because the printing material gradually wears away.

This process is not generally recommended for external direct mail but is useful for bulletins and announcements to keep costs down.

Direct-plate Offset. Small offset presses, such as the A. B. Dick and Multilith, can be used not only as "photo-lithography" presses but will also print by the direct-plate process. The only difference is in the method of preparing the original plate for the machine. But direct plate is so frequently used in the reproduction of letters that it is worth describing.

In the photo-offset process, a photograph is taken of the material to be reproduced, and the film negative is placed against a sensitive plate, which is exposed and then "fixed" and placed on the offset machine.

In the direct-plate process, no negative is used. Instead, the material to be printed is placed, generally by typing, directly on a paper "mat." The image is typed through a carbon ribbon, and the deposit left on the mat has the characteristics of the material used for the original stone lithographic process. That is, it rejects water and attracts ink.

A previously prepared image may be put directly on a paper mat through the process of Xerography, too. This is the method of producing a similar deposit of the image through an electrostatic process. In Xerography, previously prepared material may be enlarged or reduced just as in photo-lithography. The process uses a camera but not a negative.

The preparation of a paper mat by Xerography is somewhat less expensive than the preparation of a metal plate through exposure to a photographic negative. It is thoroughly satisfactory for reproduction of letters and similar material.

Some types of office copying machines can also be used to prepare satisfactory mats or plates for direct-plate offset.

Skill Makes a Difference

Excellent machines are available for all of these methods, many of them in small sizes for use in the office. Most of them are capable of producing extremely fine work. However, anyone interested in a successful direct mailing program should remember that the real measure of duplicating excellence is provided by the personnel operating the machines. Any investment in equipment is wasted unless an investment is made in a skilled operator at the same time. If this is not practical, it is far better to purchase the reproduction necessary for a direct mail program from outside sources. Unless highly skilled operators are available internally, outside sources will be far more economical, effective, and less troublesome in the long run.

Quality and Process Choice

Many factors, including economy, will dictate your choice of duplicating methods. There is a good chance, in most cases, that the method you choose will be less important in determining results of your mailing than will be the *quality* of reproduction which you get from that method, and it is certainly less important than the quality of your message.

For instance, there is good reason to believe that an automatically typed letter, especially when the letter writer takes into consideration the opportunity for "personalization" which is available when he is using automatic typewriters, will produce better results than other types of letter reproduction. It is also the most costly.

Part of the effectiveness is probably due to the "personalness" of the automatically typed letter, with its specific references to the reader. But part of it is due to the fact that the letter writer feels more "personal" when he is writing a letter that is to be automatically typed. If a letter sounds as if it were a form letter, automatic typing won't save it. If a letter rings with humanness and sincerity, one of the less expensive processes is often just as effective in the long run.

18

How to Think about Envelopes

A Matter of "Hello"

The envelope your mail wears is the "dress" of your mailing. It's the "hello" a mailing says as it lands on a reader's desk. It's that vital first impression which can count so much in arousing interest. Many people never see the envelopes. Secretaries and mail rooms open the mail. But in giving the mailing a better chance with the person who does open his own mail, as well as in getting selective attention with the secretary, an envelope can be of importance.

Many interesting things have been done with envelopes lately—from die cuts on both sides to a full-face, plastic-covered die cut on the address side, with a four-color illustration (as a letterhead) showing through. The address, in this case, is put on the back of the envelope.

Special effects, according to the Envelope Manufacturers Association of America, have also been obtained through printing, through design, through a difference in shapes, sizes, styles, and papers.[1]

In fact, many effective subscription promotions rely on the impact of the envelope to get the reader inside, into the letter. They use all the imaginative dimensions possible to attract attention—"oversize, undersize, odd shapes, styles, colors, weights"[2] . . . and various uses of copy.

[1] *Envelopes: Their Use and Power in Direct Advertising*, DMAA Research Report, Envelope Manufacturers Association of America and Direct Mail Advertising Association, New York, 1956, p. 3.

[2] *Ibid.*

(Chapter 8 on Attention describes a *Reader's Digest* letter which used a half-finished story to get the reader inside, where the story was completed.)

No envelope is, however, best at all times for any given type of job. If you set down rules which put a "must" in the use of types of envelopes, you cut out variety and the use of creative imagination. The wisest thing is to have an open mind about envelope selection. Such a view leads to more interesting and more effective envelope uses.

How to Choose Envelopes

The job an envelope must do is the basis for its selection. When you are planning your mailing and considering its format based on the purpose of the mailing, you should consider how much of a job you want your envelope to do. And consideration should be given to the outgoing as well as to the return envelope, consideration based on the function you wish each envelope to perform.

The following envelope check list [3] can be used to help you determine which functions you wish an envelope to perform for you. Since each mailing has its own envelope requirements, this chart can be of use to you in envelope selection.

ENVELOPE CHECK CHART

Jobs performed by outgoing envelopes	Very important A	Desirable B	Unimportant C
From a utility standpoint:			
To transport the contents			
To protect the contents			
To identify the addressee			
To carry the postage			
To identify the advertiser			
To conceal the advertiser			
From an advertising standpoint:			
To arrest attention			
To arouse curiosity			
To make a favorable impression..			
By return envelopes			
From a utility standpoint:			
To offer a vehicle for response ...			
To provide the advertiser with a means for handling replies			
From an advertising standpoint:			
To stimulate reader response			
To leave a favorable impression ..			

[3] *Ibid.*, p. 2.

Envelopes: A Definition by Size and Dimension

This next table names some of the various types of envelopes available to you. It also indicates the physical characteristics of size and dimensions. These are standard sizes. And . . . it's advisable to stay with the standards . . . as a matter of keeping costs down.

Standard Commercial and Official Envelope Sizes [4]

Designation	Size in inches
6¼ Commercial	3½ × 6
6¾ Commercial	3⅝ × 6½
7 Commercial	3¾ × 6¾
7¼ Monarch	3⅞ × 7½
8⅝ Check	3⅝ × 8⅝
9 Official	3⅞ × 8⅞
10 Official	4½ × 9½
11 Official	4½ × 10⅜
12 Official	4¾ × 11
14 Official	5 × 11½

Envelopes: A Definition by Opening and Seam [5]

Many ways of defining or describing envelopes can be used. Here, the first definition will be on the basis of how an envelope is put together.

Open-side Envelope. The flap or opening is on the long side. The flap may be sealed for use in a first-class mailing, or it may be tucked in for a third-class mailing.

Open-end Envelope. The flap or opening is on the short side. And the flap may be sealed in a first-class mailing, or tucked in for a third-class mailing.

Diagonal-seam Envelope. The seams start at the two lower corners of the envelope and run diagonally upward. Used as a *Pennysaver Envelope,* this one may have the flap sealed and one end unsealed, to permit

[4] Courtesy Mead Paper Company, 118 West First Street, Dayton, Ohio.

[5] New U.S. Post Office regulations, becoming mandatory Jan. 1, 1963, will put some crimps in what you can do with envelopes. Here are the new regulations:

1. The minimum-size envelope to be mailed will be 3 × 4¼.
2. The envelopes must be rectangular in shape, not square.
3. A width-to-length–ratio requirement of one to 1.414 or greater for all first-class and third-class envelopes, cards, and self-mailers.
4. All envelopes must be fully sealed. This will eliminate the postage-saver envelope. However, rates will not be affected . . . if you print this (or something similar) on your envelopes: "Postmaster: May be opened for postal inspection if necessary."

third-class mailing. A spot of gum is usually placed on the open flap to "discipline" the contents better.

Center-seam Envelope. The seam is in the center and on the bottom of the envelope. This type of seam is used in the open-end envelopes and in clasp envelopes, where the flap is closed with a metal clasp for use in third-class mailings. The center seam envelope is, of course, sealed for first-class mailings.

Side-seam Envelope. The seams are on the side of the envelope. This seam position is good for many printing jobs. Because the seams then do not interfere with the printing surface.

Envelopes: The Unusual

Some new (and some not so new, but still "different") envelopes can be used to create various types of special effects. Prominent among these are . . .

Window Envelopes . . . for the "Peek-a-boo" Message. Window envelopes can be used to arouse curiosity by giving a peek-a-boo at something inside the envelope. Although this type of envelope has been around for some time and is not necessarily new to the mails, it can be used for unusual effects. For the window envelope, once the bearer of bills, notices, checks—strictly first-class—mail matter—is now used widely in third-class mail. And it is effective, through giving a reader a peek at what's inside, in arousing curiosity, and in getting him into the enclosed mailing. Besides having attention-creating value, the window envelope has other advantages to the user. They are:

1. The window envelope eliminates duplicate addressing costs.

2. It removes the necessity of matching personalized letters with envelopes. Just insert. And let them be "off." Because window envelopes have been, through public experience, bearers of things important to people—news from insurance companies, government agencies, banks, and the like—they are accepted by readers as having "prestige" or "importance" overtones. And they have proved successful for many mailers, often more successful than regular envelopes. You have many styles of window envelopes from which to choose. Here are several:

a. The Glassine Window: The glassine covers the window die cut and is used to protect the mailing piece and permit reading of the address.

b. Cellophane: Cellophane is used for the same purposes as glassine, but it costs more than glassine.

c. Acetate: Acetate is used for the same purposes as glassine and cellophane. But it, also, costs more than glassine.

d. The Open Window: In the open-window type there is no material covering the die cut. Cheaper. Works well. But the open die cut may give you trouble on inserting and mailing machines.

Postal Regulations for window envelopes require that: [6]

1. The address window must be parallel with the length of the envelope.

2. The proper place for the address window is in the lower portion of the address side of the envelope.

3. Nothing but the name, address, and any key number may appear through the address window.

4. The return address *should* appear in the upper left-hand corner of the envelope, but is not required.

5. If the return address does not appear on the envelope, and the delivery address does not show through the window, the piece will be handled as dead mail. If your name is inside first-class mail, the mail will be returned to you at a cost of 10 cents per piece.

6. The address disclosed through the window must be on white paper or on paper of a very light color.

7. When used for registered mail, envelopes must have panels covering the opening. If transparent panels are glued to the envelopes, they may contain only matter without intrinsic value. If the panel is part of the envelope, the envelope may be used for all registered mail.

8. Windows other than address windows in envelopes may be placed on the face or back of the envelope, any shape or size. But they must leave the required space on front for addressing: 3½ inches clear space at the right end of the address side of the envelope.

You Can Use Odd-shaped address windows in the regular or special positions—to increase your attention and interest values. If you use an odd-shaped window, however, put it parallel (by postal regulations) to the length of the envelope.

More than One Window, permissible by postal regulations, can also be used effectively. These windows can call attention to coins, attention devices, stamps, drawings, etc., on the mailing piece inside. And the second (and/or third) window can be used on either side of the envelope. Be sure it doesn't, however, interfere with stamp cancellation, indicia, or return address.[7]

Here are some ways you can use windows to get more effective impact. Use the space *behind* the window, which is otherwise blank when the envelope's contents are removed, for an advertising message. Such as:

1. A "Thank You" to customers, when you mail "invoices, monthly statements, maturity premiums, collection and dividend notices." [8] Thank-

---

[6] "U.S. Postal Guide, 1958 Edition," *Envelope Economies*, Tension Envelope Corporation, Kansas City, Mo., 1958, pp. 7, 9.

[7] *Envelopes: Their Use and Power in Direct Advertising*, p. 8.

[8] *Ibid.*, p. 22.

ing a reader in advance in this type of circumstance does not presume. He expects to receive such mailings . . . and also may appreciate the courtesy. For example, "Thanks . . ." or just plain . . ."Thank you."

2. An Announcement of special sales, to customers or prospects, can use the space behind the window. For example, "During June, all golf equipment, ¼ off."

3. An Ad for Special Departments, to promote these departments at appropriate times of the year, or when something is new. For example, "Visit Our New Sports-goods Department."

4. Invite Orders by Phone. Use a picture of a reader phoning you for an order. And use your phone number. For example, "We invite your phone orders" or, "Our personal shopper can help you. Dial 4567."

5. Spotlight your Trademark, Brand Name, and Slogan. Everywhere you can do so, your trademark, as the identifying symbol of your company, store, etc., should be promoted. So put it in your window envelope. For example, "This trademark guarantees you money-back satisfaction" or "At General Electric, Progress Is Our Most Important Product." [9]

"Special" Envelopes—for the Unordinary Job

Many envelopes, called "specials" by the manufacturers, are available to do an effective job for you. Here are a few:

Coin-return Envelopes. Available in many sizes and styles, the coin-return envelope has a special pocket for coins. And it can be used whenever you want the "shekels" to return by mail. These envelopes have been successful for various purposes: short-term magazine subscriptions, premium offers, photo and film mailing, accident insurance policies, etc. Usually tailor-made to do a specific job, this type of envelope can be obtained from the envelope manufacturers for any purpose you may devise.

Bound-in Reply Envelopes. This type of envelope is inserted and "bound in" to prevent loss in magazines and catalogues. Some, which are durable, gummed, and perforated in a center line, appear in different parts of the publication, usually front and back.

Two-way Envelopes. This type of envelope carries your message to the reader and brings it back. The most popular style uses a long seal flap which folds around the return envelope and covers the address on the outgoing mailing. The flap, which can carry a sales message and a reply or order blank, can be torn off, kept, or inserted in the envelope . . . and the envelope then returned.[10]

[9] *Ibid.*
[10] *Ibid.*, p. 24.

The "Zip-Opener" Envelope—for Drama, Difference

Produced by the Connelly Organization,* the Zip-Opener envelope offers you a change of pace, a different, a dramatic impact. The envelope has stitching along the top edge, a half-circle die cut in the center of the top edge. The thread runs through the die cut, to make it easy for your reader to grasp it . . . pull . . . and zip his envelope open. The self-opening feature can be dramatized with lead-in copy on the envelope, with illustration—to give you more attention value.

Connellys offers a Pull Tag which can be attached to the thread. When the envelope is opened, the tag, or as many tags as you wish to pay postage on (and you can form a whole series of messages in one envelope with the use of more tags), pops out on the thread. This type of tag-and-thread combination can be used as a complete mailing, which leads to an action reply card in the envelope. It can also lead to an action card, which is the last tag attached to the thread. The Zip-Opener is a natural for:

1. Announcing a new address.

2. Announcing a new telephone number.

3. As an attention-getting enclosure with a letter. For example, some banks use it in their mailing of statements . . . to feature other services and departments. Or, some mailers have used gum . . . cigarettes, etc., to correlate this attention "gimmick" with their main sales point or copy opener on an enclosed piece of mail.[11]

Envelope Copy . . . Lead-in to Sales

If you use envelope teaser copy to help draw the reader inside to the letter or message, handle its creation in the same way you would an attention copy opener in a sales letter (Chapter 8). The requirements are the same: Get the reader's attention. Give him an incentive to read. Get him interested.

Some people are of the opinion that a teaser line on an envelope can increase your readership. Because ". . . it sets the stage for the sales message, creates a mental picture, makes your prospect drool receptively."[12] The idea these people have is that you get two tries with your reader—one on the envelope and one in the letter.

But this assumes a similarity of circumstance and letter-opening habits among your readers, which isn't necessarily true. Nothing is absolute about how people receive and handle their mail. Your wisest attitude,

---

* See SOURCE LIST for address.

[11] Published with permission of Tom Connelly, President, the Connelly Organization and its subsidiary: Zip-Opener Corporation, Philadelphia, Pa.

[12] *Envelopes: Their Use and Power in Advertising,* p. 18.

then, should be to base your decisions about the envelope teaser line on the testing you do.

With some people, your return address is enough to get the letter read. With others it can be enough to get the letter thrown away. In this case, the person more than likely identifies himself as a nonprospect. That makes it a list problem. Since most businesses are ever alert to the mail they receive, the question of teaser lines or no teaser lines with businessmen becomes academic—until you test. If, however, you use a teaser line, have it do these things (see Chapter 8 for requirements of a copy opener):

1. Command attention, develop reading incentive, and gain interest.

2. Be integrated with the copy opener of the material enclosed in the envelope. A "leap" in logic or coherence between your envelope teaser line and the copy opener on the enclosed piece destroys the continuity and, thus, your pattern of persuasion.

Here Are Some Examples of envelope copy which will be of interest to you . . . especially in getting ideas for use in your own mailings:

1. *The Reader's Digest* used two glassine windows on the face of an envelope (3⅝ by 8⅜ inches). One window was for the address. The other, to the left of the first, had two pennies pasted to the reply card inside. Above the pennies, on the reply card—showing through the window—this copy could be seen: "Here's your change." On the glassine itself, over the pennies, in red ink, the copy read, "Offer expires September 25."

Below the second window, other copy stated, "Important Dated Material Enclosed." Below the address window, the envelope copy had this to say: "If mailed by September 25, This Card Will Bring You the New Reader's Digest Condensed Books—Regular Price $2.44—for Only 8 cents!"

The copy opener of the enclosed letter was a restatement of the offer on the envelope.

2. Multi-Ad Services of Peoria, Illinois, used this challenge to get a reader to open an envelope. The envelope copy read, "Why don't you throw this thing away now? It can't do anything for you—BUT MAKE MONEY!" The top of the first page of the enclosed leaflet then offered this line: "So you're Interested? Take a look at the newest idea in the field of Graphic Arts . . . 'Ready-to-go-Layouts'." (An art portfolio.) Good lead. Good integration of envelope teaser copy and inside copy opener. Good effect.

3. Foote and Jenks, Jackson, Michigan (makers of vanilla), used an envelope (3⅞ by 8⅞ inches) with three pennant-shaped, cellophane-covered windows on the face. The back of the envelope was used for the address. In the pennant-shaped windows were pennants colored blue, then orange, and then blue. The pennant windows had copy (one word each) which read, "TRY . . . TRIANGULAR . . . TESTING."

When the envelope was opened, the mailing piece was a folded, pennant-shaped piece. The inside copy read, "The next time you compare flavors," to correlate with the window copy. The copy continued this way, "Try Triangular Testing. To put it simply . . . try three samples . . . coded blind . . . *in your product* . . . two of them flavored alike!"

Many other ways of creating teaser or lead lines can be developed for use on envelopes. The few we have here will give you a starting point from which to generate your own ideas.

Envelopes and Color

Here we offer you the general attitude which will help you in selecting envelope colors. It is based on the idea that what works for someone else, for another product or service, for one time of year and its various affective circumstances such as weather and news events—as against another time of year—will not necessarily work for you. No color tests are given here. Because color is such a sensitive animal, it's not readily possible to transfer its use from one occasion to another. Too many of the world's circumstances intervene. You should test colors as you test other parts of mailings. These, then, are the suggestions on color we offer . . . for color on your outside and inside envelopes:

To Figure the "Where" of Using Colors on Your Envelopes, use this listing as a means of planning color application to your envelopes. You can produce some interesting results with these ideas . . . for they are based on the use of color and on those things which bring color to an envelope: [13]

1. Use display window envelope to let color of enclosure or illustration show through.

2. Try using a background (simulated water-mark effect) tint design or illustration on the envelope.

3. Use colored artlining, printing on the inside of envelope.

4. Print teaser copy, such as "Confidential" or "Air Mail Reply Requested" or "Urgent—Open Immediately" on face and seal flap of envelope in color. (Remember, the seal-flap copy is the last thing seen by the addressee before getting to the enclosures.)

5. Use colored paper and colored return address.

6. Use colored return envelopes to separate them from others which recipient might save. (Consult post office about colors.)

7. Use advertising-style envelopes, with advertising display covering an entire face or back. Caution: Be sure to leave the required space for the address, postage, postmarks, etc., on the address side.

[13] "Color for Your Advertising," *Envelope Economies,* p. 3.

8. Use unusual-shape envelopes, long and thin, square. (Consult post office for limitations.)

9. Try Kraft Envelopes, envelopes with clasps, Tension Ties. (Tension Tie is the registered trademark of the Tension Envelope Corporation. It is a string-and-button closure for envelopes.) Kwick Klasp (a registered Tension trademark for a clasp closure), or unusual-shape flaps or methods of closure.

10. Use commemorative stamps on outer envelopes.

11. Change style and color of indicia.

12. Use postage meter.

The DMAA offers you the following suggestions as a color guide.[14] But be sure to talk color decision with the person doing the art work. You're paying for his talents. Use them.

1. Deep colors suggest stability, sturdiness, dependability.

2. Tints suggest speed, lightness, and sheerness.

3. Pure colors (bright reds, purples, greens) draw attention to low-price items.

4. Subdued colors—as maroon, cinnamon brown, teal, green, and dark blue, suggest more expensive merchandise.

5. When two colors are used, complementary and analogous colors work well together—a tint of one and a shade of the other. Colors of approximately the same strength and area rob the copy of a point of interest. Good complementary colors are dark brown and light blue; dark red (maroon) and light green. Dark blue and light blue; brown and tan; peach and maroon, are excellent analogous colors.

One Case Study of interest in envelope color was made by Mr. Dean H. Doyle, president of Doyle Stationery, Inc., Marshall, Missouri. Let him tell you about it.

As you no doubt recall, several months ago, you (Tension Envelope Company) twisted my arm and talked me into giving you an order for 50,000 three-color, creative-design catalogue envelopes in which to mail my Sno-white napkin offer. Inasmuch as I mail out samples of these napkins with the mailing, I did not think that the outside envelope would have any effect on the results of the mailing. I am glad to say that I was wrong.

We tested your envelopes against our white catalogue envelopes with one-color, black corner card and permit indicia. I mailed a total of 28,000 to an outside rented list we had never used before, using every other name. All enclosures were exactly the same in both envelopes.

For every dollar my black-and-white envelopes produced in sales, your three-color, creative-design envelope produced $1.82. Profit-wise this means that we made $66 per thousand on the names mailed in the black-and-white

---

[14] *Envelopes: Their Use and Power in Advertising*, p. 20.

envelopes and $168 per thousand on the names mailed in the three-color envelopes.

I am going to continue testing, of course, but it looks very much as if your creative design is by far the best deal. If other lists pan out the way this first list did, it would enable us to double our net profits.

Mr. Doyle's experience shows that color can make a difference . . . and in his test *did* make an appreciable difference. Note, however, in his last paragraph that he plans to continue testing. Just because a test works once . . . doesn't mean it will necessarily work the second, third, etc. times. So . . . our advice to you on the use of the color available to you in envelopes is: TEST.

19

How to Think about Postage
and Postmarks

As in many other areas of direct mail, you have a number of choices when you decide what *style* of postage to use. You may use printed indicia, a metering device, or postage stamps.

Printed Indicia

If economy is your only criterion, or if you are using a printed piece, you'll probably use the printed indicia. These markings are printed in a "box" at the same time that your envelope or mailing piece is being prepared, so the application of this postage costs nothing extra.

It is necessary, however, to obtain a permit, for which a fee is charged, from the post office where the mailing will be made and to print the number of that permit as part of the indicia. You do not have to pay the postage charges until the mailing is delivered to the post office (it cannot be mailed in a collection box). At that time you must be sure to have enough money in your numbered account to cover the postage.

Here's one other caution when using the printed indicia: If you distribute some of the pieces outside of the mail, either do not print the indicia on them or else cross off the indicia box before distribution. It is illegal for anyone except the U.S. Post Office to distribute mail with indicia on it . . . and this even includes handing a piece over the counter of your store.

The Postage Meter

The second least expensive way of applying postage is by postage meter. With this method you print the exact amount of postage needed on the envelope, usually at the same time it is being machine-sealed. The printing mechanism is a meter which records the amount of postage you use on each piece and subtracts it from the total credit you have in the meter. You buy this "credit" at the post office ahead of time, and it is locked and sealed in the meter. Metering is only slightly more expensive than printed indicia, and most mailers prefer it.

Neither the printed indicia nor the metered impression leave much leeway for creativity, although some permissible variations of the indicia are better looking than others. Perhaps we should also mention the possibility of using the postage meter "ad space" for a message or design. This is printed, at the same time as the postage, in a small space to the left of the metered postage.

Postage Stamps

You have some opportunity to increase favorable attention or improve design when you affix postage stamps for postage. Many mailers feel that the use of a stamp "upgrades" their advertising, and this may especially be true when a letter itself is unusually personal. Some mailers use commemorative stamps regularly just for variety. There always are new ones available, since the U.S. Post Office issues a score or more every year. Other mailers use commemoratives to upgrade the design of their envelopes or mailers . . . since most commemoratives have a striking appearance.

Still other mailers make their bid for attention by using strange denominations. Eight seldom-seen, ½-cent stamps, for example, on a letter which would ordinarily carry a standard, four-cent stamp, are bound to cause some comment when received.

Special delivery, registered, or certified letters can be used with good effect to emphasize the importance which you place on the message. Naturally, you'll want to use these when there is a factor of speed or importance involved that is obvious to the recipient, too. If the message seems trivial to him, however, the use of special postage may backfire and create an unfavorable image of your organization.

The Glamour of "Faraway" Places

As the song says, people are intrigued by "faraway places with strange-sounding names." This is especially true if the names appear as postmarks on the letters they receive.

Couple the above with the fact that the United States is full of post offices with the strangest of names, and you have a tempting opportunity for the advertiser looking for a different, yet effective direct mail approach.

Apropos P.O.s. One advertiser who has taken advantage of this opportunity is Price Brothers Company, Dayton, Ohio, supplier of prestressed concrete building units, concrete blocks, and concrete sewer and pressure pipe.

For years now, Price Brothers Company has been "visiting" its sewer-pipe prospects via four or five attention-getting direct mail pieces a year. Recently the company and its agency, Yeck & Yeck, began searching out U.S. Post Offices with names that fit the key selling features of its pipe.

As a result of this search, letters were soon being mailed from Limestone, Tennessee; Waterflow, New Mexico; Strong, Mississippi; and Economy, Indiana.

Home-town Flavor. Each mailing discussed the selling features indicated by the postmark. For example, the first letter read, "If the founding fathers of Limestone back in 1857 had mixed up a batch of concrete and buried it in the ground, it would be a better piece of concrete today than on the day they buried it. . . .

"The sand, gravel, water, and limestone in concrete all come from the ground, and when you put them back they're right in their own element. Concrete actually gets harder and harder the longer it is buried.

"You can try this out for yourself. Next time you install a water line, use concrete pressure pipe. And if you care to dig it up for a look after 100 years, you'll find that it's harder and stronger and a better piece of pipe than the day you buried it. . . . You can guess what pipe I recommend—Price pipe (made with limestone). If you want some, just drop us a line in Dayton, Ohio, or Hattiesburg, Mississippi."

The second letter, postmarked Waterflow, New Mexico, explained that ". . . when water runs over certain materials, it causes them to corrode and tuberculate. . . . If it happens in a pipeline, the capacity of the pipe is cut down and sooner or later you have to clean it out.

"Funny thing, though, about concrete. It seems to be exactly the right material for easy water flow. When water runs through a concrete pipe, a sort of slick forms that makes the water run faster and pump easier . . ."

The third and fourth letters, from Strong, Mississippi, and Economy, Indiana, also pointed up the respective mutualities between the town names and the pipe features. Again the tone of the letters was friendly and conversational.

No Envelopes. So as not to spoil the "local feel" of the mailings, no letterhead was used. Instead, to add the distinctive touch, the letters were run on an 80-pound text stock, which was perforated, gummed, and folded into an envelope. A small hole was punched out at one end of the perforation to "cue" the recipient on how to open the letter.

The main reason for making the letters self-mailers (in addition to economy) was that the recipient was certain to see the postmark.

Were the mailings successful? According to the response, yes. In fact, Price Brothers is so pleased with the technique that it recommends it to others.[1]

More Glamour: Harris-Seybold

Harris-Seybold Company, a Division of Harris-Intertype Corporation, Cleveland, Ohio, also used postmarks to create interest, add a bit of glamour, spark additional effectiveness into a mail campaign.

Using double post cards which did not supply an answer piece, they based their theme on wise sayings which were tied in with the unusual postmarks. Then a quotation was given inside the card and tied into the main selling point of the message. One double card, on the address side read this way:

A Wise Saying about *quality* from . . .

Then the postmark read:

QUALITY, KENTUCKY

Flip open the card. Find the wise saying:

"QUALITY remains long after the price is forgotten." E. C. Simmons

Now, to the copy which does the selling:

And speaking of quality . . . all the advantages of offset-print quality, register, flexibility, productivity, and economy are available with this 14½ × 20½" Harris Offset Job Press.

The smallest *professional* press in the industry, the Harris Model 120 is an easy, fast-on, fast-off press, with "big-press" features that mean more profit for you.

Here's why: It handles the wide range of stocks expected of job presses. It runs at speeds up to 7,000 sheets per hour and it has print quality comparable to larger Harrises.

Furthermore, it will outproduce any other sheet-fed press of its size. It's ideal for standard-form work, letterheads, and 9 × 12" bleed pages. And, it's excellent for multicolor work too.

Make-ready and running of the Harris 14½ × 20½" set a new "high" in operating simplicity and convenience. Over-all design makes it the heaviest and most stable of all presses in its sheet size, and features which were formerly found only on 17½ × 22½" and 23 × 30" Harris presses are on the 14½ × 20½".

[1] "Unusual Postmarks Sell Pipe for Price," *Industrial Marketing*, vol. 44, no. 9, pp. 186–188, September, 1959.

Let's check off a few of the advanced features on the Harris Model 120:
- fast-acting plate clamps
- 3-form–roller Harris inker
- full 1-inch hardened bearers give faithful print transfer
- roll-back fountain for quick dampener changes
- Harris vacuum-wheel feeding with sheet slowdown

In general, this "bread-and-butter" press will make ready faster . . . change over quicker . . . and produce more high-quality, salable sheets than any other sheet-fed offset press of its size.

Why not get the full story on this quality press from your Harris-Seybold sales representative?

Another of the cards featured this line on its address side:

A Wise Saying about *Talent* from . . .

Then the postmark:

TALENT, OREGON

The wise saying inside the double card was:

"If the power to do hard work is not talent, it is the best possible substitute for it." James A. Garfield.

The remainder of the copy read this way:

And speaking of talent . . . the Harris 17½ × 22½″ has the talent to produce run-of-the-book form work on beautiful multicolor jobs . . . to satisfy the most exacting customer. And, like all Harris job presses, the 17½ × 22½″ combines the talent of fast-on, fast-off versatility with high running speeds. Pressmen will appreciate the fast make-ready features, including a center separation feeder, that reduce starting and change-over time to a minimum . . . the sturdy inker–a big press inker on a small job press–that has the talent to give an even lay of ink . . . even when running solids. On the Harris 17½ × 22½″ all form rollers can be adjusted from the outside. Owners of the Model 122 will appreciate the quick getaway, high running speeds (up to 7,000 iph) and precision register that add up to big-bonus production and more profits. The Harris Model 122 has the talent to play any role in job printing and could easily be the press you've been looking for to round out your offset department . . . Why not investigate putting its talent to work for you? Write or ask a Harris representative to demonstrate its profit-making potential and see what it can do for your business.

Other cards used these lead lines on the address side, followed up with these postmarks, and moved into these quotations:

A Wise Saying about *Profits* by Winston Churchill . . .

Postmark:

ENGLAND, ARKANSAS

The quotation:

"It is a socialist idea that making profits is a vice. I consider the real vice is making losses." Sir Winston Churchill.

Or . . . take this example:

A Wise Saying about *Speed* from . . .

Postmark:

SPEED, INDIANA

With this wise saying:

"The speed of a runaway horse counts for nothing." Jean Cocteau.

The last card mailing . . . an accordion-folded card . . . presented this line on its address side:

A Wise Saying about Work from
HARRIS, MICHIGAN

The "inside" wise saying was:

A man does his best work on a Harris.

The copy continued, with illustrations of the various Harris presses. It concluded with an action card, which gave the reader a choice between a representative calling . . . or literature on any specific press desired.

Note in these cards the way "theme" was skillfully carried through. Note also how the theme ties in with the specific selling point being developed. And how the carry-through of theme from postmark to selling point is well conceived, well integrated in those mailing pieces where we have given you complete copy. The whole campaign had the same thoroughness, ability, competence.

How to Obtain Special Postmarks

If you have occasion to make a mailing from another post office in order to obtain an interesting postmark, it's wise to use the following procedure:

1. Determine whether or not the post office is still in existence, or will still be when your mailing arrives. The U.S. Post Office is constantly combining or eliminating post offices, and the ones with unusual and appealing names are often small. Your own postmaster can give you this information, which you certainly should get before writing your mailing.

2. Phone or write the postmaster (the superintendent of mailing in first-class post offices) and discuss your mailing with him (or her). This is especially important if your mailing is at all large and if you want a particular mailing date.

Phone if you can, for this long-distance attention gives the postmaster a feeling that the mailing is important. During the conversation, be sure to discuss the *purpose* of mailing from his post office (i.e., to get an interesting postmark on the mail) and tell him of your concern that every postmark be readable. This is very important. It doesn't take much of a cancellation for the postmaster to do his duty, but to serve your purpose you need a clear, complete impression. Ask him to send you a sample if he will.

Also tell him, "When we use another post office, it's our custom to stamp the envelopes before sending them to you and to send you a check for an equivalent amount of stamps which you will mail back to us. Is this the way you'd like us to do it?"

(Most small-town postmasters will appreciate this. Their pay depends upon the total business they do, and they appreciate the fact that you are thinking about them. Large city post offices will be more likely to tell you not to bother.)

If you have plenty of time, of course, and don't want to phone, you can simply write and tell him you're planning the mailing and want to be sure it will be handled O.K. and enclose a stamped envelope for his reply. You'll get his sample cancellation on his return.

3. When the time comes to ship the mailing to him, be sure it's in good shape for handling at the other end. Have the envelopes facing the same way, etc. If your mailing is large and the post office is small, he may have the neighbors in to help. . . . In any event, you want to make it easy for him.

Put a note reminding him of the date, etc. either on the outside of the shipment or inside the box. You can send the shipment parcel post, express, or truck, but give it plenty of leeway ahead of your mailing date, and be sure to indicate the date you want the mailing made on the note to the postmaster. It's also a good idea to include an envelope addressed to yourself. Then you know when the pieces arrive.

4. It is also possible to get a certificate of mailing from the postmaster when you make bulk mailings. Just fill out a copy of Post Office Form 3606, put on enough postage to cover the fee (15 cents for the first thousand, 3 cents for additional thousands), and put it with your statement of mailing. The postmaster will return it to you after verifying the count.

5. Rules are somewhat different if you are getting a first-day cover celebrating a special event or a first-day cancellation. In these cases, you check with your postmaster for specific instructions.

A Guide to Unusual Post Offices

The United States Postal Guide will give you an almost unlimited number of unusual post offices. With these post offices, you can use your own creative imagination to develop all kinds of effective advertising ideas. The list given you here is brief. But it will give you a perspective on what is available to you. Here you are: [2]

Christmas Promotions

Santa Claus, Ind.
Jolly, Tex.
Joy, Ill., Ky.
Holly, Calif., Mich., W. Va.
Goodwill, W. Va.
Hollytree, Ala.
Snowflake, Ariz., Va.
Snowball, Ark.
Snoeshoe, Pa.
Mistletoe, Ky.
Noel, Mo., Va.

New Year Greetings

Many, La.; Happy, Ky., Tex.
Goodyear, Ariz.

St. Valentine's Day

Valentine, Ariz., Nebr., Tex.
Friendship, Ark.
Romance, Ark., Mo., W. Va.
Sublime, Tex.
Hon., Ark.
Delight, Ark.
Groom, Tex.
Platinum, Alaska
True, W. Va.

Fourth of July

Flag, Ark.
Fireworks, E. St. Louis, Ill.
Independence, Mo., Calif., La., Kans., Ky., Iowa, Miss.

Insurance, Life, Auto Accident

Mutual, Md., Okla.
Accident, Md.
Auto, W. Va.
Bird in Hand, Pa.
Miracle, Ky.
Hazard, Ky., Nebr.
Thrifty, Tex.
Driver, Miss.

Special-sale Promotions

Early, Iowa
Gee, Ky.
Eek, Alaska
Hasty, Ark., Colo.
Hurry, Md.
Luck, Wis.
Loco, Okla., Tex.
Novelty, Mo.
Nuttsville, Va.
Call, Tex.
Utopia, Tex.
Weeks, La.

Food or Grocery Promotions

Birdseye, Ind.
Beetown, Wis.
Bread Loaf, Vt.
Chicken, Alaska
Chili, Ind.
Cucumber, W. Va.
Dairy, Ore.
Coffee Springs, Ala.
Lamb, Ky.
Lemons, Mo.
Soap Lake, Wash.
Tea, S. Dak.
Tomato, Ark.
Fancy Farm, Ky.
Fried, N. Dak.
Java, S. Dak., Va.
Pie, W. Va.

Bank or Savings Loan Cos.

Fort Necessity, La.
Friendly, W. Va.
Dinero, Tex.
Dollar Bay, Mich.
Doorway, Ky. (to investments, etc.)
Bucks, Ala.
Fort Deposit, Ala.
Okay, Ark., Okla.

[2] Bette Macon, "Postmarks Can Sell for You," *Advertising Requirements,* vol. 5, no. 6, p. 53, June, 1957.

Gold Bar, Wash.
Fairchance, Pa.
Cash, Ark., Va.
Access, Ky.

Names of Foreign Places

Brussels, Ill., Wis.
China, Maine, Tex.
Siberia, Ind.
Sweden, Ky.

Famous People

Kipling, N.C., Ohio
Mozart, Ark.
Jenny Lind, Ark.
Hemingway, S.C.
Keats, Kans.
Chopin, La.
Voltaire, N. Dak.
Cinderella, W. Va.
Tarzan, Tex.
Dagmar, Mont.
Chloe, W. Va.
Brutus, Ky.

People Everybody Knows

Old Joe, Ark.
Clara, Miss.
Clem, Ga., W. Va.
Clint, Tex.
Eddy, Mont., Okla., Tex.
Edsel, Ky.
Peggy, Tex.
Gladys, Va.
Herbert, Ala.
Lucy, La.
Mary, Ky.
Minnie, Ky.

Miscellaneous

Booth, Ala., Tex., W. Va.
Book, La.
Boring, Md., Ore.

Bromide, Okla.
Bunch, Ky., Okla.
Champ, Md.
Channelview, Tex.
Cool, Calif.
Coward, S.C.
Coy City, Tex.
Crook, Colo.
Daylight, Tenn.
Dewdrop, Ky.
Dimple, Ky.
Dye, Va.
Dwarf, Ky.
Equality, Ala., Ill., Ky.
Earth, Tex.
Era, Tex.
Fine, N.Y.
Gay, Ga., Mich., W. Va.
Gas, Kans.
Grit, Tex.
Goodnight, Tex.
Gravity, Iowa
Holder, Fla., Ill.
Hippo, Ky.
Hyacinth, Va.
Humble, Tex.
Kidder, Ky., Mo., S. Dak.
Kodak, Ky., Tenn.
Laws, Calif.
Lone, Ky.
Lovely, Ky.
Loyal, Okla., Wis.
Man, W. Va.
Media, Ill., Pa.
Minor, Va.
Mix, La.
Molt, Mont.
Mold, Wash.
Tell, Tex.
Truth and Consequences, N. Mex.
Tumtum, Wash.

20

How to Develop "Idea" Mailings

The chances are that most of your direct mail is fairly normal . . . that is, it consists of letters, folders, or self-mailers that look much like the rest of the mail your prospect gets. Chances also are that this is as it should be. Most problems are fairly normal.

Occasionally, though, you may run into a problem that needs a little more "impact." You want your message to stand out from the rest of the mail . . . or to be kept or remembered. So you say to yourself, "I need a new idea for this mailing. What can I do that's different?"

Well, while it's difficult to come up with a really "new" idea, it's usually possible for you to produce something that does have the characteristics you went after in the first place . . . attention, retention value, or memorability.

There are a number of ways to approach this problem, of course. One is to keep a file of all the unusual mailings you and your friends have ever received, paw through it when you want ideas, and adapt something that strikes your fancy at the moment.

You can extend that file by jotting down all the variations you have seen or can think of . . . and by adding to it from time to time. Then, when you need ideas, you return to this check list and take off from there.

To help you develop such a list, we have arbitrarily set up thirteen categories. You can set up more. Using those categories, we've had a private "brain-storming" session, simply setting down every variation under these categories which, offhand, we can remember seeing (and a few we haven't seen yet) in twenty-some years of watching direct mail.

We suggest you come to this check list whenever you need an idea for an "unusual" mailing and take a look. Add ideas in the margins as you get them, even if they don't fit your present problem. They may help next time. Most times you'll have the idea you need before you even finish reading the list. Here are some starters:

Think about Mailings that Use Unusual Stock

1. Graph paper
2. Day-glo paper (red-letter day)
3. Wallpaper
4. Sandpaper
5. Pressure-sensitive post card
6. Cloth
7. Wood . . . ⅛-inch plywood . . . paper
8. Aluminum foil
9. Transparent paper (cellophane, etc.)
10. Translucent paper (carbon copy, etc.)
11. Blotting paper
12. Phonograph record
13. Ribbon that talks a message when you run your thumbnail over it
14. Cork
15. Canvas
16. Wood veneer

Think about Using Unusual Shapes, Sizes, Designs, or Folds

1. Simulated IBM card
2. Simulated membership card
3. Giant letter, telegram, or card
4. Circular (round in shape) letter
5. Letter or card die-cut into the shape of some object
6. Formal invitation (regular size, giant, or miniature)
7. Triple post card, with address showing, plain or die-cut
8. "Snap-box," which snaps into a cube when opened
9. Fold 8½- by 11-inch sheet longways for self-mailer
10. Trim a single-fold piece a little narrower at the fold to give it a butterfly look when opened
11. Deck of cards—fifty-two messages
12. Train-ticket format
13. Yellow page of phone-book format
14. Simulated entertainment poster (movie, variety show, opera, ballet, hillbilly)

Think about Die Cuts, Punching, Defacing in Your Mailings

1. Pop-ups
2. Cards cut to special design
3. "Circular" (round in shape) letter, or zigzag letter
4. Envelope: die-cut all the way through to let color show through on both sides
5. Punch hole in paper and make it apply to message
6. Burned-edge letter
7. Preerased letter
8. Half letter: Cut the overrun of a previous letter in half, and on blank side, write a short letter which may start, "Maybe we got only half of our story across to you."

Think about Unusual Layouts

1. Reverse letter (read in mirror)
2. Upside-down letterhead
3. Fancy reply cards or envelopes
4. Four-page letter or self-mailer
5. Handwritten letter or note
6. Shorthand on letter or envelope
7. Imitation telegram or imitation phone message
8. Music and words to a song
9. Stock certificates
10. Jig-saw puzzle
11. Name of letter writer in top position on letterhead; company name subordinated
12. Format of "wanted" signs in post office, using fingerprints and front and profile photos to introduce salesmen—"WATCH FOR THIS MAN" . . .
13. Calendar page used as a memo (handwritten), but printed on a card stock and used as a mailing card
14. Magazine cartoons (reprinted with permission), used as a source of inexpensive but effective art
15. A photo used to fill the whole top fold of the letter, 8½- by 11-inch sheet; then accordion fold used, leaving the picture the first thing you see
16. In place of letterhead, attention-getting picture . . . no letterhead at all
17. Page out of dictionary
18. Wedding or party invitation
19. Label from bottle or can
20. Empty cigarette package
21. Instruction tag

22. Candy wrapper
23. Ticker tape
24. Yellow paper from wire service, like AP
25. Last will and testament
26. Child's building block
27. Garden-seed packet
28. Page from language dictionary
29. Insurance policy
30. Claim check
31. Birth certificate
32. Passport
33. Savings book (bank or savings-and-loan)
34. Three- by five-inch recipe card
35. Sheet music
36. Map
37. Ad reprint
38. Magazine covers
39. Recipe
40. Menu
41. Paint paddles
42. Checkbook
43. Shelf paper
44. Printed sticker or decal
45. Credit card
46. Gift wrapping
47. Place mats and doilies
48. Crepe paper and streamers
49. Paid bill
50. Shoe or cereal box
51. Instruction sheets
52. Sheet of trading stamps
53. Paper towels
54. Soap box
55. Napkins
56. Roll of film wrapper—with spool print on inside of paper—to be unrolled as film
57. Adding-machine tape
58. An *offbeat* greeting card
59. Film positive
60. Silk screen on wallpaper or cloth
61. Overprint in bright color on old telephone-directory pages
62. Sheet of sandpaper or emery cloth
63. Giant shipping label (like one on product)

64. Overprint on company form (credit memo)
65. Paper party hat
66. Cardboard milk carton
67. Christmas wrapping paper
68. Kite paper
69. Newspaper.mat (reversed)
70. Embossed on thin metal (like name plate or even packaging stickers)
71. Printed on a piece of building material (aluminum, floor tile, felt paper, etc.)
72. Lobster or spaghetti bib, big coaster, etc.
73. On wrapper that goes around product
74. White shipping or mailing bag
75. Plastic bag
76. Corrugated packing board
77. Zipper reply card

Think about Unusual Copy Style

1. Radio, TV, or movie script
2. Shorthand notes on envelope or on a tip-on addressed to the secretary
3. Telegram format and style
4. Newspaper clipping
5. News ticker
6. "TIME style"

Think about Using Special Processes

1. Invisible ink
2. Burning message
3. Fragrance
4. Cabala (erasable) process
5. Fingerprints
6. Wet message

Think about Adding Something Unusual

1. Gadgets
   a. Glimericks
   b. Vari-view
   c. Gold-plated items
   d. Flower seeds
   e. Third-dimension paste-on
   f. Plastic gadget on post card, catalogue, or reply card
   g. Useful item which becomes gift when removed
   h. to z. (Their number is legion.)

2. Photos
   a. Snapshots
   b. Postage-stamp size
3. Foreign money
4. Fragrance
5. Special stamp
   a. "First-day cover" on envelope
6. Special seals
   a. With ribbons attached for important announcements

Think about Using Unusual Containers

1. Tubes
2. Bags
3. Shape-conforming plastic
4. Cellophane envelopes, tubes, or bags
5. "Zip-velope"
6. Double-window envelope
7. Boxes (unusual)
8. Plastic bottle

Think about Unusual Mailing Processes

1. Foreign mailings
2. Special postmarks
3. Messenger-boy delivery
4. Registered letters

Think about Using Specialized Stock Material Available

1. Printed personalized calendars and other "reminder advertising" material
2. Texas bucks, safety bucks, magic bucks, and the like
3. Flash cards
4. Zip envelopes with tag attachments
5. Bordered blanks
6. Giant letter or wire
7. Global letter
8. Holiday letterhead
9. Colorful-stock letterhead
10. Double-window envelopes
11. Zip envelopes with stock art

Think about Reply Cards

1. Two-color
2. Product or object in light half-tone screen behind the copy
3. Stylized art

4. Extra small or extra large cards

5. IBM card punched

6. Check squares in reverse (white in color band or color squares to check)

7. Very large type, one-line signature

8. Two-color underlining of copy

9. Plastic mail box on reply card

10. Smith-Corona, London, used a carrier pigeon as a reply device . . . got 100 per cent return

Think about Envelope Impact

1. Die-cut all the way through, so color of enclosure shows both front and back

2. Money showing through double window. ("The price is $1.98. . . . Send us $2. . . . Here's your change.")

3. Put a shorthand note on the envelope or on a tip-on addressed to the secretary

4. Photograph on back of envelope repeated inside as letterhead

Think about Unusual Art

1. Enlarged sections of photographs

2. Surrealistic art

3. Child's drawings

4. Doodles

5. Three-dimension art

6. Photographs of puppets

21

How to Buy Art and Layout

If you've ever had a carpenter paint your house or a painter work out the locations for your lighting fixtures, you know that there is more than one skill in home building.

The same thing is true in commercial art. One artist is a layout genius. Another an illustrator. A third a top-flight retoucher. Then, of course, there's the "handy man" of commercial art, who can do anything reasonably well. The "all-round" artist is often like the handy man around the house. He's a jack of all trades. Master of none.

And if you've ever watched a student in an art museum, copying an Old Master, you'll notice a "slight" difference in the results.

As you buy art and layout for direct mail, you'll want to keep those facts in mind.

You may want to "buy" your art by putting an artist on your payroll. If you do, you'll usually hire a "handy man." That's fine, if your quality requirements are not very high, if you need work in a big rush, or if you have a lot of routine art work like paste-up to be done.

Except in those cases, however, an artist (or even a good-sized art department) hired to create direct mail is likely to be a false economy if a good art studio or a reasonable supply of free-lance artists is nearby.

Such artists work by the hour. Most of them can give you an estimate of the cost of your job before they start it. They will take longer, in elapsed time, to do a single rush job than your inside artist will. But if

235

you have a good deal of work, you'll get the whole batch done faster through a studio. Because they'll be able to put more men on the job. One of the art studio's best selling points is that they have a lot of man-hours on tap when you need them. Then, too, experience may prove that your staff artist is a whiz in laying out catalogue sheets, but everything he does looks like a catalogue. Or that he's a brilliant cartoonist. But incapable of designing a simple letterhead and a total loss at figuring out how much space your copy will take up. Or at choosing a type face that fits your message.

Many good artists are like that—brilliant in one field, rather sad in others. That's another reason why art studios and specialists prosper. But the real reason that studios and specialists are preferable, of course, is— *they are better.* While your "handy man" is doing a fair job of layout, illustration, and retouching, three studio specialists knock out a sparkling layout, sharp illustrations, and smooth retouching. When you see the final results, side by side, you get the same impression as you did in the art museum—watching a student copy an Old Master.

The very finest illustrators, cartoonists, retouchers, and fashion artists may be found outside the studios, operating as free-lancers. If you want top-quality work and can't be satisfied in the studios, you might look among the free-lancers. (There are free-lance handy-man artists, too, if your requirements aren't too strict, but these comments are about the skilled specialist who has found he can live on his specialty.)

If you are just starting to buy art for direct mail, or are not satisfied with your present art, and are in or near a city of any size, take a day or two to improve your sources. You can't beat or bludgeon better art out of a poor artist. The best way to improve art is to improve your source.

Start with a personal visit to the studios. And be sure you talk to the boss. Call ahead and let him know you're coming. Tell him what kinds of work you expect to need, and let him show you what the studio has done. But be sure he takes you through the studio. As you go, look at the work each man is doing and the kind of "scrap" he has around. You'll see the differences among the artists and be able to guess where each man is best. Ask if the studio ever goes outside for special help. Form a mental picture of the variety of skills the studio has. There's no use talking price at this point. Because an artist's hourly rate means nothing to you.

Take a little different approach with the free-lancers. Ask them to come to you. Tell them you're looking for sources for occasional spot work, that you've heard they're outstanding in a particular field, but you have forgotten which. They'll tell you. Then ask to see a few samples of their work in that area, plus anything else they think is especially good. They'll be glad to come in and spread samples on your desk. You can draw your own conclusions.

Don't bother to visit a free-lance artist. His workroom would probably depress you. The reason you visit the studios is that, otherwise, you deal with a "contact" man. And he is trying to satisfy you on a particular project. In such a case, you may never find out what skills the studio *really* has.

Talk things over with your art source. When you order layout and art, you'll need more than a purchase order unless the need is very simple. Sit down with the artist or studio contact man and go over the problems. Your artist can often make very valuable contributions to the success of your direct mail if he knows what you are trying to do. So tell him as much of the story as you can. Who is getting the piece. What it's supposed to do to them. Give him some "direction" if you want to, some rough sketches of your own, a sample you like, a statement about what you *don't* want, or simply let him tackle the problem himself. It will usually cost you less if you "direct" him. You'll often get brand-new ideas if you let him strictly alone. Take your choice.

But *be absolutely certain to give him a deadline.* A good artist or studio is usually overloaded with work, and "as soon as you can" is just another word for "never."

When it comes to cost, artists and studios vary. Most are willing to give you a quotation before they begin a job. But their quotes and their prices are usually based on hourly rates. It's an old axiom (not always true, of course) that, in his specialty, the highest-rate artist is the cheapest in the end. A top-flight cartoonist, for example, can do a better cartoon in ten minutes than a mediocre one can in two hours, maybe two years. In any event, don't ever let a high hourly rate scare you away. Almost every commercial artist that ever lived started at a minimum wage and worked his rate up. It's high for a reason—his performance and ability.

22

Jobs Letters Can Do for You

The Versatile Letter

The letter is the persuasive salesman of direct mail . . . the most personal format of this most personal medium. No other format of direct mail quite compares with a letter. It is the most widely used form. In general, it is conceded to be the most effective. And many believe it is the most difficult form to do well. Other formats have their place, of course. They can be more colorful, or carry more illustrations and information; many forms are less expensive in quantity, etc.

In fact, even when the letter is used, it is frequently only part of a mailing. It is often accompanied by a folder or other insert which fully explains the product and by a reply device of some sort. However, the letter is used for so many purposes in direct mail you can almost say, "Use a letter every time, and you won't go wrong."

While that might slightly overstate the case, there are some areas where a letter is practically required for success . . . or where it is certain to increase the value of the mailing appreciably. Here are some of those cases:

1. When you want to make a complete sale.

2. When you want replies or inquiries.

3. When you are writing to "protected" business officials whose mail is well screened before delivery.

4. When you can use the value of a more personal approach. We'll touch on more of them in our discussion of letters.

Different problems, however, call for different *kinds* of letters, and it is a lack of understanding in this area that causes many of the "copycat" failures in direct mail. Imitative advertisers receive or read a good letter and proceed to adapt it for their own purpose. Often, however, their problem is different. And they find themselves trying to drive a nail with a screwdriver. The letter which worked well in the job for which it had been tailored falls flat when out of its element.

Types of Letters

With this in mind, let's classify letters into different types, look at their functions and their characteristics, and show some examples.

Our first broad division is between "Mail-order" letters, used to complete a sale, and "Advertising or Sales-promotion" letters, which are used to move a person *toward* a sale . . . but not necessarily to complete it.

The Mail-order letters (see Chapter 28) must replace a salesman completely. The Advertising or Sales-promotion letters are designed to assist or support a salesman, in the same way that publication or broadcast advertising assists and supports him.

These basic differences in the two types of letters are very important when judging results. The Mail-order letter (seldom used without a folder and reply card of some kind) must be judged largely on the number of sales traced directly to it. The success of the others can be judged only on readership, reaction, inquiry response, etc. Because other elements intrude between the letter and the sale.

If you'll keep in mind the fact that these classifications have no scientific basis, but are simply developed out of experience . . . and that you are not *required* to classify every letter you read or write into one of these categories, you'll find them quite helpful.

Before you begin a letter, for example, you can say to yourself, "What kind of letter is required here?" and read the characteristics of that type of letter. You'll find it will help you do the right kind of writing job.

Or, after you have written a letter, you can compare its characteristics with others of its "type." This may indicate something overlooked or overdone and help you with rewriting.

Here, then, are our classifications of letters.

The Announcement Letter

The Announcement Letter Is Used for moving announcements; price changes; additional items; personnel changes, etc; any kind of change or situation which you wish to announce.

Here is a letter chosen by Dartnell Service * as one of the twenty best letters of the year it was used. It makes an announcement in a human-

* See SOURCE LIST for full name and address.

interest fashion . . . by letting the reader know a new "face" will soon call on him.

WESTERFIELD PHARMACAL CO., INC.

11 St. Mary Street, Dayton 2, Ohio

A NEW FACE AT YOUR OFFICE DOOR

That's what you'll be seeing one of these days.

It will be a pleasant face . . .

. . . the face of Mr. Sidney Wilson, a man who has spent many enjoyable years building friendships among the doctors of New York State.

Perhaps he's already a friend of yours. Then you'll note a new sparkle in his eye. For he's enthusiastic over his new job. And he'll have some new things to tell you.

He'll tell you that his headquarters will be Hamburg, from which city he'll pay you regular visits.

He'll tell you that he's now representing Westerfield, and about its fine line of pharmaceuticals, including injectables and specialties.

He'll tell you how glad he'll be to help in any way he can.

And we know he'll serve you well, in a courteous and efficient manner.

He'll be dropping in soon.

Another example of making an announcement is found in these two letters. They show how "those days when nothing goes right" can be exploited to your own advantage, even when lightning strikes twice. We think you'll enjoy these letters. They were written years ago, around 1946. First was the problem of announcing a number change in the middle of the year. Here's how that was done:

GRAPHIC SERVICE

846 South Main

Dayton, Ohio

Me and the Telephone Company "has been in a fight."

Naturally, I was in the right.

Naturally, the Telephone Company won.

I said, "Our line is too busy too often, and I either want you to show us how we can quit talking so much or else give us one of those two-way jobs like the National Cash Register or Wright Field."

The Telephone Company said, "Your trouble is, you have too much business nowadays . . . you ought to have less business."

"What do you want me to do?" I asked, "Go back to the days when I didn't pay your bills?"

"Say no more," said the Company, "you'll have another phone. If one is busy the other will ring. After today your number is Fulton 1166."

"Oh, no," I said. "Fulton 8211's our number. It's always been our number. Everybody knows it's our number. We won't give it up. I don't care who you are, you big bully . . . Our number stays Fulton 8211."

"Fulton 1166," it said.
"Fulton 8211," I said.
"Fulton 1166 . . ."
"Fulton 8211 . . ."
I had the last word . . . because at this point, I hung up.

           ✿   ✿   ✿

This afternoon a man came in the office with a screwdriver.
"Who are you?" I said.
"I'm here to take out your telephone, I understand you don't want it any more. . . ."
Well, that's why I'm writing this letter to you. After today, our telephone number is Fulton 1166.

Call it often.

Unfortunately, this number change became better known to customers than it did to Bell Telephone employees, for when the new telephone book came out, it listed the *old* number for Graphic.

At about the same time, John and Bill Yeck, who owned Graphic, were just organizing Yeck and Yeck (which, while destined to grow into a well-known organization, was at that time operating from the same offices as Graphic). Somehow the telephone people had skipped this listing entirely. Hence, this second letter soon went out:

"You're one in a million," said the Telephone Company.
We blushed prettily . . . then stopped. Wasn't this the same Company that gave us a fast bit of number changing not long ago?
Still, that sounded nice. "Thanks," we said tentatively.
"The Ohio Bell Telephone Company is one of the world's outstanding financial organizations," the Company boomed. "It pays dividends to millions of stockholders. It utilizes the world's most advanced technical knowledge in its subsidiary, Western Electric. It has plush-lined rest rooms for its female employees. It is a dream come true."
We wondered what this had to do with us. "Continue," we said.
"Our publishing ventures are classics in their field," said the C., its vest buttons popping. "We publish directories at the drop of a hat, with millions of names in little two-point type. Such things as listing 'Yeck and Yeck' and 'Graphic Service,' both with the same new telephone number, are pie. We do everything through channels, and verbal orders don't go. We have more complicated systems for answering questions than the Army, and in our great publishing ventures, we have *less than three errors per thousand* listings."
"Nice," we said, "but when we have one error in a thousand some kill-joy wants to know 'why?' What's this long speech to us?"
"You're one in a million," said the Telephone Company.
We began to feel faint.
"Look," the Company continued quickly, "we gave the quick shuffle to your 'Yeck and Yeck' listing and it didn't get in the new book at all. And Graphic

Service's number change must have stuck to the bottom of some printer's beer glass, for it reads Fulton 8211, not 1166. Think how absolutely and utterly unique this makes your organization. Only three people in a thousand get any errors at all, and you get two . . .

"You're one in a million."

That's us.

P.S.   Honestly, we're not proud. We'd rather be common, ordinary people with our name in the book. But, since we're not, would you mind writing it in. That's right . . . Fulton 1166 . . . call it often.

Characteristics. The announcement letter is usually rather short, concise, and clean-cut. It carries its news in the opening paragraph or headline. Then the *meaning* of the news and its benefits or value *to the reader* should be stressed. If the benefits are strong enough to justify prominence, they can come first, and the "facts" of the case can follow.

On the other hand, if your benefit is really a rationalization (you've been forced to move to the edge of town and away from most of your customers, so you want to stress "plenty of free parking space"), always emphasize the facts as your "news" and let the rationalized benefits tag along. Because . . . when minor sales points are exaggerated in value, they become negative factors.

Whether the facts are in the opening or not, it's best to draw attention to them by some mechanical device: *Italicize the new address and moving date* . . . PUT THE ITEMS ADDED TO YOUR LINE IN CAPS . . . indent the paragraph that tells the facts, etc.

But don't close your letter without including a selling idea.

The Attention-getter Letter

1. *The Attention Getter Is Used* to illustrate or dramatize a sales point. It's difficult to open a mind to the appreciation of a new product. It's just as hard to impress people with the virtues of a particular product or service. This is especially true when you try to convince readers of the *abstract* qualities of a product: economy, richness, silence, etc. Often, you will try to do this by comparison, or by saying, "In other words . . ." Or, you might find yourself trying analogy. Sometimes this is difficult to do with words alone . . . but easier when you can add nonverbal symbols of some sort to your letter. If these illustrations are dramatic or unusual, they can serve as attention getters as well as illustrate the sales point.

But be sure they tie in directly and quickly with the *one* most important idea you want to get across.

Here is an example of using an attention getter to dramatize a sales point. The letter has a one-inch, plastic "smokin'-type" pipe in the space for the inside address. Note how this pipe is related to the product—Price Pipe—and the "peace and contentment" which both kinds of pipe bring to "Waterworks Men."

PRICE BROTHERS COMPANY
1932 East Monument Ave., P.O. Box 825
Dayton 1, Ohio

[Plastic Pipe]

Here's the *second* best kind of pipe to bring peace and contentment to waterworks men. The kind you sit by the fire with, and tap on the arm of a rockin' chair.

What's *first* best—for peace and contentment?

Well, Price Pipe. Here's why.

With Price Pipe in your water lines, your waterworks men get *years*, not hours, of peace and contentment. Probably not even your youngest will live to see the day when Price Pipe gives trouble.

That's because three things go together to lick water-line problems: Long Life; Great Strength; Sustained Capacity. And Price Pipe meets all three of those requirements, *better than any other type pipe.*

There's no "big bust" in the middle of the night—for anything less than an earthquake. There's no worry about a tough cleaning or lining job after 15, 20, or even 50 years. As for long life, you just can't beat concrete, buried in the ground. And the steel cylinder makes it plenty strong.

So I think Price Pipe tops the rockin'-chair type for contentment . . . and you'll be happy and contented with Price Pipe right off, too. It's so easy and fast to install that your new Price line will be operating before you know it.

You'll enjoy reading our new 16-page booklet, "Laying Instructions for Concrete Pressure Pipe." Each step is illustrated with a photograph or drawing. It is easy to read and easy to understand. You'll want one for your files . . . and maybe some for men in the "field."

If you think you'd like *years* of peace and contentment . . . of trouble free, full capacity service,

Think first of Price.

2. *The Attention Getter Is Used* to ensure reading of the letter. This is probably the most common reason for using attention-getting letters. And the least necessary. By and large, direct mail is used as a selective method of advertising. It is mailed only to people who are presumed to have an interest in the product, service, or individual sending the letter.

The fact that it has been received in the mail *guarantees* "attention" from all but a lunatic fringe of society. (Almost everybody gives their mail enough attention to evaluate it.) So in most cases the real problem is to retain the reader's interest. Or, you might say, to keep the reader from throwing the letter away.

Actually, the addition of a poorly chosen attention getter sometimes works against this. It selects, from among the readers, those people who are interested in a gadget or trick rather than those who are interested in the particular product. Many users, by their choice of attention elements, limit the impact to the job of getting attention alone, without any sales-point tie-in. While this may amuse some readers, it's seldom necessary and adds little if anything to the effectiveness of the mailing. For example, a letter arrives in the mail. On the envelope is a drawing of a man about to put a wastebasket in a safe. Under it are the words, *"If you throw this letter in the wastebasket, put the wastebasket in the safe."*

In our opinion, this is a great attention getter. Can't imagine many people throwing the letter away without opening it. But then it's hard to imagine many people throwing away a good-quality *blank* envelope, either.

If they open the letter with a chuckle, this has some added value. (No one disputes that.) But it also requires a pretty important announcement in the letter to avoid a let-down . . . and, unless there *is* a very important announcement inside, the memory value of the envelope (which recipients will remember indefinitely) will not carry over to the product advertised.

3. *The Attention Getter Is Used* to make the letter memorable. This is an entirely legitimate use of a gadget or other attention getter. It is particularly valuable when the letter is designed to sell a personality or an impulse-purchase item. Anything presented in an out-of-the-ordinary way will naturally be remembered longer.

This memory is likely to be reinforced by future contacts, too. When you send a good, attention-getting letter to a group of local people, you should be prepared to have them greet you on the street with comments about "that letter you sent" and expect to be introduced, possibly years later, with, "This is the fellow who sent that ——— letter I told you about." Obviously, if memorability is your problem, the attention getter you use must have impact. A routine use of a common gadget will not do the job.

A series of letters using common or "usual" gadgets or die cuts will possibly prove to be a memorable *series* of letters, but you can often get your name or product more readily recognized and remembered with one truly unusual mailing a year than you can with twelve ordinary gadget letters.

The attention getter in the next letter was an excellent device to make the letter memorable. No matter how the reader looked at it, he couldn't lose. The "gadget" was a pair of dice in a cellophane bag, attached to the letter in the position of the inside address. However, the dice were "loaded." No matter how the reader rolled them, they came up seven. It's an interesting letter:

CONTINENTAL TOOLING SERVICE, INC.
19 West Fourth Street . . . Dayton 2, Ohio

Roll 'em . . . you can't lose.

We call these gallopin' dominoes "Continental" dice because you aren't gambling when you use them. You're going to win every time.

. . . and that's our aim at Continental Tooling . . . to make sure that you do win every time . . . by getting tool design that is *good;* as foolproof as possible; yet economical to buy and to use.

So we try to get and keep the best designers in Dayton . . . and Dayton rates pretty high in tool design. We make the most of past experience with hundreds of all kinds of jobs, digging through our knowledge and our files for the best and most efficient ideas. We want to make every Continental job an investment, not a gamble.

Three types of people "invest" in tool design at Continental. Those who go outside for all their design work; those who have a temporary overflow; and most important of all, those old-time, top-flight designers who know the value of a fresh approach to a tough problem.

Next time *you* have overflow or a design problem that needs a fresh approach or a tool that isn't producing at the rate you think it should, give us a chance to help you. It won't be a gamble.

Well, use the dice; you'll enjoy them. Use Continental; you'll enjoy working with us, too. In either case, you can feel sure of one thing . . .

The venture is sure to be profitable,

You can't lose.

4. *The Attention Getter Is Used* to get a laugh. There's still room for a bit of the old-time medicine-man technique in selling some products. Entertain 'em first. Then persuade them to buy. So one additional use of attention-getter letters is to elicit that chuckle . . . and, with it, to line up the reader on "your side."

The next example gets a chuckle from the way it "makes a landing" in the reader's home. Part of a campaign which promotes "keeping hubby happy" with salesmen's wives, to help the salesmen perform better, this was a most unusual mailing piece (see Chapter 26 for a study of the Knipco campaign). The chuckle starts from this mailing—a 4- by 10-inch piece of green cardboard in a 4½- by 10⅜-inch end-opening, clasp envelope—with the curiosity aroused by a line on the outside which says, "Air Mail All the Way." The chuckle develops as the letter flies out the end of the envelope as soon as the clasp has been opened. The card had been inserted with a taut rubber band attached next to the clasp.

Here's the example:

I want to save your time.

I couldn't resist writing to tell you how wonderfully all you wives are treating your Knipco-selling husbands this fall (Esther Soderberg of Lake Geneva,

Wisconsin, must be a real charmer. I've sent her 35 checks so far), but it's getting so close to the end of our check-signing spree that . . .

I hate to have you waste the time it takes to pull a letter from an envelope when you could spend it keeping hubby happy.

So I won't write again . . . except when saying, "Enclosed find check" . . .

and, 'til November 30th, I'm ready and anxious, any time you give the word, to make many more $5 checks . . .

"Fly" your way.

5. *The Attention Getter Is Used* to widen readership. In spite of the fact that direct mail is a "selective and personal" medium, the lists available are not always entirely accurate as far as buying influences are concerned. They can't be. In some families, father makes the decision. In others, it's mother. Occasionally, the kids join in.

The same is true in business. In one firm, the chief engineer must be sold. In another, the purchasing agent. In a third, your product just happens to be a special interest of the president. And, occasionally, everyone in the place is a prospect . . . even though you have only one of them on your list. In such cases a dramatic, unusual attention getter will increase readership and interest in your product. But it has to be so good that the person receiving the mail can't keep it to himself. He simply has to show it around. When used to widen readership, the attention getter has general and wide interest, is truly unusual, or has a "pass-on" quality.

Here is an example of a dramatic attention getter (a Viewmaster, three-dimensional viewer with six full-color photos of a pleasant young lady demonstrating the advertised product), which should get "news" of the letter passed around. In fact, the letter suggests showing the attention getter to others. The use of this "gadget" is adequately justified, also, in the copy. But, read the letter. You'll see how you can widen readership by means of attention getters:

HUFFY MOWER
The Huffman Manufacturing Company
Dayton 1, Ohio

Dear Mr. _____:

LET ME LEND YOU BETTY.

Betty knows how to sell Huffy Mowers.

She takes mowers out and *demonstrates* them. She shows folks how easy the Huffy is to run . . . she shows prospects what the Huffy will do for them. She proves it's *fun to run.*

Folks watch her demonstrate . . . and they *sell themselves.*

If I could send Betty, in person . . . let her stand in Housewares all day, or take people out on a lawn somewhere . . . you'd sell mowers by the gross.

But I can't. There isn't enough of the gal to go around.

So I've done the next best thing. I've caught her in the act—on three-dimension color film—and put her in this Viewmaster.

Betty-in-action is part of a display that hooks right on the floor model of a Huffy. She takes up no floor or counter space, but she does *help you and your salespeople sell faster and easier*. In fact . . . she often makes the sale.

. . . prospects take a look at Betty's demonstration and *almost sell themselves.*

Betty's whole display comes free with an order of 24 Huffy Mowers or can be purchased separately with smaller orders.

The price-protected, profit-producing, popular Huffy Mower will be one of your hottest items this spring . . . particularly with the tireless, effective Betty on hand . . .

To help you sell.

P.S. I'd like to give you this copy of Betty-in-action, but obviously it's impractical to give copies away and then try to make them part of a deal. Show it around, see what your salespeople think of it. In a few days Mr. R. E. Utz will drop by to pick up Betty and answer any questions you may have about the Huffy Mower.

6. *The Attention Getter Is Used* to sell the boss (the man who O.K.s the mailing). Direct mail, along with all other forms of advertising, would probably do an even better job if it could concentrate on selling the prospect. Unfortunately, in many cases, it cannot.

First, the "boss" must be sold on using the advertising. And sometimes the boss is quite concerned about "attention." When you have a boss who doesn't believe in conventional direct mail, you often find that he will O.K. a good attention getter.

Characteristics. In the "attention-getter" field, the world is your oyster. This is the home of the surprising phrase, the gadget letter, the die cut, the funny-fold, the pop-up, the "circular" letter (a round sheet of paper), the scented letter, and many, many others (see "Formats" for ideas).

The Attention-getter letter is built around the attention getter, whatever it may be. The trick is to use the attention getter functionally, so that it reinforces the sales story and does not replace it. The attention getter wastes money when it says, "Look at me. You've never seen such an unusual letter. You'll never forget this letter. You'll probably want to send out one like it yourself," but fails to impress you with the name or the value of a product or service.

These letters, at their best, have a sort of singleness of purpose. The attention element, if it is to be successful, *must lead directly into the most important point of your letter.* A good, dramatic attention element—used properly—can lend a sledge-hammer force to the impact of one sales point.

The Benefit Letter

The Benefit Letter Is Used for the "what-it'll-do-for-you" approach to the reader. It is the basic advertising and sales-promotion letter for any *new* product or service . . . or for any one which has a *demonstrable difference* over its competitors.

Here is an example of a Benefit letter. Note that, through the use of the unusual layout, the reader's problems can be emphasized . . . and the profit-making solutions well pointed up:

DUMPCRETE DIVISION

Maxon Construction Company, Inc.

131 N. Ludlow Street   Dayton 2, Ohio

"It's getting tougher and tougher,"
ready-mix men are saying . . .
        "to squeeze out a decent profit between cost and selling price."

You may be saying the same. If you are, you know the answer . . . lower costs and higher production. But how to get it? Look at *these* ideas:

YOUR PROBLEM	A SOLUTION
Rising costs of materials	Users say they can save $1 a yard with the lower-cost Dumpcrete. A dollar a yard can add up pretty fast—to *your profit*—in spite of soaring material costs.
Higher equipment costs	You can save over half with Dumpcretes.
Increased upkeep, repair and operating expenses	The Dumpcrete has no motor or other complicated moving parts and requires no day-in–day-out attention . . . so maintenance and repair costs drop way down.
Rising labor costs	In some localities Dumpcrete drivers are on a lower rate—the difference helps you keep costs down.
Equipment down time	In extremely cold or rainy weather agitating equipment isn't good for much. But Dumpcretes stay on the job hauling sand, gravel, coal, earth, mortar, or other materials.
Waiting time at the job	Here's an interesting and unexpected advantage of the Dumpcrete. Some contractors will keep a truck mixer grinding away at the job until they are good and ready for it. Dumpcrete users tell us, "Our customers know they can't keep us waiting all day. So they plan their pours better, and we have less waiting time."

YOUR PROBLEM	A SOLUTION
Demands for greater production on big jobs	Contractors often want their concrete "all at once." You can get an extra load a day from the Dumpcrete because of its faster loading, hauling, and discharge time.
High cost of delivering small "cleanup" loads	The light-weight and low-cost 2-yard Dumpcrete handles small loads at rock-bottom cost. It's a swell utility body, too.
Maintaining load-to-load uniformity of concrete	Careful control at the central mixing plant, plus Dumpcrete hauling, delivers uniform air-entrained concrete without appreciable changes in air content, temperature, or slump—the high-grade product that contractors always ask for.

The Dumpcrete and air-entrained concrete are a profit-making combination for ready-mix men everywhere. Put this team to work for you. Send the card for more information, without obligation, today . . . so tomorrow you can
Increase your profits too.

Characteristics. The Benefit letter starts right out, in the first sentence or in the running headline, by announcing the product's *most important benefit to the reader.* (A series of letters for a product with more than one significant benefit may use a different benefit in the head each time.)

After the benefit is stated, in strong, interesting, understandable terms, the letter proceeds to make the benefit statement believable. It tells the reader *how* the product produces the benefit for him. It explains how *easy* this benefit is to get . . . through purchase of the product, and how to go about getting it.

Somewhere in the letter all the other major benefits of the product will be listed. And, finally, the letter will urge the reader to action, usually giving some reason for prompt action. If you have a sales problem and are in doubt about the type of letter to use, then stick to the Benefit type.

And, when you use this approach, whether you are trying to make the entire sale or not, you can experiment with some of the "formulas" mentioned in the Mail-order chapter, such as Henry Hoke's PPPP (Picture, Promise, Prove, Push) or the famous AIDA (Attention, Interest, Desire, Action) of advertising in general (if you think of "attention" as calling attention to your strongest benefit).

Or, if you'd like a more expanded guide to a good Benefit letter, you might follow the outline used at Yeck and Yeck, Dayton, Ohio.

1. Put yourself in the other fellow's shoes.
2. Be sure the proposition is *clear* and *attractive* to the prospect.
3. Tell him what the product will do *for him.*
4. Tell him *exactly* what to do next.
5. Tell him *why* he should do it now.

Obvious as these admonitions seem to be, they are often overlooked or slighted. But they are all important for successful direct mail. Let's look at them, one at a time.

Put yourself in the other fellow's shoes. This, of course, is "Rule No. 1" in all efforts to persuade another, whether in advertising or not. Surely the salesman or the advertising man, whose business is persuasion, should understand this basic need.

Unfortunately, many don't. Company president, sales manager, advertising manager, and copy writer are frequently found presenting the case for a product from the point of view of the *seller* instead of that of the *buyer*. The writers talk about what they (or their boss) think is important . . . or about what they think the buyer *ought* to consider important, instead of those things in which the buyer actually *is* interested.

Eric Smith of Smith and Hemmings, Los Angeles, is one of the ablest and most highly respected direct mail practitioners in the country. He's a practical psychologist, who understands people and what makes them act as they do.

Smith cautions against taking prospects' knowledge of the proposition for granted. In discussing retail direct mail, he has summed up this admonition nicely with: "You've got to take your prospect by her little hot hand and lead her through the steps of the sale."

If more direct mail people had as vivid a feeling for the *people* at the other end of their mailings, their results would improve considerably.

With this need in mind, we can say that the whole recent idea of "motivation research" is good. And without passing judgment on the accuracy of the findings of some psychologists in this area, it's safe to say that *any* consideration of the motives or point of view of the reader is a good thing.

Be sure the proposition is clear and attractive to the prospect. The "proposition" (you might call it the offer) is the most important part of a mailing piece. It tells the reader what he can expect to get. And what he must give for it.

It should be spelled out completely and clearly . . . and then, looking at it from the point of view of the buyer, it should appear to be a real *bargain* for him. If it doesn't, you haven't presented enough facts, or you need to be more persuasive or convincing. If you aren't offering a bargain to the buyer, don't bother to make the mailing. You'll be throwing money away.

"Bargain" doesn't mean a special low price, necessarily, though that would classify as a bargain. The "bargain" reaction appears in the buyer's head when he decides that the thing you offer is worth more than the time, trouble, or money you are asking for it. By this definition, a "bargain" must be obvious to the buyer before *any* sale is made . . . so it's your job to make your proposition appear to be a bargain to him.

Tell him what the product will do for him. At the heart of making a proposition attractive to a buyer is the old question, "What'll it do for me?" Unless you can answer that question satisfactorily, there is no reason for the buyer to buy. It's a complete, convincing answer to that question that makes any sale possible.

Tell him exactly what to do next. If you've done a good job so far, the sale is "made," but it hasn't yet been completed . . . and, unless the buyer knows exactly what to do next, it may never be. He doesn't necessarily know! You'd better tell him.

Salesmen face this same danger when selling in person. They "make" the sale in the other fellow's mind, but fail to "close." They don't ask for the order, so they don't get it. Bill Gove, former sales manager of Minnesota Mining, used to call this the "British" way of selling. He said he felt this was the key difference between sales success in England and America.

Mr. Gove points out that typical British salesmen hate to ask for the order. "I've shown them the product," they say, "I've demonstrated its value; told them how it would help them; given the price and delivery. If they're going to buy, why won't they buy of their own free will and accord?"

"I don't know *why* they won't," says Gove, "but they won't."

The same thing is true when you are selling through the mail. Don't wait for the reader to figure out what to do, even if it is only to sign a card. Tell him . . . exactly.

Tell him why he should do it now. If you are one of Bill Gove's "British" type, you might say, "Why push him? Why not let him buy at his own speed? Why should he decide to buy and then not do it?"

Perhaps the real reason in both cases is inertia. The difference between decision and action. The buyer must not only decide to buy, mentally, he must act, and it's our job as persuaders to get him actually to take the action. This means making it as *easy* for him as possible.

So be sure to include in your copy complete instructions on the step you want the reader to take and the reason for taking it now. Make it the best reason you know. But if you don't have a good reason, don't try an obviously "phony" one. Because this will weaken conviction. If you lack any better reason, you may have to fall back on, "Do it now before you forget." That's not much of a reason, but it's better than nothing.

23

More Jobs Letters Can Do for You

The Mood Letter

The Mood Letter Is Used when the writer wants to mix emotion with fact in selling. This type of letter has the same objective that a salesman has when he takes a prospect to lunch or prefaces his sales talk with a bit about the weather. Its objective is to relax the reader, or, in some cases, to get him into the correct mood for the "pitch" (for example, a request for donations). Actually, emotion of some sort is part of almost every sale . . . all motivations for buying have an emotional base—happiness, pity, greed, fear, or some other. And the mood letter attempts to bring out this emotion.

Here's a comment about a humorous mood letter written some years ago:

This letter isn't written just to be funny. . . . To be "human," yes . . . to read "easy," of course . . . to enjoy reading, naturally—but not just for a laugh. Letters like this are written to sell things, and the "sell" is always there. Sugar-coated, perhaps, but the point we want to get across is solidly pounded into the letter.

Really, they're "mood" letters.

The important thing in selling is to make people happy before you get to the "sell." By the time they reach the selling sentence in these letters they *want* to believe it . . . because they're in a happy mood.

Ask any salesman if the mood is important when he's selling a new prospect
. . . he'll tell you, "Naturally, get 'em happy."

One thing is certain . . . a salesman who is never heard, an ad that is never
read, cannot get results. YECKOPY is read from stem to stern . . . the
readers are in a happy mood . . . and they want to believe the sell.

That, I am told, means sales. Sales means profits. Profits mean salaries.
Salaries mean prosperity. Prosperity means happiness. Happiness means sales
. . . Oh, oh! That's where I came in.

It's hard to describe the mood desired when dealing with egg-heads
and beatniks. But here's an example of an outfit selling recordings by
mail that gave what might be called a "screwball" mood a try. The
envelope for this letter had a "drowning" hand clutching the air from
beneath the water. The same hand appears as part of the letterhead. On
the envelope was this suggestion, "Burn this." But on to the letter:

MAELSTROM
53 State Street
Room 1010
Boston 9, Massachusetts

Never mind how we got your name. The point is, we got it, and furthermore,
WE KNOW HOW HOPELESSLY DEPRAVED YOU ARE!

We plan to take advantage of your warped sense of humor and lack of moral
fibre to try to foist upon you from time to time various items—books, records,
useless gift items, etc.,—by which we think you might be amused to such an
extent that you will be willing to buy them from us.

Now, wait a minute, don't throw this away yet. You might as well read it,
because you're on our list, and we're going to be sending you these letters
until you read one. As we were saying,

MAELSTROM is *not* a Something-of-the-Month Club! We're not even a club.
We'll be peddling only whatever comes along that looks good enough to recommend, so it may be a few weeks or a few years between selections.

MAELSTROM is *not* giving away anything free! Anything you get from us
(except these nondescript sheets of paper, which we print up cheap) you will
have to shell out hard cash for.

MAELSTROM is *not* taking a loss in order to perform a service! At least, not
if we can help it. We're in this strictly to make MONEY off *you*.

If you don't want the items, we'll let it go at that—but don't get the idea
that we're through with you. In any event you'll hear from us again concerning
future selections, as will any of your friends whose names you are unprincipled
enough to send us behind their backs.

Please don't get the idea that we are showing favoritism just because we are
devoting a whole page to Tom Lehrer. Golly, no. It is simply that he is a great
artist, a brilliant wit, and is looking over our shoulder while we write this.
Besides, we owe him some money.

Since bad news travels fast, you may have heard that Mr. Lehrer has recently recorded some new LPs. We list below the new and the old, as logically as we can under the circumstances. . . .

The MAELSTROM letter is the first page of a leaflet. On the remaining pages, the copy describes the various albums available. And always in the same light, "screwball" mood.

The Blended Mood. An interesting mood can be created by making a "blend" of several types of mood. Blend, in this type of writing, becomes Impact's Mixmaster. It becomes a process of smoothly intermingling the various levels of the reader's conscious and unconscious reaction.

Skilled blending of moods can take the laughter of a man and leaven it with anger. It can poke at things nostalgic and wrap them in a "right-now" urgency. It can strike at a man's defenses and lay bare his resistance. It can swing from the pinnacle of a man's pride to the depths of his defiance. It can take anger and frustration and tie them with the knot of hope. It can take hurt and assuage it with the impulse of generosity. It can entangle a man's feelings with his belief. It can create a mood combined of meanness, of magnificence, of tenderly outraged manhood, of an open generosity springing forth defensively.

The blended mood is used every day, successfully—particularly in charity appeals. It can be used in any kind of advertising—to strike deeply at the core of a man. Because the strings on his own reaction harp are plucked all at once.

As an example of this type of copy, take this letter from Boys' Town. Its mood effect is produced by throwing a monkey wrench into the reader's self-satisfaction of conscience. Note how the reader is swung from one side of his nature—a revulsion toward circumstances which abuse a child—to another side of his nature—the desire to "give a guy a break." The letter:

FATHER FLANAGAN'S BOYS' HOME
BOYS' TOWN, NEBRASKA

My dear _____:

How much is a homeless boy worth? Today thousands of proud, productive citizens, who live in the large cities and small towns across the nation were, only a few years ago, homeless, destitute boys. Many are skilled mechanics in the various trades; others are farmers, business and professional men.

These men came to Boys' Town as young boys, of all races and religious creeds. They all had the same qualification—they were homeless! They were sad, sensitive, with many heartaches because some tragedy had robbed them of their home and parents. Some wandered along the crossroads of the nation, their only home in some empty freight car. The shrill shrieking of the whistle as the train plowed forward was the only mother's lullaby they had ever heard. Others, who had been in trouble, came to us with snarls on their faces, with eyes that were hard, sullen, and suspicious.

How much are their lives worth today—to themselves, their wives and children, and to the nation?

Here at Boys' Town we continue, year after year, to rebuild the lives of homeless, deserted boys. You know of our work—your contributions in the past show that, for which I am eternally grateful. We help them solve their problems, we educate them in our schools, and teach them a trade. The mental and moral training they receive here teaches them to become stalwart, wholesome citizens.

As Christmas approaches, won't you help me provide for more homeless boys who have no other place to go? I am enclosing your 19__ Boys' Town seals. Any amount you care to send will help me care for more boys, and let me serve as your Santa Claus to my family of almost 1,000 who are here now. I want them to be happy because they've already had life's share of grief and hardships. Will you kindly do this now?

Thank you, God bless you, and may your own Christmas be doubly happy because you have brought happiness to our homeless, helpless boys.

> Sincerely
> /s/
> Father   Wegner

Another example of blended mood is found in the "Sea-of-Galilee" letter. Written by Bruce Barton, this letter combines a "happy" mood with a "sad" mood. Well blended, the moods seem to flow together, mix, intertwine, then rise to an effective "punch" at where the reader's feelings lie.

On such moods, mixtures, blends, are good appeals built. Here you are:

There are two Seas in Palestine.

One is fresh, and fish abound in it. Splashes of green adorn its landscape. Trees spread their branches over it and stretch their thirsty roots to sip of its life-giving waters.

Along its shores children play, as children played when He was there. He loved this sea. He could look across its silver surface as He spoke His parables. And on a rolling plain, not far away, He fed five thousand people.

The River Jordan forms this Sea with sparkling waters from the hills. So it laughs in the sunshine, and men build their houses near it, and birds their nests, and every kind of life is happier because it is there.

The River Jordan flows on south into another Sea.

Here there is no splash of fish, no fluttering leaf, no song of birds, no laughter of little children. Travelers do not pass, unless on urgent business which might take them there. The air hangs heavy above its waters, and neither man nor beast nor fowl will drink of it.

What makes this mighty difference in these neighbor Seas?

Not the River Jordan—it empties the same good water into both. Not the soil in which they lie, nor the country 'round about.

This is the difference:

The Sea of Galilee receives but does not keep the Jordan. For every drop which enters it, another drop flows out. The receiving and the giving go on, day after day, in equal measure.

The other Sea hoards its "income" jealously. Every drop it gets, it keeps.

The Sea of Galilee gives, and lives. The other Sea gives nothing. It is named "The Dead Sea."

There are two kinds of people in the world . . .

There are two Seas in Palestine.

Numerous fund raisers and others have used this example of mood as an introduction in a letter . . . then followed it with the appeal and an action close.

Characteristics. The Mood letter starts with a story, poem, experience, or description that is generally interesting and easy to read. (Remember here: you don't have quite the same restrictions on "selection" that you have in publication advertising. In publication advertising an interest device that is too general may not select your best prospects from the crowd. In direct mail, you have selected them beforehand. And they know it. "Selection," in publications, means the reader must decide *to read* an ad. In direct mail, it means he must decide *not to read* it.)

The beginning of a mood letter does not need to have any apparent connection with your product. And length is not a factor. As long as the copy remains interesting and easy, you can continue. At the end of your "story," however, you need smooth and easy transition to your sales pitch. And your story should have clear and effective application to a reason to buy or to act. Your beginning, in other words, should serve not only as an attention-getter and mood-producer, but also as an illustration of one of the buying reasons.

It's true, you see, with all these various methods of getting attention, that the method itself should not stand apart from the message but should lead into it naturally. If this is not done, the reader can easily stop reading the letter when you suddenly switch to your "commercial" . . . and he probably will.

Most mood letters, perhaps, aim for a happy mood . . . and this can hardly hurt in almost any case, for most of us are more willing to act when we are feeling happy. A sad mood, however, might be better in raising charity funds, and a nostalgic mood for raising funds from college alumni.

The Request Letter

The Request Letter Is Used to produce some kind of action that does not lead directly to a sale. This is often a request for information.

This next example is an excellent request letter. Written to educators asking information, it offers an unusual type of reward for doing as asked:

O'BRIEN–SHERWOOD ASSOCIATES INC.
Marketing Research
230 Park Avenue   New York 17, New York

Dear Educator:

College newspapers and magazines, like most publications, rely in part upon the support of advertisers for the revenue necessary to their operation.

The advertising these publications carry depends upon the personal buying and product-use patterns of their audiences including both students and faculty. We have been asked to determine these patterns among faculty members.

May we have your answers to the few, brief questions on the back of this letter?

As an expression of our thanks to you and the other educators cooperating in this study, we shall contribute $1,000 to a national charity—on behalf of "College Educators." Your vote will help determine which charity is to receive this sum. Please indicate your choice on the other side of this letter.

It is not necessary for you to sign this letter, and you have our assurance that you will never be identified with your responses in any way.

For your convenience we have attached a preaddressed and postage-paid envelope.

May we thank you in advance for donating a few moments to what we hope you will consider a mutually desirable objective.

Sincerely,

O'BRIEN–SHERWOOD ASSOCIATES INC.

Members: American Marketing Association
American Statistical Association

The following is also an excellent request letter. After over a quarter-century of experience in getting answers to questionnaires, Fact Finders Foundation, 2617 South Broadway, Los Angeles, finds this straightforward approach still the best, as indicated by this letter in behalf of a client:

FACT FINDERS FOUNDATION
2617 S. Broadway   ·   Los Angeles 7, Calif.

Date

Will you do me a favor . . .

. . . and take just a few moments to answer *any* or *all* of the brief questions on the back of this letter? Your answers are important and will be carefully read and considered.

One of the country's leading manufacturers of accordion folding doors, the Curtition Corporation, has employed us to learn the opinions of prominent contractors and architects regarding folding doors and especially about Curtition folding doors.

Our client is interested in doing everything possible to give those in the architectural and building industry the type of product and service you desire. This is the purpose of this survey.

Your signature is *not* required unless you would like more information or the results of this survey.

Sincerely,

/s/

Robert L. Baier

Director

When firms such as Fact Finders, whose continued existence depends upon successful surveys by mail, determine that this style of letter does the best job, we can be safe in following it when we have requests to make.

Characteristics. Obviously, the Request letter asks for something, frequently some kind of a response, so it must be clear, concise, and friendly. Since it is asking for something, it will give a logical reason for the request. And then ask for it. It will avoid any obvious sales pitch.

If it asks for a simple response, the number responding can be increased by enclosing a government postal card on which the response and the person's name have been automatically typed.

A "survey" letter, for example, should be of this type. Explain why you're asking, ask, and get out of the way. Some writers believe that a dime or a quarter (and lately a dollar bill) will get them more answers when attached to a letter of this type ("for your trouble"). But there is good reason to believe that the words, "I wonder if you would do me a favor," at the beginning of the letter will get just as good a response from men in business offices, where letter answering is the rule rather than the exception. When dealing with housewives or men who are not in offices, the payment is undoubtedly effective.

The Handshake Letter

The Handshake Letter Is Used to encourage the reading of or calling attention to, additional material sent with the letter. This kind of mailing is often used when you need to get a good deal of information across, and must use a booklet, folder, catalogue, or similar piece to do the job. The situation then becomes one where the letter is a supplement to the folder rather than the other way around. (This is not the normal situation. Usually, the letter carries the brunt of the selling load, and the booklet or folder is an additional reference piece.)

Here's an excellent example of the Handshake letter, in penscript with a picture of a lovely young lady smiling at the reader:

Picture of	From the desk of
Lovely Young	HELEN HOLMES
Lady	

You say you'd like my phone number? Why surely—it's Ravenswood 8–1065. Won't you phone your order *collect* after you've looked through this catalogue? Or mail your order to me . . . for my personal attention. I'll be listening for that phone to ring . . . I'll be watching each day's mail for your order or for just a note from you to me.

Helen

Precision Equipment Co. . . . 4411 Ravenswood Avenue . . . Chicago

The next letter example, used to introduce a folder, presents another interesting approach to get the folder read:

DURING PROHIBITION

. . . 'tis said, one enterprising Piggly Wiggly store owner posted this sign near his display of Welch's Grape Juice:
    "Be careful not to add 10 lbs. of sugar and let set for 10 days in a cool place or this may turn to wine!!"
To this old-time "advice," I'd like to add an up-to-date thought for you:
    *Be careful not to read the rest of this folder thoroughly and then snoop around for Plastrip * uses in your plant, or it may turn into the most profitable reading you've done this year.*
If you reject my "advice" and come to suspect that Plastrip may save big money for you as it has for others, you'll probably insist on using the card enclosed.
But don't do it unless you're prepared to have your company make larger profits as a result. Remember . . .

You've been warned.

Made by PT Protective Treatments, Inc., 420 Dellrose Ave., Dayton, Ohio

* T.M. Reg.

Characteristics. This letter should be relatively short, generally, because it doesn't want to compete with or take the place of the material it accompanies. It should be as friendly as a handshake or greeting.

Most important, it should talk about the advantages of the accompanying material to the reader and encourage him to read or inspect it immediately. It should not summarize the accompanying material or do anything to make it easy for the recipient to decide not to read the material. Because of the nature of the folder or other material, however, the letter may have to carry a request for action.

The Original-contact Letter

The Original-contact Letter Is Used to announce a new product or to introduce a new firm. It is any contact with a prospect who can be assumed never to have heard of you.

Here is an example:

HUFFY MOWER
The Huffman Manufacturing Company   ·   Dayton 1, Ohio

Dear Mr. _____:

I want to put my cards right on the table. I'm convinced, after its second year on the market, that the HUFFY MOWER is a red-hot item in the hardware field. I'm not alone, either. Wholesalers, dealers, consumers, and research firms are backing me up.

A. A. Powell, of C. W. Farmer Company, for example, wrote me: "You have the greatest selling mower on the market."

Stores like Maas Brothers in Tampa, write: "We put 50 out on free trial and *only two came back.*"

Consumers are saying it with dollars. They went for the HUFFY like cracker-jack. Neighbor sold neighbor. They bought us out.

A Marketing Bureau wrote, "Statisticians estimate only 7½% of national market for low-price power mowers now satisfied . . . with a constant in-crease in consumer preference for rotary type . . . now with a sales ratio of *3 to 1* over reel type (in some sections)."

But we've just received a report from an independent market-research firm, Stewart, Dougall and Associates, that tops them all. They talked to retail dealers and salesmen all over the country. The *summary* was 35 pages long, but what it said was: "*This is it.*"

You know what all that means. It means that consumers, and hardware dealers, will be looking and asking for the 19__ HUFFY. It's the "hot" product of the day.

But Stewart, Dougall point out . . . and we're quick to agree . . . that a good product is only half the battle. To have long-term success we need quality in the product *and* quality in the distributing organization. That means *limited, top-flight distribution.*

That's why I'm writing you.

We believe that top-flight distribution in hardware selling means selling through fewer than 100 wholesalers, of which you are one. Stan Lamb, our territory manager, may have told you that already. I want to emphasize it now.

We want you with us.

We want you with us this year . . . because this is our year. This is the year we have to serve every territory in the country—including Winston-Salem. And I'm confident that as soon as you know *as much about the HUFFY and the solid profit it is bringing wholesalers as I do, you'll want to be with us, too.*

It's easy, of course, for a manufacturer to be enthusiastic, but you probably know someone personally in Dunham, Carrigan & Hayden Co. of San Francisco, Igoe Brothers, Inc. of Brooklyn, Stowe Hardware & Supply Co. of Kansas City, Florida Hardware Co. of Jacksonville or in dozens of other "top-flight" whole-salers who handled the HUFFY in 19__. If you don't, someone else in your organization might. (For that reason, I'm writing this same letter to your mower buyer.)

Then I'll leave it to you.

But we must have someone in the Winston-Salem area soon. We don't like to continue to refer your hardware dealers to other trading areas for HUFFYS. And this is the time of the year when we'll be forced by events to decide what to do. In the next few weeks we'll have to complete our 19__ distribu-tion pattern. I'm sure you appreciate that . . . and understand why I'm anxious.

As I've said, we'd prefer to work with you . . . but (much as I'd enjoy it) I don't expect this letter to be answered with an order for two carloads. I'll be satisfied if you'll simply agree with me that the subject is worth looking into.

The best way to look into the Huffy market is through the neutral eyes of that Stewart, Dougall market-research summary. It's not for publication, but I can send you a confidential copy to look over. Then you can tell us whether you think there's a spot for the Huffy in your *future*.

Wouldn't you like to see that report soon? We have to move fast this month and we don't want to move without you if we can help it . . . so I'm taking the liberty of slipping a post card in this letter. Just initial it and I'll have Mr. Lamb stop in with the report. He can answer any questions you have and, I'm sure, show you that, with Huffy Mowers, there are . . .

Plenty of profits to share.

Characteristics. This letter is long, full of information, friendly, personal, and promises a benefit to the reader early in the letter. It is a strange thing that most people believe a "first" letter to a prospect should be short . . . when the fact is it has the best opportunity for success and by far the most to gain, when it is long.

The reason's clear when you think about it. You have a certain opinion or impression or "image" of the companies or firms you know. In many cases you have a pretty good "mind set" on what their products can do for you. Normally, you've formed this image during your first contacts with them. And, while you may change these first impressions, it turns out they were easier to form than they are to change.

So, if you get a long letter, with lots of information in it, *after* you "know" a company, the letter itself must be interesting all the way . . . or you begin to skim through it. On the other hand, if you get a long letter from a company you've never heard of, but which promises you a benefit for reading the letter, you have no prior knowledge to fall back on. So curiosity, or at least an open mind, drives you ahead.

So the first letter follows the sales manager's constant advice to "touch all the bases." You take the time to explain everything necessary carefully, without short cuts. But you must also remember that the reader is forming an opinion about the kind of company you represent as well as about the products you sell. Your personality should emerge from the letter; and the reader should feel you are a pleasant, friendly person and that you represent a company that's easy-to-do-business-with . . . as well as a source of profit or satisfaction to him.

The Reminder Letter

The Reminder Letter Is Used to keep everlastingly in touch with prospects. It is used to keep the name, the values, and the availability of a product or service continually before prospects.

Here are several examples of Douglas B. Mahoney's Cordial-contact letters, written for Horner Pharmaceuticals of Quebec. Mr. Mahoney, as advertising manager, has used Cordial Contact most effectively with doctors. His copy is quiet, restrained, erudite, dignified. But it comes up off the page with the warmth of story telling, slips quietly into the commercial, rides through a wisp of soft sell. And then is on its way. Its impression is one of quiet, soft-spoken sincerity . . . which implies a doctor can have confidence in Horner.

This letter, typical of the style used, tells an interesting story before it slips quietly into the soft-sell commercial:

FRANK W. HORNER, LIMITED
5485 Ferrier Street—Montreal, Canada

Dear Doctor:

"Give them any colour as long as it's black."

The late great Henry Ford is remembered by millions for many things. An automotive genius, foe of unions, champion of the common man, and coiner of phrases. He was ever in the public eye because of his remarkable contributions toward a better way of life.

And as sayings go, the above Fordism gets pretty close to expressing his penchant for practicality. Sacrifice frills to put a good product within the reach of every purse. Millions bought Fords.

In some respects, Horner came close to this philosophy in solving a tough pharmaceutical problem. A small sacrifice yielded a solution that gives you a relatively foolproof form of administering ammonium chloride. It's a tablet that takes this irritating salt through the stomach safely and ensures dissolution in the small intestine. The trade name is Dalitol.

Dalitol is no beauty . . . not from the outside. For here is the sacrifice. There's no teardrop design; no exquisite colour . . . Dalitol's innocuous exterior will win no fashion award. But underneath lies the functionalism.

Dalitol is a true enteric tablet—not just enteric-coated. Beneath the light, resinous coating, the active mass is impregnated with an enteric excipient. This resists gastric HCl, but dissolves easily in the alkaline contents of the small intestine.

When you prescribe Dalitol you ensure absorption of 7½ grains of NH_4Cl. For urine acidification, congestive failure, premenstrual tension, or whenever you must mobilize the sodium ion.

Prescribe inexpensive Dalitol in bottles of 100.

Here is another Horner reminder letter, to give you an idea of the continuity of style:

Dear Doctor:

There once was a man who never was.

You may have heard the bizarre account of this soldier who was D.O.A. at the recruiting office. How a corpse called "Major Martin" played such a big role in World War II.

Equipped with courier's pouch and bogus invasion plans, he was launched from a British sub and floated ashore in Spain. As surmised, these documents reached the Germans, who were completely deceived. This simple stroke changed the whole course of the Italian invasion in Allied favour.

Yet the plan, now hailed as inspired, almost died at birth. Because the top brass felt this simple scheme was much inferior to several complicated and more dangerous ones put forth.

The whole story is captivating in itself, but is even more fascinating to us for the pharmaceutical parallel it suggests. This comes with a new Horner agent that bids fair to change the course of treating nonfebrile oral infections. Bionets, with their simple formula, avoid the complications and dangers of antibiotic therapy yet are more effective.

Thanks to Bicetonium,* a potent new germicide, Bionets provide broad antimicrobial activity without the risks of antibiotic boomerangs. Unlike most other lozenges, Bionets destroy pathogens on contact. And they cover not only gram-positive and gram-negative bacteria, but also the fungus organisms that so often complicate antibiotic treatment. With *nonantibiotic* Bionets there's no worry about side reactions.

What's more, the benzocaine content promotes rapid pain relief. You can prescribe inexpensive, peppermint-flavoured Bionets now—bottles of twenty are in good supply at all pharmacies.

* Cetyldimethylbenzyl ammonium chloride, Horner.

This next example of cordial contact is from Charles W. Groves Company (teacher and high school student mailing lists) of Michigan City, Indiana. As usual with the Groves's copy, this letter radiates the warmth, the sincerity, the "We-wish-you-well," for which Mary Lou Lewis and Peggy Greenlaw are noted in their copy. Their style, like that of Douglas Mahoney's, has a consistency—to assist in building continuity:

CHARLES W. GROVES
427 Willard Avenue   ·   Michigan City, Indiana

A thought or two . . . for April

REGARDLESS OF TAXES

any of us can hold his chin high. There's no tax on that. You and I can enjoy our good health . . . and there's no tax on that.

There is no tax, either, on the feeling of soul satisfaction derived from a job well done. Friendship; fellowship; the right to call upon the wisdom of the Great Planner. They are ours for the asking.

There's no tax on cheerful courage. Nor on confidence, or the rain. We can be proud of this America of ours . . . walk in an awakening park . . . or down a country lane and smell the odor of freshly turned earth. We are lucky to live in a country where free enterprise allows each of us to earn according to the service offered his fellow man. Who can collect tax on that brand of luck?

The service I am offering you is the skill and know-how put into our public school teacher name listing. It provides you with an accurate means of selling your service effectively, economically, through direct mail. Through our teacher lists you can reach a market of 765,000 affluent and intelligent people. It's worthwhile.

> Cheerfully

Characteristics. This type uses the soft-sell approach. Like other forms of reminder advertising, the reminder letter (or mailing card) attempts to remind the reader, in a pleasant way, of the advertiser. It makes no attempt to complete a sale or even to promote an inquiry.

The essence of reminder advertising is that it must remind, and preferably on a regular schedule. Jack Carr's famous "Cordial Contacts" are good examples of reminder letters. His formula was simple. Write a list of good prospects regularly, once a month. Begin your letter with a story, a joke, an interesting experience. And, in a lighthearted way, lead into a recital of some of the benefits of your product. Said Carr,[1]

Mail these month after month, for the sole purpose of establishing and maintaining a constant contact on a concentrated group of people, and I can tell you in exact figures what such letters will do. If the average legitimate, reputable merchant or manufacturer will compile a mailing list of 1,000 names, we'll say. Names of actual potential prospects for his product. One hundred and forty out of each thousand will respond by the end of the first year. And about an equal number for each succeeding year. Until, at the end of five years, 70 per cent of the total list will have made inquiry, come into the store, or actually become customers. The other 30 per cent of the list will have died, removed elsewhere, or through some change, no longer remain prospects.

Reminder letters don't have to be as smooth as Carr's were. The fact that you are interested enough to write regularly is important. One machine shop in the Midwest for years did all its selling with a good price and regular letters which read simply:

Dear _____:
We will have some screw-machine time available during September.

Perhaps we can characterize reminder letters by reminding you that "little drops of water wear away the hardest stone," or of the old adage that it isn't the one-thousandth blow of the hammer that breaks ·the rock but all of the 999 that have gone before.

Good reminder letters, sent month after month to good prospects, will produce business, though perhaps not on quite the exact schedule predicted by Carr. They build a reputation, make friends, and predispose the prospect in your favor. This is a good type of letter to use between

[1] Jack Carr, *Cordially Yours,* The Reporter of Direct Mail Advertising, Garden City, N.Y., (n.d.), p. 35.

salesmen's calls when salesmen can't call as often as they should. The reminder letter does not try to take the place of a salesman; it just makes another "cordial contact" for him.

The Sincere Letter

A Sincere Letter Can Be Used any time you feel "moved" to do so. As a sincere letter, this next example shows how a very sincere man felt about a situation which affected him. No need to write about it, actually. But he felt moved. He felt this way about it. So . . .

CHRYSLER CORPORATION
Airtemp Division
Dayton 1, Ohio

Good-bye.

That's a word I hate to say. For now, after four-and-a-half years in Dayton, I'm beginning to know how fine all you folks are . . . how happy I am that I came here . . . and now suddenly, I have to say "good-bye."

Believe me, it isn't easy. Particularly to members of the Dayton Ad Club, who have certainly helped make Dayton the city where I've felt most "at home."

But wild horses (in the form of an opportunity I just can't turn down) are dragging me away. I'll soon be getting into hot water daily—as Assistant to the President of the Rudd Manufacturing Company (you know, hot-water heaters since 1893) . . . and, if you're ever in Pittsburgh, Pa. and want to see me "boil," just drop in. I'll give you a "warm" welcome.

I'll be gone on the first of June (things happen fast in the Space Age), so there's a chance I won't see you again to say "Hello—Good-bye." I'll have to let this letter do it for me.

So I'm writing to you and your fellow club members . . . who took me in and made me feel "homely" in Dayton . . . who have added to my friendships and broadened my horizons . . . to say "thanks" for all you've done for me and for Chrysler Airtemp.

Au revoir. Auf wiedersehen. Hasta la vista. 'Til we meet again,

Good-bye.

Another Sincere letter, used as a morale booster, as a thank-you gesture, as a means of letting a salesman, distributor, dealer know his efforts have been appreciated, is this letter by H. M. Huffman, Jr., of Huffy Mowers.

Star Salesman E. M. Thompson
Geo. Worthington Co.
802–32 St. Clair Avenue
Cleveland, Ohio

Dear Star Thompson,

I suppose you're a star salesman to everyone. I don't know . . . but anyone who opens 4 Huffy Key Dealers is a star to me. So I hope you don't mind if I call you that.

I have a big map of the U.S. here in my office . . . a pin in it for every Huffy Key Dealer in the country. It looks awful good. Frankly, when I show it to people, I sometimes sound a little cocky.

Yet I realize that every pin in that map was put there by a wholesaler salesman . . . at least four of them by you. *You've* made that map look good, and I want to tip my hat your way with . . .

Thanks.

If you're ever in Dayton, stop in and look at the map . . . you'll get a kick out of it. And thanks again for helping it look so good.

Characteristics. This letter has a "nonprofessional" feel about it. Perhaps it could be classified as a "business" letter written by someone who is not a businessman. (Or by a businessman who is particularly moved by events. He has, for example, a new product that will do wonders for you.) Sincere letters often give what might appear to be unnecessary background, but they set the stage for the announcement or offer.

The writer's personality shines through very clearly in this type of letter. It is often written in the very heat of enthusiasm, anger, success, or sincere conviction. And the writer's mood comes through.

There is frequently an overabundance of "I" in the sincere letter. Because the writer is deeply involved. The believability of the letter, however, and the obvious conviction of the writer seems to transfer some of the conviction to the reader.

Often the objective of the sincere letter is to get the reader to read some enclosed information and to act on it. In other cases, the entire information is in the letter.

The danger, when writing a sincere letter, is that you will jerk it out of the typewriter and get it into production without sufficient review. While these letters are often written "hot" and need little or no rewriting for style, they often fail to carry through . . . by failing to tell the reader exactly what to do and why he should act now.

Without instructions, the reader is "moved" all right. But he doesn't know what to do about it. So he just spins his wheels. This is like showing a powerful, moving film to develop an emotional appreciation for the United Fund and then just expecting the audience to send in checks, with no further instructions.

The Letterhead . . . a Double Handshake

Your letterhead has a great deal to do with the impressions you make on people who receive your mail. And the term "letterhead" has two meanings. One is the sheet of paper on which you write a letter. The other is information which you print, engrave, lithograph, etc., at the top of the sheet. The letterhead, within the bounds of both its meanings, should do these things for you:

1. It should briefly and succinctly give your reader all the necessary identifying information about your firm and its products or services.

2. It should clearly identify the firm, or the person in that firm, which it represents.

3. It should give an "impact" of quality, stature, prestige . . . as reflected in the paper's quality, the quality of reproduction which produces the reading matter at the top of the page, and the way in which the message is arranged upon the page.

Your Letterhead Is You

The letterhead (both types) you use represents your company and you. Because papers, designs, colors all make an immediate impression upon the recipient of a letter. Paper, design, and color have an impact on the eye and the sense of touch. Paper's texture can tell the story of who you are, by how much you think of yourself in your choice of a personal representative—your letterhead. The same choice of colors as presented to you in the chapter on envelopes applies here.

Your letterhead's design should, to create attention, be developed upon the basis of these three principles as stated by Alta Gwinn Saunders: [2]

1. Limit [letterhead] content to essential information. . . . The *who,* the *where,* the *what* have a better chance of being seen and remembered if they are not encumbered with a mass of detail.

2. Essential elements in the letterhead [should be] . . . made to stand out by being surrounded with an ample amount of white space . . .

3. Simplify design. Simplicity of design gets favorable attention from those whom a progressive firm wishes most to please and hence induces the recipient to read the letter.

A good letterhead, then, should convey all the information necessary to identify you and to create the impression you prefer. Some additional information or material which you can add to develop the impression desired includes: your trademark, emblem, or seal; your trade name, or founding date; your products, services; and where pertinent, your committees.[3]

When you wish to design a new letterhead, take these questions as asked by the Strathmore Company of West Springfield, Massachusetts, as a guide to determining what you want.

Does [your letterhead] . . . represent the type of business you do? Expressive of style, stability, precision, or whatever the character of your business may be?

[2] Alta Gwinn Saunders, *Effective Business English,* 3d ed., The Macmillan Company, New York, 1949, pp. 29–30.

[3] *The Proper Planning and Design of Your Next Letterhead,* Hammermill Paper Company, Erie, Pa., 1958, pp. 4–7.

Does it represent the prestige of your business? Expressive of quality and product reputation?

Does it carry the right copy? All necessary information and no unnecessary details?

Is the design of your letterhead appropriate in its typography or letterhead? Different enough to be interesting . . . not too novel to become tiresome? Well designed in relation to message area and fold? Reproduced in the best printing process for its purpose?

Is the paper used in your letterhead right in these respects? In color, finish, texture, substantial feel? In size? In its weight for the purpose?

Do you have coordinated matched forms? Second sheets, billheads, etc., for uniform appearance and modern effect?

24

Direct Mail as Response Advertising

Producing a Response

It's difficult to estimate what percentage of direct mail's total volume goes into response mailings. It is, however, much greater than the percentage of response advertising found in other advertising media.

Its influence on mail-advertising techniques is much greater, too, since it is the portion of direct mail advertising that produces results. Consequently, the successful techniques of result-producing response campaigns are carefully studied by other direct mail and direct advertising people. This "professional" concern about the successful methods used by "response advertising" is not nearly as great among newspaper, magazine, radio, and TV copy writers.

Number of Responses. Direct mail amateurs are eager to study response mailings, too. And they are responsible for one of the great misconceptions about direct mail . . . that there is a certain "percentage of return" which can be expected as a result of any "good" mailing. The folklore of business is not entirely clear as to what this percentage should be, but people in general seem to "know" there is a percentage, above which a mailing is considered successful and below which it is a failure.

Approximately two seconds of thought are enough to help you realize such a mythical success point is not even sensible.

When you write to ten or a dozen personal friends, inviting them to an especially attractive affair, anything less than 100 per cent response is a failure. On the other hand, if a dealer in large-sized yachts sent out 10,000 letters, got one return, and sold one yacht, his mailing would be a huge success . . . on a return percentage of $\frac{1}{100}$ of 1 per cent.

Your particular product is probably somewhere between those two extremes. So your success point is somewhere between $\frac{1}{100}$ of 1 per cent and 100 per cent, but no "average" can possibly mean anything to *you*.

Types of Responses. In addition to this factor of "How many *returns* indicate success for you?" is the question of the type of response you desire. For the *type* of response is as important as the number. The quality of the response is important, too. You might say that responses in direct mail are weighed on a three-way scale: *Who* they come from. *How many* come. And *what* kind of response was requested.

In general, most efforts to get responses in direct mail fall into one of these areas:

1. *To get information.* This group includes mailings which are made to get correct addresses, make surveys, determine opinions, etc.

2. *To qualify prospects.* The response to this kind of mailing is a "Yes" to the question, "Who's interested in my kind of product?" It identifies the interested prospect and qualifies the responder for further, more intensive sales effort, either by mail, phone, or in person.

3. *To "open the door" for salesmen.* This is used most effectively when good prospects are known but somewhat inaccessible.

A combination of No. 2 and No. 3 is also common.

4. *To "involve" the prospect.* This is an attempt to get a response from a known or presumed prospect which will obligate him, remind or favorably impress him, or make a stronger than normal advertising contact with him.

5. *To sell by mail.* (See Chapter 1 for definition of mail selling.) Here, of course, the response is an actual order.

Common Characteristics of Response Mailings. While there is some overlapping in practice (the information you get might also help you "qualify" the prospect; the qualifying response might open the door for a salesman, etc.), you approach each of these problems in a different way. So, we shall deal with each of these five types of response mailings more in detail later. However, there are a number of common characteristics found in all five categories. Let's take a look at some of them.

A *Solid Reason for Response,* on the part of the respondents, is one important thing to remember when preparing any kind of a response campaign. The readers will not respond, in quantity, just because *you* want them to. The reader will respond only because he *wants* to do what you suggest.

Sometimes it doesn't take very much to get the reader to respond. In our first category (to get information), about all we need is a polite, reasonable, friendly request that rings true. Most people are courteous and somewhat generous. A good percentage will respond as long as you don't seem to be creating future trouble for them. On the other hand, when you ask a man to put himself into buying position ("have your salesman call") or even allow you to give him something for nothing, he must genuinely want *what* you are selling. So your "reason for response" will always be determined by the kind of response mailings you are making and the kind of person your prospect is.

Two Major Dangers Develop out of the use of response mailings, strangely enough, mainly *because* responses are produced. While the dangers are most apparent in areas 2 and 3—qualifying prospects and opening doors for salesmen—you'll find them in the other categories occasionally, too.

One danger is the queer psychological situation which the advertiser (the boss) develops. He may have been using direct mail for years, without asking for a response, simply as another medium of advertising, secure in the realization that he is getting a high percentage of readership.

Then he asks for a response. He gets, say, 4 per cent return. Suddenly he visualizes the entire remaining 96 per cent of his mailing being thrown in the wastebasket, unopened . . . and considers the mailing a failure. Not true, of course. He's still getting the same readership as before, *plus* 4 per cent action. And it's important that he keep this in mind.

The second danger comes from a lack of prompt follow-up. When a recipient returns a card asking for literature, he expects it . . . *soon*. If the advertiser promises a demonstration or a call from a salesman, the people who respond really *want* to see that demonstration . . . *now*. That's why they mailed the card.

It seems incredible, but many, many, *many* advertisers go to the expense of making a response mailing, pay, cheerfully, the postage due on the returns, and then fail to follow through. Answer 100 ads yourself and see. The fulfillment of your request, in many cases, will be long delayed. In others it will be inadequate (a bare catalogue sheet, for example, with no prices or information on how to purchase locally). In some cases, you will *never* be answered.

Naturally, response advertising which is not promptly acknowledged is *worse* than wasted money. It becomes a devilish practice of *selecting your very best prospects and systematically making them* DISLIKE *you*. Your worst enemy couldn't do a better job of discrediting you.

Obtaining Information

Obviously, practically every mailing used to get information from the recipient is, in the last analysis, a questionnaire. It may be a short, one-sentence, "Is this address correct?", or a multiquestion, elaborate government report.

Mail is used to get information in one of three major situations:

1. When it is less expensive than any other method
2. When it is quicker
3. When it is likely to be more accurate

The money-saving angle is fairly obvious. You generally have the option of getting information in person, over the phone, or through the mail. If you need the information from only a few people, locally, it's cheaper to call. When you want a response from hundreds or thousands across the country, mail saves money.

Information by mail saves time, for example, for a local businessman who wants to know what his customers think about something. He could ask them when they come in, at no cost. But this might take weeks or months. So he asks by mail.

Information by mail is generally more accurate than information obtained in other ways. In the first place, questions are printed. So they are always the same. And they don't change as the questioner becomes bored or depend upon voice inflection for correct meaning. The answers are written. So they are given more careful attention and are always available for reference.

Just as important, as far as accuracy is concerned, is that there is less reason to "fudge" on answers if there is no interviewer to impress . . . particularly if the questionnaire is to be returned unsigned.

Mailings designed to get information range from simple to highly complex. Among the simplest is a mailing to get corrected addresses for mailing lists. Suggestions for this type of information mailing are found in Chapter 5. Perhaps the most complicated type of mailing used to get information is that used for market research. This is fairly well covered in Chapter 12. The procedures and techniques covered in Chapters 5 and 12 should help in the development of any mailings of this type.

Qualifying Prospects

The use of direct mail to "qualify" prospects is probably one of the medium's most valuable functions. Yet, among the general business public, it may well be the least known and understood.

Every businessman faces this need to "qualify" prospects. There is always some section of the total market that contains a higher percentage of his true prospects than the market as a whole. If the advertiser can concentrate his efforts to inform, convince, and persuade within that segment, he'll get better results for his money.

So he buys a children's TV program if he's selling cereals; if cigars, he's not satisfied with "newspaper" advertising, he wants the sports page; or he may sell products that call for the financial page or the women's section, etc.

Naturally, when he uses direct mail advertising, he tries to be sure that the people on his list are actually qualified as prospects. His list goal motto is: "Get all our prospects *on* the list; get all the nonprospects *off*."

Most important of all, he tries to keep his outside salesmen concentrating on real prospects, preferably people who are ready or nearly ready to buy. For the astronomical cost of salesmen's calls nowadays means they simply can't be wasted on cold canvass or "suspects." So he looks for "hot leads."

Response mailings of the "prospect-qualifying" type can help him in two of his major problems: list building for direct mail advertising and the development of leads for salesmen.

These are important areas. Take the typical industrial salesman. McGraw-Hill research shows that he spends only 42 per cent of his time in face-to-face selling. The rest goes into paper work, sales meetings, service calls, waiting for interviews, and traveling. Many salesmen who travel and wait through a territory count it a good day when 15 per cent of their time is face to face. The magazine, *Sales Management*, has determined that probably 64 per cent (Get that! Almost two out of three!) of his calls are made on the *wrong person*. This means that 5 per cent or less of his time is actually spent face to face with the right prospect.

But prospects are qualified, not only by their general interest or need in a product, but by *time*. The average man with a steady job may be the "right" prospect . . . but not if he has just purchased a new car. He comes back in the market years later, but only for a few weeks. How does the salesman know?

Let's take a commercial example: You are a salesman for calculating machines. Your territory includes 8,000 small- or medium-sized offices and plants, each one a potential user of your calculating machine. Perfectly good prospects. But many of the managers never see the need. Others have just purchased machines and will be out of the market for years. Where do you begin? If you just start calling on one office after another, you'll spend a lot of days waiting for or talking to managers who "aren't interested," "haven't the need," "have just bought a new one." The cost of selling for every sale will skyrocket.

On the other hand, if you could just train each prospect to "raise his hand" when he began to think about a new calculator, you'd know where to call. Your weekly sales record would zoom. And your cost per sale would go down.

Inquiry-producing direct mail, if handled correctly, can do that . . . it can get your prospects to "qualify themselves" as worth more attention, so you can spend your time with better prospects.

To put today's typical industrial salesman in front of real prospects, talking about his product, costs money. How much it costs depends on (1) his hourly rate; (2) the cost of overhead, direction, supervision, and support given him; and (3) how much of his time is spent face to face with prospects—good, mediocre, or poor prospects.

A $3-per-hour salesman ($120 per week), who carries only an equal amount of overhead, etc., has a base rate of $6 per hour. He'll do well to spend 20 per cent of his time actually talking to prospects . . . so every prospect-hour costs $30—or 50 cents per minute—and that is *low*, not high. If he sells *every* prospect in two minutes, each sale costs $1. If he averages ten minutes on each of four prospects before he makes a sale, that sale costs $20. If he spends five hours talking to good, medium, and poor prospects before he finally makes a sale, *someone* has to pay $150 for that sale.

But if he *knows* which prospects are *hot* and, by skipping the poor ones, sees twice as many hot ones in the same time, the cost of the sale has been cut by $75. If $25-worth of marketing machinery will help him *know* which prospects are hot, you can *cut* the cost of selling by $50 per sale.

You begin to help that salesman the minute you imagine a *taximeter* on his hat, with the flag down whenever he's in front of a prospect—good, bad, or medium—ticking off "four bits" or more every minute he stands there. Once you see that taximeter, you want desperately to get your salesman in front of *good* prospects; *hot* prospects; $99^{44}/_{100}$ per cent convinced prospects. Because you begin to see what *wasted* time can do to profits.

Let's, for the sake of discussion, agree on some terminology:

1. We'll call any large mass of people which logically contains some prospects for us . . . "*suspects*."

2. We'll call any group of people who can be identified by title, position, income, or some other method as needing or wanting our product . . . "*natural prospects*."

3. We'll call any person who has indicated, himself, that he has an interest in our product or has the problem which our product solves . . . a "*qualified prospect*."

4. We'll call any person, otherwise qualified under No. 2 or No. 3, who has asked for more information about our offer or "to have a salesman call" . . . a "*hot prospect*."

Salesmen, incidentally, don't like inquiries from "suspects." They can find all the suspects they want without help. Experience shows that even a "request for a salesman to call" from a *suspect* is a waste of time in so many cases that they simply refuse to follow up any of them.

It follows, then, that if we want salesmen to follow up the inquiries we get for them, we should be careful:

1. To *avoid* asking salesmen to follow up inquiries from *suspects*. (These can be followed up by mail, in an effort to turn them into *qualified prospects*.)

2. To be certain that each salesman knows that the inquiries we send him to follow up are from *natural prospects* (which he will usually recognize himself) or *qualified prospects*.

3. To make absolutely certain that each salesman knows which of the inquiries we send him are from *hot prospects*.

To understand the true value of this kind of letter which "qualifies" prospects, we must look at the businessman's problems of marketing. Marketing has a dual function: First it must *find* real prospects for a product and, second, persuade them to buy. The first function is just as important as—and sometimes more difficult than—the second.

What's more, the first function affects the second, for there are degrees of prospects. And the "hotter" the prospect found, the easier the persuasion. The people who are assigned to "persuade" (the salesmen) know this. They know that few salesmen can profitably call on *everybody* to find their prospects. And any salesman can increase his efficiency if he limits his calls to "natural prospects" or "hot prospects."

So salesmen *like* any kind of advertising or sales promotion that gets real prospects to "raise their hands" and indicate interest. They look forward to inquiries from these people.

But salesmen *hate* inquiries from nonprospects. They shudder at the idea of driving fifty miles (or walking fifty feet) to satisfy someone's idle curiosity. So they call coupons "confetti" and the inquiry cards included in some magazines "bingo" cards . . . and they'll work up a degrading name for your reply cards, too, if you get too many inquiries from nonprospects.

There are, of course, many cases (particularly when your list is made up of known prospects in the first place . . . or names that a salesman himself has placed on the list) where you want the maximum number of replies possible, every time. This type of situation is covered in this chapter under "Door Openers."

But when you are trying to "find" qualified prospects, whether you expect to turn them over to a salesman or simply to add them to your list for intensive direct mail promotion, it's important to remember that *you can get too many inquiries* if they aren't from real prospects.

So much for the reasons for this kind of response mailing and warnings about it. How about the mailing itself? Obviously, the simplest kind of qualifying mailing is a single question: "Do you ever purchase _____?" If respondents answer "Yes," they qualify themselves as prospects. This can be and has been used successfully and shouldn't be overlooked.

An example of a simple qualifying mailing was a double post card sent to credit unions. The brief copy in this successful mailing came right to the point:

NEW CREDIT UNION
PROMOTION FOLDERS AVAILABLE

657 Credit Unions have used our education and promotion folders to increase their assets and service to members.

New folders to promote loans and savings are just being published. If you ever use promotion folders for hand-outs or mailings, you might like to see samples and prices. Just mail the attached card.

The reply card read:

OUR CREDIT UNION WANTS TO GROW

Please send us samples of your latest education and promotion folders for Credit Unions. We have approximately . . .

_____ members

_____ potential members

NAME _____

OFFICE _____

NAME OF C.U. _____

ADDRESS _____

CITY, STATE _____

On the other hand, on most occasions an approach which is not quite so abrupt will do better . . . and the more usual approach is to make an "offer" or proposition which will be interesting primarily (preferably *only*) to those who are real prospects for the product.

This "offer" is the most important factor in the mailing, for the number of responses you will get depends more upon the offer you make than upon the kind of letter or folder you write. You'll get fewest inquiries when the reply card asks for a salesman to call.

You'll increase responses if you offer to *send* information about your product. And you'll get even more if you say you will *mail* information. (The custom of "sending" the information by salesmen is well known to those who inquire.) With some products, of course, you might offer a free (or "bargain") sample.

Returns from people who ask for a salesman to call are the kind salesmen like best, of course, but they will often be quite satisfied with a list of folks who have asked for "more information" . . . if they are real prospects.

Obviously, you can increase or decrease the number of people who ask for "more information" by the *amount of information* you send with the original letter. You'll get more replies if the original mailing speaks only of the benefits of a product and carries little or no technical or price information. You will get fewer replies when price, catalogue sheet, or something similar is included. But people who ask for "more information," after they have received printed literature and have some idea of the price range on a product, are obviously "hot prospects." They are ready to buy.

If you want a great number of replies, with "warm" prospects added to the "hot" ones, you'll offer something of tangible value, free. But you'll be very, *very* careful that the offer is valuable *only* to people who use or need the product you are selling.

Assuming that your product solves some problem or satisfies some need that your prospect now recognizes, you can offer him assistance or information about that problem or need. And he's likely to respond. People who do not recognize that problem or need probably won't respond. Obviously, those who do are better prospects.

For example, a manufacturer of postage meters might offer a booklet entitled, "Seven Ways to Prevent Pilferage of Stamps in Offices," to a list of businessmen or manufacturers. Most of the people who ask for that booklet would be concerned about the problem and probably responsible for control of stamps. They would be showing no direct interest in the product itself, but they would "qualify" themselves as prospects because they need one of the benefits the product brings.

This "mix" of warm and hot prospects, who, by responding to an offer qualify themselves (by and large) as honest-to-goodness prospects, is probably the most popular with manufacturers who have a large sales force. It not only produces valuable leads for the salesmen but, by follow-up reports on their part, helps the sales manager keep tab both on salesman activities and type of prospect.

By and large (unless you make an inexcusable error in your appeals), it's safe to say that the *fewer* returns you receive, the *better* quality they are. But your objective should be to get as *many* as your sales force or place of business can handle. If you are promoting a shopping center or a retail store and make the prospect come in or make a purchase to receive the offer, the sky's the limit, of course.

Naturally, since the important step here is to produce the qualifying response, not an immediate sale of your product, you "sell" the need for response, not necessarily your product.

Naturally, if your response is going to be a request for "more information" about it, or for a salesman to call, you must develop interest in your product. But, if the response is for the stamp-stealing booklet we mentioned, your "sales" copy should be centered on the booklet, and you should say little if anything about the product. You'll do better to talk about that after the prospects are qualified.

It's reasonable to believe that few responses mean a greater percentage of good prospects, and many responses mean a smaller percentage of good prospects. This isn't necessarily true . . . although there is temporary comfort in it—if your response is small.

The quality of your response depends more upon the *selecting* ability of your offer than on anything else; so the trick is to develop an offer which is of interest only to real prospects . . . and then to work hard to make it as attractive as you can. And to make answering your letter or folder as easy as it can possibly be.

Warning: Your offer may be so good at "selecting" hot prospects that you get no returns, or very few. In that case, you'll have to make an offer which has more general interest, even if it isn't quite as selective. Actually, if you provided a salesman only with snap sales, it would be a reflection on his talent.

Let's sum up now the case for the "qualifying-prospects" approach: While this type of mailing does advance the sale and can include persuasive, convincing sales talk in the advanced stage (when searching for "hot prospects"), its basic function is a *search* for better prospects. These better prospects may become subjects for more intensive direct mail or for personal contact, by phone or in person.

Some advertisers depend upon the product itself to make the sale, and a good "prospect" is one who will try the product. Many magazines are like that. Their "qualifying" mailing actually makes a short-term, try-out sale, and the magazine itself must sell the customer. Such short-term sales are not profitable for the magazine, any more than are the other "qualifying" mailings we have mentioned; so they must be careful not to have such an offer *too* attractive. The trick is to make it attractive only to the type of people who will become customers after reading it.

Here are two prospect-selection letters. Both were successful. Note that they are thorough, long. But most importantly, they give enough information, stress benefits sufficiently, to whet the reader's desire for the "more information" which can lead to sales. This first letter is a "humdinger."

HARNISCHFEGER CORPORATION
Milwaukee, Wisconsin

Dear Mr. _____:

I've waited a long time to write you this letter. My boss, Walter Harnischfeger, spent over 15 years of hard work and a couple of million dollars in hard cash before he'd let me write it to anyone.

And I've spent a couple of months searching for the right man in Sanford before I could be sure I wanted to write it to you.

I think it's an important letter.

It's important to us at Harnischfeger because of the tremendous investment we've made in construction research and development.

It's important to you because (I hope) it will be a letter that leads you to more profit, easier, than any other letter you've ever received.

I've never met you, but I hope I will some day soon—because I've learned a lot of good things about you. I know your business and financial reputation is above reproach. I know your banker thinks a lot of you. I'm pretty sure that you are the man with whom we'd like to deal in Sanford. But since I sound so particular in writing you, it's only fair to tell you something about the company that I represent.

Perhaps the Harnischfeger Corporation (or our P & H trademark) is an old story to you. That's possible, for the company has been in the construction business for 66 years. It's run by an honest, sincere Milwaukee family, proud of its business integrity and its Dun & Bradstreet rating of AAa1. Harnischfeger is active in a lot of fields. We make diesel engines, welding equipment, traveling hoists and cranes, power shovels, etc. Now, after more than 15 years of development and experiment, we're in the housing business.

We're in it, you might say, as "partners" with local builders across the country—but with no one, as yet, in Sanford.

It's a fast-growing business, for in the past two seasons we have proved that the Harnischfeger system of home building will *cut costs, increase values,* and *bring higher profits to the builder.*

The system, bluntly, produces a house you can be proud of, at a price today's buyers are willing to pay.

That means you can sell full-sized, well-built, roomy houses in a *very* low price range. Hundreds of dollars lower than comparable houses.

More than that, builders who are using the system are *increasing* their annual profits . . . by good percentages.

How? With: (1) *Preplanning.* The Harnischfeger system simplifies many problems in purchasing, trucking, waste, and erection. (2) *Less on-site "dirty work."* (You order panelized floors, walls, trusses, gables, etc., eliminate difficult site work and get your house up fast.) (3) *A financial plan* that lets you build more houses on less working capital. (4) *System* . . . There's the real key. A system that licks most of your risks, worries, and delays, that helps you control costs more accurately, saves months on the job, and means *profits on more units in a price range that sells today.*

Even though some of the building material is panelized, nobody in your organization gets hurt. There's no change in your relations with plumbers, electricians, etc. The only fellow who stands to make less per house is your carpenter, and he gains because the system sells more houses.

Let me tell you what happened to a builder in New York State. It's an interesting and typical story.

He was a good builder . . . not the largest in his city by a long shot (he is now) but a quality one. In 19__ he built 7 conventional homes. Good homes

. . . sound homes . . . His probable profit was about $10,000 . . . but at the end of the 19___ selling season he still had two of these seven left—unsold.

In 19___ he built 39 Harnischfeger homes. After he put up a sample he *sold every house before he broke ground.* His profit in 19___—over $33,000. He's planning more Harnischfeger homes in 19___. Every man that he deals with—his subcontractors, his suppliers, his banker—has made more money with him this year.

He says, "I'm with the Harnischfeger system to stay." No wonder.

The same kind of thing can happen in Sanford . . . *will* happen in Sanford. I hope it will happen to you.

The whole story is a thousand pages long. You wouldn't want to read it at one sitting even if I took time to write it. I'll be glad to go more into detail . . . tell you exactly what the system can do for you and exact costs for Sanford. But I must know one thing: Are you at all interested? Would you like to hear more about a system that will help your building, your selling, and your bank account?

If you're open-minded, I'd like to send you some detailed literature. I'd like to send you the names of other contractors, like yourself, who have profited—in cash and in community service—from the use of this system in their cities. Then, if you become really interested, I'd like to talk to you about it in person and go into complete detail.

I know you'll want to understand the plan thoroughly before you commit yourself in the slightest, but I certainly hope you will say, "I'm open-minded" . . . because I'm so anxious to get this profitable program rolling soon in Sanford. I've taken the liberty of enclosing a card and envelope to make that step easy. There is no obligation whatsoever.

This next prospect-selection letter presents another type of problem, that of locating prospects on the consumer level. The format of this letter was note-size, 5½ by 8½ inches, to make it appeal more to the reader—the lady of the house:

BIGLEY HARDWARE
Maumee, Ohio

Break a vase—

and, as the pieces scatter on the floor, its value is lost, will never return. Repair it? Maybe. Replace it? Perhaps. Forget you ever had it? Possibly. But part of its value is gone—forever.

In the same way, value destroyed by termites is a value that can never return. An envied rug, a lovely tapestry, a priceless heirloom. . . . Suddenly beauty has become food for worms.

For termites eat more than wood, once they enter a house. They seem to thrive on the things you love the most, and they strike without warning. Since they work in the dark, hidden in the woodwork, you don't see them. You may never realize that they are in your home until long after great damage is done . . . *unless you know exactly what to look for.*

The termite is no respecter of persons. The beautiful $100,000 mansion of a millionaire is just another meal to him. And one out of every three homes in this area has termites . . . for brick and stucco houses have termites, too . . . they go after the woodwork, books, and rugs.

But termites can be beaten—if you discover them soon enough. The damage can be stopped, the termites driven out of a home and kept out—*if* you know exactly what to look for.

First you must learn how to recognize the termite's telltale tracks . . . his "entrance ways" into the house.

Termites do thousands of dollars worth of damage around Maumee every winter, and for a long time I've wondered how we could help cut down the huge repair bills they cause.

I think I've found a way to help.

One of the companies we work with has shown hundreds of people how to keep a regular check on the condition of their own homes.

Their Toledo man has agreed to teach a reasonable number of home owners in Maumee how to tell whether there are termites in their homes. He shows folks exactly what to look for and exactly where to look.

He won't rush in and out. He'll spend about fifteen or twenty minutes showing you what termites look like; what their nests and runways look like and how you can tell whether an apparently solid beam is "termite-hollow."

I've made arrangements for you to get this information free . . . without any obligation to anyone. There is nothing you must buy, either now or later.

You really can't afford to be ignorant about termites. Even if you have none now, you never know when a termite family might decide to move in.

Just mail in this card to tell me you want the information. It's free . . . and if you ever find termites as the result of it, it will be worth hundreds of dollars to you. . . . Even if you don't, the fact that you know your house is safe is well worthwhile.

Do it today.

Door Openers

When you are using a response mailing to open a known prospect's door for a salesman, you throw all those rules about offers for "qualifying" prospects out of the window . . . for you mail only to qualified prospects with this type of mailing.

The "door opener's" job is to get the salesman in. And "door opening" is used in those cases where a known prospect (or qualified prospect) is difficult for a salesman to see. The prospect may be deep in a plant, behind many closed doors, blocked by a purchasing agent, like a president or chief chemist. Or he is easy enough to reach physically but not willing to give time or an open mind, like a typical life insurance prospect. Or he is a prospect who resents a "no-purpose" call from a salesman. Or, let's face it, the prospect is "difficult" to see because the salesman is lazy or timid.

In other words, door openers are planned by sales managers with prospects who are, in one way or another, difficult to see often enough . . . for, in many fields, prospects who aren't *seen* by salesmen aren't *sold.*

In all these cases, we can increase the salesman's effectiveness by opening the door through a response mailing.

Now the *kind* of response required for a "door-opener" mailing is entirely different from the kind required by a "qualifying" mailing. In the case of the "door opener," the prospect is *previously qualified.* He may be a known prospect. (For example, a manufacturer of fan belts *knows* that certain men in General Motors are his prospects.) He may have been qualified by mail or by some other method. In any event, the only problem is to get the salesman in front of an "open-minded" prospect.

So we mail to the prospect. We make an offer. It's a booklet to tell him how others make profits, or a new kind of chemical-element chart, or a notebook-with-your-name-in-gold, or a new booklet on our product, or even a request for a salesman to call . . . though these are fairly rare. Because we want lots of responses, every one is good.

The prospect responds. He asks for the chemical-element chart, let's say. And out trots the salesman—lazy, timid, or brash—to "honor the request." And out past the Purchasing Agent to the outer lobby in his shirt sleeves comes the chief chemist, constrained to sit, out of common courtesy, for a few minutes while the salesman finally gets his chance to focus this decision maker's attention on the benefits of his product.

For nationwide programs, operated by companies with more than one echelon of organization (branches, distributors, etc.), two additional steps are always required for a truly successful door opener–response program.

First, to get blanket coverage, the offer should be made by the national organization and not left up to the branches. And the request *must* be acknowledged either by mail or phone, within forty-eight hours after receipt. It should be fulfilled by the salesman as soon thereafter as practical, but the quick acknowledgment is vital. Acknowledgments should be handled under the personal direction of the sales manager's office or assigned to a thoroughly responsible outside mailing house. These "door openers" are designed to create good will. And good will thrives on prompt attention. Slow responses hurt rather than help.

The mail acknowledgment or phone call is necessary because salesmen simply cannot follow up quickly enough every time. They're busy. It takes time for the information to reach them. They'll classify the responses by "importance" and fulfill the requests out of order. Salesmen are great fellows, but don't trust them entirely with your acknowledgments.

The second thing that is necessary for nationwide programs is a follow-up system to see that each request actually *is* fulfilled. A program of door openers can make friends. But offers that aren't fulfilled will make prospects more difficult than ever to see. Here, again, you can't depend upon every salesman. If undirected, some will delay delivery for one reason or another, until they suddenly decide, "It's too late to deliver this now. I'd look like a fool."

So some system of reporting should be included in any "response" plan which depends upon a salesman to fulfill the request.

You'll notice, with door openers, there's no need to restrict the character of the offer to something that only prospects are interested in. Such an offer is perfectly all right, because these people *are* prospects *and* anything of this nature provides a natural tie-in with a sales promotion. But if you think a reasonable proportion of your prospects will ask for a map of the United States—or of South America—and your salesmen feel they can go from the delivery of the map to a sales contact (or even, as is true in some cases, that the personal "delivery-boy" good-will contact would be worthwhile), then by all means offer a map.

Let's look at some door-opener letters which call for a response. Here's a letter from a Flexicore manufacturer to school-board members. All school-board members, nowadays, become decision makers when an architect presents his plans for a new building . . . and some board members have their own opinions even about architects. But it isn't easy for a Flexicore salesman to call, cold, on school-board members. So Flexicore sends them a series of letters, offering various booklets of interest to school-board members. One of them, aimed to interest those members who are interested in fire safety, follows. Others are beamed at members with interest in speedy construction, classroom design, etc. The delivery of each booklet leads automatically into a discussion of the values of Flexicore as a structural material for schools. Here's the letter which aims at the school-board members' interest in fire safety:

THE FLEXICORE CO., INC.
1932 East Monument Ave.
Dayton 1, Ohio

HOW ALL-CONCRETE CONSTRUCTION
WILL MAKE YOUR NEW SCHOOL FIRE-SAFE

At no cost or obligation, I would like to send you a booklet that tells how hundreds of schools across the country are now being constructed of fire-safe materials.

All these schools use the Flexicore system of precast concrete floors and roofs combined with noncombustible walls. *They will not burn.*

Insurance rates will usually tell you how fire-safe your new building really is. Here is what a firm of Chicago architects told us about a suburban school project of theirs:

"We were advised by the Board of Education that the *fire insurance rates* on the recently completed building had been *reduced considerably* by using Flexicore concrete floor and roof slabs, and they asked us to construct the new addition in such a way as to preserve that insurance rate."

I know you will agree that although the insurance rate is important, the real value of a fire-safe school is *the safety it provides the children.*

The 16-page booklet I would like to send you shows how the Flexicore system was used on eight 1- and 2-story schools in Alabama, North Carolina, New York, Ohio, Michigan, Illinois, Massachusetts, and Minnesota.

I am sure you will want this booklet, because it also tells how the mass production of these concrete floors and roofs provides a low-cost structure, and how they save on future maintenance.

Just mail the enclosed card. It is addressed to the Flexicore manufacturer in your area. He will be glad to send you a copy of this booklet without obligation.

Sincerely,

Here's a letter to farmers from a manufacturer of farm heaters. Every farmer on the list is a good prospect because he has been chosen by one of the company's authorized dealers. The dealer is eager to provide a demonstration for any of them.

KNIPCO, INC.

Suite 324   ·   Talbott Building   ·   Dayton 2, Ohio

Recently . . .

I asked one of our Key dealers, near you, for names of a few farmers who might help us find out what kind of "first impression" our new-model *portable farm heaters* make.

He sent me your name.

So I'd like to have you try one right on your farm for a day. Then after you've used it, tell our dealer what you think of it. He'll pass the word along.

Would you do that?

This Knipco heater has a hundred uses on the farm, as you'll see. It heats people, thaws frozen pipes, warms cold tractors and cars. It's great for heating farrowing houses and repair sheds. It puts out enough heat to keep you warm indoors or out, but is light enough to carry around with one hand.

Here's a chance to see, for yourself, how one of these inexpensive Knipco heaters could work for you . . . without feeling the slightest obligation to buy, since I'm the one who is asking the favor.

Of course, if you like the heater so much you insist on buying it, I'm sure we can work it out . . . but, in this particular case, I'm most interested in your first impression—good or bad.

Are you willing to try one for a day? I've made arrangements with our dealer to make one available to you. Just mail or take him the card enclosed. He'll take it from there.

Sincerely,

E. J. "Tex" Erp, President

To sum it up: The characteristics of a true door-opener letter require a response from the prospect which puts him in the position of either welcoming or graciously accepting a personal visit from a salesman. It's a fair deal. It gives the prospect something he wants (the offer) in return for something the salesman wants (a few minutes of time).

Creating Involvement

A step down the scale from the "door-opener" response is a response which might be classified as "Involvement" or "Identification." As we go through life, we find our interest caught by many organizations and people. We go to a certain school or root for a particular big-league ball club. And we become more than normally interested in anything that happens to that school or club. Or we shake hands with the Governor. He forgets it. We don't. And he gets our vote, or at least our attention, from there on in. We've become "involved" with him. He's touched us in a memorable way. A few more such contacts, and we may become a staunch supporter of his.

This is true of business firms, too. We have some kind of memorable contact with a company. We take a tour through their plant. We meet a man who works there. We read that they've given $1,000 to our favorite charity. And we are more favorably interested in that company from that time on.

A company's efforts along the lines of "public relations" are, of course, all aimed at creating this psychological "involvement" . . . for it *is* entirely psychological, of course, though very real.

Naturally, this "involvement" with a company improves sales in the long run. And, admittedly, it is developed through the slow, "soft-sell" type of selling that cannot be used by those who must sell an item quickly and be on their way. But, for companies looking for long-term customers, it has real possibilities.

Through advertising contacts—and particularly through direct mail, because it is more personal—you can "involve" people with your business, psychologically. Good direct mail, continuously directed to the same people, will make them feel they know your company. They'll begin to identify your interests with theirs. They'll "be for" you. This is just human nature.

Of course, direct mail varies in its ability to involve prospects, just as personal sales calls do. All sales managers know it pays to make calls but that calls are not enough. After-dinner speakers are fond of the sales manager who insisted on "more calls." His new salesman made five one day. "Not enough," said the sales manager. "Make more."

Twenty and thirty calls a day by the salesman brought the same response from the sales manager. Finally, one day the salesman wrote a comment on his call report, "I made forty calls today. I would have made more, but one fellow asked me what I was selling."

Sales calls, then, *aren't* all the same. Sometimes a salesman is barely able to say "Hello." At other times he gets an opportunity to make a favorable impression. (He may do this by talking about golf.) On still other calls he gets in a word or two about his product. His constant objective is to do a little more than just leave his card.

So it is with direct mail. Some direct mail just "calls." Some manages to "leave its card." It not only calls, but it is *recalled* by the recipient at a later time. Some direct mail manages to get a sales message into the reader's mind. And some makes an even stronger contact by causing the prospect to *do* something . . . like making a response that "involves" him with the advertiser.

So an "involvement" mailing which gets a response is at least twice as effective as a "cordial contact" (see Chapter 23, reminder letters). In fact, we can feel certain that an involvement mailing which *asks* for a response is probably more effective than one which does not, if the recipient so much as considers responding, whether he actually does or not. Psychologically, the name of the company and its product is stamped a bit more firmly in the prospect's mind.

Since no salesman is expected to follow up an "involvement" response, the offer can be as "popular" as you want to make it. It could be the gift of something too insignificant to justify a salesman's call . . . or (in the same way as "involvement" is often attempted in publication or broadcast advertising) a contest with prizes for the person who best finishes an "I-like-Blank-because . . ." sentence in twenty-five words or less. It could even be the offer of a sample of your product.

The "involvement" response could be a vote in a straw poll or for a "Miss Brand X." It could be in answer to a request for advice on future policies. ("As an independent distributor would you advise us to move into the widget field?") It could be, for that matter, a short questionnaire, taken more for the purpose of focusing the attention of the recipient on your company than for the information you get out of it.

Anything which gets or encourages the recipient to respond and—through this response—strengthens the image of your company in his mind fits into the category of an "involvement" response.

Direct Mail Selling

Of course, the pinnacle of response direct mail is direct mail selling itself, where a product is offered, for cash, through the mail with no salesman or middleman in between. Each response is a sale. Since this book contains a whole chapter on Direct Mail Selling, we won't go any deeper into it at this point except for this warning:

The "response" type of mailings (Qualifier; Door Openers; Involvement Responses, and Direct Mail Selling) have many characteristics in common . . . but they have many differences, too. The objectives in each area are different. And the mailings should be prepared with those differences in mind. Too many direct mail neophytes, after reading a fact-packed magazine article written by a mail-order practitioner, try to apply the lessons they've learned to other types of response mailings without respecting those differences in objectives. Don't do it.

Improving Responses

Of course, every mailer who tries for a response wants to "increase returns," and this is a perfectly sound objective . . . as long as the quality of the returns does not suffer.

If you get "too many" returns to a Qualifier mailing, for example, you won't really be qualifying. So, you'll have to make your offer even less attractive to nonprospects or lukewarm ones.

If you get "too many" returns to a Door-opener mailing, your salesmen won't get around soon enough. So you'll have to slow down the pace of your mailings. In general, however, you'll want more returns if you can get them. And there are some proved techniques to use to improve them.

One way is to improve the offer. Obviously, more people will respond if your offer is more attractive to them. So you'll want to experiment with the offers you make . . . to discover the most popular. And you'll also want to change offers occasionally.

You'll want to experiment because it is very difficult to tell which offers will have the most appeal. You'll want to change them from time to time because what appeals to one portion of your list may not appeal to another.

A manufacturer of maintenance equipment, for example, had unbounded faith in a new machine. He knew the product would literally pay for itself in a few weeks. So he was willing to make an extremely generous offer . . . an extensive, free-trial period. (In substance, he offered use of the equipment, free, long enough for the actual savings to pay for it before payment was due.) When used on a test mailing, however, this offer was a 100 per cent flop. *No* response. None.

On the other hand, a mailing to exactly the same list, with an offer which appeared *much* less attractive to the manufacturer ("We are preparing a folder on this equipment; would you like one for your files?"), pulled a successful response, with the majority of the inquiries resulting in sales. Evidently, the offer of a folder, as a first step, was more attractive to the prospect than a free trial. But this is not always the case.

As we mentioned, you'll probably want to change your offers from time to time also, as Flexicore did to school-board members (page 283), first offering information on fire safety, then quick construction, etc. Interests of the individuals on your list are different, and some will *never* respond to one type of offer . . . even if you make it a hundred times.

While the offer itself is probably the most important factor in determining the number of replies, other things are important, too. The interest in your mailing piece, the readibility of your copy, etc., are factors. For the reader must *read* and understand the offer at the very least.

The *ease* of replying is important, too. In fact, the simplest way to improve mail returns is to enclose a reply card or envelope . . . and a most obvious rule (frequently overlooked) is:

> The *easier* a card is to return, the more cards will be returned.

Since it takes no particular creative skill to make most reply cards easier to return, this may be the quickest way to improve the average mailing. Obviously, for example, fewer cards will be returned if the inquirer has to pay the postage than if it is paid for him. So a "Business Reply Card" helps.

It also appears to be universally true that more cards will be returned if a postage stamp is on them than if they are business reply cards (not because it is easier to use the card with the stamp on it, but probably because it is harder to throw the card away . . . and, if the stamp is pasted on tight, the card stays around the desk longer and simply has more chance of being used . . . on impulse, if nothing else).

Then there's the problem of filling out the card. Is there a pen or pencil handy? Is the time required available? Is the reader leaning back in his chair to read his mail, and must he lean forward to fill the card in? The thread of interest is weak sometimes. And it takes little to break it. The "overwhelming" problem of filling in the card makes the difference for some folks.

So the next "easier" step is to fill in the card, leaving only a check mark necessary . . . or requiring no action at all except, of course, mailing it. (Some mailers fear that cards requiring no action will be remailed by mistake, but this doesn't appear to be a serious factor.)

"Doing the work" for the prospect in this way can increase returns significantly . . . and so, when asking for information or making "Door-opener," "Involvement," or "Mail-order" mailings where close to 100 per cent of the names on the list are *known* prospects, it certainly pays to fill in the card. If you are working with a list that is plated, of course, it costs little to run the list on the reply side of the reply card. And the extra investment may pay huge dividends. If you are typing the addresses, or if cost does appear to be a serious factor, the use of some method similar to Sen-Bak's is worth trying. Sen-Bak uses a window envelope, a die-cut letterhead, and an "addressed" reply card which is spot-gummed behind the letterhead. In this way, the name and address, printed on the card only, shows through the "windows" and acts as address and fill-in for the letter. Another method is to use a window envelope with the reply card itself next to the window and the name and address on the reply card.

The ultimate in "response" is the card which threatens, "*Unless* we hear from you, we will send . . ." or, "Mail this card only if you *don't* want a free copy." If it's numbers of "inquiries" you're after, this one's a dandy, but it's not popular with recipients. However, you may recognize it as the "response" system used by the Book-of-the-Month and other such clubs when mailing to their membership.

25

How to Follow Up Responses

Follow-ups Are Imperative

When response mailings of the "Qualifying" or "Door-opener" type are made, they simply waste money unless the responses are followed up by sales calls or additional mailings which eventually lead to sales calls.

So no plan for such mailings should be considered complete until it is developed to the point of a sale. And no such mailings should be considered successful . . . unless they *do* lead to sales in profitable quantities.

Yet again and again we see this lack of prompt follow-up, a waste of advertising dollars, often among the country's largest companies. The magazine, *Sales Management,* once called it "Modern Marketing's Sorest Thumb,"[1] and a nine-year study by *Industrial Equipment News,* concerned with salesmen's follow-ups of publication advertising, indicated that only *14 per cent* of all inquiries were followed up, even though later questionnaires by the publication proved that more than half of the responders had been genuinely interested in the product.

Reasons for Follow-up Failure

Well, *why,* after advertisers have invested good, hard-earned cash in obtaining a satisfactory response from a mailing, do they fail to follow up and complete the sale? There's no real excuse, of course, but here are some of the major reasons:

[1] "Significant Trends: Modern Marketing's Sorest Thumb," *Sales Management,* vol. 84, no. 11, p. 17, June 3, 1960.

1. Planning was all concentrated on getting out the original piece on time. The fulfillment mailing simply fell behind schedule.

2. Advertising is the responsibility of the advertising department, and follow-up is left to the sales department, "because a personal follow-up is better." And the salesmen, believe it or not, either:

a. Are slow to follow up. So they sometimes miss the sale because of delay (and sometimes just put it off until it's too late).

b. Evaluate the card themselves as "not worthwhile" and throw it away. (There is, also, often a discouraging delay if a response is directed to an advertising department in one city and then referred to salesmen in another.)

3. Somehow, it is assumed the response will be small enough to be handled by personally typed letters in the sales department. (It takes surprisingly few responses to overwhelm sales correspondents.)

4. The planned fulfillment is too expensive for the quality of the response. (If a mailing that is supposed to *qualify* the respondents as "hot prospects" is too popular, it will pull in replies from "suspects." Salesmen, who could profitably call on "hot prospects," will find their time being wasted, in many cases, on people who are not ready to buy. They will then stop calling on *any* of the leads.) And, if a less expensive method of fulfillment does not replace the salesmen, the responses will get no reply at all.

Plan for Follow-up

In any event, it's plain to see that any response mailing needs to be part of a complete plan, which includes plans for follow-up mailings and —sometimes in "qualifying" mailings and always in "door-opener" mailings—follow-ups by salesmen. These plans must be made before the response mailing goes out, and they must be complete.

In this regard, *Sales Management*, in commenting on the "sore thumb," went on to say: [2]

The salesman has shown little promise of beefing up his own follow-up record; his field manager, more than likely already beset by far too much administrative work, probably won't *originate* action to check on every lead that comes through his office. So the home office must also assume responsibility for untangling the mess on the *salesman end*. Until this is done, increasingly important sales will continue to be lost for imaginary or trivial reasons.

Obviously, the precise plan used will be different for manufacturers who use distributors or dealers than for those who sell through their own salesmen or branches or manufacturers' representatives. And, while a mailer will find that *any* plan, if settled upon ahead of time, is better than

[2] *Ibid.*, p. 18.

no plan at all, he'll also find that a plan which takes his peculiar problems into consideration will work best.

Almost any mailer will save time, trouble, and money if he will have his follow-up program handled by a direct mail agency or competent mailing house. (A list of such organizations, for most cities of the U.S. and Canada and for major cities abroad can be obtained from the Mail Advertising Service Association, International, 622 Fifth Street, N.W., Washington 1, D.C.) Mailers who plan to use such an organization should bring them into the planning from the beginning, for their special knowledge of follow-up procedures can be helpful.

Such a plan, developed by Graphic Service of Dayton for a manufacturer of office equipment which sold through its own branches and salesmen, follows. The name "Super-Tabs" is substituted for the actual company name. But in all other respects this is a copy of the actual plan which Graphic Service prepared for the company's director of sales.

First is the copy contained on the twenty-one-page flip-chart presentation used to explain the program to company executives.

Page 1	Selling S-Ts to "B-Ps"
Page 2	Certain Business Firms Are "B-Ps" (Best Prospects) for "Super-Tabs"
Page 3	Salesmen know these "B-Ps"
Page 4	Advertising directed to "B-Ps" is More Valuable than general advertising
Page 5	Occasionally "B-Ps" become WARM PROSPECTS
Page 6	Salesmen like *warm* prospects · "warm"—thinking about "Super-Tabs" · "warm"—feeling about "Super-Tabs"
Page 7	Sometimes "B-Ps" become HOT PROSPECTS (They want a demonstration.)

Page 8	Salesmen *love* HOT PROSPECTS
Page 9	DIRECT MAIL SALES PROMOTION can help with "B-Ps," "W-Ps" and "H-Ps"
Page 10	HERE'S a Suggested Plan
Page 11	PURPOSE · "ASSISTANT SALEMAN" calling between calls · OBLIGATING MATERIAL for WARM PROSPECTS · DEMONSTRATION OPPORTUNITIES FOR HOT PROSPECTS · Informed SALESMEN
Page 12	Schedule · 6 Mailings before next June · Inquiry replies within 48 hours · Weekly reports · Follow-up letters to Warm Prospects
Page 13	LIST Development 200 "B-P" names from each salesman Coded, plated, & filed 3 × 5 "control" cards to salesman
Page 14	LIST CONTROL Size of list strictly limited Use of Control Card for additions, changes, or replacements
Page 15	BRANCH MAILING Bulletin Mailing List Request List Preparation Instructions
Page 16	TYPICAL MAILING *Letter,* containing offer *Reply Card,* containing prospect's name and salesman's code Returned to: Super-Tab Information Service 846 South Main Street Dayton 2, Ohio
Page 17	INQUIRY RESPONSE *Offer requested* *Letter* . . . mentioning all three products Two Reply Cards—Requesting product information *or* office demonstration *a.* Enclosed with letter *b.* Bound or inserted in offer

Page 18	When Inquiry is made
	a. Answer promptly.
	b. Report to Super-Tab Sales Manager.
	c. Report to Branch Manager.
	d. Original inquiry to salesman (through Branch Manager).
	e. Salesman reports to Super-Tab.

Page 19	WARM PROSPECTS
	(Inquirer)
	Monthly letters with
	"demonstration-requested" card

Page 20	This system provides:
	1. *Advertising* to *Best Prospects*
	(whether answered or not)
	2. *Inquiries* for Salesmen
	3. *Obligating Material* to "Warm Prospects"
	4. *Opportunities* for "Hot Prospect" identification
	. . . in an *organized* way.

Page 21	. . . without additional
	staff or trouble at Super-Tab.

The following material explained the system in detail and was used in connection with the presentation of the plan.

SUPER-TAB SALES PROMOTION
Direct Mail to Business Firm Prospects

Purpose:

To mail promotional material to 50,000–60,000 of Super-Tab's best business prospects, as selected by salesmen in the field, with the following objectives:

1. To serve as an "assistant salesman," carrying the Super-Tab sales message to prospects between salesman calls.
2. To make it easy for prospects to request demonstrations.
3. To offer "obligating material," of interest to prospects. Requests for this material will help identify "warm prospects" and provide a reason for a salesman's call.

TENTATIVE SCHEDULE
Super-Tab Direct Mail to Business Prospects:

Week of:

July 20:	Program presented to Super-Tab
August 3:	Program O.K.'d by Super-Tab
August 10:	Bulletin to salesmen (written by manager) and accompanying forms and instructions (written by Graphic Service) mailed to salesmen, requesting names by September 1
August 30:	Wires sent to branches not heard from, asking for intentions so print order can be established
October 5:	First Mailing (New product announcement)
November 1:	Second Mailing—"Working girls and wives have . . ." offering "Tips for Tabulators"

January 4:   Third Mailing—"New product announcement" offering infor-
                  mation
February 15:   Fourth Mailing—Offer of Tabulator's Handbook
March 28:   Fifth Mailing—Offer No. 3
May 9:   Sixth Mailing—Reoffer of whatever pulled best

INQUIRY ANSWERING PLAN

48 hours after receipt of inquiry:	Reply to inquiry—first-class mail within 48 hours (all inquiries received on Friday will be processed Friday or Saturday)
Weekly: (Tuesday)	1. Notice of inquiry to branch manager, with extra notice for salesman and original inquiry enclosed (first-class mail)
	2. Notice of inquiry to Super-Tabs
Periodically, as practical:	Two or three follow-up mailings to these "warm prospects" asking for requests for demonstrations

List Development:

The objective of the list development will be to get the names or titles of the 200 best prospects in each salesman's territory.

Salesmen will be requested, via a bulletin from Super-Tabs Sales Manager, to supply a list of 200 prospects, by name if possible, direct to the mailing house: Super-Tabs, 846 South Main Street, Dayton 2, Ohio. They will be provided with directions on how to prepare, correct, or change this list. (Exhibit A)

Card copies of the lists will be run off on 3 × 5 yellow cards (Exhibit 1) and returned to the salesman for his file. This file will show him, at all times, what names he has on his list.

List Control and Correction:

Since the factory pays for this sales promotion, we recommend that the number of mailings allotted each salesman be *strictly* limited to a predetermined figure (200 at the outset).

We believe this will have the psychological value of making the mailings seem more valuable to the salesman and will also control expenses.

We have worked out a method of list correction and control which can keep this limitation in effect and automatically police itself.

Here's how it would work.

1. Each branch manager would be allotted 200 "Mailing List Spots" for himself and 200 for each salesman. He would send these names and addresses to Dayton. (See Exhibit B.)
2. When his names arrived, they would be coded, plated, and a mailing list on 3 × 5 yellow cards (Exhibit 1) would be run off and sent to the branch manager or salesman. If a branch sent in too few names, enough extra blank yellow cards would be sent them so they could add names, up to 200 for each salesman, later.
3. The salesman's yellow card would actually become his "claim" on one series of mailings. He would use that card to make corrections or to change names on his list, simply by mailing it to Dayton.

4. If, as a matter of policy, Super-Tab wanted to add "Spots" for a given branch after the program started, we would simply supply extra yellow cards to the branch (each one becoming "scrip" for an additional series of mailings).

5. If, for any reason (postmaster notification, etc.) a name is removed from the list, a notification card (Exhibit 2) would be sent to the salesman, so that he could replace or correct the name.

Exhibit A
Instructions on List Preparation
To Branch Managers with Announcement Bulletin
HOW TO PREPARE YOUR MAILING LIST
For Super-Tabs Sales Promotion

Please prepare your lists as follows:

1. Make separate lists for each salesman.
2. Type each list either on 3 × 5 cards or 8½ × 11 sheets.
3. Begin each list with the salesman's name and branch address, thus:

    Salesman's name, SALESMAN
    Branch name
    Branch Address   Branch No. _____
    City, State

(Each salesman will receive a copy of each mailing when it is mailed to the names on his list.)

4. In addition to the salesman, include up to 200 names of prospects on his list.
5. The printing area for names and addresses on our addressograph plates is limited to _____ lines of _____ characters each. Keep your list within these limits.
6. Mail your lists, with the attached "Mailing List Request" to:

    Super-Tabs Sales Promotion
    846 S. Main Street
    Dayton 2, Ohio

This is the address of our mailing house and the address to which everything having to do with the mailing of this series should be sent.

Exhibit B
Mailing List Request
To Branch Managers with Announcement Bulletin

Attach this request to your lists of 200 prospects for each salesman. Mail the lists to:

    Super-Tabs Sales Promotion
    846 S. Main Street
    Dayton 2, Ohio

Branch Manager: (filled in at Super-Tabs)   Branch No.:
Branch:
Address:
City, State:

    Accompanying this sheet are lists for _____ salesman.
    _____Lists for_____more salesmen will follow.
    _____We have now forwarded lists for all of our salesmen.

Exhibit 1
Yellow Card: Branch File

No._____

(Space for name and address)

NEVER DESTROY THIS CARD *

THIS PERSON IS RECEIVING SUPER-TABS SALES PROMOTION.

If name or address needs correction: Make correction (print or typewrite) on this card.

If you wish to substitute another name for this one: Use this card. Cross out the name above. Print or type the new name and address on the reverse of this card.

Mail this card to:

> Super-Tabs Sales Promotion
> 846 S. Main Street
> Dayton 2, Ohio

We will send you a new yellow card with the new or corrected name and address on it.

* It represents one of a limited number of factory promotion mailings. You cannot add or change names without returning this card.

Exhibit 2
White Card: Notification Card: for List Correction

No._____

(Space for name and address)

REMOVE FROM MAILING LIST

NOTICE:

This name has been removed from your mailing list.

_____At your request.

_____Postmaster notifies us of nondelivery (see attached).

Remove the corresponding yellow card from your file and use it as instructed on that card to (*a*) correct this name or address, or (*b*) add a new name.

The typical mailing will include:

Letter: This letter will contain the "offer." If the "offer" is simply one of a product folder or a demonstration, the letter will dwell mostly on the benefits of the Super-Tabs equipment and can be considered as a piece of effective "product advertising" even when the recipient does not respond. When obligating material is offered, the letter will dwell mostly on the value of the material and only incidentally, if at all, on Super-Tabs products. Its advertising value (in the case of those not answering) is not necessarily reduced, however, since the offer, even if not accepted, creates good will.

Reply Card: This card will contain the name and address of the prospect and the salesman's identifying code.

The reply card may contain art, showing the offer or product.

The reply card will be addressed to:

> Super-Tabs Information Service
> 846 S. Main Street
> Dayton 2, Ohio

The typical response to an inquiry will include:

Letter: The first paragraph will acknowledge the inquiry and indicate that the requested information is enclosed, or being sent separately.

The balance of the letter will stress the benefits of Super-Tab equipment, with a suggestion that the reader "compare" Super-Tab with similar equipment and draw his attention to the reply card provided.

Offer: Whatever was requested.

Reply Card: A reply card, asking for more information about any or all of the equipment mentioned in the letter, and/or requesting a demonstration, will be included with the letter. When practical, a similar reply card will be bound into or fastened to the "offer" so it remains available after the letter is discarded. These cards will *not* be salesman-coded, obviously, and when returned, will be sent to the branch manager for the territory served, after requests have been answered (same general system as used for requests to original mailings).

Inquiry answering forms:

When an inquiry arrives, an inquiry answering set will be typed and the inquiry answered, by first-class mail, within 48 hours. The inquiry answering set will contain:

1. A label for the inquiry-answering envelope (Exhibit 3).
2. A white sheet, forwarded to Super-Tab Sales Department (Exhibit 4).
3. A blue sheet, which is sent to the branch manager (Exhibit 5).
4. A pink sheet, which is sent to the branch manager and passed on to the salesman. Attached to this pink sheet is the original inquiry itself (Exhibit 6). The pink sheet becomes a "report on follow-up" for the salesman and is returned to Super-Tab after the salesman has called on the inquirer.

Exhibit 3
Inquiry Answering Set: Label—for Inquirer

SUPER-TAB, Factory Address

The enclosed
material has
been requested
personally
by_____(Name and address of the
                                     inquirers are typed in
                                     this space)

_____ °
_____ †
_____ ‡

° Item requested is typed here.
† Salesman's identifying number, if known, is typed here.
‡ Date item was mailed from Dayton is typed here.

Exhibit 4
Inquiry Answering Set: White Sheet—for Super-Tab

To: SUPER-TAB—Sales Manager

This is an inquiry received as the result of direct mail sales promotion, from:

(Name and address
of inquirer here)

_____
_____
_____

_____

(Item requested, salesman's identifying
number, and date item was mailed from
Dayton)

Exhibit 5
Inquiry Answering Set: Blue Sheet—for Branch Manager

To: SUPER-TABS—Branch Manager

This is an inquiry received as the result of direct mail sales promotion. The requested information *has been mailed*. Pass the attached pink sheet on to the correct salesman for follow-up and report. Inquiry was from:

(Name and address
of inquirer here)

_____
_____
_____

_____

(Item requested, salesman's identifying
number, and date item was mailed from
Dayton)

Exhibit 6
Inquiry Answering Set: Pink Sheet—for Salesman

This is an INQUIRY from one of your BEST PROSPECTS

This inquiry was received as the result of Super-Tab national sales promotion mailings. Any material requested has been mailed. Follow up on this inquiry immediately with a price quotation and offer of demonstration.

(Name and address
of inquirer here)

_____

_____

_____

_____

(Item requested, salesman's identifying
number, and date item was mailed from
Dayton)   (over)

Reverse Side

SALESMAN'S REPORT

Super-Tab's policy of salesman support and inquiry development requires a follow-up call and report on all inquiries supplied in this manner.

Please return this report, within two weeks, to Super-Tab Sales Manager at the factory.

FOLLOWED-UP _____ Personal; _____ Phone   Date _____

Person contacted _____

Interest: _____ Active; _____ Mild; _____ None

Comments: _____

_____

                                                    (over)

THE TYPICAL "FOLLOW-UP" PROMOTION TO THE SPECIAL LIST OF WARM PROSPECTS (INQUIRERS) WILL INCLUDE:

Letter: A "Cordial Contact" (low-pressure sales letter), will stress the importance of comparing all makes of similar equipment and offer an office demonstration or free trial.

Reply Card: A reply card asking for a few days free trial or an in-the-office demonstration will be included with the letter.

When returned, these cards will be sent to the branch office for the territory served for follow-up by salesmen.

Of course, before the program could be put into operation, the branches and salesmen had to understand it. So part of the plan, as presented, included copy for the announcement to branches. It follows:

Page 1   DIRECT MAIL ADVERTISING PLAN
                SUPER-TAB

Pages 2 & 3   DIRECT MAIL CAN HELP IN THE FIRST
           3 STEPS OF EVERY SALE YOU MAKE

                                 5. CLOSE THE
                                    SALE
                       4. MAKE DEMON-
                            STRATION
              3. HELP
                  CREATE
                  PREFERENCE
       2. AROUSE
           INTEREST
    1. CONTACT

Pages 4 & 5

The most heartening words a salesman can hear when he stands in front of a prospect are

> "Super-Tab? I've been getting your mail.
> Looks like you may have some pretty good
> equipment."

An *open-minded* prospect!

That's what every salesman wants, and that is what this new direct mail program is designed to make for you . . . *open-minded prospects!*

You know that if you make enough calls on a prospect over a period of months, you can usually get him to open his mind to Super-Tab.

But *you don't have time* to make all those preliminary calls.

That's why we are recommending that you start now on this *direct mail program* that will help you make the *first* three steps of many sales:

> Contact the prospect
> Arouse his interest
> Help create preference

Your job will then be to *make the demonstration* and *close the sale.*

- - - - -

Advertising is designed to *plow the ground* for a sales call . . . to fertilize it . . . to make sure that you and your product are favorably known.

Sometimes advertising can produce an actual inquiry for you . . . but that is gravy.

At Super-Tab, we spend thousands of dollars every year in advertising, for your prospects to see and hear.

But your *best* prospects need *more* attention, and it should come to them from *you* (so they will begin to know and trust you, as a Super-Tab outlet).

For that reason, we are beginning a *Super-Tab Branch & Dealer direct mail program.*

Pages 6 & 7
Purpose:

The purpose of this program is to be sure that Super-Tab *advertising* gets to *your best prospects,* to help make the first three steps of the sale.

What it is:

A continuing advertising series, one mailing every month. Most mailings will be letters. Some will be (or include) reprints of magazine advertising. Most will include reply cards asking for a demonstration in case the mailing arrives when the prospect is thinking about our kind of equipment. These cards will come directly to you. Occasionally one will offer something of value to the recipient. . . . Upon request, you will deliver it to him (and, in the process, create a better impression of yourself and Super-Tab).

When such an offer is made, you will be furnished with a supply of the items sufficient to cover expected returns. If you need or want more, they'll be supplied at a small cost. Each letterhead will contain your company's name and address.

What do
you do?

Furnish the list. That's all.

You make up a legible list, by name and/or by company, including street address, city and zone number. Send it in. (See below.)

You may add, remove, or correct listings at any time. At the beginning of the program and once a year, thereafter, you will receive a complete list, on 3 × 5 cards, for your review and office use.

What Super-
Tab does:

We bear the cost of creating the advertising, the material that is included or given away, and administering the program. The actual production of the material will be handled by an independent mailing house.

You pay only the cost of producing, addressing, postage & handling.

Page 8
What does
this cost
you?

An average of _____¢ per name, per month.

After each mailing, we will charge your promotion account _____¢ for each mailing made.

That means, for example, that for $_____ a year you can hire an "assistant salesman" to call on your *one thousand* best prospects *every month.*

About your
list:

You may address by title or by name, as you prefer. Be sure your list is correct. Because mailings will be prepared ahead, your account will be charged for at least one extra mailing to any name you drop or change. Use the enclosed sheet and any extra paper to print or type the names, or use any other legible method. (If you use a *directory* of any sort, which covers more than one post-office address, be sure the correct post office is shown after every name.)

How to
begin:

Prepare your list. Mark your branch or dealer name on every sheet of the list. Mail it to:

> Super-Tab Branch & Dealer Advertising
> 846 S. Main St.
> Dayton 2, Ohio

Advertising, *direct* from you to *your best prospects,* once every month, is the hammer, hammer, hammer that will eventually make Super-Tab the No. 1 name in their minds. They will think of you when they think of our type of equipment . . . and that's all you need.

Page 9

ORDER FORM

SUPER-TAB

BRANCH AND DEALER

DIRECT MAIL ADVERTISING

Date

TO: Super-Tab Branch & Dealer Advertising
846 S. Main Street
Dayton 2, Ohio

Please send the monthly Super-Tab mailing series to attached list.
I understand

1. You will send out one mailing a month in the form of:
   a. Letter or ad reprint or combination
   b. Usually containing a return card addressed to me
   c. Sometimes offering something of value to the recipient that you will furnish at no charge to me
2. That you will pay all development and administrative costs and I will pay only the cost of producing the mailings at _____¢ per name per mailing
3. That the program will continue until canceled by me

Branch or Dealer_____

_____

Signed_____

This kind of advance planning ensures follow-up, right down to the point of sale. It anticipates problems and includes plans to avoid or to overcome them. Every direct mail program which includes a response-and-follow-up should begin with a similar plan.

26

Direct Mail as an "Assistant Salesman"

Low-cost Sales

One thing about sales managers . . . they aren't subtle. Sales managers know what they want. They'll tell you:

More sales . . . at a lower cost per sale.

Since they know that their *star* salesmen—even though they make the most money—sell at the lowest cost per sale, most of them try to hire more star salesmen. But they've found there aren't enough of these to go around.

Some sales managers, though, have found a "secret" way to improve the selling of their present salesmen and to multiply the effectiveness of their star salesmen so they have, figuratively, more and better salesmen . . . and can, without increasing their sales force, literally sell more at a lower cost per sale.

Direct Mail—Assistant Salesman

They use *direct mail* to do part of the salesman's spade work for him . . . not indirectly, as in direct mail *advertising*, which tries to get the prospect to come to a dealer . . . nor in *place* of the salesman, as in direct mail selling (mail order), which makes the entire sale . . . but as an integral part of the sales-department effort, to help salesmen make sales quicker and easier. We might call this direct mail "Assistant Salesmen."

These "Assistant Salesmen" act somewhat as flesh-and-blood "Junior Salesmen" do. Junior Salesmen are often teamed up with experienced salesmen in the office. Their job is to help the Senior Salesmen produce more. They make calls regularly, to educate and remind the prospects about the company's product or services. When it comes time actually to close a sale, they usually need the Senior Salesmen to help them do that.

Direct mail "Assistant Salesmen" have these same functions . . . primarily those of calling on your company's customers and prospects; educating them about your product; reminding them about your services.

Whenever your company's sales depend upon the effectiveness of salesmen—your own or those of your distributors or dealers—you can increase sales, yet cut their cost, by making the salesmen more effective. Sales managers are quite aware of this when they try to hire more experienced men, give them good training, and add incentive programs. The more a salesman knows about the product and about "selling" the better, of course.

Types of Prospects

But there's a second person present in every sale . . . the prospect. His attitude is important, too. Most salesmen have all kinds of prospects and customers, big and little, off and on, good and not-so-good.

The Prize Prospect likes your product, likes your company, likes your salesmen. He'll turn business your way every chance he gets. In connection with your business, *he* would call himself "open-minded."

Other Prospects are more like that famous McGraw-Hill "Man-in-the-chair," who is saying:

> I don't know who you are.
> I don't know your company.
> I don't know your company's product.
> I don't know what your company stands for.
> I don't know your company's customers.
> I don't know your company's record.
> I don't know your company's reputation.
> Now—what was it you wanted to sell me?

In connection with your business, this prospect would call himself "uninformed."

Still Other Prospects are "tough." Some tough prospects are rude and rough or just won't see your salesmen. Most of them, though, are just indifferent. They've developed a defense against salesmen.

A typical tough prospect will come out to meet you. He'll shake hands and smile. He appears interested . . . but busy. When your salesman explains something or makes a sales point, he nods his head. But his mind's on other things. And all the time, he knows he'll be buying from someone else.

In connection with your business, he'd call himself "neutral."

But "neutral" is just a polite word . . . and "uninformed" isn't much better. In selling, anyone who isn't "for" you is "against" you.

Although every good salesman would like to talk exclusively to "open-minded" prospects, most of them spend a good deal of time seeing, or trying to see, the more-or-less "uninformed" or "neutral" ones. . . . (And some days, it seems, even the "open-minded" friends slip slightly toward "neutral.")

These, of course, are a salesman's least effective calls.

Consequently, most sales managers agree that salesmen would be more effective if they could spend more of their time talking to "preconditioned," open-minded prospects.

Sales managers often realize, too, that:

1. Their salesmen aren't calling often enough.

2. Prospects are often unavailable or "too busy" when salesmen call.

3. Salesmen have called on some prospects for months or years without really stressing and restressing the company's best sales points.

4. Some "decision makers" in a prospect business are beyond the reach of salesmen. Salesmen *never* "get in."

5. Something more ought to be done to keep the open-minded prospects completely happy.

Direct Mail, Problem Solver

Direct mail Assistant-salesman programs can help sales managers with all these problems. For, when well prepared, such programs can help a great deal. Among other virtues:

They call regularly.

They are always pleasant and informative.

They tell the same story on every call.

They often get to see prospects when the flesh-and-blood salesmen cannot.

They can make hundreds or thousands of calls at once.

They wait patiently, without pay, until the prospect is free and ready to listen.

And, they gradually turn uninformed and neutral prospects into open-minded prospects who are *friends* of your company, your product, and your salesmen.

Naturally, your salesmen become more effective.

What's more, if your Assistant-salesman program is mailed over the signature of someone at the home or a branch office, it has the added advantage of helping the customer think of your company in broader terms than those of the salesman himself. Then, when the salesman is promoted, transferred, or leaves the company, you have a second contact with the prospect on which to build.

The Cost of Selling

When McGraw-Hill, in 1958, made a study of Industrial salesmen, it uncovered some startling facts about the cost of selling.

Salesmen worked long hours, for example, averaging eight hours and forty minutes a day. But most of this time was spent in paper work, reports, sales meetings, waiting time, service calls, and traveling. Only three hours and thirty-seven minutes per day were spent in face-to-face conversation with customers and prospects.

No wonder, then, with all these people to see and with so little time to see them in, that the cost of each sales call has gone up and up, from an average of $10.72 in 1945 to an average of $22.23 in 1958, when this survey was made. And the cost is still rising.

What's more, our average salesman finds that each of his prospect companies averaged 3.6 identified buying influences. That is, whether he was able to reach them personally or not, the salesman could list three or four people in every company who influenced the purchase of his product.

Obviously, then, with the list of prospects and customers most salesmen have to call on, multiplied by three or four to count all the individuals, salesmen don't get around to see their prospects very often. They need assistants.

Direct Mail . . . to Increase Salesmen's Effectiveness

Almost any company, large or small, can increase its salesmen's effectiveness through the use of direct mail "Assistant Salesmen." Most progressive, successful companies do use this method, though their activities are more or less "secret." It isn't that companies deliberately hide what they are doing in this area. Most of them are extremely generous with their knowledge. But mail promotion is delivered only to a selected list of prospects; so, it isn't "noticed" by competition and the public as other advertising and promotion is. Consequently, few people realize how much mail is used by business. It's simply that, unlike other types of advertising and promotion, only their prospects and customers see the mailing. Consequently, few people appreciate the tremendous amount of Assistant-salesman mail that is being used.

The library of the Direct Mail Advertising Association has hundreds of examples of "Assistant Salesmen" in its files, which can help a sales manager determine whether such direct mail would be useful to him.

Generally speaking, whenever you want to produce more sales without adding salesmen, or when you want to trim your sales force without losing sales volume, you can use Assistant-salesman direct mail profitably.

Plan for Continued Impact

When you decide to use it, though, don't start with the idea that you will "try it out" with a mailing or two. Assistant Salesmen are much like regular salesmen (who "make most original sales after the fifth call" and who call faithfully on customers whether they get an order every time or not).

Before you begin, allocate a budget and prepare a plan for at least twelve months of regular calls by your "Assistants." Schedule your mailings carefully and keep to the schedule. If your sales are strictly seasonal, you may not want to schedule regular mailings during all periods of the year, though off-season calls—when your competitors are staying home—can often be profitable.

The frequency of your calls depends on your product and on your budget, of course, but the great majority of Assistant Salesmen call monthly or more frequently.

If some of your prospects or customers are substantially more important to you than others, you may want to schedule more frequent calls on them. In any event, whatever you plan in the way of Assistant Salesmen should be designed to solve your particular sales problems, not simply be a copy of some other company's program.

Here are some things to keep in mind whenever you have Assistant Salesmen calling for you:

1. Be sure your messages reach *all* of the decision makers in your prospect company who are important to you . . . both those your salesman sees regularly and those he cannot. (No danger of "going over anyone's head" . . . Assistant Salesmen can easily avoid this problem where necessary.)

This generally means more than one person in larger companies. When developing your list, you'll rate some companies with ten times or one hundred times the potential of others. Don't slight these Very Important Prospects. Be sure every person in that company who shares in the decision to use your product is getting calls from you.

2. Some purchases are made entirely because prospects are sold on the *value* of your product to them. . . . Be sure your Assistant Salesmen point out *what your product will do for them* . . . how it will help solve *their* problems.

3. Most sales are influenced by the fact that open-minded prospects

like you. (They trust, admire, respect, have faith in, or just plain "like" your company, your product, and your salesmen.) So be sure your Assistant Salesmen are helpful, interesting, friendly, concise, and believable.

4. Your Assistant Salesman represents your company. In a way, he *is* your company to the prospect. So be sure your Assistant Salesman is worthy to represent you: is clear-spoken, neat and clean, well planned, and well designed.

Emphasize Value and Interest

Perhaps the most important of those "tips" are the ones emphasizing *value* and *interest*. Yet they're frequently overlooked, and the flesh-and-blood salesman suffers.

When Assistant Salesmen have been making interesting, valuable calls, the flesh-and-blood salesman who follow the mail know it. They get *action,* in the form of easy sales where they were difficult before. They get *reaction,* to something that was said or implied in the mailing. They get a better *reception* when their name is announced.

Your "Calls" Contain Value for the recipient when you tell or show him things he *wants* to know or *ought* to know about the benefits he receives when he uses your product or service.

Your "Calls" Are Interesting to him when they are dramatic; when they are accompanied by something of value to him (regardless of its direct connection with your product, the reminder-advertising type of thing); or when they are pleasing, fascinating, amusing, inspiring . . . or just plain interesting.

Most good Assistant-salesman mailings, of course, contain *both* value and interest.

When you follow these "tips" closely, your mailing program is almost bound to work. It could probably be considered a sales axiom to say:

Sales calls are more productive when a prospect has read something complimentary about the product or received something interesting to him from the salesman's company since the salesman's previous call.

From the files of Graphic Service, Dayton (from whom we've borrowed the designation "Assistant Salesman," which they use to identify this type of direct mail), we've also picked a few examples of such campaigns, which they have created or produced for others. In each case, of course, the mail contacts are designed to help solve a specific sales problem.

A Case Study: Assistant Salesmen

Of course, when you are selling Assistant Salesmen, as Graphic Service does, your problem is to make prospects aware of the advantages of this type of direct mail. Here's an Assistant Salesman that delivers a message about Assistant Salesmen.

GRAPHIC SERVICE

846 S. Main Street

Dayton 2, Ohio

A salesman stopped to see us in the fall of '58.

"Dear Friend," he began, "We are pleased to acquaint you with the latest addition to our carbon-paper line. It has been named John Q. Higglebeck Century Carbon in honor of our firm's illustrious founder and our one hundredth year in business. Please be assured that your order for any amount will receive our prompt and courteous attention."

Then he left . . . and he's never been back.

❖   ❖   ❖

Naturally, we made that up. No *salesman* ever talked like that.

What he really said was: "Good morning. How's the golf game lately and isn't this weather terrible? You'll be interested in this new carbon paper we've just added. It stays blacker longer but at the same time it doesn't smear all over the second sheet the way the stuff you've been using does. Rub your finger over it there. No smudge. Watch what happens when I crease it a dozen times! No cracks. It's the best carbon paper I've ever seen and look what the folks up the street say about it. Do you want six boxes or twelve? Still have a good supply? O.K. I'll be back in a couple of weeks. Here are a few sheets of this *good* paper . . . try it out."

That sounds more like a salesman. He's friendly . . . he talks about the product's advantages . . . and he keeps calling back.

Yet in some companies, even today, the only help salesmen get is through sales letters that sound something like the Higglebeck letter above.

At the high-cost-of-good-salesmen today, they need more support than that. Salesmen need bona-fide "assistant salesmen" who call between calls and *really* help sell.

The enclosed card, for example, is an "assistant salesman" for us—because it offers useful information to help *you* sell.

Mail it. Learn "How to Increase Your Salesman's Effectiveness by Mail." There's no charge or obligation of any kind . . . but it's chuck-full of good ideas that can be turned into added sales for you.

Sincerely,

The Reply Card with that letter read as follows:

Of course, I'd like to

    INCREASE SALESMEN'S EFFECTIVENESS.

So I'd like a copy of your booklet,

    How to Increase Your Salesman's Effectiveness by Mail.

I understand there's no charge or obligation.

This particular Assistant Salesman asked for a response, of course, as some such mailings do, and might more properly have been included in the chapter on "Response Mailings," but since it's part of the Assistant-salesman story, we've included it here.

A Case Study: Printing Equipment

Let's take the Dayco Corporation's problem. Their Printing Equipment Division sells printing rollers and other equipment to printers. They have a handful of salesmen and thousands of good prospects. So it's a long time between calls. Worse than that, their product is hard to "sell" on a call. Because printers buy new rollers when they need them, not on impulse. So the job of both the salesman and his direct mail assistant is to keep the printer in a happy, friendly frame of mind regarding Dayco. Then, when he needs rollers, he'll think of Dayco favorably and give the salesman a ring.

Dayco has accomplished this through the years with mailings of what they call "Remember Whens," interesting, humorous cartoons about the "good old days."

Each cartoon is in a folder with the description of one Dayco product for printers and a reasonably humorous write-up about the cartoon. A lighthearted letter with a reply card goes along.

As you know, advertising departments tend to tire of a campaign after a year or two. Sales managers are less likely to do that if the campaign is effective. The salesmen won't let them. They haven't let this campaign stop.

After about fifteen years of the "Remember When" series, with six scheduled mailings a year, Dayco expanded the program, cutting the "Remember Whens," back to four and adding four special or unusual mailings to top prospects.

Their approach to the additional series was to choose a type of printing piece that was not normally used for advertising (typical examples: a record jacket, a child's coloring book, a book jacket, gift wrapping paper, etc.), then to write all the copy on the piece in a lighthearted, humorous vein about Dayco products.

The Record Jacket, for example, was entitled "Music to Make Money by," by "The Happy Printer and His Band." The cover featured a photo of a smiling printer, plus small sketches of Dayco products. The reverse of the jacket described the "music" in terms of those products. Here's an excerpt:

OPUS 1:   Rolling in Wealth

Through the opening strains of this movement is heard the tinkling of coins, gradually increasing in volume, reminiscent of the money saved when using *Dayco Rollers.* The constant theme in the background recalls the steady beat of a busy press accompanied by the whistle of a Happy Printer. Musical raindrops, heat waves and cold chills intrude, fortissimo, then fade, but the theme continues without a break . . . as the firm, soft, velvet touch of Dayco rollers leads to constant upbeat of profit.

OPUS 2:   Split Your Troubles in Two

Pianissimo, and hesitant, as printers often do initially, the musicians approach Dayco multicolor passages. Suddenly, one section of the strings picks up notes of the "St. Louis Blues," while strains of the "Red, Red Robin" come from the other side. Miraculously, each melody comes loud and clear, without interference or overlap from the other. Then, in rising crescendo, the welcome sound of a cash-register bell begins to ring as the profit music of *Dayco's Color Separators* and *Fountain Dividers* becomes fully understood.

OPUS 3:   Blanket Your Troubles Away

Through the measured beat of a clicking printing press, the dissonant sounds of sixteenth notes remind listeners of a series of pinholes in offset blankets. Suddenly, the long, low moans of a rusty slide trombone, the beat of a kettledrum with the skin slit and the dull ting-tong of a triangle partly submersed in a pan of dirty oil, call to mind balky blankets that have suddenly gone tacky and dead. A hush, then a brilliant, clear note signals the appearance of *Dayco Offset Blankets.* Finally, led by the strings, the entire orchestra blends its sweet, smooth, swinging tones in reprise of the Happy Printer melody, an indication of supreme satisfaction with Dayco Blankets, their smooth surface, controlled stretch, and long, long life.

FINALE: Many a Happy Day (co)

In a superb blending of the three earlier movements, reflecting *Dayco Products in Every Position on Every Press,* the symbolic cash-register bell becomes louder and louder, harmonizing with a rising and rousing rendition of the Happy Printer theme, which quickly fades into the "everafter" distance, promising THE END of your troubles.

The Book Jacket in this series was for "The Mystery of the Printers' Profits," a "whodunit" by a Happy Printer . . . where it turns out that the "mystery" (described on the back cover) is, "Who put those extra profits in the printing business?" The culprit turns out to be Dayco.

The Child's Cartoon Book followed the same light, humorous vein, with cartoons and captions telling the history of "The Happy Printer and His Dog." The captions themselves tell the story fairly well:

Once there was a printer who was very unhappy. (Cartoon shows dog trouncing his owner at checkers on this page.)

Mainly because he had trouble with his form rollers.

He'd tried umpteen different kinds and brands, in his life. None of them worked right all of the time. (Cartoon shows huge stack of rollers on a rack.)

He had summer rollers, winter rollers, rollers for special inks, rollers for rain, and rollers for partly cloudy.

He even called the weather man for predictions whenever he started a run of over 3,000. Nothing seemed to help.

Finally, even his dog laughed at his printing.

"I could do better than that," said the dog.

So the printer took him at his word and used the dog as a form roller for a while. (Cartoon shows press running with dog in form-roller position.)

This really worked better than his old roller. But it gave Hans sore feet, so he went on strike.

Just about that time, the printer received a card from Dayco—like this one: (Reply card was attached to this page). He sent it in and found out how *good* a roller can be.

He put Daycos in every position on every press he had.

Now everybody's happy . . . with bigger profits for the printer and lots of juicy bones for Hans. (Cartoon shows old roller rack full of selected bones.)

Hope you'll join the many, many happy printers who use Dayco Rollers in every position on every press.

Along with Dayco Rollers, Dayco Fountain Dividers
Dayco Color Separators
Dayco Offset Blankets
. . . are profit producers, too, you know.

Other Pieces, including a reusable, all-purpose greeting card and "The Check-stubs of a Happy Printer," continued the series. Each piece was designed to create an impact when it arrived and apparently did just that, for after the first few mailings one of the company salesmen reported: "Don't stop the advertising. I used to spend a half-hour on every call just reminding the prospect who I was and warming him up. Now he's warm when I come in. The other day one fellow said to me *'Thanks* for sending me your advertising.' I never thought I'd live to see the day."

Another long-term user of Assistant Salesman is the Flexicore Co., Inc., with headquarters in Dayton. In the late forties, Flexicore began to promote a new product—prefabricated floor sections made of concrete. They had a few licensees across the country and were promoting through publication advertising. A quick analysis showed that while Flexicore licensees appeared to be selling the Flexicore system to contractors and builders, their sale was very difficult unless the architect specified Flexicore units in the beginning.

Architects are easy to reach by direct mail, and so began a long-term program to sell architects on the value of Flexicore construction and to make it easy for them to use it.

The main selling job was done through case histories, showing how other architects used Flexicore for many varieties of buildings. The first ones were simple, one-page, black-and-white affairs which went out monthly. And these mailings were titled "Flexicore Facts."

The value of these regular calls by Assistant Salesmen, in this case to educate the prospect gradually to the many uses of the product, became more and more apparent. And the "calls" became more elaborate, two-color, six-page descriptions of Flexicore uses. After a dozen years of regular mailings, the campaign was considered more valuable than ever.

In addition, each piece carries an AIA file number on it to encourage the architect to file it . . . and, because they carry specifications and details that he can't get anywhere else, he does. Because there was some doubt about this after a few years of the series, one of the manufacturers had a survey made. Over 50 per cent of those surveyed said they actually *filed* the Facts.

Even more important, they have become a sales kit for salesmen. And all eighty-five "Flexicore Facts" plus "Flexicore Idea Files" and "Design and Data" mailings, which sometimes ·take their place in the mailing series, are kept *in stock*, in each sales office.

Any salesman heading, say, for a meeting with a school board, just turns to a quick index, which tells him that Facts Nos. 7, 28, 37, 40, 51, 52, 62, 67, 70, 81 and 85, each demonstrating different benefits for different types of schools, might come in handy at the meeting.

The Flexicore sales manager uses direct mail in other ways . . . for special mailings to school boards, builders, etc., but this constant hammer, hammer, hammer on the architects is the basic use.

A Case Study: Water Pipe

Another Midwest user of Assistant Salesmen is the Price Brothers Company. This organization sells water pipe, the large kind that brings the water from the reservoir into town.

They have tough competition, of course. And because they sell to municipalities, politics and advertised bids are problems. On top of that, Price Brothers sells a comparatively new type of pipe. So the two old stand-bys of government-type purchases—"proved performance" and "low bids"—don't help much. At first, Price Pipe often couldn't meet the specifications, written for cast-iron pipe.

Then direct mail Assistant Salesmen went to work for them. They visited waterworks engineers and consultants, municipal officials, and employees, telling the Price Brothers' story.

They hammered away at the superiority of Price Pressure Pipe, regularly, as Assistant Salesmen, at an *economical* cost per call, to keep all prospects aware of Price Pressure Pipe, and to convince prospects that prestressed-concrete, steel-cylinder, pressure pipe belongs in the specifications.

Direct mail isn't expected to sell a single foot of pipe. Its objective is to keep the ground cultivated; so, when plans are made for a pipeline and the Price Brothers' salesman arrives, he'll be regarded as a friend who sells an acceptable type of pipe.

After thirteen solid years of consistent reiteration of the three major virtues of Price Pipe—long life, great strength, and constant flow . . . through interesting, friendly, pleasant letters, which tell the same story in new and fresh ways—the Assistant Salesmen were working harder than ever.

This series was also mentioned in Chapter 19, concerning postmarked mailings. Here's a letter example, one of a long series that reiterated the special qualities of this unusual pipe:

PRICE BROTHERS COMPANY
Prestressed Concrete Pressure Pipe
1932 East Monument Ave.
Dayton 1, Ohio

THERE'S A GIRL IN OUR OFFICE . . .

She files things. Forms and records and letters like this. I've noticed, though, that she doesn't just file. She reads every letter through . . . and, as she reads, she constantly shakes her head . . . sideways.

The other day she stuck that head in the door. "Begging your pardon, Mr. Price," she said, "but could I ask you a question . . . and no offense?"

"Certainly," I answered. "Having trouble with the files?"

"No sir," she said, patting her poodle-cut, "it's with the letters. I'm not sure I know what they mean. Now take this one. You talk about *sustained capacity* because of the absence of *tuberculation* and *corrosion*. Frankly, I don't get it."

"It's one of the reasons our pipe is so much better," I tried to explain. "Some other kinds of pipe don't *last* as *long*, they aren't as *strong* and their *capacity* isn't—ah—*sustained* because they corrode and—er—tuberculate. See?"

"Corrode, I get," she said, "because I've seen corrosions in the hills on Dad's farm, but tuberculation," she said, pityingly, "is of the lungs."

I saw I'd better take another tack.

"Look," I said. "Suppose your husband came home from work every week and tossed $80 in your lap. This goes on week after week. You depend on it. Suddenly, it's only $75. Then $70. What would *you* call that?"

"Divorce," she said flatly.

"Aha!" I said. "But if it's a pipeline, you can't divorce it. You're stuck with it . . . and, if you have pipe that—ah—gucks up, it's going to cut down on the amount of water it delivers every week . . . just like a husband who goes from $80 to $75 to $70."

"Well," she said, heading for the files, and another round with the alphabet, "*that's* simple enough. Next time you write those people a letter, why don't you say it like that? You'd get farther. I bet they'd send in more cards, too."

What else could I do???

Here it is.

Harry S. Price, Jr.
Vice-president

A Case Study: Electronic Equipment

Ledex, Inc., a manufacturer of component parts for electronic equipment, rotary solenoids, stepping and selector switches, etc., has an interesting sales problem and an unusual use for Assistant Salesmen. They have thousands of potential buyers and only a small handful of salesmen. But that's not unusual in the electronics business. Their surprises come through the unexpected uses which other people find for their products.

Consequently, the major assignment for their Assistant Salesmen is to encourage designers and engineers to "think about" using Ledex switches and solenoids in totally new and different ways. The following letter is one of a series of calls designed to do this. The card asking for further information is for the use of those new on the list who are not acquainted with the Ledex line, but the calls continue to the entire group, whether inquiries are received or not:

LEDEX INC.
123 Webster Street
Dayton 2, Ohio

I'll bet there's a young engineer . . .

. . . in your organization who will take a special interest in the enclosed Ledex Leaflet 4.

I say this because, of all the products we make, our Rotary Selector Switch seems to be the one that sets young engineers (and old ones too) to dreaming up simple solutions to complex problems.

He'll be interested in Leaflet 4 because, at a glance, it explains what a Rotary Selector Switch is, gives some idea of sizes, speed of operation, methods of control . . . and how you can get nearly unlimited switching combinations by varying decks and circuitry.

For example, your young engineer might figure out that he can sit at his desk with a 1-deck, 24-position control (smaller than a pack of cigarettes) and operate a 24-position remote selector switch in the basement next to the main electrical panel. With it he can control 24 lighting or power circuits.

And he'll need only 6 wires to connect his control with the remote switch.

Then if he adds a 1-deck, 10-position control in tandem on his desk, and substitutes an 11-deck, 24-position remote switch in the basement, he'll be able to control 240 circuits. He'll need 10 wires for this setup.

If you can get him thinking like this, it won't be long until he is developing some space-saving circuitry combinations for your products.

For more information about our rotary switches, just initial the card and drop it in the mail.

Sincerely,

Gerald Leland
Vice-president–General Manager

A Case Study: Plumbing

An example of the use of Assistant Salesmen by a local wholesale plumber concern with plenty of competition, who wanted to hammer away at the excellence of its service, is the Pickrel Brothers' campaign. This consisted of a series of eleven cards, each with a dramatic "gag" picture of one of the three brothers, enthusiastically entering into the spirit of the copy beneath. One showed a brother, in chef's hat, flipping a valve; another had a ball player swinging a bat; others showed a fireman on a fire truck; one of the brothers hopping a freight car; etc. The copy below the picture tied in. Here are some samples:

1. (Photo of Jim Pickrel riding a freight car)

Jim Pickrel's ridin' high.

Off on another buying trip, Pickrel Brothers' world traveler spares no expense to bring you the broadest possible selection of plumbing and heating supplies. Undisturbed in the spacious expanse of his private car "XRT 346587," Jim will complete plans for an even better season ahead. His shopping list guarantees you a full selection of top-quality products. If Jim's "abroad" when you call, Dave, Dick, Bill, or John will high-ball your order through for you.

2. (Photo of Dick Pickrel swinging a baseball bat)

Dick Pickrel's gone batty.

Yes sir. With baseball season on us, he's unlimbered the old pogo stick and claims he aims to bat 1,000. Fact is, every one of us expects to make a hit with you every time you pitch a plumbing or heating problem our way. We're "old pros" and always deliver in the clutch. If Dick's out giving pointers to Ted Williams, just look for Dave, Jim, Bill, or John. They'll produce.

3. (Photo of Jim Pickrel flipping a valve over a pancake griddle.)

Jim Pickrel's gone high-hat.

But he's really cooking on the front burner when it comes to short orders . . . or long ones. Whatever your plumbing or heating needs—we can fill the bill. Satisfied customers, who've had a helping of our courteous and friendly service, keep coming back for more. You'll like it too. If Jim's sweating over a hot pipe-fitting à la Pickrel, Dave, Dick, Bill, or John will rustle your order. They know the recipe.

4. (Photo of Dick Pickrel hopping on a bicycle.)

Gangway!

The sidewalks on our street clear fast when Dick Pickrel hops on his Huffy for a deadline delivery. Willing to break his neck instead of a promise, Dick pedals over whenever trucks seem too slow. He draws the line at bathtubs though (they keep falling over his eyes), so give us a couple hours warning when you're doing a new house. If Dick's burning up the boulevard when you call, turn to Dave, Jim, John, or Bill.

5. (Photo of Bill Hanby leaping from the barber chair half shaved.)

Bill Hanby is in a lather!

He's just had word that a Pickrel Brothers' customer needs help, and he's on his way. He'll stop anything to prove that you'll get friendlier service, better quality and more complete selection at Pickrel Brothers. Just try and see . . . and if Bill's on the run for somebody else, Dave, Dick, Jim, or John will drop what they're doing for you.

6. (Photo of Dick Pickrel peeking from behind old-fashioned cash register)

Dick Pickrel thinks he's his own grandpop.

It can't be helped. We've tried so hard for old-fashioned service that poor Dick finally went overboard and posted old-fashioned prices. Better rush over for your plumbing and heating supplies before Dick finds out what's happened to costs in the last fifty years. Hurry. He may recover any day. If Dick's over at the blacksmith's, ask for Dave, Jim, Bill, or John. They'll treat you right too.

7. (Photo of "Doc" Pickrel with stethoscope to boiler)

Doc Pickrel has the right prescription . . . for customer satisfaction. Just the healthiest products, loving care for every detail and siren service in emergencies. That's why Pickrel products are always in fine shape, and why Pickrel customers keep coming back for dose after dose of friendly Pickrel service. Y'all come. If Doc's giving a physical when you call, just ring for Dave, Jim, Bill, or John. They've fingers on the pulse, too.

8. (Photo of John Holloran floating toy boat in bathtub)

Rub-a-dub-dub, just testing the tub.

That's John Holloran. Never satisfied 'til he knows every Pickrel product will satisfy in use . . . and the only way to test a bathtub—you guessed it; sail in it, naturally. John's enthusiastic; wants to test all the time. But when he says a thing will satisfy, you can count on it: he's not all wet. If somebody's pulled the plug on John, just whistle for Jim, Dave, Dick, or Bill.

9. (Photo of John Holloran riding fire truck with package under arm)

John Holloran's no false alarm.

Always ready to grab a handy hook and ladder for faster delivery, our friendly fireman's pulled many a perspiring plumber out of the fire by supplying a hard-to-find item, quick as a spark. A demon for speedy service, with a burning desire to satisfy, John's red hot to help you. If he's putting out a fire when you raise an alarm, just ask for Jim, Dick, Dave, or Bill. They have helmets, too.

10. (Photo of Jim Pickrel peeking out of a manhole)

Visit our bargain basement!

Jim Pickrel's picked a dandy . . . but any basement's a bargain if it's loaded with plumbing and heating products from Pickrel Brothers. Not because Pickrel prices are the country's cheapest, but because they're all honest bargains—top quality at reasonable prices, plus friendly, snappy service. Try it . . . once you have, you'll agree. If Jim's completely out of sight when you come in, just look for Dave, Dick, Bill, or John.

11. (The three Pickrels and rear view of lovely, blonde "model")

Ho hum! . . . just a routine order at Pickrel's. But Jim, Dave, and Dick try to be as smiling and helpful as if this customer were as important as you.

Everyone of us aims to please, regardless of the size or shape of the order . . . but just watch all five of us beam when you walk in. And if the trio above happen to be out delivering the sink trap for the lady, Bill and John will work three times as hard to prove you're welcome.

A Case Study: Salesmen's Incentives

Estimating properly the "power of a woman," one manufacturer used Assistant Salesmen to help develop salesmen's incentives—on the home front. Combining the power of feminine persuasion with a reward of checks to the wife for a husband's performance, the manufacturer obtained 600 new dealers for his products in the first two months this "Assistant-salesman" plan was used. He paid out $3,000 in rewards to eighty-six wives who helped their salesmen-husbands do a better job. But, of course, he automatically received every dollar (and more) in the additional sales made before the rewards were earned. Because the campaign was so successful originally, the idea was continued and has been used to persuade wives to help husbands bring home the bacon for a number of years.

The manufacturer, Knipco, wanted to push a portable heater to the farm market. The letters were sent to the wives of the salesmen who worked for twelve wholesalers, who sold to dealers. The dealers, in turn, sold to farmers.

The campaign appealed to wives to start a husband out on a successful selling day by setting his mood in an aggressive mold with a "Cheery Word at Breakfast." The first letter in the series explains the campaign's purpose very well:

Letter No. 1

This is how it all started.

Not long ago, I went to a sales managers' convention. One of the speakers, who seemed to know everything about everything, kept us awake one afternoon with a statement something like this:

"A cheery word at breakfast is what makes the salesman's day. Find the noble wife who sends her husband off in the morning with enthusiasm for his work and you'll find a successful man. The top salesman's wife takes an interest in his problems. She cheers him in the morning and applauds him at night. She is his star, his jewel, his all-in-all. She is the guiding beacon of the family partnership. It is the *wife* who turns the stumbling salesman into a shining star. She should get the credit . . .

". . . or at least a little cash."

Since then, I've checked this theory with a few wives, and find it quite generally accepted. When wives please salesmen, salesmen try to please wives . . . but wives seldom get the credit they deserve and the cash they receive is usually secondhand . . . perfectly good, but sometimes inadequate.

Well, your husband's firm is selling Knipco heaters this fall, and his particular problem, this month, is to sign up more "Knipco Dealers" (they give him an original order for three heaters). Naturally, we'd like to see him sign up as many as he can, as soon as possible.

That's why I'm writing you.

We'd like to have you, as the "guiding beacon" of your partnership, interested in Knipco, and, if your team is successful in establishing Knipco dealerships, we want to be sure that you get the credit, and . . .

A little cash as well.

That's why you'll find $150 in $5 checks enclosed. They're yours . . . and there are more where they come from if you need them. These are perfectly good checks . . . all they need is a satisfactory signature—and we'll be happy to provide that.

The enclosed sheet shows you how to arrange for the signature.

But your first step is:

Follow that speaker's advice; keep your husband happy; running in high gear; ready to conquer the world. Be sure he has a *"Cheery Word at Breakfast"* every morning (if he's out of town, better write him a note) . . . and if you'll just sing out *"Nab another Knipco"* when he leaves the house, you'll keep his energies on the right track.

Whenever he does "Nab another Knipco," reach for a check. Start it on its way . . . first to his sales manager, then to me.

My pen is full of ink, and there is no limit to the number of checks I'm willing to sign, under these conditions.

I'm sure you'll be able to handle the problem of disposing of them without any real difficulty.

I think that's the whole story. I have only one more thought to add. These are *good* heaters. Users *like* them. Dealers make more money when they carry them. So whenever your husband "Nabs another Knipco," he honestly does a real favor for the dealer, the dealer's customers, himself, his firm, and . . . until October 31st, certainly . . .

For *you.*

E. J. 'Tex' Erp,
President

Another letter, in the same light, near-playful vein, sent wives a small packet of stickers which read, "Nab Another Knipco Dealer." The letter then presented means by which the wife could get the message on the stickers across to her husband:

Letter No. 2

Dear CWABer:

Emergency!

One wife with a stack of unsigned checks called me long-distance yesterday.

"Look," she said, "this 'Cheery Word at Breakfast' idea is great . . . except that my star boarder wakes up every morning with a king-size, no-filter-tip grouch on. If I'm cheery it just makes him worse, so I learned, long ago, that he likes the Quiet Type. That's me. So he goes off each morning without thinking of Knipco. Can you help me?"

No sooner said than done. We're sending her a handful of the enclosed "Nab-another-Knipco" stickers . . . and made a few extra for you.

They'll stick most anywhere . . . on the sport page of the newspaper, the bathroom mirror, under the bacon, on his car windshield or speedometer, under the coffee cup, on his shoes—there must be a million places in *your* house.

Try a few. They may start more of those $5 checks rolling your way.

Hope so.

E. J. 'Tex' Erp

A later letter used an inventive layout to focus the emphasis on the wife's reward for using the "Cheery Word" to help her husband "Nab Another Knipco Dealer":

Letter No. 3:

Dear Mrs. 5-dollar checks:

I don't know about yours, but I am beginning to see five-spots before my eyes & every "three-heater" dealer your husband signs up brings out another one. Since we have extra time he still has a couple more

weeks to go
to grab hold
of plenty of
Knipco money
for you . . . be
sure he gets
those cheery
words in the
mornin' to keep
him Nabbin' those
Knipco Dealers all
day through and
spawnin' $5 bills

All you
ha ve to do
is to gr in
wh en ev er
you can

Then he will nab & you can do your Christmas shopping early . . . on Knipco checks

E. J. 'Tex' Erp
President

The Knipco approach was unusual. And it was unusually effective. It made Assistant Salesmen of wives, the enlistment of their services being based on the idea that incentives "at home" can help a salesman be more successful "on the road."

These letters were "interesting" in the unusual approach they used and in the chatty, friendly style of the copy . . . and in the various devices used to illustrate persuasion points. For example:

One letter carried a plastic mirror. The copy read:

> Know this woman? She's one of my favorite people. I like to send her checks.

Another letter carried a rubber band. With this copy:

> We're in the home stretch. This is the final week of our CWAB "Nab-another-Knipco Month."

The "value" presented to wives for this cheery-word effort is in the cold, hard cash which increases their power of the purse.

Assistant Salesmen Need a "Manager"

One final thought about Assistant Salesmen. They need a good *manager*. You're most likely to find the best one for you in a direct mail agency or acting as an independent direct mail consultant. That's because this particular "managerial" skill is relatively rare. The Assistant-salesman–manager job requires skills different from those used by the typical Sales Manager. For "Mail-men" are different creatures from "Male-men." Their message must be carefully prepared. They must anticipate all objections, decide on their entire story ahead of time, and tell it all at once, without boring. They contribute no personality of their own. It must all be prepared for them. Whereas sales managers are most successful when they lead their salesmen to greater *self*-development, the Assistant-salesman Sales manager must take care of every tiny detail, much as if he were tying the shoelaces and wiping the nose of every member of the sales force.

Neither is the typical Advertising Manager nor his typical Advertising Agency prepared for this particular job. Communication through the mail to a company's known prospects and customers requires a "friend-to-friend" technique that is entirely different from the "stranger-to-stranger" communication of mass media. And few advertising technicians understand both.

A skilled Assistant-salesman manager who can help you will easily be worth the trouble and cost of finding him, of course, for you'll be multiplying his skills hundreds of thousands of times every time your Assistant Salesmen call. In this area, even more than with regular salesmen, it pays to hire a "star."

27

How to Solicit Funds

Need Is Primary—to Planners

When it comes to giving to "worthy causes," whether that cause is a church, a welfare agency, an alumni association or some other educational, charitable, or religious organization, the "need" is always primary in the thinking of the people who are preparing the campaign. They generally want to discuss the "budget" (which is never large enough) and deal with what might be called "conclusions."

That is, people closely connected with an organization have given a good deal of thought to its financial problem, have done a good deal of reading, and have come to some conclusions which they feel strongly about. Typical conclusion: "We simply *must* have $25,000 additional."

Unfortunately, these conclusions don't mean very much to most givers.

"Heart" Is Primary—to Givers

Major givers (foundations, men who give up to their "income-tax-deductions" limit, and perhaps some trained accountants and engineers) do give on the basis of a demonstrated need and carefully broken-down budget. Most people, however, giving relatively small amounts to many similar organizations, give, literally, from the heart. They give without reason, purely on emotion.

Any one of a number of emotions may trigger their giving. Pity can do it. A sense of duty can do it. So can humor and fond memories. In fact, any emotion which allows the small giver to *identify* himself or his interests with a particular cause is enough to produce gifts.

Once the giver has established a habit of giving to a particular cause, the habit often takes over, and the size of his gifts can be increased simply because the organization is increasing its program or needs more money to keep it at the same level.

All Aid Is Divided into Four Parts

The fund-raising efforts most commonly encountered in America are of four types: welfare, health, churches, schools and colleges. We'll take up examples from the several types, in that order.

Welfare . . . Hope for Others. Welfare letters offer a bit of hope for a better, happier, more productive life. And from the talents of Emily Klinkhart, director of development, American Foundation for the Blind, Inc., comes a most unusual, hope-for-others, fund-raising letter. Based on the oddity which braille is to people who can see, the letter "involves" the reader physically by having him run his finger over braille . . . and it "involves" the reader psychically—to create an emotional impact—through illustrating how difficult it can be for a blind person to tell the date.

The Foundation mailed a pocket-sized braille calendar—developed by a blind New York insurance man—with a letter signed by Bennett Cerf. The mailing went to 210,000 names, using eight lists which had been rented on a one-time basis from intellectual magazines and luxury-product houses. A house list of lapsed names over three years old was also used.

The eight lists rented by the Foundation were *The Reporter Magazine,* Lewis & Conger, Plummers, Mark Cross, Doyle Stationery, Kozak's, Rodale's *Word Finder,* and a compiled list of 48,700 names obtained from a large list compiler.

Returns were 10,751 out of the 210,000 . . . with $35,521.71 brought in at a cost of $23,697.90. To those who contributed, a "thank-you" note was sent, and it said "thanks" both in print and in braille.[1] While this may seem a high cost for contributions, you must remember that mailing to new lists such as these is simply a "search" for people who have an interest in helping the blind. Once found, they will continue to contribute in future years for a very small cost in contacts.

Here, then, is the letter . . . and the "thank-you" note:

[1] "Sight at Their Fingertips," *The Reporter of Direct Mail Advertising,* vol. 23, no. 6, p. 67, October, 1960.

AMERICAN FOUNDATION FOR THE BLIND, INC.
15 West 16th Street, New York 11, N.Y.

Good Neighbor:

Just shut your eyes and run your fingers along the raised dots on the enclosed calendar. This will show you how blind people can look up a date in advance.

But using a braille pocket calendar is not quite as simple as this may sound. Let me explain.

Braille is bulky. Consequently, this little calendar is only a reference tool. It has on it the word "Calendar," the year, and the day of the week on which the first day of each month falls. That's all—no more. If it had every day of every month on it like the usual pocket calendar underneath it, it would be twelve pages long and 4 by 5½ inches in size.

Naturally a blind person cannot tuck a bulky article like that in his pocket, so he must calculate the rest of the dates mentally. For example, he must remember that the eighth, fifteenth, twenty-second, and twenty-ninth of a month always fall on the same day of the week as the first day of that month.

But enough of that. Blind people often are required to make greater use of their memories and sense of touch than you do. In addition, they count heavily on their sense of hearing.

These then are some of the clues on how thousands of blind Americans compensate to make up for lack of sight. And they look to this national research and resource center to find newer and better ways to help them to do this. Please do give today and keep the doorway to progress for blind people at AFB wide open. We will be grateful to you all year long.

Very sincerely yours,

Bennett Cerf, Chairman
Braille Calendar Project

P.S. The Foundation sends these calendars without charge upon request to blind people every year. We hope you will accept your copy with our compliments too.

The "thank-you" note:

Dear Friend:

Many blind people use braille to write. Thus AFB thinks it is fitting to say thank you for your fine gift both in print, which you can read, and in braille, which they can read.

Best wishes.

Very sincerely yours,

M. Robert Barnett
Executive Director

Health . . . Heartbreak and Hope. One of the most effective health letters ever used in an appeal for funds to combat cancer was developed out of the "heart" of a man. Because of the heartbreak of a man.

One day in Washington, D.C. an envelope arrived at the Cancer Fund offices. In it was a piece of paper which contained a woman's engagement and wedding rings. No message. No identification. No written word. Just a soiled dollar bill.

But in the unwritten language of simplicity was the "heart" of a man. The rings, once the bond which formed a marriage, were now offered—as a measure of help to others.

The fund-raising letter developed from this gift used the envelope in which the rings arrived, the sheet of paper, and the rings in a picture on the letterhead. Written with gentle quietness, the copy has an impact which leaves the reader deeply touched. It presents him with a quiet challenge. Judge for yourself: [2]

> I almost wish we had not been sent one contribution that came in last week's mail. It lives with me. It gives my mind and soul no peace.
>
> The mails were heavy that day. The campaign was under way. There were hundreds of letters . . . donations . . . questions . . . offers to help . . . appeals for help. And in that great mass of mail there was one envelope . . . a commonplace stamped envelope. The address was typed.
>
> In the envelope was a plain piece of soiled paper. Carefully wrapped in the paper we found a dollar bill, an engagement ring, a wedding ring.
>
> There was no name. No return address. No message. Just those three well-worn items.
>
> No message?
>
> Yes, there was a message . . . an overwhelming, heartbreaking message. And if the anonymous sender had found it in his heart to put his feeling in words, I can see that message too . . .
>
> "This is all that's left. God spare others from the agony she knew . . . the anguish I know."
>
> Are you fighting Cancer? Have you given?

Here's a letter which shows how contributions to the Cancer Fund have given a degree of success. And how, properly financed, greater success is possible. The letter was written as a local case study to bring things closer to home. It offers a promise by showing that the enemy, cancer, is being, in some cases, whipped. But it brings out clearly the ground that yet has to be covered, the degree of cure which is possible. It shows how the person who benefited from help behaved in return.

This letter, mailed in 1958, to a list of 2,100 donors who had contributed between 1948 and 1955 but not since . . . and to others who had never contributed before—received 74 replies. The average contribution was $6.30. Total contributions, $466. And it cost only $75.92 to put the letter in the mail and bring back replies:

[2] Margaret M. Fellows and Stella A. Koenig, *Tested Methods of Raising Money*, Harper & Brothers, New York, 1959, p. 189.

AMERICAN CANCER SOCIETY, INC.
Champaign County Chapter
310 W. Church St. Champaign, Illinois

April, 1958

You wouldn't know it . . .
only her close friends do . . . that the friendly, gray-haired woman you may have met on one of our Champaign-Urbana streets had cancer nine years ago. Next fall she and her husband will celebrate their golden wedding anniversary.

Those nine years since she had prompt, early treatment for cancer have been pleasant ones. She remembers her brush with man's cruelest enemy—cancer—and has for years directed a small group of women in the making of cancer dressings for the American Cancer Society. Most any evening . . . you can find her preparing dressings . . . as she and her husband sit before the TV set.

She heeded the danger signal of cancer and went straight to her doctor. The American Cancer Society is alerting people to guard themselves. But not enough are being reached, as the following figures show:

Kind of cancer	Present cure, per cent	Possible cure, per cent
Uterine	55	70
Breast	46	81
Rectal	25	77
Mouth	36	65
Skin	90	95
Lung	4	34

Your check mailed today will be your promise that the fight will go on. It is your investment in more research, better service for patients, more effective education—an investment which pays off in LIVES saved.

Sincerely yours,

G. W. Manley
Crusade Chairman

Help for the Hand of God. One of the appeals which can be effective in getting results from church mailings for funds is to illustrate how man can help the Hand of God its mysterious wonders to perform. Men of faith want to share. They'll give of time, of effort, of money to help other men find the intangible out of which they have built faith, and hope, and serenity—into peace.

The pattern for such a letter is based on simplicity itself:

1. Show the need. Illustrate why and where help is needed.

2. Show how the "goodness" of men moves the Hand of God—unto assistance.

3. Ask . . . quietly, because God's work is not raucous . . . for help.

This letter, from the Westminster Presbyterian Church, Dayton, Ohio, is an illustration of how the Hand of God is manifested in the missionaries who do the work in those faraway corners of the world for those who would have their beliefs and their aid extended to others through their church. This letter is brief, to the point, appeals to the reader to help the missionary carry on his work.

Dear Partner-in-Westminster:

When a flood spreads devastation in India, famine fans out in its wake.

As starvation spreads, men despair . . . and then, here and there, the Hand of God seems to reach down with food and clothing and shelter.

"Providence," in the person of our missionary in India, is doing Christ's work among those who need.

Our Westminster partnership, through the combined gifts of all of us, supplies the food and materials that spell a new life to the victims.

But the need, this year, and our opportunities to serve, are greater than ever. And, more than ever, is the need for a substantial pledge from each member.

Won't you let us know we can count on yours . . . soon?

This next letter uses hands—the hands of man helping man—as its theme to appeal to the reader to help the Hand of God. The contrast between empty hands, groping hands, twisted hands, pleading hands, reaching hands, missionary hands, and "hands warm with the love of the Saviour" gives a blend which is rare. The letter follows the same pattern as the Westminster letter. It has great depth because of its "hands" figure of speech which is well and thoroughly worked out.

WORLD VISION, INC.
117 East Colorado Boulevard
Pasadena, California

Dear Friend:

All over the world—literally—empty hands reach out to World Vision.

Some are the hands of the blind, groping uncertainly for a touch of warmth and love.

Some are the hands of the leprous, twisted into pathetic claws, pleading for someone to display the love that Jesus always showed for the leper.

Some are baby hands, reaching out for the strong clasp of half-remembered parent hands—hands now stilled by death.

And some are missionary hands: hands warm with the constraining love of the Saviour; hands that bind up wounds and offer healing medicines; hands that hold forth the Word of Life and point the way to Heaven. But these too are empty hands. They have given all they have, and now they too reach out to us.

So now we too must reach out. We must reach out to *you*. We cannot ignore the pleading hands stretched out to us. Please—won't you help us help them? Our hands are empty too—until you fill them so that we in turn can fill the hands of others.

Gratefully yours,

Budget Needs and Soft Sell developed a unique, low-pressure, successful mail campaign for the Westwood Community Methodist Church of
Los Angeles.[3] The "boom" in Los Angeles' growth left no room for a
"bust" in the support of Westwood's Methodist programs of mental health,
Bible classes, Little League, and other programs. To maintain and operate
the church and its programs, it was necessary to double their budget to
$180,000. And . . . they did.

Using simplicity, a seven-week series of mailings was sent to members
and to people who were not members. Unusual were the series' points:

1. No direct response was requested until the last mailing.
2. The campaign was built around two actions.
    a. A representative would call to answer questions about what the
    copy described as the Unified Budget Plan. The copy prom-
    ised . . .

    "The 'Answer Man' carries no blackboard ledger or quill. He
    will not visit you to record the pledges you may wish to pledge
    . . . and he carries no leather pouch to collect pieces of silver or
    gold. Pointedly . . . he cannot accept any tithes you may wish
    to give. That business is between you and God."

    b. On a day designated as Loyalty Sunday . . . people were asked
    to make pledges. The campaign's last post card said:

    "Sunday, May 5th, is *Loyalty* Sunday. On this day, by our
    presence, we demonstrate to our church, to each other, *and to
    ourselves,* our *determination* to support Westwood Church . . .
    and to sustain our church in its work. And it is on this day that
    each of us will show by our presence and by our pledge . . .
    whether we think our church is worth 'buying.' Is it?"

Simplicity and theme gave the design of this campaign its successful
impact. The theme was "Church for Sale." And the church and its services
were "sold" to the people on the list. The envelopes had a picture of the
church, with a sign, "Church for Sale!" running across the steeple. The
letterhead had "Church for Sale!" emblazoned across the top, with a
picture of the church to the left. Next to the picture of the church was
a sign which read, "Valuable Going Concern." Below the picture and the
sign was a list of the committees working for the fund drive. At the bottom of the letter's first page was this: "Ask the ANSWER MEN about a
Church for Sale!" Here, then, is one of the letters:

Dear Fellow-member:

It may be news to you, but we are going to sell Westwood Community
Methodist Church! At least, we are going to try. We're going to sell the

---

[3] "How a Church Was 'Sold' through a 'Unified Budget Plan,'" *The Reporter of
Direct Mail Advertising,* vol. 20, no. 8, pp. 24–25, December, 1957.

grounds, buildings, traditions, the services—yes . . . even the chimes in the spire.

Certainly it would leave a void in our lives to drive down Wilshire and find only a sprawling, weedy lot where Westwood Methodist's lighted spire now points toward the skies. Each of us would know a loneliness in our individual spiritual lives. And if that gives you a sharp twinge, it's understandable—but don't let it because we're going to sell it TO YOU!

Until now, only a relative handful of our members have shared the *full satisfaction* of maintaining our church and its activities . . . men and women who have expended more on the "luxury of giving" than on fleeting pleasures of the moment. Down the years, they (and you may be one of them) have supported our church to the very best of their ability. Today, it's doubtful whether they really miss the excess worldly goods or entertainment that their pledges might have purchased.

Now, with the new Unified Budget, the rest of us have a unique opportunity to share in this rich satisfaction. No longer can the "luxury of giving" be limited to a handful of members. Today, through our new "blueprint for living and growing" . . . through our improved *Unified Budget,* each of us will be able to participate in full measure. What *we do,* individually and collectively, will determine what the *Church can do! We are* the Church—and the success or failure of our Church to grow depends on us—and what *we do*—and upon how *sold* we are on the goals that we may achieve by working together through our *Unified Budget* plan.

The success or failure of our new "blueprint for growing" rests with just one person. With YOU.

Will you "buy?"

Meantime, please remember—the Westwood Community Methodist Church —its services and its future—are for sale.

Sincerely yours,

Robert P. Carson
General Chairman

P.S. Please keep this letter as there are more to come. When the series is completed, I will ask each of you to read each one through just once more, beginning with the first and continuing through to the last. After that, it will be up to you to show whether we have been successful in selling *you* our Westwood Church—the grounds, the buildings, the traditions, services—and a promise of the future.

Notable in this campaign are the well-molded qualities of Impact, Simplicity, Theme. And upon these qualities the foundation of Westwood Methodist's future was built . . . successfully.

Education . . . the Nation's Future. In an effort to maintain standards, develop scholarships, expand physical plants and services offered . . . and many other things . . . private and public schools use a great deal of fund-raising mail. Education, dedicated to preparing youth to ensure properly the nation's future, uses many means to obtain the funds to do so. The approaches, the appeals are various.

Here we've included quite a few case studies, using this section to illustrate some techniques which might well be considered for all types of fund raising.

Proof of Performance was a successful appeal used by Cranbrook School, Bloomfield Hills, Michigan, to ask for money to continue its scholarship fund. The appeal ". . . was based on the actual records of Cranbrook boys—first, those alumni who had had scholarships at Cranbrook; next, a present scholarship student; last, an outstanding scholarship applicant." [4]

The campaign, which won the *Time-Life* Award for the "Direct Mail Effort of the Year" in 1959, was most successful. The needed funds were raised. And its success was based on the "Product" it sold. As the judges who granted the award said: "This school is selling people, its product. Its whole appeal is completely human. The mailings are so interesting one can't help but read them through; they combine emotion and logic to a remarkable degree. Cranbrook glorifies the product rather than the plant, and the effect is personal." [5]

Note that "Cranbrook glorifies the product rather than the plant." The product being the performance of young men who have been given a chance to produce. Much better it is to define the net results of what contributions create in terms of things human. In terms of qualities people, contributors, admire—determination, effort, achievement. Cranbrook has proved its ability to produce high-calibre men by the performance of the youth it trains. So much wiser it was to define that which is Cranbrook in terms of that which Cranbrook produces—able men.

The first of the five mailings, sent out January 8, 1959, was composed of:

1. A 9- by 12-inch first-class manila envelope. In place of a return address, this copy was found:

> For Your Consideration—Case Histories: C. R. A., '55, R. P. F., '48, W. J. C., '55 [initials of three alumni].

2. A note-sized letter, which carried this copy:

Look at the case histories of these typical scholarship boys who have graduated from Cranbrook.

You share in their achievements—if you have contributed to the Memorial Scholarship Fund.

These are only three of the hundreds of boys who have received scholarship aid—boys who would not have had a chance to attend Cranbrook without your financial assistance.

[4] "Alumni Campaigns Win Awards," *The Reporter of Direct Mail Advertising*, vol. 22, no. 12, p. 35, April, 1960.

[5] *Ibid.*, p. 39.

Our present scholarship students (there are 38 of them!) have the same potential. And like Chet, Dick, and Walt, they also need your support. Please contribute now. Send your check today in the enclosed envelope.

3. A 3¾- by 3⅜-inch card, which had this copy:

Dear Alumnus:

Again this year, as a basis for continued giving, alumni are asked to contribute *at least* $1 for each year since they graduated from Cranbrook.

CONTINUED giving is as important as the amount that you give to strengthen this Fund.

4. A postpaid envelope pledge card which read:

THIRTEENTH ANNUAL CALL

The Cranbrook School Memorial Scholarship Fund

Continued giving is as important as the amount that is given. I hereby contribute to the Thirteenth Annual Call of the Cranbrook School Memorial Scholarship Fund by:

ENCLOSING $_____ herewith;

PLEDGING $_____ by April 15, 1959

So that we may personally
thank you for your gift,
please verify this address:

Gifts are deductible for income-tax purposes. (Please make checks payable to: Cranbrook School.)

5. Three data sheets, called Alumni Records, which pulled all the prestige plugs of performance to prove the young men who had graduated from Cranbrook went on to a further and a higher level of performance. Such names as Harvard, Amherst, such symbols as Phi Beta Kappa and General Motor's National Scholarship were used (in the "Worthy-word" technique, actually) to show the levels of performance of these young men.

The second mailing, sent out January 28, 1959, was composed of:

1. The same type of envelope, with this copy in place of the return address: "For Immediate Action."

2. A note-sized letter which read:

Dick needs your help if he is to stay at Cranbrook.

Read his record. He is representative of all 38 scholarship boys at the school today.

Each has the same high potential. Each is depending on you for the money to continue his scholarship.

Please send your contribution to the Memorial Scholarship Fund today so that there will be funds available for each of these boys. Send your check now in the enclosed envelope.

3. A card, same size, which said this:

Dear Alumnus:
Again this year as a basis for continued giving, alumni are asked to contribute *at least* $1 for each year since they graduated from Cranbrook.
CONTINUED giving is as important as the amount that you give to strengthen this Fund.

4. A sheet called: "Cranbrook School, Student's Cumulative Record." This was the record of a student now enrolled at Cranbrook. The symbols of his performance were spotlighted this way: Average 94.6 per cent, Honor Roll, Awarded Scholarship.
5. The same postpaid envelope with pledge card.
The third mailing, sent out February 18, 1959, presented the case of a deserving applicant for scholarship funds. The mailing was composed of:
1. The same type of 9- by 12-inch manila, first-class mail envelope. In place of the return address was this copy: "Urgent."
2. A note-sized letter:

We may have to say "No" to Robert—unless you say "Yes" to us.
Read about this boy. He is a scholarship candidate for next year. He needs help to come to Cranbrook.
Please help him by giving right now.
Send your check today in the enclosed envelope.

3. An application form, with the student's picture, which gave this information (Answers have not been included):

CRANBROOK SCHOOL
Bloomfield Hills, Michigan

Application for permission to compete for a Cranbrook Scholarship

THE SCHOLARSHIP COMMITTEE
Cranbrook School
Bloomfield Hills, Michigan

I hereby request that your committee consider my son as a candidate for one of your awards. The following information is freely given to aid your committee in considering my son's candidacy.

Name of Candidate _____
Date of Birth _____ Height _____ Weight_____
Name of Parent or Guardian _____
Resident Address _____
Business of Parent or Guardian _____
School now Attending _____

How would you classify the family's economic status? _____

What honors has he won in school or in other organizations?

_____

_____

If the candidate has ever earned any money, explain how he did this, etc.

_____

Give any other information that will help our committee formulate a clear concept of this boy's ability, personality, and general desirability _____

_____

_____

_____

Signature of Parent or Guardian _____

4. The same postpaid reply envelope and pledge card.

Cranbrook's fourth mailing, sent March 18, 1959, was a letter with the same reply device. Here's the letter:

CRANBROOK SCHOOL MEMORIAL SCHOLARSHIP FUND
—Established 1946—
Cranbrook School
Bloomfield Hills, Michigan

Dear Friend of Cranbrook:

Without your help we can't make it.

Right now we cannot help all of the 38 boys who have just been selected for scholarship aid for next year. Boys who show every promise of resembling those whose records we sent you: Andy Anderson, '55, at West Point; Scott Swan, '48, at Cambridge University in England; Dick Felton, '55, at Amherst; John Hamilton, a prefect at Cranbrook this year, and Bob Gieselman, one of the 38 who has applied for aid.

Their outstanding records have encouraged 788 alumni and friends to contribute to this year's 13th ANNUAL CALL to date. These generous contributions have brought us within $5,700 of the amount needed to help these 38 boys, but we can't make it without your help.

If you, and others to whom we are writing this letter, will contribute a minimum of $10 now, we will make our goal.

Please don't delay! These boys are waiting to hear from us.

The final mailing, fifth, was sent out on May 28, 1959. It was a copy of the *Cranbrook Alumni News.* And it reported on the success of the fundraising campaign.

Nice job. And successful. Its product was people and their performance. It proved to alumni that their pride, implicitly, in Cranbrook was worthy. It was a good example of the helping hand being extended and gratitude being returned through performance, competence, capability.

Believability through Proof

In fund-raising letters you can show your reader how the contributions already made (contributions from the reader or from others) have been used successfully. And, with such use of evidence, you can increase the believability of your copy. A most important quality, believability. And necessary if your appeal is to work.

One such letter, which proves the valuable use of alumni contributions to the academic achievements of intelligent and deserving students, is this letter which the University of Illinois Foundation used to ask alumni for funds. It brought in approximately $7 for every $2.50 invested in putting out the letter. Here are the figures: from a mailing list of 80,000 alumni, 821 replies were received. The letter brought in $14,106.78 at a cost of $2,554.05. The percentage of return was small, yes. But dollar returns were excellent. Just shows how little percentages mean.

The letter proves that a "chance" given youth on the campus will develop the "bright young minds" so necessary to the rather cloudy future mankind faces. The letter, most wisely, also points out how five of the six highest-ranking students in the 1959 graduating class had been able to go to school because of scholarships. And that graduating class numbered 3,016.

Such academic performance shows ability and appreciation, and proves the contributors were well rewarded in return for their gifts.

UNIVERSITY OF ILLINOIS FOUNDATION
Illini Union, Urbana

July 1, 1959

Dear Illinois Alumnus:

Five of the six highest-ranking students in this year's graduating class here at the University were able to go through school because of scholarships.

More than 700 of the 25,000 enrolled in the University this last year got some help from scholarship funds. These 700 constituted some of the brightest minds in the student body. Many of them would not have had a chance at a college education if it hadn't been for a little financial help.

Half of all the unmarried men students in the University this year and a third of all the unmarried women students get no help from home. I report this to show you that this is a serious, purposeful bunch of youngsters. They are here to prepare themselves to take important places in business and industry or in the profession, and they have little time to waste.

A tragic note is that, right now, the scholarship fund has been used up. There isn't a penny on hand—and the start of the fall semester is only weeks away. All funds have been allocated, and applications keep piling up.

Telling these needy and high-ranking high school seniors that there are no funds is a tough job.

There is nothing that can be done unless—

Unless your contribution comes to the rescue.

A gift of $500 will make it possible for a well-qualified young man or woman to get a University of Illinois education. Ten dollars or $5 or $50, coupled with other gifts, will do the same.

A check from you, earmarked for scholarships, will be multiplied in value many, many times. It will be one of the best investments you ever made.

Cordially,

James C. Colvin
Executive Director

Forceful Simplicity

Simplicity has great force in all things—from the language of Lincoln's Gettysburg Address, to the modern table silver and furniture the Danes create, to the ways you can plan and design campaigns to raise funds. Maybe some things simple will do a more effective job for you, maybe not. But, in developing a scope from which to project plans, consider the simple, unornate, unostentatious. An answer to a problem may lie there.

One good example of the use of simplicity is the fund-raising campaign of the Alumni Association, Clemson College, Clemson, South Carolina. Clemson decided to get a forceful, simple approach. They decided that their *ideal* program for asking for funds would be:

1. To send a post card which asked for money
2. To get an envelope back with a check in it.

Prior to 1956, the highest number of contributing alumni at Clemson for any one year was 1,385. And previous efforts to solicit funds had not been as good as Clemson desired. These solicitations had been relatively "dressed-up" mailings with postpaid reply envelopes which had been preaddressed.

Since Clemson—as a state-supported school—couldn't use state money to conduct its alumni program, the alumni themselves had to supply the funds for the program. Here's how Clemson went about getting these funds . . . as told by Mr. Joe Sherman, director of public and alumni relations: [6]

We felt that the first step in the development of a long-range alumni annual giving program should be increased active membership (payment of "dues") and [that we should] concentrate on raising money amounts only after alumni interest had increased. The "dues" for active membership in the Clemson Alumni Association have always been $5 a year. And *still*, the record number

[6] Joe Sherman, "Switch to Post-card Simplicity Boosts Alumni Membership . . . and Lowers Cost," *The Reporter of Direct Mail Advertising*, vol. 21, no. 8, p. 24, December, 1958.

for any single year was only 1,385 . . . while the potential of good alumni addresses in our files (the number of alumni being solicited) [was] approximately 14,500.

In July of 1956 the active membership was 800. And it looked as if this figure would reach or exceed the 1,311 for 1955. Using a campaign of simplicity, Mr. Sherman sent out a two-cent (remember those days!) post card. It stated, simply:

> This is a statement you have overlooked
> —For your 1956 Clemson Alumni Association dues $5

Results: By September 11, 1956, active membership was 1,500. One more simple post card was then sent out. It read:

Reminder—The Alumni Association Honor Roll of active members is now being prepared for the printer. If you are to be on the Honor Roll, your 1956 membership must be activated before December 31.

Results: On December 31, 1956, active membership stood at 2,118—a new record. To simplify office procedure and record keeping, the cards mailed to the alumni, and returned, became the keys to finding the class to which each alumnus belonged. (All individual contributions are kept by graduation years.) Clemson also uses the same cards returned by the alumni for address changes, for records in acknowledging the contribution. And Clemson does this by letting the alumni pay the postage—thereby saving a considerable sum.

The alumni get the cards, are asked for a contribution, and are asked to pay the return postage. Mr. Sherman tells this story, as to the alumni attitude toward paying the postage: [7]

Recently, we had to get an active membership vote to amend the association's constitution. We mailed the ballot with no postage-guaranteed envelope. The return was over 50 per cent. And now we are mailing a self-mailer for officer election. The part of the card that comes back to us has a box for a stamp and the message: "Place 3¢ stamp here." I expect at least a 75 per cent return.

Here is an example of the type of card which Clemson uses. The illustration on the left one-third of the card was of a prehistoric male human, stone hatchet in hand, well dressed in prehistoric loin cloth and hairy skin. The copy:

> Before Paying You a Visit

I thought you'd like to know who's calling . . . and why.

It's about your 19___ Clemson alumni membership that will enable us to have a better alumni program and a finer Clemson College.

[7] *Ibid.*, p. 25.

A Loyalty Gift of *at least* $5 ($3 if you graduated in the last five years) will do it . . . and if you can send more, it will be credited to your name in the Alumni Loyalty Fund.

Make check to: CLEMSON ALUMNI LOYALTY FUND

Mail to: Clemson Alumni Association

Don't keep my picture—it's the only recent one I have. Verify the accuracy of your name and address on the other side and return it with your loyalty gift.

To show the effectiveness of Clemson's card campaign in raising the number of alumni who contributed, take a look at this chart:

TIME TABLE OF RESULTS [8]

Number of members	Reached on these dates		
	1956	1957	1958
800	July 6	Feb. 7	Jan. 10
1500	Sept. 11	Mar. 12	Feb. 3
2118	Dec. 31	May 3	Mar. 10
3492		Dec. 31	Aug. 12

Mr. Sherman's departure from the more complex mailings was done with a calculated risk. The results show that risk was worthwhile. In this case study you may find an answer to a fund-raising problem. But, in any case, consider simplicity in the various areas where it can apply. It may pay off for you, too.

Using Nostaljoy

"Ago" is a funny time of life.

Things were better then, or at least it seems so now . . . kind of. Just go to Meredith Wilson's *The Music Man* some time and see. Everything is fun if it's long enough ago . . . and this wonderful, mystical, rose-colored hindsight is usually referred to by a most pedestrian word —nostalgia.

Now Webster equates nostalgia with "severe melancholia . . . enervating homesickness," and he has the right . . . since the *algia* part is from the Greek, meaning pain . . . but this is at once too narrow, too deep, and too painful for today's mine run of hindsight. Most people, we believe, think happily and a bit blissfully of the old swimmin' hole, Cokes at the corner drugstore, the "first" car ever owned, the "ideal" girl or boy one knew at eighteen. Jerome Cowle compares it to "running through the attic, or taking out an old photo album." We referred, earlier, to "fond memories."

[8] *Ibid.*, p. 24.

So the kind of "ago" that affects people pleasantly and does so well for some fund raisers *can't* be nostalgia. Perhaps the language is lacking a word and waiting for us to set it right. Let's try. How about "*nostaljoy.*"

For this is the emotion that, like the sundial, recalls "only the sunny hours" and smiles, now, at the disappointments and temporary tragedies of the past. This same emotion has the power to get a letter read; to open the heart . . . and the purse . . . when it "involves" the reader's roots with the cause of the writer.

Jerome Cowle notes three levels of "nostalgia" (and we won't trifle with the word as he uses it). They're built on something like the degrees of emotion you go through when you read those columns in a newspaper which take you back, then farther back, then farther back yet with the items which were of interest in those years.[9]

1. *Contemporary nostalgia*—the kind that makes people want to read about things that happened just a few years ago. For example a Korean War veteran reading a novel of that period.

2. *Formative nostalgia*—concerning the things that happened in your formative years, whether to you directly, or around you: what people were wearing when you were a child, what they were reading, singing, eating, drinking. A clear-cut example is the sure-fire response that a cocktail-lounge pianist gets when, late in the evening, he starts playing all the old-time tunes.

3. *Historical nostalgia*—covers the reminiscences you've heard from your grandparents, or read in books, or seen in movies. Like the bloomer girls, Carrie Nation, high-button shoes, rushing the growler from the neighborhood saloon, quilting bees, box socials, barn raisings, and so on.

Advertisers (and fund raisers) can use all three kinds of nostalgia with good effect. What may be historical nostalgia to a person of twenty-five might be formative nostalgia to a person of fifty. Contemporary nostalgia is sure-fire for every age group.

The use of nostaljoy as the warp and woof of the tapestry of persuasion shouldn't be restricted to fund raising. As you weave any kind of letter, your designs of belief and conviction can be woven into the fibre too.

A note of caution in the use of memories, however. They can be overdone. People don't act just because of this appeal alone. . . . "Most people want a good logical reason, over and above the appeal of nostalgia and loyalty, for giving. . . ."[10]

This letter from Stanford University uses a light nostaljoy appeal to help get across the need for funds. The copy "involves" the reader by "taking

[9] Jerome M. Cowle, "The Importance of Being Nostalgic," *Printers' Ink*, vol. 262, no. 3, p. 84, Jan. 17, 1958.

[10] Fellows and Koenig, *op. cit.*, p. 244.

him back" to those things which are Stanford—Big Game, Stanford's motto, "The Wind of Freedom Blows," and other reminders. It's a good example of using "mood" (Chapter 23) lightheartedly to combine an almost spoofing touch of the nostaljoy with the implication of what Stanford can no longer offer—if gifts are not given.

The letter kindles the spark of competition which exists between Stanford and the University of California. Helps the "flame" grow by the use of a Cal grad's daughter as the writer of the letter. But, very carefully the letter points out what gifts are needed for. A well-balanced appeal.[11]

THE STANFORD UNIVERSITY FUND

Dear Friend of Stanford:

"My daddy was a Yale man . . ." so an old song starts.

Well, *my* daddy was a *Cal* man, but he sent his two daughters to Stanford to lower the grade average (his most effective sabotage, since he had no sons to offer to the Cal football team).

During football season he is our enemy, but for most of the year, we think he is pleased down to the tips of his toes (encased in Blue-and-Gold Big-Game argyles) with the opportunities his daughters have had: a stimulating education, often in small classes with fine professors; the fun of campus living; and a basic outlook summed up by Stanford's motto, "The Wind of Freedom Blows."

And our sturdy Golden Bear of a father knows, too, that he got a bargain—two educations for the price of one. He knows that every dollar *he* spent on us, the University matched with a dollar from alumni and friends.

As you know, perhaps better than I, Stanford's endowment in 1891 was the largest of its time. Today, however, income from this endowment meets only 14.5 per cent of Stanford's operating costs. 50 per cent of these costs are covered by tuition, so a large portion of the rest MUST come from gifts.

You are one of many thousands of alumni who, in the past, have expressed their belief in Stanford with their generous gifts to the Stanford University Fund. This, then, is just a reminder that the need is greater than ever. So, *once again,* won't you please dig down into your loyal Indian pockets?

A More than Doubled Loyalty Fund for Miami University, Oxford, Ohio, in six years was achieved with letters like the ones which follow. In addition, they have provided $279,000 for an Alumni Chapel . . . brought Miami to second place among state universities in the percentage of participation of alumni in an alumni fund.

The philosophy behind them is this: Alumni give emotionally . . . not for personal, economic gain. So they should get appeals that produce an emotional mood which will help them react. The people who create Miami's fund-raising campaigns believe in the emotion of nostaljoy,

[11] *Ibid.,* p. 202.

for without this warm feeling, how can faraway alumni be expected to give?

This first letter bases its appeal on the nostaljoy which burning leaves create in the fall. Moving on from the nostaljic opening, the letter discusses some of the things achieved through the Loyalty Fund . . . which is asking for more support.

I smelled something Saturday.

Burning leaves.

Next to fresh bread baking, nothing brings me any better memories than the smell of burning leaves.

I was in Oxford where leaf smoke fills the air every fall, watching Miami beat Ohio U. and, in addition to my sniffer, all my other senses got a workout. I *saw* four new buildings going up, including the new administration building and the Student Center. I *heard* the yell in the stadium and bells over the campus after the game. I *tasted* one of Tuffy's toasted rolls—had a hot chocolate at the Purity . . .

And I *felt* good.

Not only because I was in Oxford, and Miami was winning—which is always fun—but because I saw some of the things our Alumni Fund is doing. John Dolibois, our Alumni Director, grabbed me before the game and introduced three of the bright kids who are in school on Fund scholarships. They were smart, sincere, and grateful . . . and none of the three would have been in school without those scholarships. He showed me the results of a couple of faculty research jobs made possible by Alumni money. We went through the library and peeked in the "browsing" and "listening" rooms that Alumni money helped put there . . . he showed me a dozen other things the Fund does.

Believe me, when you see those tangible, practical results with your own eyes, you know that the Alumni Fund is a good thing . . . and I was darn glad I've been a regular giver to it.

Before I left, I told John I'd like to write a note to Alumni who haven't yet shared in this year's Fund . . . and have him send it to you. He said "Sure," and this is it.

That is all I want to say: *If you liked Oxford and Miami while you were in school, don't leave it.* Keep roots there through your Alumni Fund. Your money will do a whale of a lot of good even if you never see the results of it. And if you do visit Oxford and see some of the things the Fund does, you'll keep giving as long as you live.

But take a tip: do it now, while your mind's on it. Use the envelope . . . act on your most generous impulse. Grab a pen or pencil and give now.

You'll be glad you did.

Lloyd O'Hara, '39
President, Alumni Fund Council

The next letter uses a humorous appeal to wrap a request for funds into a pleasant package. Light, cheerful, the letter isn't as specific as the previous letter in stating how funds have been or will be used, except for aid to "worthy students." But it brought in excellent results.

Dear Miamian:

I remember a special train, some years ago, coming from Cincinnati to Oxford on a Thanksgiving evening. Everyone was feeling wonderful (guess why), including a cute, young, smiling redhead who was collecting money for "a worthy cause."

She gathered quite a bit of loose change on her way through the train . . . and wasn't a bit abashed when someone asked her to name the worthy cause.

"Me," she said, and went on counting the cash.

Now I don't know whether you contributed to the "worthy cause" of some Miami gal while in college, or not. In any event, you're probably ladling it out, fairly generously, to many, many, *really* worthy causes today. Most of us are.

That's good. And I hope that, this year, part of your "contribution" money will go to support higher education. If so, there's no better place, I'm sure, than the Miami Loyalty Fund.

Loyalty Fund gifts are just as "tax-deductible" as any . . . and while you can designate the use of any money you send, most of the undesignated money goes to help really worthy students who would not otherwise be able to get a college education.

If we were on a train, from Cincy to Oxford, and I (disguised as a cute, young, smiling redhead) shook the enclosed envelope under your nose with a little sweet talk about a *really* worthy cause, what would you do?

　　　　　　　　　　　　　　　　　　　　Well! Do it now.

This letter brings nostaljoy, under the alias of "fond memories," right out into the open in an effective appeal for funds.

Dear Miamian:

This letter is about Miami.

I like to write letters about Miami, but they go slow.

Whenever I write about Miami, I think about Miami. . . . And when I think about Miami . . . I stop writing!

That's because I have what lyric writers call "fond memories." Fond memories cause pause between paragraphs.

Probably *you* have fond memories of Miami, too . . . and I doubt if I'd write anything in the next paragraph that equals the fun of one memory. So let's spend the next eight lines thinking about the *best* Miami experiences we've ever had. I'll think about mine; you think about yours.

❖　❖　❖　❖　❖　❖　❖　❖　❖　❖　❖　❖

❖　　　　　　　　　　　　　　　　　　　❖

❖　❖　❖　❖　❖　❖　❖　❖　❖　❖　❖　❖

Now we're both in the mood for the *purpose* of this letter: to tell you that if you have "fond memories" of Miami, the Miami Alumni Loyalty Fund is your dish. For just three-bucks-or-up, depending on your own feelings in the matter:

  . . . You can join with the rest of us to do important things for Miami—in the way of scholarships, faculty research, campus improvements, and all the things alumni like you and me ought to do,

  . . . and, at the same time, keep in constant touch with the campus and all your "f.m.'s," through the Alumni Magazine and other contacts and privileges.

The story of the Fund, in a nutshell, is in the enclosed folder. The envelope is for your name and contribution. The time is now. Dig as deep as you can. You'll never regret it.

Sincerely,

To Put a Fund-raising Letter Together

When you write fund-raising letters, use the same techniques you would use in a sales letter. Writing with complete familiarity with your problem and a thorough understanding of your purpose:

1. Use the sales-letter formulas (Chapter 28).

2. "Involve" your reader (Chapters 3, 10, 24).

3. Remembering (Chapter 3) that "readership is largely a matter of product interest," . . . select a perspective on your fund-raising problem which has "product interest" to a reader.

4. Try the various copy styles (Chapter 14), particularly in a series of letters.

5. Think in terms of a variety of formats (Chapter 16).

6. Use enclosures . . . if the situation is such that an enclosure is warranted: if there is the necessity of illustration, further development, and the desire for a shorter letter.

7. Use case histories as you would testimonials in a sales letter. Use case histories of success, of hope, and use occasionally the case where success *could have been,* had help been given in time. Limit your cases, not only to the reader's home town, not only to the reader's own block, but to his neighbor, and to the chances as they affect him. Quietly, of course.

8. Use the Creative Impact of Mood (Chapter 23).

9. Use the "Pleasant Picture" and the "Oh, No, Not" persuasion techniques (Chapter 10).

10. Use prestige names. Your committees can have an important influence, when used locally or nationally. Care, however: don't use so many committee names the letter looks like a small plot of grass surrounded by an enormous hedge.

11. Supply a return envelope. And on this reply envelope boil down

your most powerful appeal to throw one more request toward the reader's generosity. However, in letters which are highly personalized, letters which go to the people who have made large contributions previously, letters which go to friends, don't use a reply envelope. They don't expect it.

12. ·Consider the impact of your letterhead (Chapter 23). And, occasionally, vary the size of your letters—for a change of pace, a "difference" (Chapter 13).

13. Use a P.S. for "one more try" . . . to get your appeal across. The National Jewish Hospital, Denver, used this P.S.—in simulated handwriting—to bring the realities of its appeal closer to home.

During the minute it took you to read this letter, a total of eight people died somewhere of tuberculosis and forty-three were infected.

28

How to Sell by Mail

Selling by Mail

When a sale is completed through the mail without the use of salesmen or dealers, that is direct mail selling—or selling by mail.

The term "mail-order selling" is deliberately avoided in this chapter because it includes all means of selling where the order comes through the mail: newspapers and magazines, radio and TV, car cards, etc. The emphasis in this chapter is on advertising which goes through the mail to the prospect and brings the order back through the mail.

Why Is Buying by Mail Popular?

People buy by mail for a variety of reasons, which can probably be boiled down to three basic ones:

1. *Exclusiveness.* People like to buy by mail because the product they receive can be different from what their neighbors or friends have obtained locally. Some products, like the Christmas Letters for customers sold by The National Research Bureau, Inc., Chicago, are offered on the basis that no one else can buy them. Other products, although of the same type as products available locally, offer different designs, patterns, colors, types of fabrics, etc., when sold by mail.

2. *Convenience.* To some people, the availability of a product sold by mail is the important reason for buying. These busy people, who lack

time to shop, can conveniently obtain goods by mail. Sometimes transportation is poor, or too expensive on top of the price of goods or services. And some people are unable to shop easily because of physical disabilities. Another convenience, or availability, reason for buying is that buyers sometimes don't know where else such items can be obtained.

3. *Price.* To the buyer, the price for the items or services offered to him can be obtained, usually, at a saving over local buying. Or, if not at a saving, with some special inducement which he can't get locally except at a price in addition to the product he buys. Book Club–dividend books, a free book upon joining the club (or at discount), are examples.[1]

Eight Fundamental Laws

According to Earle A. Buckley, there are eight fundamental laws which make for successful selling by mail. These are Mr. Buckley's laws: [2]

1. Have a product in demand by the type of people on your mailing list. The product should have a low delivery cost and enough markup to allow for profit.

2. Develop the most attractive proposition you can: in the product you choose, in the price at which you sell, in the means of payment which you offer—approval, cash, c.o.d., etc.

3. Give a pleasing impact to your mailing in every way possible; so that the people on your list will *want* to read it (see Chapter 3 on How to Increase Readership).

4. Tell your story with sincerity, with believability, and so "involve" your reader that you convince him that he wants the benefits you offer him.

5. Prove any claims about a product's performance or desirability and give an unqualified guarantee that claims are true. (See Chapter 10 on Belief.)

6. Make your list comprise as close to 100 per cent prospects as possible.

7. Test all mailings before sending to a large list. Then, when sent to the list, time their arrival as favorably as possible.

8. Build your reputation for offering good value, for dealing with integrity, so that people will have confidence in your firm and your offers.

Cullinan's Eight Points

George Cullinan of the Cullinan Organization, Chicago, lists eight points which he considers imperative in planning and carrying out a pro-

---

[1] Robert Stone, *Successful Direct Mail Advertising and Selling,* Prentice-Hall, Inc., Englewood Cliffs, N.J., 1955, p. 17.

[2] Earle A. Buckley, *How to Sell by Mail,* McGraw-Hill Book Company, Inc., New York, 1938, p. 8.

gram for selling by mail. Mr. Cullinan has a formula which he calls, "The formula for growth in Direct Mail profits." And that formula is: [3]

The right product . . . at the right price . . . to the right list . . . at the right selling cost . . . with the right methods of buying . . . at the right time . . . in the right markets . . . with the right creative-selling techniques.

The word "right" in this instance means "profitable" or "most profitable."

The Order of Importance of these Cullinan points is (1) Product, (2) Price, (3) List (4) Selling Cost, (5) Method of Buying, (6) Timing, (7) Markets, (8) Creative Techniques. The immediate inference from this order is that, in selling by mail, one must adequately analyze and competently plan the product and the sale before getting into the creative aspects, which are actually a culmination of all the previous thought and effort given to a problem. It's the same principle you found in the copy chapters: You cannot express a selling idea until you are thoroughly familiar with the whole background which develops that idea.

The Right Product

Your product is the service or the merchandise that you offer. And it must be acceptable to the specific "public" to which you offer it, in reasonable volume, or you have nothing to start with. The right or most profitable product can be determined by test. In selling by mail, this testing is rather simple (although it may be fairly costly, too). Because, in selling by mail, your order cards, blanks, envelopes, etc., are keyed. Results, then, can be measured easily. The main point is not to guess. But to test.

The Types of Products or Services adaptable to selling by mail fall into three categories. They are:

1. *Merchandise* . . . including manufactured products purchased for resale (specialty items, office supplies, novelties), articles manufactured at home or in a small shop (curios, necklaces, hand-woven rugs), and agricultural commodities (livestock, fruits, nuts, eggs, chicks). There is no predetermined limit. Very successful mail-selling operations sell such "normal" things as shirts and neckties.

2. *Information* . . . in the form of instructions and educational literature on a wide range of subjects. Particularly effective are the "How-to" offers which give information on making money . . . preserving health . . . developing ability to speak in public, etc.

3. *Services* . . . in the form of personal, professional, business services which help solve problems of prospects nearby . . . or in other parts of the country. This type of service can extend from the copy writer who offers his talents . . . to the printer who offers his facilities for the ex-

[3] George Cullinan, "The Formula for Growth in Direct Mail Profits," Speech, Philadelphia Direct Mail Day, Apr. 20, 1960.

pression of these talents. It includes the consultant . . . whose abilities and perspectives can prove profitable to those who use them.[4]

The Characteristics of Products and Services . . . that are adaptable to selling by mail are based on those things which tend to attract the prospect. Some of these are: [5]

1. The product or service should fill a need. Particularly, if you are going to follow up with other products and services to the same prospects, should you offer things which fill a long-time need. Novelty products are often "fads" . . . and the need or desire for them can disappear.

2. The product or service should have "mass" appeal . . . so that you can hit at larger markets for greater profits.

3. The product or service should have "class" appeal . . . so that you can develop a readily definable type of prospect . . . who can be reached by mailing lists.

4. Products and services should have the quality of Repeat Sales. Since the sales which follow the original sale are usually obtained at less selling cost . . . the repeat business should give you a higher profit margin. Some advertisers actually buy the first order at a loss . . . to make the profit on repeat business.

5. Products should be analyzed on the basis of their perishability. The delivery plans for fruits, chicks, etc., those items which can perish in transit toward delivery, must be thoroughly analyzed on the basis of how to ship at low cost and how to ship so they arrive intact. Many people have solved such problems most effectively and profitably. But this area of the process of exchanging your products for prospects' dollars must be thoroughly thought out—*before* you make any offers to sell by mail.

6. Products must be mailable. Brittle, fragile products must be analyzed on the basis of shipping costs, which can affect selling costs. If the cost of getting a product to a prospect is too high because of high postage or shipping costs, it will be that much harder to sell it by mail.

7. Products should be easily assembled by the receivers. The buyer's satisfaction may vary according to the complexities involved in putting the product together—when received.

8. Products should be readily, promptly available to the seller from his supplier—to facilitate the prompt filling of the seller's orders.

9. Products which are seasonal give special problems. These products don't give you year-round repeat business, but they can be profitable. Particularly as part of a line of merchandise.

---

[4] Nelson A. Miller and Joseph H. Rhoads, *Establishing and Operating a Mail-order Business,* Industrial (Small Business) Series no. 46, Marketing Division, U.S. Department of Commerce (n.d.).

[5] Irvin Graham, *How to Sell through Mail Order,* McGraw-Hill Book Company, Inc., New York, 1949, pp. 32–36.

Pricing a Product

Pricing a product involves the consideration of your selling price, your costs (including your product costs and mailing costs), and your desired level of profitability. These three considerations are somewhat interdependent, and your failure to give proper recognition to each may result in an unsuccessful venture.

Your Selling Price frequently cannot be established by you alone. Thus, when a competitive situation exists, recognition must be given to prices at which competing products are sold. You cannot expect to set your own price, for example, where comparisons of quality between your product and that of a competitor are obvious. On the other hand, if your product is unique or if quality comparisons are difficult or impossible to make, you may be able to establish your price, basing it upon the value placed on the item by the purchaser. Regardless of the selling situation which you anticipate, you must give careful consideration to the probable price your product will be able to command in the market.

Your Cost Price includes two important elements: cost of the product and mailing costs. The cost of your product must include all the costs you incur from the purchase or the manufacturing stage to the delivery of the product to the buyer. This cost would include, for example, the basic manufacturing or purchase cost of the item; costs of shipment to your plant; postage or shipment from your plant to the customer; wrapping materials, boxes, cartons; allowance for losses by damage, refusals, c.o.d., replacements, gifts, etc.: labor costs of assembling, packing, and shipping; storage costs; and overhead costs, such as rent, salaries, utilities, traveling expenses, supplies, insurance, taxes, accounting and legal services, research, and many others in special circumstances. In determining the cost of your product, you must consider all elements of cost, since the omission of any item of cost from consideration could lead to an unwise decision on pricing or production volume.

The other element of cost which a mail seller must consider is the cost of selling. This cost element may vary greatly and thereby cause some problems in pricing a product. On a total-cost basis, your cost of selling would include all costs of your mailings. On a cost-per-order basis this total cost of mailing is divided by the number of orders received. Since the number of orders to be received from any mailing effort may vary greatly, your cost per order is extremely difficult to anticipate.

Your Profit will be determined by the difference between your selling price and your total costs. You may use several guides to measure your profit, such as your markup, gross profit, and net profit. Markup is the difference between the cost of your product and your selling price. The cost of your product in this connection would include all costs of purchase or manufacture and all other costs necessary to get the product delivered to the customer, but would not include the expenses of selling or mailing.

Markup is generally expressed as a percentage of your selling price. For example, if you can produce and deliver a product for $2, and your selling price is $6, your markup is $4, or 66⅔ per cent. According to some mail sellers, merchandise or services of a staple nature should bear a markup of from 25 to 40 per cent depending on the average unit value of the item or items. Prices on merchandise which is of a promotional, novelty, or fashion nature generally must bear a markup of 50 to 65 per cent if you expect to earn a profit.

Gross profit is the difference between your selling price and your cost of manufacture. Gross profit differs from markup in that gross profit is generally expressed in dollars and is generally related to your total sales rather than the sale of a specific item. Markup is the "gross profit" on a given item, and, as noted above, is generally expressed as a percentage of your selling price on the item involved.

Net profit may be described in several ways. It is gross profit less all selling costs, including advertising and mailing costs. It is your selling price minus your costs and expenses—all costs and expenses. While both markup and gross profit are important considerations in setting a selling price, only if you have a net profit will you consider your venture a success.

The question still remains: How should you price your product? Assuming for the moment that your competitive position enables you to be able to set your selling price, you should initially give consideration to your break-even point.

The Break-even Point in a mail-selling effort, according to Bernard Gould, consultant in mail selling, comes when ". . . the number of orders multiplied by the selling price . . . equals the number of orders times the sum of the delivered goods plus the cost of the completed mailing." [6]

In the terms we have developed above, the break-even point is that point at which your total sales equal your total costs, that point at which your selling price times the number of orders you receive is equal to the cost of your product delivered times the number of orders you receive plus your selling and/or mailing costs.

The following example will illustrate how to use the break-even–point analysis in a given situation: [7]

[6] Bernard Gould, "Mail-order Mathematics: Determining the Break-even Point Is Fundamental in Successful Mail-order Operation," *Printers' Ink*, vol. 222, no. 8, p. 47, Feb. 20, 1948.

[7] *Ibid.*

$$N = \text{Number of orders needed to break even}$$
$$SP = \text{Selling price}$$
$$C = \text{Cost of goods delivered}$$
$$MP = \text{Cost of mailing piece—in the mail}$$
$$100\ MP = \text{Cost of 100 mailing pieces in the mail}$$

Assume, first, that you expect to mail 10,000 pieces at $0.08 each, that you expect to have a unit selling price of $7, and that the cost of your item delivered is $4 ($2 cost to produce and deliver, $0.35 operating costs, and $1.65 selling cost or cost per order).

The break-even–point formula would be applied as follows:

$$N \times SP = N \times C + 10{,}000MP$$
$$N \times \$7 = N \times \$4 + 10{,}000\ (\$0.08)$$
$$7N = 4N + 800$$
$$3N = 800$$
$$N = 267$$

N would be interpreted as follows: You would have to receive 267 orders from your 10,000 mailings in order to break even, in order to have your total revenue from your sales just equal your total costs. On a percentage basis, you would have to have a return of 2.67 per cent in order to break even. Thus, with a product which costs $4 each and which you can sell for $7 each, you must be able to anticipate a 2.67 per cent return from your mailings (when the cost per mailing piece is $0.08) if you expect to break even.

You can also use the break-even–point analysis to help you set your selling price. Assume that you have a product which has a delivered cost of $4 per unit, as above, and that the cost of your mailing will be $800 (10,000 units at $0.08 each). Also, assume that you have analyzed the market situation and expect to have a 4 per cent return from your mailing, or a return of 400 orders. Using the above formula, you would find that the selling price per item would have to be $6 for you to break even.

$$N \times SP = N \times C + 10{,}000MP$$
$$400 \times SP = 400 \times 4 + 10{,}000\ (\$0.08)$$
$$400SP = 1{,}600 + 800$$
$$SP = 6$$

If you then decided that a price of $6 per unit was not out of range from a competitive point of view, you might decide to proceed with the venture. If a price of $6 was too high, you might halt your plans, while if the $6 price was below the competition, you might sell for more than $6 and anticipate a net profit.

Pricing Your Product is not a simple task, not one that can be reduced to a simple formula. You must give consideration to all the variables, including your competitive market position, your costs of the product, your mailing costs, your expected return from the mailings, and your expected, or hoped-for, net profit. You must also recognize that in some instances it is wise to take a loss on the first order because of anticipated profits from return business. Or, you may be willing to take a loss on the first order because the repeat order may involve an item having greater profitability to you.

Probably the most important warning for you to retain is that *all* costs must be considered when you are pricing your product. The omission from consideration of any significant cost element may doom your venture to failure.

And that's how you price a product for selling by mail.

Another Point of View

Remember though—that's not the only way. Like everything else in mail selling, it depends on circumstances. For example, Jerry Hardy, Director of *Life's* Book Department, came up with an interesting story at the Direct Mail Advertising Association Western Convention, San Francisco, May 4, 1960. Mr. Hardy took to task the idea that saving money was the only appeal people would respond to. And he gave convincing examples of how . . .

People will respond to an offer of substantial convenience at a reasonable cost.

First examples pointed out were Book of the Month and its cousins, Fruit of the Month, Doll of the Month, Volume-at-a-time Encyclopedias, Art Education by the Month, Piano lessons by the month, and others. All of which *offer substantial convenience* at a reasonable cost.

Mr. Hardy feels that mail sellers give up too easily in their research to offer substantial convenience. And he feels they're shackled by what they know. Because too many mail sellers believe, *falsely*, that . . .

   . . . certain things cannot be sold by mail. Because they never have been.
   . . . the market for a product is limited to a certain economic group. Because that is where the product has been selling.
   . . . we need a three- or four-times markup. Because we've always had one in previous mailings.

But some competent person didn't believe these things. So he came up with a whale of a different type of offer—which was successful. And which had a markup of only 50 per cent. If he'd believed in the "shackling" type of experience, he'd never have tried it. But, he didn't. So he succeeded.

The offer was a complete home-movie outfit, Bell & Howell, for $149.95. The offer included an electric-eye meter, an 8-millimeter camera, an instruction book, a supermoderator projector with a 400 take-up, a film catalogue, a movie-magazine subscription, a magazine of about the same type of subscription list as *Sunset,* a 30- by 40-inch floor-model projector screen.

The price is about the same you would pay in a camera shop. No great saving in money.

But an interesting device went with this offer. The offer included one roll of color film and one roll of black-and-white film. To top it off, the mailer offered to supply the buyer with all the black-and-white film, one roll at a time, that he could use for two years—FREE. The buyer could send in his black-and-white film for development. Pay the same development cost as he would locally. He would receive in return his developed film plus a free roll.

To quote Mr. Hardy:

Here is an offer I knew was wrong the moment it was presented to us. How are you supposed to go about selling a movie outfit by mail when everyone knows the customer will insist on a demonstration in his local camera store? And when every neighborhood in the land has a camera store? How are you going to sell a $150 package to a group of women who belong to a book club that supplies them with best-selling fiction at $1 per 400 pages?

The only thing we knew about the dollar club to which . . . [the advertiser was] . . . trying to persuade us to make this offer was that people like entertainment and had a dollar a month. It didn't sound like an ideal project for a $150 movie outfit. How are you going to make money where they only give you a 50 per cent markup? The whole thing seemed ridiculous.

It was. Except it worked.

The movie outfit was sold to numerous lists: encyclopedia lists, for example; and book-club lists, which pulled from 1 to 2 per cent. It was successful, in Mr. Hardy's opinion, for these reasons:

1. Many Americans have money and kids. That's what you need for home movies. You don't need talent.

2. The black-and-white film added a compelling element of service . . . which provided a reason why people should want the outfit, right now.

3. The lists, book clubs, and encyclopedias, represent a relationship between a producer and a consumer which has been extended beyond the thing which the producer produces himself. People who have this relationship with a group of consumers have begun more and more to market other people's products either under their own or someone else's name.

To quote Mr. Hardy further:

I believe we will see more and more examples of high-priced, good-quality . . . merchandise sold to book-club lists, even encyclopedias, perhaps even magazine lists, with sales being made at markups much more nearly akin to traditional retail markups but with offers of service added.

Some examples of high-priced items which are now being offered successfully to club lists were mentioned by Mr. Hardy: Cannon towels at $39.38; an art-instruction course, which offers nothing free and which requests you to sign a commitment to spend $48 (this offer, incidentally, works most successfully. Of those who sign up, 94 per cent continue); a biography of Teddy Roosevelt at $15; a Jewish encyclopedia at $22.50.

Mr. Hardy continues:

The evidence, then, is that the tendency toward much higher prices for much, much higher quality is beginning to pay off. Even five years ago most such offers would have been unthinkable. Now they are beginning to be commonplace.

Thus does Jerry Hardy sum up a point of view you should analyze when considering selling by mail:

Substantial convenience at a reasonable cost . . . may open a market for you with higher-priced items at markups more near to the traditional retail markup.

The Mail-selling Offer

Your "offer" is the way you present the product, its benefit, and its price, in terms of the reader's desires, needs, wants, etc. And it should be stated so fully to the advantage of the prospect that only inertia or the lack of money will keep him from buying. A successful offer will break through the inertia with the desire it creates for a product or service by skillful description of the benefits offered—by free trial, by samples, by exclusiveness, etc. And the prospect's lack-of-money problems can be overcome by the method of purchase offered the prospect.

We shall define several kinds of offers to show you various ways to approach the problem. Offers, actually, can be combined in many ways. The only restrictions would be your own ingenuity in devising an offer and the feasibility of the idea itself.

Free-trial Offer. This type lets the prospect take a look at the product, lets him try it, free, before he decides he wants to buy it. There is usually a time limit within which the prospect must make up his mind. The chief advantages of the free-trial offer are: the prospect gets a chance to see the product before he buys, and the mailer keeps the good will of the prospect. And, of course, a good product has a chance to sell itself.

This example of a free-trial offer was made by Goldblatt's Department Store, Champaign, Illinois. It's the opener of a letter:

FREE! Trial Offer! SAVE $100

An EASTMAN KODAK MOVIE OUTFIT, plus Money-saving Coupon Envelopes for New Color Film and Processing. Try it for FUN for 15 days FREE without cost or obligation to you.

(The $100 saved is to be on new film and processing.)

Later in the letter the offer develops into a free-trial, time-pay offer in these paragraphs:

All this is yours to use for 15 days—right now—without any cost or obligation to you. If, after 15 days, you decide you enjoy taking and showing movies as much as we think you will, and you want to keep the outfit, then it's yours for our low, low price of $169.95, plus a small carrying charge.

As a preferred customer, we will add the movie outfit to your account with *no money down* and you'll have two full years to pay at terms of only $8.80 per month. Yes, Goldblatt's generous long-term time-payment plan lets you own this complete Eastman Kodak Movie Outfit with *no down payment.* Imagine owning and enjoying this complete outfit for only a few pennies a day!

Gift (or Premium) Offer. This type of offer tells the prospect he will receive "something to boot," something in addition to the main product offered if he buys. This gift can be parlayed into sales. Because people like the idea of getting something for nothing. For example, the book and the record clubs attribute part of their success to their "gifts" (either outright or at a fantastically reduced price) when one joins the clubs. The "dividends" of books or records have the same appeal, even though they may not be obtained until a specified amount of merchandise has been purchased.

The type of gift should be related to the product in such a way that it increases its value, or it should have a relation to the reader's business or professional interests, or habits.

This paragraph, from a *Changing Times* letter, offers a gift if the reader will subscribe. It also points out how the gift is of "professional" value to the reader.

By agreeing to try the Kiplinger Letter now, you can get a 3-month trial subscription, a $6 value, for just $4. And at no extra cost, you will also get the KIPLINGER EXECUTIVE-ACTION-KIT for 19___. This 5-part portfolio will help you increase your earnings and savings in the months ahead.

Here's another type of free-gift offer. The mailing includes free cartoon art, which the reader can use in any way he sees fit. The opener of the letter, from American Marketing Services, Inc., Boston:

The seven FREE cartoons enclosed
are yours to reproduce and use
with the compliments of the new
YANKEE CLIPPER

This get-acquainted sample sheet is our way of demonstrating the originality and quality of the 162 cartoons contained in VOLUME II of THE YANKEE CLIPPER.

Cartoon art has many appropriate uses. Direct mail pieces . . . newspaper ads . . . meeting notices . . . cartoon letters . . . contest announcements . . . bulletins . . . magazine illustrations . . . sales presentations . . . printed literature.

Then, in a later paragraph, a free-trial offer is made:

So, if you want stimulating ideas for printed promotion . . . if you want professional cartoon art at your fingertips for less than 10 cents per cartoon . . . mail your check for $15 right away. If you are not completely satisfied with your purchase, mail THE YANKEE CLIPPER back to us. We will refund your money the same day the book is received in our office. Fair enough?

Limited Offer. This type of offer has a stated date beyond which the offer is no good. The idea is that an impulse toward action can be stimulated if the reader knows he has to make up his mind right away. People like to "get in on things." And the time limit on an offer can appeal to this.

If you use a limited offer, be sure your expiration date has sufficient leeway to permit the mailings to reach your readers and give them time for consideration.

As an example, here is part of a *Look* letter. It is a combination of a money-back guarantee and a time limit (not specific) based on the possibilities of events forcing a withdrawal of the offer.

And it's so easy to start LOOK coming. Just check the "BILL-ME" box on the certificate made out in your name, along with the special GOLD SLIP enclosed— and mail them in the postage-free AIR-MAIL envelope . . .
        . . . and we'll send you THE NEXT 40 ISSUES of LOOK (a $6 single-copy value) and bill you for just $3. The certificate itself pays the rest!
OR—if you prefer, you may enclose your $3 along with your certificate. Either way, you receive LOOK for 18 months for just 7½ cents per copy.
You take no risk whatever. You may cancel your subscription and receive full refund on all remaining issues due you at any time. But we offer this MONEY-BACK GUARANTEE in full confidence that it's something you'll never want to use . . . that just a few issues will, instead, make you a long-time friend of LOOK.
But one more thing. The possibility of higher postage rates is still with us, and we may be forced to withdraw this low price at any time—so, please, mail your order now . . . *while this special rate is still in effect.*

"Proof-of-the-pudding" Offer. This type of offer, which might be called "free-sample," can be used successfully when you can send a sample which illustrates the qualities of your product. The New Process Company (in Warren, Pennsylvania), for example, is famous for its swatches, which display the quality of the various types of clothing they sell. New Process is a skilled and successful user of the mails. Their samples of shirt materials, slacks materials, etc., have been part of their successful efforts. Because when you offer a sample, you have the overtones of the free-trial offer. You lay your claims on the line, with proof. Such a method of merchandising builds up the reader's confidence in you when he knows you have enough confidence in your product and *in his judgment* to offer proof which he can analyze himself.

This example of a "Proof-of-the-pudding" offer sends along a sample of the booklet which is being sold. The booklet, illustrated on the letterhead, is "2001 Household Hints and Dollar Stretchers." The letter, to bank executives, suggests the bank use the booklet as a gift to depositors and to prospective depositors. After reading the booklet, the reader can judge its value for himself. Here's the offer:

(Picture of the booklet here)　　TO: *The Bank Executive*
in Charge of NEW BUSINESS:
With this little give-away booklet, you can boost savings deposits up to 20 per cent within weeks! And at a new low in costs!
This is no guess! It's been done.

The reason you can know in advance that "2001 Household Hints and Dollar Stretchers" will pull in *new* accounts and stimulate increased deposits from *old* accounts is just this:

Michael Gore, well-known writer of consumer-service material and author of this booklet, published a similar booklet back in the late forties. It was not as complete as "2001 Household Hints"—not as appealing—and was printed on cheap newsprint. But this old booklet was an instant success. Three million copies were printed for leading companies over the country. It was used by large banks and small banks—and was consistently popular.

"2001" is brand-new . . . finer . . . more authoritative . . . but AT THE SAME OLD PRICES!

(Institute for Business Research, A Division of Keller-Crescent Co., 20–28 S.E. Riverside Dr., Evansville 8, Indiana)

Money-back Guarantee. This type of offer, where a buyer can purchase a product, look it over, make up his mind to keep or return it, has been successful in mail-order selling. It is also a requirement of such newspapers as the Chicago *Tribune* and other newspapers before they will accept an ad in their mail-order sections. And it's effective when you can't use a free-trial offer.

Your reader knows you have faith enough in your product to let him try it and to return his money if he doesn't like it. Such offers smack of integrity and trust. They defer to the reader's judgment, always a good selling perspective.

This offer is similar to the free-trial offer in that the purchaser has a chance to judge the product's merits. The only difference is he pays before he gets the product.

This next example from the Haband Tie Company has a powerful money-back guarantee. It doesn't limit the guarantee in any way. This attitude, which shows confidence in the reader, builds reader confidence in the Haband Tie Company's product.

> Haband doesn't make a guarantee lightly. When I say these new Argyles will "live forever," I don't mean you can hand them down to your children's children even unto the third or fourth generation. I mean these socks will outlive and outlast any other sock you ever had on your foot. Will still look their best when ordinary socks are matted, rough, and out of shape.
>
>> Pick six pair from the enclosed circulars—*any* 6 pair. You can have two pair of the heather-mixture Argyles, two pair of the all Nylon plain colors and two pair of the heavy plains. Or, three pair of Argyles and three of the plains. Or, *all six* in any size, shape, number, knit, or color. ANY 6 PAIR is the plainest way I can say it. 6 PAIR FOR ONLY $4.95, FULL PRICE FOR ALL SIX PAIRS. (And still cheaper by the dozen, only $9.69 for any 12 pair.)
>
> Make your check for the $4.95 or the $9.69 (the latter could be almost a lifetime supply depending on your age, but don't let them bury you in a pair of Argyles). Check off your choices by number on the order blank. Slip it in the return envelope and drop it in the mail. You will get the socks in the next few days. You will GET YOUR MONEY BACK, EVERY CENT, ANY TME—a week, a month, or a year—if you don't FOR ANY REASON like these socks better than any socks you ever saw in your life.

"Pay-as-you-go" Offer. Some merchandisers have found it advisable to extend the payments for a product over a period of time so that people who prefer to "pay as they go" can buy on a time-pay plan. Book companies are notable for offering expensive books on a time-pay plan. Particularly interesting is the *Great Books of the Western World* which Britannica Press offered, successfully, on an easy-payment plan.

Discount Offer. The discount offer lets the purchaser decrease his unit price as he increases his quantity in ordering. It also is used to discount the purchase price to various trades or professions. For example, book companies offer (usually on the reply card) a 10 to 20 per cent discount on the purchase price of books sold to the teaching profession.

"First-in-line" or Charter Offer. For those people who consider themselves *avant garde* in the use of products as status symbols, for those people who wish to be "first in line" for something, for the type of person manifested by those people who "camp" in line at ball-park windows to get World Series tickets, the "first-in-line" or charter offer is effective.

It's particularly good when you have a new product which has an appeal to a highly selective audience.

This example is from the reply form for an offer made by Britannica Press, a division of Encyclopedia Britannica, Inc., Chicago. The product is a set of two books, *The Britannica Library of Great American Writing.* This is a combination of three types of offers:

First-in-line because it is a prepublication offer of a first edition.

Pay-as-you-go because of the extended terms of payment.

Discount because it gives a price reduction under the publication price.

Please enter my reservation for the giant two-volume BRITANNICA LIBRARY OF GREAT AMERICAN WRITING from the First Edition.

When it arrives, I may examine it for seven days free. At the end of one week, if I don't agree that this magnificent two-volume library will bring my family a lifetime of reading adventure, I will return it and owe nothing. Otherwise, I will send only $2.95 plus a few cents for postage and handling, and then $3 a month for the following three months. (This represents a full $3.05 cash saving under the $15 price after publication!)

"Combination" Offer. This offer is included to throw emphasis on the idea that you can combine most of these offers into an interesting and successful offer. Each offer doesn't have to be used exactly as defined here. For example, your charter offer can have a time limit. Your "pay-as-you-go-offer" can have a free-trial period and a money-back guarantee based on a time limit after the product is received. Your own ingenuity, combined with your merchandising strategies, can give you any offer combination you want.

This example of a combination offer was made by Goldblatt's Department Store, Champaign, Illinois. The offer combined *free trial* with a *time limit* to decide on the purchase, a *free gift*, and *pay-as-you-go.* This copy is taken from the reply card, which also carried an illustration of the product—a set of golf clubs:

15-DAY FREE-TRIAL EXAMINATION
The 24-Pure Nationally Advertised
ROLL KING Pete Cooper Complete
GOLF OUTFIT

Ship me immediately my RK Golf Outfit and my FREE Socke Tool Kit. After a 15-day trial I agree to pay just $5 per month plus a small carrying charge until the $79.95 purchase price is paid, or I will return the outfit. I may keep the Socke Tool Kit in either case.

No Money Down! Only $79.95 for this complete outfit, including a nationally advertised Roll King Golf Cart, matched and autographed Pete Cooper irons and 2 woods, Scotch Plaid Bag, one dozen liquid-center balls, Satin-finished Head Mitts, Subscription to *Golf Digest* . . .

Be sure to include my free 14-Piece Socke Tool Wrench Set.

The Mailing List

George Cullinan says that if a person has bought from you within the previous thirty-six months, he belongs on your customer house list. If, however, he has never bought from you, or last bought from you more than thirty-six months ago, he is part of a promotional list. According to Mr. Cullinan, also, a customer list should buy 2½ to 5 times as much as the average promotional list. Promotional lists vary in value, too, because some can pull orders at higher rates than others. Selection of promotional lists, and a balance between high-pulling house or customer lists and lower-pulling promotional lists can make or break a mail-selling effort, even with good merchandise properly priced.

The House List should be your greatest source of new business. You should use it more than promotional lists and can often mail repeatedly—three or four times, up to twelve times a year—even with the same merchandise.

Your house list should be kept by age—twelve months, twenty-four months, etc. And it should be kept up-to-date and added to whenever possible. One of the best ways to increase the number of names on your house list is to use the "friend card." Send cards to the people on your house list, asking for names of their friends who might be interested in what you offer. You'll probably find that these cards will produce your best and lowest-cost-to-obtain customer. Diner's Club and *Changing Times* are two examples of advertisers who use the "friend card" to build lists. Caution: A total of five names per card seems best. More than that, and the quality declines.

Any Promotional List should be tested before you use it for timing, quality, pull, and cost of sell. If you use a marginal list, qualify your prospects first. Use the inquiry approach—to cause the suspects on the list to raise their prospect hands. Then send your future promotion only to them.

Probably the best piece of advice you can follow in regard to lists, whether you are brand-new or an old hand in the mail-order field, is this: consult a good mailing-list broker. He'll have the know-how, the sources, the abilities to help you find the promotional lists that will work for you.

Methods for Customer Buying

Your reader's method of buying from you can be directed by the type of offer you make, as you will recall from the discussion of types of offers. The method you encourage can also make a difference in the returns you get from a mailing. But, first, to some of the various methods of buying:

1. **Cash with Order.** This is where you get the check or money order before you ship the product ordered or begin the service purchased.

The Advantage of getting the money on the barrel head before shipment is that you get away from c.o.d. forms and problems and the records necessary for c.o.d. or open account. If you use cash with order, most people who sell by mail advise that you ship postpaid.

The Disadvantage of cash with order is that it almost certainly will pull the least response in orders and the lowest average order.

2. **C.O.D.** You accept the order, ship, and have the mailman collect for you. Usually pulls more orders than cash with order. According to George Cullinan's experience, ". . . c.o.d. pulls 25% more than cash at about the same average order." But, also according to Mr. Cullinan, c.o.d. is treacherous. Most people prefer the lesser cash business because of the problem of c.o.d. refusals, which often wipe out the advantage of the additional pull in net business. The handling of refusals is so costly that the profits on c.o.d. business are generally less than in the cash business . . . despite the superior original pull.[8]

The Disadvantage of c.o.d. is the increased cost to the buyer, through his paying the postal' or shipping charges. You also encounter refusals, which create a bookkeeping problem.

3. **On Approval (Trial Offer).** This lets the buyer receive the product, look it over, decide if he wants it—usually within a definitely stated period of time.

The Advantage is the buyer's ability to test, to examine, to use the product before he makes up his mind.

The Disadvantage is that the person "approving" the product may not stick to his bargain and pay for the merchandise. In that case you're up the creek, paddling a collection canoe.

4. **Charge Account and Credit.** Here you let the prospect buy. You ship. Then bill him later.

The Advantage is, according to some experienced mail sellers, that charge accounts (call it credit, if you wish), pull more orders than either cash with order or c.o.d. Some believe that charge accounts pull about twice as many orders as cash. And with at least a 50 per cent higher average order. Credit, or time payments, according to these people, pull twice as many orders as cash at twice the average order, or four times as much annual business as cash.

The Disadvantage again is the possibility of collection problems, plus the fact that you have money invested in accounts payable.

Timing

When to Mail, from the customer-acceptance point of view, is important, but not difficult. The time a mailing arrives at its destination can have an effect on the advertising's success. Everything from hang-overs

[8] George Cullinan, Speech quoted.

to hot dogs and hot days can affect a prospect's attitude toward life, ability, and your pursuit of profits.

You can increase your chances by getting your mail on prospects' desks on the day, in the week, of the month most favorable to you. Since you want your mail to arrive when it'll be well received by readers, try to stay away from Monday and Friday. Monday's mail delivery can be large—and your competition, thereby, increased. On Friday, if the prospects are normal (meaning human, of course) they're getting ready to clean up their desks at the office, or ready for the relaxation at home for the week end.

Other days to avoid are holidays and days before holidays. Edward N. Mayer, Jr. says, however, that the period between Christmas and New Year's has been profitable for some people who sell by mail. Also, if you have gifts which are good for last-minute giving and you *can* deliver the goods on time, the late Christmas-rush period might work for you. Otherwise, avoid that time. If you're selling for Christmas giving, particularly to business lists, you might find it advisable and profitable to mail as early as August. The National Research Bureau, Inc., offers a Christmas song book as a gift for businessmen to give. Their advertising which sells this song book arrives in late August, annually.

The months, particularly for seasonal goods, should be selected so your mailings hit prospects ahead of the time when they would be using your product.

Some people say summer vacation time will cause your returns to fall off. George Cullinan's experience has been that July and August do not fall off. According to Mr. Cullinan, the readership of advertising is highest in the winter time—except for direct mail, which maintains its readership in the summer. From readership come orders.

The order of the various months, rated in decreasing sales productivity, according to Robert Stone, is:

January	March
February	November
September	April
October	December
August	May
July	June

How Often to Mail is another area which you must settle for your own product. When you are ready to determine what frequency of mailings is best for you, try what Robert Stone calls "Test Control."

"Test Control" means "extracting from a given list a representative quantity of names. These names become the 'control group.' All tests are made against the 'control group.' " [9]

Here is an example:

1. You have 4,000 inquiries for your product.
2. Out of the 4,000, you select 1,000 representative names. They become your "control group."
3. You mail one follow-up letter to the control group each week for five consecutive weeks.
4. You use the remaining 3,000 names to test other frequencies against the "control group," such as—five mailings two weeks apart; follow-up No. 1 in one week, then the remaining follow-ups two weeks apart; follow-up No. 1 in two weeks, then the three remaining follow-ups three weeks apart; and so on. (There are many combinations which can be tested, but naturally you will test the most logical.)
5. By carefully recording the response from each mailing against the control group, you will, over a period of time, establish a pattern which will indicate the best frequency of mailing. You have tested three different sales letters. Letter A brings an exceptionally high return, producing more than its quota of orders the first time you mail it. Neither Letter B nor C meets quota.

Now your question is: How often can I repeat Letter A to the same list and at what frequency? Your procedure might be something like this:

a. Set up a "control group" comprising 10 per cent of the representative names on the list.
b. Mail to the "control group" each thirty days until your per cent of return drops below quota.
c. Mail against the "control group" at intervals of two weeks, six weeks, eight weeks, ten weeks, and twelve weeks.
d. By keeping close records you will determine (1) the number of times you can mail the same letter to the same list at a profit and (2) at what frequency. Many mailers are surprised to learn that an above-average sales letter can be mailed profitably to the same list three to four times. And rarely will a letter that pulls second best in original tests match the results of the better-pulling letter when the better-pulling letter is mailed over the identical list the second time.[10]

Creative Techniques

The means of developing mental and visual impact with your prospects have been discussed earlier. Here, however, we want to add several more items which can help you develop effective mailings.

These are selling description and copy formulas. Selling description will help you pipe effective selling imagery from your own reservoir of

[9] Stone, *op. cit.*, p. 60.
[10] *Ibid.*, pp. 60–61.

knowledge into your prospect's pool of desire. The copy formulas, given you under mail selling, where they have greatest validity, will help you make sure all the plumbing connections in your pipe of persuasion are tight and in order.

Selling Description

In describing the benefits your product or service offers a reader, you should offer him ideas which will impinge upon his total ability to react —psychically and through his senses. To get full coverage of his reaction abilities, you should appeal to as many of his sensibilities as possible through both "Psychological Description" and "Physical Description." Neither can stand alone. Each must reinforce and bolster the other for the greatest effectiveness.

Psychological Description plunges into the psychic area of reader personality. It recognizes that people buy things to get what these things do to or for them. For example, the American housewife buys the myriad of household gadgets to help her do her chores. But she wants the time such gadgets save to be with her family, her friends—to devote to other interests. She wants the savings she can have through the economies she can achieve for doing other things: making her home more attractive, entertaining her friends, etc. Because she wants the recognition of her ability, the appreciation from family and friends which accrue to her for her expression of self in décor and entertainment:

The American man wants a car for transportation, yes. But, as we pointed out in an earlier chapter, he also wants a car as a symbol of his ability to perform. He wants a car, also, for the time it saves him over public transportation.

A man wears clothing to keep warm, or cool, as the case may be. But he also dresses according to his concept of what is proper for the self-image he carries in his mental strongbox—of executive, or sportsman, or even of defiant rebel.

An example of psychological description is this excerpt from a letter of The National Research Bureau, Inc. The psychological description comes in the benefits of self-esteem, the desire for the good will of one's fellow man, the wanting to have friends—and to think of them at Christmas.

This copy also offers to help a man play his "role" more effectively (see Chapter 8 on Attention):

Your customers see you
differently at Christmas time . . .

   . . . and if you could only see each one of them in your own mirror . . .
you would see a host of friends.

For no business can last long without friends. And who can place a value on these customer friends of yours? All through the year you deal with your customers on a business basis. You ask for business, you get orders, invoice and collect. Some of your customers drift away . . . *others are tied closer to you.*

But at Christmas time—your customers see you differently. The Christmas spirit extends beyond the home . . . *reaches out to those with whom you do business.* Lasting and profitable friendships are cemented during the holiday season.

And it is with this thought in mind—*building lasting friendships at Christmas time*—that we have set aside the enclosed executive Christmas-greeting letter for you. The letter expresses your thanks, your appreciation . . . *and it reflects the holiday spirit in good taste.*

Physical Description takes account of what people perceive with their senses. It gives details of size, shape, color, length, breadth, texture, taste, sound, odor, and the like. To know the physical details about what one is selling, a writer has to learn how to use his senses. At least four sense appeals are used in the description of the following brand of tomato juice: [11]

Perfect red-ripe tomatoes selected from the world's finest crop—pressed and packed the day they are picked—give Heinz Tomato Juice that matchless, natural fresh flavor. It's unadulterated—just the pure, tender pulp and sunmellowed juice with only a pinch of salt added. You get all the food value of the ruddy, fully ripened Heinz tomato at the height of its scarlet goodness—all of its essential health-giving vitamins—even its delicate aroma.

Freshness, tang, zest—these are the things that make Heinz Tomato Juice an excellent appetizer—a splendid drink with any meal.

If you have ever eaten a big, luscious, ripe tomato right off the vine, you have tasted the rich garden-fresh flavor that makes Heinz Tomato Juice deliciously different. Sip a chilled glass of this full-bodied, full-flavored juice, and you'll realize that this is tomato juice at its best—pure and wholesome as nature made it.

Copy Formulas

These copy formulas are to help you create order and direction in your selling letters. They are particularly adaptable to those letters which ask for action from the reader—mail-selling letters, inquiry producers, etc.

In using these formulas, it is advisable to subordinate them to the flow of the creative impulse. Creativity can produce effective letters which may violate all the so-called rules and formulas. Use them, then, as guides, road maps, a compass, to lead you from the beginning of your process of persuasion into the asking of action by your reader:

[11] Alta Gwinn Saunders, *Effective Business English,* 3d ed., The Macmillan Company, New York, 1949, p. 327.

Formula 1: A General Formula.

1. Write with the ease with which you talk.
2. Learn your letter-writing faults.
3. Remember four essentials of a good letter: clearness, brevity, courtesy, and believability.
4. Read your letter aloud. Then rewrite it if it doesn't ring true.

Formula 2: AIDA. Attract *Attention,* build *Interest,* create *Desire,* demand *Action.*

Formula 3: DDPC. Start by being *Dramatic,* continue by being *Descriptive* (of your product or service), continue further to be *Persuasive* (about the benefits the reader will receive if he accepts your offer), and end by *Clinching* the sale.

Formula 4: AIDPPA. *Get Attention,* then build *Interest,* include *Description* of product and *Persuade* the reader to buy, reaching a climax with *Proof* of what the product has done for others and will do for him, and ending with the all-important demand for *Action.*

Formula 5: PPPP. Start by painting a word *Picture* of what your product or service will do for the reader, *Promise* that this picture will come true if the product is bought, continue with *Proof* of what the product has done for others, and end with a *Push* for an order or a demand for immediate action of some sort. (This formula comes from Henry Hoke . . . whose whole creative life has been devoted to making direct mail better.) [12]

Formula 6: The Egner Formula. Frank Egner, formerly vice-president of The McGraw-Hill Book Company, developed this formula. It is adaptable to mail order, to soliciting of inquiries, to many types of letters.

1. Write a headline (or first paragraph) to evoke desire as well as get attention.
2. Add an inspirational lead-in.
3. Give a clear definition of the product.
4. Tell a success story about the use of the product.
5. Include testimonials and endorsements from satisfied customers.
6. List the special features of the product.
7. Make a statement of the value to the purchaser.
8. Devise an action closer that will make the reader want to buy immediately.
9. Conclude with a P.S. rephrasing the headline.[13]

Formula 7: The Fox Formula. Merral A. Fox, president of Fox Advertising Co., Baltimore, Maryland, gave this method of writing a sales letter to

[12] *How to Use the Mails for Sales,* Bureau of Business Management, University of Illinois Bulletin, vol. 51, no. 65, University of Illinois Press, Urbana, Ill., May, 1954.

[13] Edward N. Mayer, Jr., *How to Make More Money with Your Direct Mail,* 3d ed., Printers' Ink Books, New London, Conn., 1957, p. 86.

The Reporter of Direct Mail Advertising. Here it is, as he wrote it: [14]

I mentioned whatever came to my head at the convention, Henry, with the exception of the pretty legs on a girl in the front row. As for a description of my talk:

It was as simple as this: Working on the assumption that nobody was going to read my letter, no one was interested in my copy, not a soul cared a hoot about what I had to say or what I sell, I took it on from there, and did my best to arouse their interest.

The first paragraph, as you know, is always a tough one. So I put as much of an electric shock in it as possible to get them into the second paragraph.

There, I exploded a little bombshell to keep their interest aroused, and to get them into the third paragraph.

When they reached the third, I had an opportunity to do a little selling.

I didn't take advantage of their good nature, so I kept my selling paragraph as short and as concise as possible.

I wooed them into the fourth, dropping a Fourth-of-July firecracker to keep up the momentum, put a bit more commercial in it, and prayed that they would get to the fifth paragraph . . . where I asked for the order.

I hope that is what you want to know.

Formula 8: The Stone Formula. Robert Stone, vice-president of The National Research Bureau, Inc., Chicago, developed this next formula. It, too, is adaptable to mail order, inquiry solicitation, and other types of letters: [15]

1. Promise a benefit in your headline or first paragraph—*your most important benefit.*
2. Immediately enlarge upon your most important benefit. (Here's where problems arise. If your opening is too "strong" . . . possibly farfetched . . . you have a difficult time moving into the development of the benefit.)
3. Tell the reader *specifically* what he is going to get. (This has to do with completeness in the physical and psychological description of the product. . . . Here is where you blend the physical description with the psychological benefits.)
4. Back up your statements with *proof* and *endorsements.* (Use here testimonials and endorsement of former users, or of present users of your product or service. Or use the "word" of prestige personalities whose endorsement is credible. You can also use case histories, success stories, pictorial appeals showing the product in use, when feasible, or any official recognition you have received—awards, honors, and the like.)

[14] "How to Write a Sales Letter," *The Reporter of Direct Mail Advertising,* vol. 17, no. 8, p. 29, December, 1954.

[15] Stone, *op. cit.,* pp. 99–101.

5. Tell the reader what he might lose if he doesn't act. (This draws a contrast between the positive of the benefits and the negative of not having the benefits. One effective principle of copy is offering a reward—the reader obtains a benefit if he buys—or posing a threat—what might happen if the reader doesn't buy. In this type of situation, you blend the reward and the threat to create contrast . . . and desire.)

6. Rephrase your prominent benefits in your closing offer. (Here you give a last "punch" toward a reader's desire . . . to help him make up his mind.)

7. Incite action—NOW. (*Ask* for action . . . give reasons why the reader should act—NOW.)

Copy Check Lists

Here are copy check lists which were devised by two of the ablest men in direct mail. These check lists are more effective if used *after* writing copy, to determine if everything you want to tell is included. The first one was developed by Harrie A. Bell, the second by Maxwell C. Ross, director of advertising, Old American Insurance Company, Kansas City, Missouri.

The Bell Check List. Harrie A. Bell developed a check list which he considered valuable in writing advertising copy. "A final check list" . . . according to Mr. Bell, "may be helpful." Presumably you will start to write copy after you have clearly established your purpose. With this in mind, you have these four goals to achieve: [16]

1. You will naturally have to *awaken interest* in your first few words. Sometimes—in fact, almost always—your interest-arresting headline is not complete in itself. It invites further perusal, so—

2. You must instantly *bridge over* from your catch-line heading to the subject you are going to discuss. This joining up of headline and text should be a reasonable and sensible process. If it is not, then your headline is too "farfetched," and readers may feel they have been tricked—a bad start to make when you seek their confidence. Having made your logical transition from heading to initial copy—

3. You must *begin to prove your point,* and keep on until you have done so. You must cite your facts, verify what you say, and introduce your complete case. Here is where your powers of persuasion begin to work. In this section of your copy you concentrate on the process of creating desire, so that—

4. You can *point clearly to the action* you desire, and persuade your reader to take action. To make it easy for him to do so, you must tell him in specific terms *how he can do it.*

The Ross Check List. This check list is divided into two parts: (1) Copy Techniques, or the over-all pattern of a letter, and (2) Copy Editing,

[16] Harrie A. Bell, *Getting the Right Start in Direct Advertising,* The Reporter of Direct Mail Advertising, Garden City, N.Y., (n.d.).

aimed at correcting possible flaws. It is presented to you in the words of Mr. Ross:

Copy Techniques

Point No. 1: Does the lead sentence get in step with your reader at once? You do this by talking in terms of things that interest your reader—not in vague generalities or of things *you* want. You put yourself in his place! (I can't think of a better way to say it than this—get in step with your reader.)

Point No. 2: Is your lead sentence more than two lines long? (In our case, we hope not.) Experience has shown . . .(Old American) . . . that our best letters have one- or two-line leads. But if it takes three lines or four lines or even more to get in step with your reader, use them.

Point No. 3: Do your opening paragraphs promise a benefit to the reader? Lead with your best foot forward—*your most important benefit.* If you have trouble with your opening paragraph, try writing your lead at least six different ways. Then—when you get *six* down on paper you are quite likely to have at least one pretty good lead somewhere among them.

Point No. 4: Have you fired your biggest gun first? Sometimes it's easy to get confused in trying to pick out the most important sales point to feature in your lead. But here is one way to tell. Years ago Richard Manville developed a technique that has been of great help. When you are pondering over leads, ask yourself this test question: "Does the reader want more X or more Y?"

Let me give you an example of how this works. Take two headlines, "How to avoid these mistakes in planning your house" and "How to plan your house to suit yourself." Ask yourself the test question, "Which do people want the most?" It becomes obvious, then, that more people want to plan their house to suit themselves rather than simply to avoid mistakes. In this case, the one headline was 16 per cent better than the other.

Take another pair, "Don't swelter this summer" and "Now every home can afford summer cooling." Well, by applying the test question, you already know the answer, but do you know by how much? The second ad, which promised summer cooling, was 300 per cent better.

Or these two, "Your pair of Ben Hogan golf shoes will outwear any other brand," as opposed to "Cut three strokes off your score by wearing Ben Hogan golf shoes." Any real dyed-in-the-wool golfer will buy a new pair of shoes every summer if it will lower his score.

So—tell your reader how what you have to sell will bring him pleasure . . . or save him money . . . or increase his knowledge . . . or better his standard of living (or for that matter, any one of a score of things he wants) and you will have him on your side.

Point No. 5: Is there a BIG IDEA behind your letter? You may wonder what the difference is between firing your biggest gun and this BIG IDEA. In our case, for example, the big gun may be the introductory offer on an insurance policy, but the big idea behind the letter is that here is a company which makes insurance available to the older people of our country. The *big idea* is important. My private guess is that the *lack* of a big idea is why letters fail.

Point No. 6: Are your thoughts arranged in logical order? In other words, have you put the cart before the horse? It's a fundamental copy-writing truth that your reader anticipated what you're going to say. So it may help to think of your reader as a passenger in a motorcycle sidecar—and you as the driver.

You can take him straight to his destination—surely and swiftly and smoothly. Or you can dawdle along the way, over side roads, bumps and curves, sometimes making such sharp turns that he may go shooting off down the road without you. Unless you follow a charted course and make his ride as pleasant as possible, too often he will say, "I'm tired. Let me off." This is another good reason for having a check list to follow.

Point No. 7: Is what you say believable? Here is a chance to offer proof and use testimonials to back up what you have said in your letter. Also, in our case we triple-check to make sure the reader doesn't misunderstand. (Notice I didn't say "true" instead of "believable." What you say may be true, but not necessarily believable.)

Point No. 8: Is it clear how the reader is to order—and did you ask for the order? This is especially important in the insurance industry, where filling out an application can sometimes be complicated. You'd be surprised how easy it is to write a letter without asking for the order!

Point No. 9: Does the copy tie in with the order form—and have you directed attention to the order form in the letter? This latter point is particularly important, we think. So we call our reader's attention to the next important step in the transaction by saying something like this, "As you look at the enclosed order form, you will notice that, etc." Do something to get the reader's attention to the order form, because this is a *key step*.

Copy Editing

Point No. 10: Does the letter have "you" attitude all the way through? You can tell easier than you think. All you have to do is put yourself in the other fellow's place. As the little poem goes, "When you sell John Jones what John Jones buys, you must see John Jones through John Jones's eyes."

Point No. 11: Does the letter have a conversational tone? I'm not going to tell you that you should write as you talk, because your letter might sound pretty weird if you did. Ed Mayer says, "Write with the ease with which you talk." Or—to put it another way—write as you would talk if you could edit what you are going to say. And that's what you have a chance to do here.

Point No. 12: Have you formed a "bucket brigade" through your copy? This will take a little explaining. If you study the works of master letter writers, you will notice that all their letters have *swing* and *movement*—a joining together of paragraphs through the use of connecting links. Some of these connecting links are little sentences like, "But that is not all" . . . "So that is why" . . . "Now—here is the next step" . . . "But there is one thing more."

You can find literally dozens of ways to join your thoughts like this—in short, to take your reader by the hand and lead him through your copy—and to avoid what I call "island paragraphs" that stand all alone—and are usually just as dull as they look to the reader. In fact, the next time you run across one of those deadly dull letters, see if it isn't because it lacks this bucket-brigade technique.

Point No. 13: Does the letter score between 70 and 80 words of one syllable for every 100 words you write? This is one of the most important check points to follow in writing effective copy. It isn't that people don't understand the meanings of words—they just can't cope with the way they are used. Their vocabularies are adequate, but their patience isn't.

Point No. 14: Are there any sentences which begin with an article (*a, an,* or *the*)—where you might have avoided it? This is another one of our own ground rules. And we don't always follow it to the letter. But we like to try—because we think sentences which *begin* with those words are frequently robbed of their strength.

Point No. 15: Are there any places where you have strung together too many prepositional phrases? This is an important check point because it's so hard to catch when you write your first draft. Now is a good place to catch them—for overusing prepositional phrases is another strength robber.

Point No. 16: Have you kept out "wandering" verbs? You can often make sentences easier to read by rearranging them so that verbs are *closer* to their subjects. When you let verbs wander too far away from their subjects, you make understanding more difficult for your reader.

Point No. 17: Have you used action verbs instead of noun construction? You gain interest when you do this. Instead of saying, "This letter is of vital concern to . . ." say, "This letter vitally concerns. . . ."

Point No. 18: Are there any "that's" you don't need? Using too many "that's" is another strength robber. Eliminate as many as you can . . . but be careful. Read your copy aloud to make sure you haven't trimmed out so many that your copy will slow down the reader.

Point No. 19: How does the copy rate on such letter-craftsmanship points as (*a*) using active voice instead of passive, (*b*) periodic sentences instead of loose, (*c*) too many participles, (*d*) splitting infinitives, (*e*) repeating your company name too many times.

If you're going to split infinitives; if you're going to use the passive voice; if you're going to do these other things, don't do them too often. Moderation in copy is a great virtue.

Point No. 20: Does your letter look the way you want it to?

  a. Your letter should assume the same proportions as the sheet upon which it is placed.

  b. It should not be crowded.

  c. The paragraphs should be short—not over six lines at the most. (Not a hard and fast rule)

  d. Appearance can be helped by indenting and sometimes numbering indented points or paragraphs.

  e. Use italics and capitalization sparingly, thereby reserving emphasis for spots where needed.

  f. Use punctuation (dots and dashes) to increase reading ease.

Source List

This list includes the names of companies and other sources of services which were mentioned in the text, but for which we gave you no addresses. If you should want their help, here's where to get in touch with them:

Cabot-Letter (Responda Letter)
910 West Van Buren Street
Chicago 7, Illinois

The Connelly Organization, Inc.
1010 Arch Street
Philadelphia 7, Pennsylvania

The Dartnell Corporation
4660 Ravenswood Avenue
Chicago 60, Illinois

The Reuben H. Donnelley Corporation
Direct Mail Division
2000 South York Road
Hinsdale, Illinois

Goes Lithography
42 West 61st Street
Chicago 21, Illinois

R. L. Polk & Co.
Howard Street
Detroit 31, Michigan

W. L. Ponton, Inc.
44 Honeck Street
Englewood, New Jersey

Postal Bulletin
Superintendent of Documents
Government Printing Office
Washington 25, D.C.

Reply-O-Letter Co.
7 Central Park West
New York 23, New York

Sen-Bak
1355 New York Avenue, N.E.
Washington 2, D.C.

Arthur Thompson & Company
109 Market Street
Baltimore 2, Maryland

U.S. Department of Commerce
Washington 25, D.C.

Bibliography

Books

Aurner, Robert R.: *Effective Communication in Business*, 4th ed., South-Western Publishing Company, Cincinnati, 1958.

Baker, Robert A.: *Help Yourself to Better Mail Order*, Printers' Ink Books, New London, Conn., 1953.

Bedell, Clyde: *How to Write Advertising that Sells*, 2d ed., McGraw-Hill Book Company, Inc., New York, 1952.

Bell, Harrie A.: *Getting the Right Start in Direct Advertising*, The Reporter of Direct Mail Advertising, Garden City, N.Y. (n.d.).

Bentley, Garth: *Editing the Company Publication*, Harper & Brothers, New York, 1953.

Bernays, Edward L. (ed.): *The Engineering of Consent*, University of Oklahoma Press, Norman, Okla., 1955.

Bernstein, Theodore M.: *Watch Your Language*, Channel Press, Great Neck, N.Y., 1958.

Bettger, Frank: *How I Raised Myself from Failure to Success in Selling*, Prentice-Hall, Inc., Englewood Cliffs, N.J., 1949.

Britt, Steuart Henderson: *Selected Readings in Social Psychology*, Holt, Rinehart and Winston, Inc., 1950.

————: *Social Psychology of Modern Life*, rev. ed., Holt, Rinehart and Winston, Inc., New York, 1949.

Buckley, Earle A.: *How to Sell by Mail*, McGraw-Hill Book Company, Inc., New York, 1938.

Burton, Philip Ward, Bowman Kreer, and John B. Gray: *Advertising Copy Writing*, Prentice-Hall, Inc., Englewood Cliffs, N.J., 1949.

Caples, John: *Making Ads Pay*, Harper & Brothers, New York, 1957.

Carr, Jack: *Cordially Yours*, The Reporter of Direct Mail Advertising, Garden City, N.Y., (n.d.).

Cassels, J. W. W.: *How to Sell Successfully by Direct Mail*, rev. 3d ed., Business Publications Ltd., in association with B. T. Batsford, Ltd., London, September, 1956.

Clarke, George Timothy: *Copywriting: Theory and Technique*, Harper & Brothers, New York, 1959.

The Robert Collier Letter Book, 6th rev. ed., Prentice-Hall, Inc., Englewood Cliffs, N.J., 1950.

Converse, Paul D., Harvey W. Huegy, and Robert V. Mitchell: *Elements of Marketing*, 6th ed., Prentice-Hall, Inc., Englewood Cliffs, N.J., 1958.

De Voe, Merrill: *Effective Advertising Copy,* The Macmillan Company, New York, 1956.

Dimnet, Ernest: *The Art of Thinking,* a Premier book, Fawcett Publications, Inc., New York, 1955.

Dunn, S. Watson: *Advertising Copy and Communication,* McGraw-Hill Book Company, Inc., New York, 1956.

Eastman, Max: *Enjoyment of Laughter,* Simon and Schuster, Inc., New York, 1936.

Egner, Frank, and L. Rohe Walter: *Direct Mail Advertising and Selling,* Harper & Brothers, New York, 1940.

Fellows, Margaret M., and Stella A. Koenig: *Tested Methods of Raising Money,* Harper & Brothers, New York, 1959.

Flesch, Rudolf: *The Art of Clear Thinking,* Harper & Brothers, New York, 1951.

————: *The Art of Plain Talk,* Harper & Brothers, New York, 1946.

————: *The Art of Readable Writing,* Harper & Brothers, New York, 1949.

————, and A. H. Lass: *The Way to Write,* Harper & Brothers, 1949.

French, Elbrun: *The Copywriter's Guide,* Harper & Brothers, New York, 1959.

Graham, Irvin: *How to Sell through Mail Order,* McGraw-Hill Book Company, Inc., New York, 1949.

Gunning, Robert: *The Technique of Clear Writing,* McGraw-Hill Book Company, Inc., New York, 1952.

Hattwick, Melvin S.: *How to Use Psychology for Better Advertising,* Prentice-Hall, Inc., Englewood Cliffs, N.J., 1950.

Hayakawa, Samuel Ichiyé: *Language in Thought and Action,* Harcourt, Brace & World, Inc., New York, 1949.

Hotchkiss, George Burton: *Advertising Copy,* Harper & Brothers, New York, 1949.

James, William: *Some Problems of Philosophy,* Longmans, Green & Co., Inc., New York, 1940.

Kilduff, Edward Jones: *Words and Human Nature,* Harper & Brothers, New York, 1941.

Laird, Donald: *What Makes People Buy,* McGraw-Hill Book Company, Inc., New York, 1935.

Lapp, Charles L.: *Successful Selling Strategies,* McGraw-Hill Book Company, Inc., New York, 1957.

Lucas, Darrell Blaine, and Steuart Henderson Britt: *Advertising Psychology and Research,* McGraw-Hill Book Company, Inc., New York, 1950.

Martineau, Pierre: *Motivation in Advertising,* McGraw-Hill Book Company, Inc., New York, 1957.

Mayer, Edward N., Jr.: *How to Make More Money with Your Direct Mail,* 3d ed., Printers' Ink Books, New London, Conn., 1957.

Menning, J. H., and C. W. Wilkinson: *Writing Business Letters,* rev. ed., Richard D. Irwin, Inc., Homewood, Ill., 1959.

Messner, Richard: *Selling Printing and Direct Advertising,* Fred W. Hoch Associates, Inc., New York, 1947.

Miller, Clyde R.: *The Process of Persuasion,* Crown Publishers, Inc., New York, 1946.

Miller, George Lafline: *Copy: The Core of Advertising,* McGraw-Hill Book Company, Inc., New York, 1949.

————: *How Advertising Is Written—and Why,* McGraw-Hill Book Company, Inc., New York, 1945.

Nauheim, Ferd: *Business Letters that Turn Inquiries into Sales,* Prentice-Hall, Inc., Englewood Cliffs, N.J., 1957.

Osborn, Alex F.: *Applied Imagination: Principles and Procedures of Creative Thinking,* rev. ed., Charles Scribner's Sons, New York, 1957.

Payne, Stanley L.: *The Art of Asking Questions,* Princeton University Press, Princeton, N.J., 1951.

Perrin, Porter G.: *Writer's Guide and Index to English,* Scott, Foresman and Company, Chicago, 1950.

Poffenberger, A. T.: *Psychology in Advertising,* McGraw-Hill Book Company, Inc., New York, 1932.

Preston, Harold P.: *Successful Mail Selling,* The Ronald Press Company, New York, 1941.

Rudolph, Harold F.: *Attention and Interest Factors in Advertising,* Funk & Wagnalls Company, in association with Printers' Ink Publishing Co., Inc., New York, 1947.

Samstag, Nicholas: *Persuasion for Profit,* University of Oklahoma Press, Norman, Okla., 1957.

Sandage, Charles H., and Vernon Fryburger: *Advertising: Theory and Practice,* 5th ed., Richard D. Irwin, Inc., Homewood, Ill., 1958.

Saunders, Alta Gwinn: *Effective Business English,* 3d ed., The Macmillan Company, New York, 1949.

Schramm, Wilbur (ed.): *The Process and Effects of Mass Communications,* University of Illinois Press, Urbana, Ill., 1954.

Shidle, Norman G.: *Clear Writing for Easy Reading,* McGraw-Hill Book Company, Inc., New York, 1951.

Shurter, Robert L.: *Written Communication in Business,* McGraw-Hill Book Company, Inc., New York, 1957.

Smart, Walter Kay, Louis William McKelvey, and Richard Conrad Gerfen: *Business Letters,* 4th ed., Harper & Brothers, New York, 1957.

Stebbins, Hal: *Copy Capsules,* McGraw-Hill Book Company, Inc., New York, 1957.

Stone, Robert: *Successful Direct Mail Advertising and Selling,* Prentice-Hall, Inc., Englewood Cliffs, N.J., 1955.

Turner, Howard M., Jr.: *Sales Promotion that Gets Results,* McGraw-Hill Book Company, Inc., New York, 1959.

Uzzell, Thomas H.: *Narrative Technique,* Harcourt, Brace & World, Inc., New York, 1923.

Wales, Hugh G., Dwight L. Gentry, and Max Wales: *Advertising Copy, Layout, and Typography,* The Ronald Press Company, New York, 1958.

Weir, Walter: *On the Writing of Advertising,* McGraw-Hill Book Company, Inc., New York, 1960.

Wilkinson, C. W., J. H. Menning, and C. R. Anderson: *Writing for Business,* 3d ed., Richard D. Irwin, Inc., Homewood, Ill., 1960.

Wolff, Janet: *What Makes Women Buy?* McGraw-Hill Book Company, Inc., New York, 1958.

Wright, Milton: *Managing Yourself,* McGraw-Hill Book Company, Inc., New York, 1949.

Young, James Webb: *A Technique for Producing Ideas,* 7th ed., Advertising Publications, Inc., Chicago, 1951.

Booklets

Chait, Lawrence G.: *Those Little Golden Lists,* R. L. Polk & Co., Detroit, Mich., 1955.

"Color, for Your Advertising," *Envelope Economies,* Tension Envelope Corporation, Kansas City, Mo., 1957.

DMAA Presents the Story of Direct Advertising, Direct Mail Advertising Association, New York, 1956.

Direct Mail Advertising: What? Why? When? How? Mail Advertising Service Association (International), Washington, D.C., (n.d.).

Doppler, William Arkwright: *Testing: The Scientific Approach in Direct Mail*, Direct Mail Advertising Association, New York, 1953.

Envelopes for Just about Everything that Gets Mailed, Direct Mail Envelope Co., New York, January, 1956.

Envelopes: Their Use and Power in Direct Advertising, DMAA Research Report, Envelope Manufacturers Association of America and Direct Mail Advertising Association, New York, 1956.

Handbook of Industrial Direct Mail Advertising, National Industrial Advertising Association, New York, 1954.

Hoke, Henry: *How Direct Mail Solves Management Problems*, The Reporter of Direct Mail Advertising, Garden City, N.Y., 1954.

———: *How to Think about Direct Mail*, The Reporter of Direct Mail Advertising, Garden City, N.Y., 1951.

———: *How to Think about Mail Order*, The Reporter of Director Mail Advertising, Garden City, N.Y., 1954.

How to Build Sales by Mail, Cavanagh Printing Company, St. Louis, (n.d.).

How to Put Action into Your Direct Mail, Creative Division of James Gray, Inc., New York, (n.d.).

How to Work with Mailing-list Brokers, Direct Mail Advertising Association, New York, (n.d.).

Kleid, Louis: *Mail-order Strategy*, The Reporter of Direct Mail Advertising, Garden City, N.Y., 1956.

Letter Reproduction: How to Select the Process for the Purpose, DMAA Research Report, Direct Mail Advertising Association, New York, 1960.

"Mailing Lists and Regulations," *How to Plan Printing to Promote Business*, no. 9, S. D. Warren Company, Boston, (n.d.).

Miller, Nelson A., and Joseph H. Rhoads: *Establishing and Operating a Mail-order Business*, Industrial (Small Business) Series no. 46, Marketing Division, U.S. Department of Commerce. (n.d.).

More Business through House Organs, rev. ed., S. D. Warren Company, Boston, May, 1951.

The Proper Planning and Design of Your Next Letterhead, Hammermill Paper Company, Erie, Pa., 1958.

Ross, Maxwell C.: *How to Work with Mailing Lists*, Direct Mail Advertising Association, New York, (n.d.).

Sand and Spray, House Organ of Chalfonte-Haddon Hall, vol. 3, no. 1, Atlantic City, N.J., Spring, 1957.

The Three R's of Direct Mail, The Reply-O-Letter, New York, (n.d.).

"U.S. Postal Guide, 1958 Edition," *Envelope Economies*, Tension Envelope Corporation, Kansas City, Mo., 1958.

Vahle, Kurt: "Does the Outside Affect Inside Readership?" *Convoys*, vol. 12, no. 2, pp. 3–10, Cupples-Hesse Corporation, St. Louis (n.d.).

Bulletins

Adman's Alley *Almanac*, American Marketing Services, Boston, October, 1960.

Bolles, Edgar W.: "Good Business Writing Makes Good Sense," *The ABWA Bulletin*, vol. 22, no. 4, American Business Writing Association, Urbana, Ill., January, 1958, pp. 5–15.

"Direct Mail Case Studies," *DMAA Research Bulletin*, vol. 1, no. 3, Direct Mail Advertising Association, New York, July, 1959.

"Direct Mail Readership," *DMAA Research Bulletin*, vol. 1, no. 4, Direct Mail Advertising Association, New York, October, 1959.

"The Handling of Advertising by its Recipients," *DMAA Research Bulletin*, vol. 1, no. 2, Direct Mail Advertising Association, New York, May 11, 1959.

"How to Develop Ideas," *The ABWA Bulletin*, American Business Writing Association, Urbana, Ill., February, 1948.

How to Use the Mails for Sales, Bureau of Business Management, University of Illinois Bulletin, vol. 51, no. 65, University of Illinois Press, Urbana, Ill., May, 1954.

Mayer, Edward N., Jr., and Earle A. Buckley: "Let's Make Direct Mail More Profitable," *Bulletin of the Buckley Institute*, vol. 1, no. 17, Philadelphia, (n.d.).

"Research into Direct Mail Advertising," *DMAA Research Bulletin*, vol. 1, no. 1, Direct Mail Advertising Association, New York, 1959.

"The Use of Mailed Questionnaires," *DMAA Research Bulletin*, vol. 1, no. 5, Direct Mail Advertising Association, New York, April, 1960.

Periodicals

"Alumni Campaigns Win Awards," *The Reporter of Direct Mail Advertising*, vol. 22, no. 12, p. 39, April, 1960.

Armour, Richard: "Of Humor and Humor Writing," *The Writer*, vol. 69, no. 10, pp. 301–303, October, 1956.

Bott, Leo P.: "Ad Industry's Need: Fewer Mimics, More Gimmicks," *Printers' Ink*, vol. 266, no. 9, p. 92, Feb. 27, 1959.

Brown, June: "Creative Articles Are Fun," *The Writer*, vol. 70, no. 3, pp. 20–21, March, 1957.

Clark, William A.: "Why I Love My Wife," *Monsanto Magazine*, vol. 39, no. 2, p. 28, May, 1959.

Cowle, Jerome M.: "The Importance of Being Nostalgic," *Printers' Ink*, vol. 262, no. 3, p. 84, Jan. 17, 1958.

Dawson, Cleo: "The Women Who Work for You," *The Rotarian*, vol. 91, no. 3, pp. 12–14, September, 1957.

DeLay, Robert F.: "It Can Be Done: Let's Put More Science into Direct Mail," *Industrial Marketing*, vol. 42, no. 10, pp. 50, 53, October, 1957.

"The Effectiveness of Direct Mail as a Pure Advertising Medium," *The Reporter of Direct Mail Advertising*, vol. 19, no. 12, pp. 24–28, April, 1957.

"Family Buying Decisions: Who Makes Them, Who Influences Them?" *Printers' Ink*, vol. 264, no. 12, pp. 21–23, Sept. 19, 1958.

Gaupp, Les W.: "Sales Pitch Shapes Redesign of Stationery," *The Post*, vol. 35, no. 4, p. 26, Mail Advertising Service Association (International), Washington, D.C., August, 1956.

Gould, Bernard: "Mail-order Mathematics: Determining the Break-even Point Is Fundamental in Successful Mail-order Operation," *Printers' Ink*, vol. 222, no. 8, pp. 46–47, Feb. 20, 1948.

"How a Church was 'Sold' through a 'Unified Budget Plan,'" *The Reporter of Direct Mail Advertising*, vol. 20, no. 8, pp. 24–25, December, 1957.

"How to Write a Sales Letter," *The Reporter of Direct Mail Advertising*, vol. 17, no. 8, p. 29, December, 1954.

Kidd, Elizabeth J.: "Sexual Behavior in American Advertisers," *Printers' Ink*, vol. 244, no. 11, pp. 41, 43, Sept. 11, 1953.

Lufkin, Dudley: "Just Two Short Paragraphs on a Post Card," *The Reporter of Direct Mail Advertising*, vol. 19, no. 8, pp. 16–17, December, 1956.

Macon, Bette: "Postmarks Can Sell for You," *Advertising Requirements*, vol. 5, no. 6, pp. 51–54, June, 1957.

Mahoney, D. B.: "The Eldest Is Always Called 'Percy,' Dear," *The Reporter of Direct Mail Advertising*, vol. 17, no. 11, pp. 16–18, March, 1955.

————: "There Is Method in Our Advertising Madness," (reprint), *Ontario Medical Review*, February, 1959.

"Marketing's Eternal Challenge: The American Housewife," *Printers' Ink*, vol. 263, no. 12, pp. 46–48, June 20, 1958.

Mathus, Kenilworth H.: "Use Action Urges in Your Coupon Copy," *Printers' Ink*, vol. 237, no. 12, pp. 58–59, Dec. 21, 1951.

Mayer, Edward N., Jr.: "Direct Mail Advertising," (reprint), *Harvard Business Review*, vol. 29, no. 4, July, 1951.

McGinnis, Frank: "What the Client Expects from His Agency in Direct Mail," *The Reporter of Direct Mail Advertising*, vol. 21, no. 9, pp. 20–22, January, 1959.

Raymond, Leonard J.: "Taking a Reading on Direct Mail Readership," *The Reporter of Direct Mail Advertising*, vol. 18, no. 6, pp. 12–16.

Shaw, Howard Dana: "How to Start to Write a Letter," *The Reporter of Direct Mail Advertising*, vol. 11, no. 10, pp. 12–16, February, 1949.

Sherman, Joe: "Switch to Post-card Simplicity Boosts Alumni Membership . . . and Lowers Cost," *The Reporter of Direct Mail Advertising*, vol. 21, no. 8, pp. 24–25, December, 1958.

"Sight at Their Fingertips," *The Reporter of Direct Mail Advertising*, vol. 23, no. 6, p. 67, October, 1960.

"Significant Trends: Modern Marketing's Sorest Thumb," *Sales Management*, vol. 84, no. 11, pp. 17–18, June 3, 1960.

"Simple Letter Campaign Puts Fire under Hubby and Dollars into the Christmas Fund," *The Reporter of Direct Mail Advertising*, vol. 20, no. 8, pp. 26–28, December, 1957.

Starch, Daniel: "Do Top Copy Writers Get Top Readership?" *Printers' Ink*, vol. 254, no. 3, pp. 32, 34, Jan. 20, 1956.

Trilling, Diana: "The Case for the American Woman," *Look*, vol. 23, no. 5, pp. 51–54, Mar. 3, 1959, pp. 51–54.

True, G. Herbert: "How to be Creative," *Printers' Ink*, vol. 258, no. 1, pp. 19–23, Jan. 4, 1957.

"Union Bag-Camp Paper Corp. Campaign Is Top Direct Mail Leader of 1957," *The Reporter of Direct Mail Advertising*, vol. 20, no. 6, pp. 28–33, October, 1957.

"Unusual Postmarks Sell Pipe for Price," *Industrial Marketing*, vol. 44, no. 9, pp. 186–188, September, 1959.

"Will Customers Take a Chance?" *Business Week*, no. 1339, pp. 82, 87–92, Apr. 30, 1955.

The Wolf Magazine of Letters, The Wolf Envelope Company, Cleveland, pp. 11–12. April, 1958.

Speeches

Cullinan, George: "The Formula for Growth in Direct Mail Profits," Philadelphia Direct Mail Day, Apr. 20, 1960.

Hardy, Jerry: "The Club Plan of Selling: How It May Fit into Your Business," Direct Mail Advertising Association Western Convention, San Francisco, May 4, 1960.

Ziegler, Ferd: "What's the Big Idea in Direct Mail?" Chicago Direct Mail Day, May 25, 1956.

Index

381

Fund raising, health appeals, 325–327
  planner's point of view, 323
  religious appeals, 327–330
  simplicity, 336–338
  welfare appeals, 324–325

Gaupp, Les W., 183
Geddes, Huntly H., 19
General Motors, 153–155, 158, 159
Goes Lithographing Co., 194
Goldblatt's Department Store, 354, 355, 359
Gould, Bernard, 350
Gove, Bill, 251
Graphic Service, 48, 72, 73, 183, 184, 240–242, 292, 309, 310
Greenlaw, Peggy, 126, 138, 263
Grolier Society, 52
Groves, Charles W., Co., 84, 101, 126, 137, 138, 263, 264
Guarantee, 139, 140, 357, 358

Haband Tie Company, 358
Hardy, Jerry, 352–354
Harnischfeger Corporation, 278–280
Harris-Seybold Company, 222–224
Hart Schaffner & Marx, 91, 92, 118, 119
Hayakawa, S. I., 93
Hoke, Henry, 142, 249, 366
Horner, Frank W. Ltd. (Horner Pharmaceuticals), 23, 96, 98, 100–102, 262, 263
Huffman, H. M., Jr., 265
Huffman Manufacturing Company, 161–163, 246, 247, 259, 260, 265, 266

Ideas, copy, 84, 85
  creative, 228–234
    art, 234
    containers, 233
    copy style, 232
    design and folds, 229
    die cuts, etc., 230
    envelopes, 234
    layout, 230–232
    mailing methods, 233
    reply cards, 233, 234
    special materials, 233
    special processes, 232
    stock, 229
    unusual, 232, 233
Illinois, University of, 139, 335, 336
Imagination, copy, 86–96
Impact, copy, 94–96
Impressions, advertising, 3–5
  direct mail, cost per contact, 4, 5, 70
Industrial Equipment News, 290

Inquiries (*see* Response advertising)
Inside mailing room, disadvantages, 74–77
Interest, causes of, 32–37
  (*See also* Copy, interest)
Involvement, personal, 35–37, 133, 134, 270, 285, 286
  with product interest, 35–37

James, William, 129, 130
Journal of Commerce, 104

Keller-Crescent Co., 357
Kettering, Charles, 45
Klein, B., & Co., 42, 132
Klinkhart, Emily, 324
Knipco Co., 124, 125, 245, 246, 284, 319–322

Laird, Donald, 117
Layout, direct mail, 30–32
  (*See also* Formats)
Ledex, Inc., 316
Letterheads, 266–268
Letters, 238–268
  announcement, 239–242
  attention getter, 242–247
  benefits, 248–251
  Cabot, 148, 149
  check lists, 343, 368–371
  cordial contact (*see* reminders, *below*)
  format, 191–194
  formulas, 365–368
  fund raising appeals, check list, 343
  handshake, 258, 259
  mood, 252–256
  original-contact, 259–261
  religious appeals, pattern for, 327
  reminders, 261–265
  requests, 257, 258
  as research tool, 153–167
  sincere, 265, 266
  when to use, 238, 239
Lewis, Mary Lou, 263
Life, 146
  Book Department, 352
Look magazine, 110, 113, 145, 146, 356

McCall's magazine, 121, 124, 125, 172, 173
McCann-Erickson, 99
McGinnis, Frank, 133
McGraw-Hill Book Company, Inc., 111, 176, 177, 273, 305, 366
Maelstrom, 253
Mahoney, Douglas B., 23, 25, 98, 99, 262, 263